Hugh Roberts is the Edward Keller Professor of North African and Middle Eastern History at Tufts University. Before joining Tufts he was the director of the International Crisis Group's North Africa Project. His previous publications include *The Battlefield: Algeria 1988–2002* and *Algérie-Kabylie.*

'In *Berber Government: The Kabyle Polity in Pre-colonial Algeria*, Hugh Roberts brings to bear his unbeatable knowledge of Ottoman Algerian history and politics as well as his equally impressive gift for social theory. He provides a convincing map of the structures, legal system, and complex social networks that had generated a self-governing Kabyle Berber polity by the advent of French colonial rule.'

Edmund Burke III, Research Professor (Emeritus) of Modern Middle Eastern and World History, University of California, Santa Cruz

'Shattering the views of Orientalists and nativists alike, this massively erudite and ruthlessly precise book takes the reader on an exhilarating detective hunt through barely-known sources, exposing a rich political history of Berber self-government that generations of researchers have missed. This is a landmark study that decisively changes the received wisdom on Berbers, Algeria, and the political history of the region. It is one of the best books I have read in Middle East Studies in recent years.'

John Chalcraft, Associate Professor, Department of Government, LSE

'Hugh Roberts's book is sharp, exhaustive, detailed and poignant. It fills an important gap and its general point about the institutional richness of Kabyle politics (and the primacy of politics more generally) is made with devastating effect. The book does not just track and explain 500 years of "the Kabyle polity" (though it does that) but also explores the logic of how and why the polity transformed as it did when it did. There is no arguing from first causes or flaccidly conceived "cultural tendencies". Roberts alerts us to multiple possible readings of every turn of events, and marshals evidence for his way of understanding each one of them. What makes this intellectually satisfying is the way these are brought together, the way empirical rigor and sometimes bewildering specificity is rendered sensible via a broader logic of institutional forms understood and acted upon in particular cultural ways. Neither the culture nor material conditions explain political life. Political life is undertaken by political actors, whom we get to know through Roberts's description, and these actors employ the institutional resources available to them in culturally sensible ways in their historically specific moments. Eric Wolf long ago complained that European scholars conceive of Others as "people without history". Roberts's book is a potent antidote to that. I have not read anything like it.'

David Crawford, Professor of Sociology and Anthropology, Fairfield University

'Thoroughly researched and well written, this much needed study fills an important gap in the history of the Berbers of Algeria. Roberts challenges the work of scholars such as Ernest Gellner and Pierre Bourdieu demonstrating that the Kabyle polity was much more complicated than they originally claimed. Dense in detail and comprehensive in structure, Roberts's fine contribution to the historiography of the area is indispensable reading for anyone interested in the development of political structures in the pre-colonial Maghreb and, more particularly, in the Kabyles of Algeria.'

Patricia M.E. Lorcin, Professor of History, University of Minnesota-Twin Cities

Berber Government

The Kabyle Polity in Pre-colonial Algeria

Hugh Roberts

I.B. TAURIS

LONDON · NEW YORK

New paperback edition published in 2017 by
I.B.Tauris & Co. Ltd
London • New York
www.ibtauris.com

First published in hardback in 2014 by I.B.Tauris & Co. Ltd

ISBN: 978 1 78453 766 1
eISBN: 978 0 85773 689 5

A full CIP record for this book is available from the British Library
A full CIP record is available from the Library of Congress

Library of Congress Catalog Card Number: available

To Salah, Ibrahim and Amar Oumohand, their families,
and the people of Ath Waaban

and in memory of

Dr W.W. Cruickshank, Head of Classics at St Paul's School, London,
and David Montgomery Hart

I have also tried to show that social relations really exist only in and through the ideas which are current in society; or alternatively, that social relations fall into the same logical category as do relations between ideas. It follows that social relations must be an equally unsuitable subject for generalisations and theories of the scientific sort to be formulated about them. Historical explanation is not the application of generalisations and theories to particular instances; it is the tracing of internal relations.

Peter Winch, *The Idea of a Social Science*, 133

Contents

Preface

This book has its origin in a discovery I made while carrying out fieldwork in the Jurjura mountains of Kabylia in the summer of 1975 and it can be seen as a development of the vision of Kabylia and the view of the scholarly literature on Kabylia which I stated in necessarily summary form in the thesis I submitted to Oxford University in 1980.[1]

The discovery I made was that central features of Kabylia's traditional socio-political organisation continued to have significance in independent Algeria. Not only traditional solidarities but also traditional institutions and practices still played a role in the political life of the region, despite the changes in the political and socio-economic context since the end of the colonial era, and the evidence I found suggested that the Algerian authorities were taking these realities into consideration in their approach to governing the region. This discovery triggered several trains of thought.

One of these concerned my understanding of the Boumediène régime, the FLN state and the Algerian political elite. Finding that the regime was treating the political traditions of the countryside with a measure of respect, I decided that it was a mistake to conceive of the regime and the state as standing in clear-cut opposition to the conservative tendencies in the society. The notion of a conflict between a radical modernising government and a conservative and tradition-bound society seemed misconceived. On the contrary, I came to the conclusion that the regime itself had conservative as well as modernising impulses, that the FLN state itself was partly founded on and informed by some at least of Algeria's longstanding political traditions, and that the national political (including military and administrative) elite was also animated in part by these traditions and the patterns of behaviour they impelled.

The second and third trains of thought concerned the character of Kabyle society and led in different directions. My fieldwork in Greater Kabylia had suggested to me that the society of the central Jurjura – that is, of the districts of Aïn el Hammam and Larba'a n'Ath Irathen – was an unusually politicised society.

---

1   Hugh Roberts, *Political Development in Algeria: the region of Greater Kabylia*, Oxford University, D.Phil., 1980.

These districts correspond to the historic territory of a very particular element of the Kabyle population known as the *Igawawen*. I accordingly began to explore the origins and constituent features of the distinction between the society of the Igawawen and that of the rest of Kabylia. An analysis of the data provided by the nineteenth-century French authors Hanoteau and Letourneux on the distribution of the population of Greater Kabylia *c.* 1868 enabled me to discover a most interesting variation in the settlement patterns of the population and one which underlined the cultural and political differences between the Igawawen and the rest. This complex of differences, of which I offered a preliminary analysis in a working paper published many years ago,[2] forms a key element of the argument of this book and will be discussed in depth in subsequent chapters.

The third train of thought led me into a disagreement with the late Ernest Gellner, who pioneered the application of Evans-Pritchard's segmentarity theory to the Berber populations of the Maghrib. My discovery that some of the traditional political institutions of Kabyle society still featured in local political life led me to suppose that they had also played an important role in the pre-colonial period and that the political organisation of pre-colonial Kabylia involved *institutions* and not merely the 'balance and opposition' of kinship groups and the mediating role of saintly lineages that were the central elements of Gellner's model. I concluded that the segmentarity theory of Berber political organisation did not really apply to Kabylia. In addressing this issue in my doctoral thesis, I did not claim that my findings refuted Gellner's theory; I was willing to accept that his model applied to the populations of the Central High Atlas in Morocco and very possibly to other Berber populations. I suggested simply that Kabylia was different, and that, if Gellner's model defined the rule, Kabylia was an exception to it. The impression I had during the examination of my thesis in 1980 that Gellner had accepted this point turned out to be mistaken, however. In an article published in 1985,[3] he made it clear that he considered that this theory applied to Kabylia as much as anywhere else. I accordingly decided that I had not made the case for my view of the matter sufficiently thoroughly in my thesis and that it was necessary to do so in depth.

The book I set out to write was begun in the autumn of 1989, when four chapters, in which I provided a reconstruction of the Kabyle polity as this existed at the moment of the French conquest, were written. These chapters, discussing in detail the economic life, settlement patterns, system of law and

---

2   Hugh Roberts, *Notes on relations of production, forms of property and political structures in a dissident region of Algeria: pre-colonial Kabylia*, University of East Anglia, Development Studies Discussion Paper No. 38 (1978), 33 pp.

3   Ernest Gellner, 'The roots of cohesion', *Man*, 20 (1985), 1, 142–55, reprinted in Ernest Gellner, *Culture, Identity and Politics* (Cambridge: Cambridge University Press, 1987), 29–46.

political organisation of pre-colonial Kabylia, were the product of many years of prior research and reflection and written very quickly. Copies were sent to Ernest Gellner, Fanny Colonna, the late David Hart and Henry Munson but not otherwise circulated. They have become Chapters 1–4 of the present work and, beyond polishing and some elaboration of particular points, no revision to the central argument of this part of the book has been made since 1989. The second part of the book, comprising Chapters 5–8, offers an account of the history of Kabylia during the Ottoman period, in an attempt to explain the historical development of Kabyle political organisation. I had not done all of the research necessary for these chapters by the time I began the book in 1989, and I had no opportunity to undertake this for many years. From 1990 onwards, I was obliged, in order to make a living as a freelance writer and consultant, to give my complete attention to the political crisis in Algeria and it was only in 2002, following the at least provisional re-stabilisation of the Algerian state, that I could consider this crisis was over. By then I was working for the International Crisis Group as director of its North Africa Project and it was only after leaving ICG in 2007 that I had the time to undertake the additional research and writing needed to complete this book.

The new interpretation of the Kabyle polity put forward in this book is not based on my exploitation of a previously unknown goldmine of archives and the claims I make for the second part of the book in particular, in which I have sought to open up new lines of thinking and enquiry, are necessarily tentative. I have long worked on Kabylia but am not an Ottoman specialist, and the circumstances in which I wrote this book, without the benefit of connection to any academic institution or any financial support, precluded research in the Ottoman archives. Since the Ottomans never governed the Igawawen, I am not sure that this seriously vitiates my arguments; I suspect that if there are important archives still to be explored, they are those of the major *zawāyā* and saintly lineages in Kabylia itself. Now that Algeria has begun to produce some Ottoman specialists of its own, it is to be hoped that they will turn their attention to Kabylia and manage to tap whatever primary sources remain to be tapped. In developing the ensemble of hypotheses I have put forward about the history of Kabylia since 1509, I have relied on the existing literature in all its variety and my own fieldwork, supplemented by consultation of the French archives in respect of the population of the central Jurjura during the early colonial period, plus a range of other sources, including the Algerian press and the internet. The work of piecing this information together has been oriented by the knowledge of Kabylia I have acquired in the field. I have conducted research in Kabylia in 1972, 1973–4 (when I spent a year teaching English at Bouïra on the southern edge of the region), the summer vacations of 1975 and 1976, November–December 1983, and during shorter visits in 1992, 1997, 1999, 2003, 2006, 2011 and 2012. In addition to the main towns, I have stayed in the following villages: Ath Waaban (repeatedly, in 1975, 1976 and 1983), Ath

Wahlan, Darna, Iferhounen, Ikhelouien, Isikhen ou Meddour and Tigzirt (Ath Yenni) and the township of Souq el-Jemaʿa. I have also visited Agouni Gueghran, Ath Abbas (Ath Wasif), Ath Agad, Ath Hawari, Ath Hichem, Ath Lahcène, Ath Larbaʿa, Ath Mislaïen, Ferhoun (Akfadou); Guenzet (Ath Yala); Ighil Bouchen, Irjaounen n'Bour, Irjaounen n'Techt, Jemaʿa n'Saharij, Mezwara (Akfadou), Selloum, Tamjjout, Taourirt Mimoun, Tifilkout, Timeghras and Werja.

I have benefitted from discussing my work on Kabylia with many scholars, colleagues and friends and it is a pleasure to acknowledge their help. They include Lahouari Addi, Fazia Aïtel, Karima Aït Meziane, the late Mahfoud Bennoune, Khelifa and Tassadit Bouzebra, Ken Brown, Terry Burke, Fanny Colonna, David Crawford, Katerina Dalacoura, Abderrezak Dourari, Ihsane El Kadi, the late Bruno Etienne, the late Ernest Gellner, Michael Gilsenan, Slimane Hachi, Mohammed Harbi, the late David Hart, John Harriss, Arezki Himeur, John King, Jean Leca, the late Peter Loizos, Mohamed Lakhdar Maougal, the late Mohamed Mazouni, Thierry Michalon, Martha Mundy, Henry Munson, Dermot Murphy, Karim Ouaras, Salah Oumohand, Roger Owen, Robert Parks, Hassan Remaoun, the late Mohamed Brahim Salhi, David Seddon, Susan Slyomovics, Khaoula Taleb-Ibrahimi, Shelagh Weir, Raoul Weexsten, Tassadit Yacine and Sami Zubaida. I owe a special debt to Michael Gilsenan, with whom I was able in the early stages of my research to discuss at length my conviction that the segmentarity thesis did not apply to Kabylia; to the late David Hart, for his unfailing encouragement, his warm hospitality at his home in Spain and the wonderful correspondence he kept up, and to Omar Lardjane of Algiers University, for obtaining a copy of Al-Warthilani's *Rihla* for me.

I have many debts to those who assisted my fieldwork in Kabylia; first and foremost, to the people of Ath Waaban for their hospitality and especially to Salah, Ibrahim and Amar Oumohand and the late Mme Taos Oumohand. I would also thank the Benabderrahmane family of Ath Wahlan; Dr Cécile Clément, formerly of Aïn el Hammam; M and Mme Idir Hammoudi of Ikhelouien, Isikhen ou Meddour and Bouïra; Salah Iboukhtouchen of Jemaʿa n'Saharij; Saïd Khelil of Tizi Ouzou; Cherif Labraoui of Tigzirt n'Ath Yenni; Hamid Messahel of Iferhounen; Farès Oudjedi of Akfadou; Mouloud and Rachid Aït Oumghar of Ath Sidi Braham and Bouïra; Dr Pierre Radisson of Lyon, formerly of Aïn el Hammam and Souq el-Jemaʿa, Mohamed Brahim Salhi and Saliha Salhi of Tizi Ouzou and Mme Cherifa Zarraf of Jemaʿa n'Saharij.

I have three other special debts to honour. The first is to the late Bruno Etienne for the warm hospitality he showed me when I turned up, a stranger and wholly unannounced, at his villa in Hydra one evening in the summer of 1974 and for his subsequent insistence that I spend time at the Centre de Recherches et d'Études sur les Sociétés Méditerranéenes (CRESM) in Aix-en-Provence. The second is to the late Jean Déjeux for his friendly encouragement and his generous willingness to open the library of the Centre Diocésan in Algiers for me on Sundays, the only day in the week that I could get to Algiers while teaching at Bouïra in 1973–4. The third is to my publisher, and especially to Iradj Bagherzade in person, for his faith in this project and his patience with it, and to a succession of Middle East editors, most notably Abigail Fielding-Smith and Maria Marsh, for all they have done to help bring it to fruition.

None of the above bears any responsibility for the views let alone the errors that may be found in this book.

My last debt is to all the members of my family, for countless acts of kindness and support but also and above all for accepting the path I have been on and wishing me '*bonne route*' at every juncture.

A Note on Transliteration

I have followed standard practice where Arabic words are concerned, retaining both the 'ain and the hamza as well as diacritical marks.

The transliteration of Kabyle words and names is a complicated problem to which there cannot easily be a consistent solution. Until recently most Berber dialects were unwritten. With the rise of the Berber Cultural Movement in Kabylia in the 1980s, this began to change. *Thaqbaylith*, the Kabyle dialect of *Thamazighth* (i.e. Berber), is now a written language, employing an alphabet devised by the French missionary White Fathers in Kabylia in the later colonial period. This has become the instrument of Kabyle poets, song-writers and academics and has acquired moral authority, to the point that it now verges on 'politically incorrect' to employ any other way of conveying Kabyle words. But for a historian addressing English-speaking readers this alphabet poses serious problems.

The first is that, while mostly employing Roman letters, it does so in an idiosyncratic manner; in many cases, the sounds they are intended to convey as an alphabet of the Berber language are not those they convey in French or German or Spanish, let alone English. Thus the letter 'c' is actually to be pronounced 'sh' (e.g. *amcic* represents the Kabyle word for 'cat', actually pronounced 'amshīsh') while the letter 'x' is to be pronounced 'kh' (e.g. *axxam* represents the Kabyle word for house, which is actually pronounced 'akhkham'). In addition, a number of Greek letters are used to convey sounds that individual Roman letters cannot convey. *Thaqbaylith* includes a letter that is the exact equivalent of the Arabic *ghain*, which is pronounced as a Parisian 'r' and conventionally transcribed as 'gh'; this is represented in the White Fathers' alphabet by 'γ', the Greek gamma, while the Kabyle equivalent of the Arabic '*ain*, conventionally transcribed as a single inverted apostrophe: ', or as a superscript 'ᶜ' (viz.: ᶜ), is represented by 'ε', the Greek epsilon. Finally, this alphabet reproduces the French inability to pronounce the 'th' sound (as in 'thorough') that is such a familiar part of English as well as Arabic and an even more frequent feature of the Berber language in its Kabyle variant. Thus the words it writes as *taddart, tajmaat* etc. are in fact pronounced *thaddarth, thajma'th* etc. I therefore use this alphabet only when quoting from authors who employ it and otherwise treat it here as I treat the Arabic alphabet, as something to be respected but transcribed for my readers' convenience.

But at this point I encounter another set of problems arising out of the way the French themselves have rendered Kabyle words and names. The Berber word that is the counterpart of the Arabic *Banu* or *Beni*, meaning 'the sons of' and frequently encountered in the names of tribes and villages as well as families is conventionally written *Aït* by the French, but this is not how it is pronounced in Kabylia, nor is this adequately conveyed by the White Fathers' alphabet, which renders it as *At*. In fact, it is pronounced *Ath* and numerous Kabyle authors now actually write it as *Ath*, as do many local authorities when representing the names of municipalities or villages on road signs or official documents. My impression is that *Ath* is superseding *Aït* in general Kabyle usage and my own usage will reflect this. But I shall also employ the French form *Aït* in certain contexts: first, because it occurs in much of the scholarly literature; second, because it is the form used in the official registers and records of individual family names. Thus when referring to a well-known Kabyle tribe I write its name as Ath Yahia, but when referring to one of its most eminent sons, I write his name as he and the government write it, Hocine Aït Ahmed. This two-track solution is precisely that employed by some contemporary Kabyle authors, notably Abdelhafidh Yaha in his memoir of the war of liberation.

Otherwise I have mainly made do with the French way of transcribing Kabyle words, with two exceptions. Where the French use 'ou' to convey the sound of a 'w' I employ a 'w'; thus I write Igawawen for Igaouaouen and Waguenoun for Ouaguenoun. Possessing only a soft 'j', the French routinely harden this with the letter 'd' to convey the 'j' sound in Arabic and Berber. But English has a hard 'j' of its own, so in place of Djurdjura, for example, I write Jurjura.

List of Illustrations

List of Maps

List of Tables

List of Tables

CHAPTER 1

~

Considering Kabylia

The object of this study is the ensemble of political arrangements which the populations of the mountains of Greater Kabylia in northern Algeria contrived in the pre-colonial period for the purposes of governing themselves as sovereign communities independent of the central power, the Ottoman Regency of Algiers. These arrangements have been discussed over the years by many other authors in numerous works. I am presuming to add a further book to this literature because, dissatisfied with the understandings of these matters that have been in circulation to date, I wish to propose a new interpretation of the nature of the Kabyle polity in the pre-colonial period and an explanation of its genesis.

The analysis of the political organisation of pre-colonial Kabylia is a matter of considerable confusion. It is my conviction that this confusion arises from two main sources, the lacunae in the analyses of the French colonial ethnographers, notably Hanoteau and Letourneux and Masqueray,[1] and the decision of more recent scholars to abandon what was valid in the work of their nineteenth-century predecessors and to substitute theoretical models that are less able than those they supplanted to do justice to the Kabyle polity. The rest of this book undertakes to make that case by dealing with the lacunae in question and thereby resolving the outstanding difficulties in the analysis of the political organisation of pre-colonial Kabylia, so that the constitutive principles and inner logics of the Kabyle polity of the later Ottoman period may at last be fully understood.

Greater Kabylia

The region called, in French, *la Kabylie* owes its name to the corruption of the Arabic word *qbā'il*. A plausible interpretation of this derivation identifies

---

1   Adolphe Hanoteau and Aristide Letourneux, *La Kabylie et les coutumes Kabyles*, 3 volumes (Paris: Challamel, 1872–3, 2nd edition 1893); Émile Masqueray, *Formation des Cités chez les populations sédentaires de l'Algérie* (Paris: Ernest Leroux, 1886); republished with an introduction by Fanny Colonna by the Centre de Recherches et d'Études sur les Sociétés Méditerranéenes, series 'Archives Maghrébines' (Aix-en-Provence: Edisud, 1983).

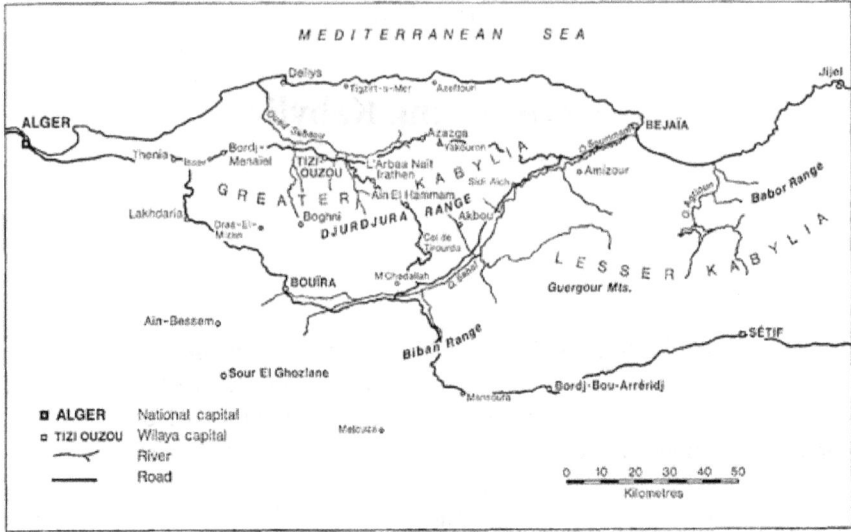

Map 1.1: The Kabylias.

it with the plural of *qabīla*, an Arabic word conventionally translated as 'tribe', so that *el-qbā'il* designated 'the tribes' as distinct from the supposedly non-tribal or de-tribalised populations of the towns and their immediate environs. A more speculative interpretation suggests that the word is derived from the Arabic verb *qabila*, meaning 'to accept', so that *el-qbā'il* designated rather the people who 'accepted Islam' – that is, the indigenous Berber-speaking inhabitants of North Africa who were converted to the faith of their Arab conquerors. Both interpretations have been current in Algeria and Kabylia in recent times, although it should be noted that the word *qabīla* appears in the Kabyle language, in the Berber form *thaqbilth*, to refer to the largest unit of political organisation, which the ethnographers have rendered by 'confederation', a fact which favours the first interpretation above.

'Berber' is primarily a linguistic term of classification, indicating those who speak one of the Berber dialects as their mother-tongue. Since the rise of the Berberist movement in the 1980s, the term *amazigh* (literally: 'free man'; plural: *imazighen*) has become the fashionable (Berber) term to apply to all things and persons that are Berber. It was previously used to indicate the Berbers of the Middle Atlas and the Central and Eastern High Atlas in Morocco and was not in general use in Algeria.

It was the French who reserved the term 'Kabyle' to refer principally if not exclusively to the inhabitants of what is now known as 'la Kabylie'. It appears that *el-qbā'il* was used by the townsfolk of pre-colonial Algeria to indicate all hillsmen without distinction, a practice that survives in some places.[2] Otherwise, in Algeria today, 'Kabyle' refers to the Berber-speaking inhabitants of that part of the Tell Atlas, the coastal chain, that extends from the edge of the Mitija plain south-east of Algiers to the Babor mountains south-west of Jijel. The small Berber-speaking population of the Chenoua massif west of Algiers used to be called 'les Kabyles du Chenoua' but are now usually referred to by their Berber name as the *Ichenwiyen*. Other Berber-speakers in Algeria are known by other names, notably the Mzabis of the northern Saharan region known as the Mzab and the Tuareg of the Ahaggar and the Tassili n'Ajjer mountains in the far south, while those of the Aurès and Nememcha mountains in eastern Algeria and the high plains immediately to their north are known as the *Chaouia*, an Arabic word meaning 'shepherds' or 'sheep people'. Thus the range of reference of the word 'Kabyle' has steadily been reduced and its focus sharpened. It is not clear when the contemporary usage became established but it certainly predates the French conquest[3] and the inhabitants of what is now known as *la Kabylie* or, in Arabic, *Bilād el-Qbā'il*, have long referred to themselves as *Leqbayel* (singular: *Aqbayli*) and to distinguish their dialect of the Berber language from others by the term *Thaqbaylith*.

Strictly speaking, there are two Kabylias, Greater and Lesser. The population of the former is almost entirely Berberophone while in the latter both Berber- and Arabic-speaking populations are present in roughly equal proportions. Most authors further distinguish the Berberophone districts of Lesser Kabylia, consisting of the Soummam valley and the Biban, Guergour and Babor mountains from the Arabophone region to the east of the Wad Agrioun – that is, the mountainous hinterland of Jijel, usually referred to as 'la Kabylie orientale'. This study is primarily concerned with the region known as *la Grande Kabylie* (in Arabic: *el-Qbā'il el-kubrā*), the mountainous country to the east of Algiers, bounded by the Mediterranean to the north and the Jebel Jurjura to the south and divided from *la Petite Kabylie* by the main ridge of the eastern Jurjura and its north-easterly extension in the lesser ranges of the Akfadou district.[4]

---

2 For example, Nedroma in western Algeria; see Yahia Rahal, *Histoires du Pouvoir: Un géneral témoigne* (Algiers: Casbah Éditions, 1997), 29.

3 Diego de Haedo, *Topographie et histoire générale d'Alger*, translated into French from the Spanish text (Vallodolid, 1612) by Dr Monnereau and A. Berbrugger, *Revue Africaine* (1870–1); republished with introduction by Jocelyne Dakhlia (Saint-Denis: Éditions Bouchène, 1998), 56–9; Thomas Shaw, *Travels and Observations Relating to Several Parts of Barbary and the Levant* (Oxford: Theatre Editions, 1738), 36.

4 Several authors represent the Soummam river as the frontier between Greater and Lesser Kabylia; this is mistaken. The populations of the west bank of the Soummam are part of Lesser Kabylia no less than those of the east bank; it is the watershed ridge of the Jurjura and its north-easterly extension that forms the boundary between the two regions.

The region is extremely mountainous, dominated by the grandiose summits of the Jurjura, which attains a maximum altitude of 7,500 feet (2,308 metres) with the peak of Tamgout n'Lalla Khedija. Inhabited by Berber-speaking arboriculturalists and petty craft manufacturers for as long as anyone can remember, more densely populated than any other part of the Maghribi countryside, famed for its tradition of political independence, it has long attracted the attention of scholars, journalists and other observers. These include the imposing trio of Ibn Khaldun, Karl Marx and Émile Durkheim and, more recently, the – also imposing – duo of Pierre Bourdieu and Ernest Gellner. It has also produced its own chroniclers and numerous Kabyle and other Algerian writers have contributed, in increasing numbers in recent decades, to the endless debate on the region, its people and its traditions.

The Kabyles and the other Algerian Berbers

The Berber-speakers of North Africa do not possess a common territory or a common economic life and there is much variation between them in cultural and even linguistic terms. In Morocco, there are three main Berber dialects, those of the Chleuh of the south-west, the Imazighen or Berraber of the centre and south-east and the Rifians of the north,[5] and there are other cultural differences between their respective speakers. In Algeria, the dialects of the Kabyles, the Chaouia, the Mzabis and the Tuareg are all distinct. *Tamahaq*, the dialect of the Tuareg, is not intelligible to the other groups and, although Kabyles and Chaouia may understand each other's speech with relative ease, there is a noticeably greater Arabic influence in *Thachawith* than there is in *Thaqbaylith*.[6]

There are also religious differences. The Kabyles, the Chaouia and the Tuareg are all Sunni Muslims of the Maliki rite, but the Mzabis are Ibadis, adherents of a dissident sect whose only other North African members are to be found in the Berber-speaking populations of the island of Jerba off Tunisia and the Jebel Nefusa in Libya. More recently, religious differentiation of a kind has developed between the Kabyles and the Chaouia. The latter were strongly influenced by the Islamic Reform movement of Sheikh Abdelhamid Ben Badis and the Association of the *'ulama* in the 1930s and 1940s,[7] whereas this had a more limited impact in Greater Kabylia.

5　Ernest Gellner, *Saints of the Atlas* (London: Weidenfeld & Nicolson, 1969), 12–13.
6　Pierre Bourdieu, *The Algerians* (Boston, USA: Beacon Press, 1962), 27.
7　Fanny Colonna, 'Rituels et Histoire: à propos d'un ancien pélérinage aurasien', in Ernest Gellner, Jean-Claude Vatin *et al.*, *Islam et Politique au Maghreb* (Paris and Aix-en-Provence: Éditions du CNRS, 1981), 95.

Thus it is a mistake to speak of a Berber community as such in North Africa as a whole or even in Algeria as a whole. But there is a Kabyle community. The Kabyles possess a common language, a common territory and a common culture and they have long been conscious of this fact. They also differ from the other Berber populations of Algeria in several important ways.

First, the Kabyles are by far the largest of Algeria's Berber populations. The 1966 census gave the Kabyle population as numbering 1,180,000, compared with approximately 400,000 Chaouia, 60,000 Mzabis and 15,000 Tuareg, but these figures undoubtedly underestimated the Berberophone element of the Algerian population at that time, assessing it in all at 17 per cent of the total. Subsequent censuses have not differentiated between those who speak Berber as their mother-tongue and those who do not, but it is now generally admitted that Berber-speakers make up between 20 and 27 per cent of the total population. Since this stands at 38 million today (2013), we can estimate there to be between 7.6 and 10.3 million Berbers in Algeria and in the Algerian diaspora abroad, of which between 5 and 7 million are accounted for by the Kabyles.

Second, they are not at all remote from the national capital, Tizi Ouzou being less than 60 miles (92 km) from Algiers, compared to Batna, the capital of the Aurès region (about 400 km), Ghardaïa, the capital of the Mzab (about 600 km) and Tamanrasset, the capital of the Ahaggar Tuareg (2,060 km). In addition, there is a large Kabyle element – at least 25 per cent and possibly approaching 40 per cent – in the population of Algiers itself.

Third, like the Mzabis but unlike any other Berber group in Algeria, the Kabyles have a highly developed commercial tradition and there is a large Kabyle diaspora; this is both much larger and more diversified than its Mzabi counterpart.

Fourth, unlike the Mzabis or the Tuareg, the Kabyles have been accustomed, for several generations, to engage in labour migration to France (and to a lesser extent to Belgium, Germany and Switzerland). In this the Chaouia have resembled them to some extent, but in quantitative terms Kabyle labour migration has far surpassed that of the Chaouia: the *wilayāt*[8] which provided the most emigrés in 1966 were Setif (which then included the western and central districts of Lesser Kabylia – the present *wilāya* of Bejaïa – and was 40.5 per cent Berberophone) and Tizi Ouzou (i.e. Greater Kabylia, 81.8 per cent Berberophone); these accounted for 24.8 per cent and 20.5 per cent of Algerians resident abroad respectively, compared with the *wilāya* of Batna

---

8 *Wilāya*, plural: *wilayāt*, is the term used in Algeria for province or governorate, the equivalent of the French *département*. The Algerian counterpart of a governor or *préfet* is called a *wali*. This word has the root meaning of 'protector' or 'guardian' and is also used of *mrābtīn* (holy men) who are the patron saints of particular localities.

(44.5 per cent Berberophone), which accounted for a mere 5.6 per cent.[9] And in recent decades Kabyle communities have established themselves in North America as well.

Fifth, Kabylia received preferential treatment in educational provision during the colonial period. As Fanny Colonna has pointed out, however, the Mzab and the Aurès were also, initially, offered above average educational opportunities by the French, but proved less receptive to these than the Kabyles. In the case of the Chaouia, the often dispersed habitat and the prevalence of transhumance may account for their relative failure to take advantage of French schooling. In the case of the sedentary, urban-dwelling, Mzabis, it was a matter of explicit resistance. The seven cities of the Mzabis,[10] as a consequence of their religious particularism, had long possessed their own developed educational system, which survived into the post-colonial era, and their populations shunned the educational services of the infidel French. The Kabyles were also entirely sedentary, like the Mzabis, but lacked both any particular religious fervour and all but rudimentary educational institutions of their own.[11] There were no major obstacles to Kabyle acceptance of the opportunity of cultural development, with its implications of upward social mobility, offered by the French once this had ceased to be associated with the enterprise of religious conversion. By no means all Kabyles underwent this particular process of cultural change directly and it was not until after the Second World War that French schooling was generalised throughout the region. But a large number of Kabyles did respond eagerly in the early period, with the result that, for example, of those Algerians of rural[12] origin studying at the École Normale at Bouzaréah near Algiers between 1883 and 1939, 89 per cent were from Kabylia, and 77 per cent were from Greater Kabylia alone.[13]

There thus developed a substantial Kabyle intelligentsia, Francophone and modernist and linked to both the migrant workers in France and the villages of the Jurjura and the Soummam valley whence these came. This combination of the experience of French education and that of mass labour

9   According to the 1966 census figures, cited in Stephen Adler, *International Migration and Dependence* (London: Saxon House, 1977), 164.
10 That is, the five cities of the 'Pentapolis' – Ghardaïa, Beni Izguen, Bou Noura, El Atteuf and Melika – plus the two newer cities to the north and north-east of these, Berriane and Guerrara.
11 Fanny Colonna, *Instituteurs Algériens 1883–1939* (Paris: Presses de la Fondation des Sciences Politiques, 1975), 107–8.
12 That is, 'rural' only in the sense of 'non-urban', i.e. not from the large European and traditional Muslim towns.
13 Colonna, *op. cit.*, 106.

migration to France was undoubtedly an important factor underlying the sixth major difference between the Kabyles and the other Berber populations, the immensely greater role which the Kabyles played in the nationalist movement and the leadership of the wartime National Liberation Front (*Front de Libération Nationale*, FLN) and the National Liberation Army (*Armée de Libération Nationale*, ALN).

Kabylia not only constituted one of the six military regions (*wilayāt*) of the ALN, *wilāya* III, it also provided most of the commanders of *wilāya* IV (the Algérois), the first commander of *wilāya* VI (southern Algeria) and the successive commanders of the important *Fédération de France du FLN* (FFFLN). In addition, it was a Kabyle, Abane Ramdane, who emerged as the overall political leader of the FLN in 1955-6 at the same time as the architect of *wilāya* III, Belkacem Krim, emerged as the most influential of the ALN commanders. It was Abane who organised the celebrated first congress of the FLN, held in the Soummam Valley in August 1956, which endowed the revolution with a national command structure and a sophisticated political platform, and it was the organisational structure and system of ranks developed in *wilāya* III that were then generalised to the ALN as a whole. That the Kabyles subsequently lost their commanding positions in the national leadership of the FLN-ALN has been a matter of resentment in Kabylia ever since, but it cannot be seriously disputed that their contribution to the liberation of Algeria was enormous.

The full story of the Kabyles' role in the national revolution and the establishment of the independent Algerian state cannot be told here and is in any case reasonably well known.[14] But the point to be grasped is that the capacity for leadership they displayed was by no means simply a function of French cultural influence. For the remarkable receptivity of the Kabyles to the opportunities proffered by the French presence and the colonial order remains to be explained and it can be satisfactorily explained only if proper account is taken of the peculiar nature of Kabyle society and culture at the moment of the colonial impact. For the specificity of the Kabyles vis-à-vis not only the Arabophone but also the other Berberophone populations of Algeria was already an established fact long before 1830.

---

14 William Quandt, *Revolution and Political Leadership: Algeria 1954-1968* (Cambridge, Mass. and London, England: MIT Press, 1969) and 'The Berbers in the Algerian political elite' in Ernest Gellner and Charles Micaud (eds), *Arabs and Berbers: from tribe to nation in North Africa* (London: Duckworth, 1972), 285-303; Mohammed Harbi, *Le FLN: mirage et réalité* (Paris: Éditions J.A., 1980), chapters 10-13; Hugh Roberts 1982, 'The unforeseen development of the Kabyle question in contemporary Algeria', *Government and Opposition*, XVII, 3 (Summer 1982), 312-34.

Pre-colonial Kabylia and the academy:
I. The unresolved controversy and its revival

The distinctiveness of Kabyle society would be more widely appreciated today if the insights of its nineteenth-century observers had been built on by their twentieth-century successors. The former lacked the theoretical panache of the latter, but they had eyes to see and extensive knowledge of the region and what they saw and described was a remarkable society of numerous, unusually large, rigorously ordered and fiercely independent villages. What they were unable to do was to provide a fully satisfactory explanation of this society. Instead of making good this lack, the most influential twentieth-century writers on Kabylia have taken the (assumed) theoretical naivety rather than the empirical accuracy of their predecessors' accounts as their point of departure and, armed with sophisticated theory but only superficially acquainted with the region, have proffered alternative accounts of Kabyle socio-political organisation which have in common the fact that they travesty it.

At issue are the characterisation of the society of pre-colonial Kabylia and the way in which its political organisation is conceived. These would not be at issue – or, at least, they would not be an issue of contemporary political significance – were society in post-colonial Kabylia fundamentally different from that which existed prior to 1830. But, while different in many observable ways, it has not been *fundamentally* different. The general context of Algerian society and politics has been different in many important respects and the events and processes which have wrought these changes have had their repercussions upon Kabyle social and political life. But, in Kabylia, these changes have, at any rate until recently (the 1990s),[15] taken place within an evolutionary process of development marked by a high degree of continuity.

Kabylia largely escaped the trauma of social disintegration engineered by French colonialism in many other parts of Algeria. Its steep hillsides and narrow valleys did not attract European settlement and its system of land tenure was left alone. In neither the political nor the cultural sphere was surgery practised upon it and in the economic sphere it was

---

15 Population growth and infrastructural development (electrification, road-building and the proliferation of modern at the expense of traditional housing) had modified the external aspect of Kabyle society by the early 1990s, but the intense dislocation and disorientation occasioned by the terrible violence of the 1990s has had a deeper impact, including a discernible demoralisation of elements of the society. For a sensitive account of a Kabyle village in the throes of these changes, see Judith Scheele, *Village Matters: knowledge, politics and community in Kabylia, Algeria* (Woodbridge, Suffolk and Rochester, New York: James Currey, 2009).

Figure 1.1: Men of Ath Lahcène (Ath Yenni)
conversing in their *thajma'th*, June 2011.

left largely to its own devices, with the colonial administration seeking at most to regulate from a distance, rather than exploit or transform, the economic activities of the population. An important cultural development occurred, the generalisation, amongst the male population, of the French language and so of access to European culture. But this development was not imposed upon Kabylia by the colonial authorities; it was achieved by the Kabyles themselves in their own way, as part of their characteristically practical response to changed external circumstances, and did not occur at the expense of their Berber mother tongue. It was therefore not experienced as a rupture.[16] There has been no global societal rupture of any kind in Kabylia, which is why the traditions which animated Kabyle resistance to the conquest in 1857 and 1871 were available to animate Kabyle participation in the modern nationalist movement from the 1920s onwards, in the war of national liberation from 1954 to 1962 and the rebellion of 1963–5[17] and are explicitly invoked or at least tacitly remobilised, together with other traditions of extraneous origin, by the various tendencies of Kabyle activism and dissidence today.[18] Knowledge of pre-colonial Kabyle society and of its political organisation and traditions is therefore indispensable to an understanding of the complex politics of the Kabyle question in post-colonial Algeria.

This point has long been overlooked. For most of the period since the early 1970s and especially since the remarkable protest movement in Kabylia known as *Tafsut Imazighen* ('The Berber Spring') in 1980, academic, journalistic and political interest in Kabylia and the Kabyles has been mainly focused on the question of identity. Where nineteenth-century observers were preoccupied with understanding Kabyle political organisation, late twentieth-century commentary and scholarship largely ignored what some scholars call the 'morphology' of Kabylia – the study of its social and political forms – in favour of a preoccupation with the question of identity, notably with regard to language and oral traditions.[19] In fact, however, there has always been a relationship of one kind or another between the two.

---

16 Unlike the transformation of the Irish peasantry into a society of English speakers at the expense of the Gaelic language and in a profound rupture with the culture of Gaelic society.

17 That is the unsuccessful revolt against Ahmed Ben Bella's government led by Hocine Aït Ahmed under the banner of a new party, the Socialist Forces Front (*Front des Forces Socialistes*, FFS) and which was mainly based in Kabylia. See Ramdane Redjala, *L'Opposition en Algérie depuis 1962*, t.1: *Le PRS-CNDR et le FFS* (Paris: L'Harmattan, 1988).

18 For an excellent discussion, see Mohamed Brahim Salhi, 'Modernisation et retraditionalisation à travers les champs associatif et politique: le cas de la Kabylie', *Insaniyat*, 8 (May–August 1999), 21–42.

19 Prior to the 1980s, both French and Algerian scholarship had produced some very valuable studies of other aspects of the sociology and anthropology of Kabylia, notably René Maunier's fine monograph *La construction collective de la maison en Grande Kabylie*

In the work of the nineteenth-century French authors, with its often admiring discussions of the Kabyle 'republics', there was a strong tendency to present the 'democratic' aspect of Kabyle life – notably the leading role of the *jemaʿa* (plural: *jemāyaʿ*), the representative assembly of the village or tribe – as a major, if not the major, feature distinguishing the Kabyles from 'the Arabs' and thus to conceive of the Kabyles' political traditions as a central aspect of their distinctive identity. At the same time, unable for a mixture of reasons to provide a serious, historically grounded, explanation of these traditions, French authors tended to present them as rooted in and expressions of the timeless Berber character, a choice of explanation that encouraged and merged with a romantic stereotype of the sturdy democratic Berber, as opposed to the negative stereotype of the shifty Arab prone to extravagance and despotism. Thus the French explanation of the Kabyle republics by reference to *la génie berbère* was not only a surrogate for historical explanation (which would have required them, most inconveniently, to investigate and acknowledge the influence of the Ottoman Regency on the political history of Kabylia) but also one which involved a transfer of political virtue from a set of institutions to the intrinsic 'genius' of a 'race'. Quite apart from all the other flaws and drawbacks in this explanation, it involved refusing to admit the element of Arabo-Berber ancestry common to most Arabophones and Berberophones in Algeria and overlooking the fact that the Arabic-speaking hillsmen generally had similar political institutions and traditions to those of the Berbers, if in less elaborate and less striking versions.

In the literature on contemporary Kabylia and especially apropos of the emergence of the Berberist movement militantly articulating identity demands (chief among them the demand for recognition of the Berber language), there has been a strong tendency to link the identity issue to the question of forms of government via the postulate that Berberist contestation of the nationalist orthodoxy of the independent Algerian state has been intrinsically pluralist *and therefore democratic* in character, a view widely canvassed by the Berberist movement itself but also widely endorsed in academic and media commentary. This literature has for the most part, however, entirely ignored

---

(Paris: Institut d'Ethnologie, 1926); Camille Lacoste-Dujardin, *Le Conte kabyle* (Paris: Maspero, 1970, 2nd edition 1982) and *Un village algérien* (Algiers: SNED 1976); Ramon Basagana and Ali Sayad, *Habitat traditionnel et structures familiales en Kabylie* (with a preface by Mouloud Mammeri; Algiers, Mémoires du Centre de Recherches Anthropologiques, Préhistoriques et Ethnographiques, XXIII, 1974); Aïssa Ouitis, *Les contradictions sociales et leur expression symbolique dans le Sétifois* (Algiers: Documents du C.R.A.P.E., III, SNED, 1977); Mohand Khellil, *L'Exil kabyle* (Paris: L'Harmattan, 1979) and Mohamed Brahim Salhi, *Étude d'une confrérie religieuse algérienne: la Rahmania à la fin du XIXe siècle et pendant la première moitié du XXe siècle* (thesis for doctorat de 3e cycle, Paris, École des Hautes Études en Sciences Sociales, 1979).

the old issue of morphology and with it the question of Kabylia's political traditions.[20] Thus a 'democratic' character has been ascribed to the Kabyles in recent decades primarily as a function of the fact that the Berberist conception of their identity has been opposed to and subversive of the official conception of the Algerian national identity as 'Arabo-Muslim', which ignored the Berber aspect.[21] It has had little or nothing to do with the political organisation of Kabyle society in the pre-colonial era and the political traditions that have sprung from this, which have long been generally ignored.

In recent years, however, it has finally become impossible to continue to overlook these traditions. In the summer of 2001, a new popular protest movement emerged in Kabylia, federating so-called 'Coordinations' in the six *wilayāt* of the Kabylia region[22] in the wake of widespread rioting in which over 120 young Kabyles were shot dead by the gendarmerie. This movement was based on the villages of Kabylia and mobilised their political traditions, above all the tradition of the village council or assembly, the *jema'a*.[23] While the Janus-like couplet of names it gave itself – *Le Mouvement citoyen* ('The Citizens' Movement') on the one hand and *Les 'aarsh* (generally understood to mean 'The Tribes') on the other – was mystificatory and deeply ambiguous to say the least (was the movement modernist and democratic or 'tribal' and backward-looking?), the fact that it mobilised traditional solidarities and forms of political organisation and behaviour was unmistakable and excited much comment.

That the Algerian press and some academic observers were impelled by this development at last to talk about Kabylia's political traditions by no

---

20 An issue and a question which, however, I addressed in my doctoral thesis, Oxford University, D.Phil., 1980 (unpublished in book form but subsequently given limited circulation under the title *Algerian Socialism and the Kabyle question*, University of East Anglia, School of Development Studies, Monographs in Development Studies No. 8, June 1981) and more recently in *Co-opting Identity: the manipulation of Berberism, the frustration of democratisation and the generation of violence in Algeria*, London School of Economics, Development Research Centre, Crisis States Programme Working Paper (1st series) No. 7 (December 2001), 46pp.

21 That is, up until November 1996, when a revision of the Algerian constitution at last formally acknowledged the Berber dimension – *l'Amazighité* – of Algerian society alongside the Arab and Islamic dimensions.

22 That is, the *wilayāt* of Tizi Ouzou and Bejaia, which encompass the greater part of Greater and Lesser Kabylia, and the *wilayāt* of Boumerdès, Bouïra, Bordj Bou Arrerij and Setif, which include the western, southern and eastern fringes of Kabylia respectively.

23 For a detailed discussion of this, see the report, based on some 70 interviews conducted in the region, which I wrote for the International Crisis Group, *Algeria: Unrest and Impasse in Kabylia*, Middle East/North Africa Report No. 15, Cairo/Brussels (10 June 2003), 41pp, especially chapter V, 'The Peculiarity of the Coordinations', section D: 'Structure and spirit: the projection of the jema'a'.

means signified that these were finally being adequately understood.[24] The eruption of these traditions into the political arena through the medium of the *Mouvement citoyen/Les 'aarsh* took the Algerian political class and intelligentsia but also most academic specialists by surprise.[25] The abrupt resumption of the old debate on the morphology of Kabylia accordingly witnessed a corresponding reanimation of the spectrum of irreconcilable *idées fixes* which had defined the positions staked out by rival points of view on this subject a century earlier. These had included the notion that the Kabyles, being democrats in some sense and having their own code of law distinct from the Islamic *Sharī'a*, were radically different from the 'Arabs' and not 'really' Muslims and so natural candidates for assimilation into the French national community, a view which had eventually provoked its equally simplistic and dogmatic counter-claim in the assertion (developed in the 1930s and 1940s but which I encountered in Algeria in the early 1970s) that 'the Berbers' were simply an invention of French colonialism, as well as more sophisticated reactions.[26] A similar polarisation of the debate has occurred in recent years. Thus in 2001 a French scholar, Alain Mahé, published a long study[27] which argued that the Kabyle *jema'a* had been usefully modernised with the aid of the developing fluids furnished by France during the colonial era and accordingly could and should form the basis of a reconstituted democratic Algerian state today. But the same year that witnessed this surprising reassessment of the Kabyle *jema'a* by French scholarship simultaneously produced its antithesis in the shape of a book by an Algerian author, Kamel Chachoua, himself a native of Kabylia, which vigorously denied the significance attached to the *jema'a* by the nineteenth-century authors (and so, by unavoidable implication, by subsequent authors

---

24 In response to what I considered a misleading article on this matter ('Une tradition très ancienne' by Ahatim Idir) published in the Algerian daily *El Watan* on 23 May 2001, at the height of the disorders in Kabylia, I submitted an article, 'A propos de la jemaa et de la Kabylie', to *El Watan* which declined to publish it; it was subsequently published in full on the website Algeria-Watch (www.algeria-watch.org/farticle/kabylie/roberts_jemaa.htm).

25 A notable exception is Azzeddine Kinzi, whose dissertation 'Tajmaat du village Lequelaa des Aït Yemmel: étude des structures et des fonctions' (Mémoire de Magistère, Institut de langue et de culture amazighes, University of Tizi Ouzou, 1998) I have unfortunately been unable to consult.

26 The interesting attempt by a prominent member of the Association of the *'ulamā'*, Tawfiq el-Madani, to counter French assimilationist theses by claiming the Berbers came originally from west Asia and were Semites and thus cousins of the Arabs has been explored in depth by James McDougall in his book *History and the Culture of Nationalism in Algeria* (Cambridge: Cambridge University Press, 2006), especially chapter 5.

27 Alain Mahé, *Histoire de la Grande Kabylie XIXe-XXe siècles. Anthropologie historique du lien social dans les communautés villageoises* (Paris: Éditions Bouchène, 2001).

as well), identified this view with the long discredited assimilationist myths about the Kabyles and insisted that the *only* institutions that pre-colonial Kabyle society had possessed were the *zawāyā*, the religious 'lodges', which bore witness to and guaranteed Kabylia's Muslim character.[28] Since these two mutually exclusive views of pre-colonial Kabylia and its institutions bore the imprimatur of the same French academic institution (the École des Hautes Études en Sciences Sociales in Paris),[29] their virtually simultaneous publication strikingly illustrated the confusion that has vitiated the discussion of Kabylia in contemporary Algerian and Berber studies.

Both the nineteenth-century and the early twenty-first-century polemics over these matters have testified to the extent to which a number of extremely septic issues have dominated the consideration of Kabylia's institutions and traditions. This is, of course, an important part of the reason why this entire subject matters. But the revival of these polemics also testifies, most eloquently, to the fact that the earlier controversy was never properly concluded. Rather, what happened is that, in the course of the twentieth century, the terms of the scholarly debate on the political anthropology of Kabylia were changed as a new paradigm supplanted the old. But the new paradigm was even less well equipped than its predecessor to account for the complexities of Kabyle society and its political organisation in the pre-colonial era, which is why the matters originally in dispute – the nature and significance of the *jema'a*, the relation of religion to politics in Kabyle society and the character of Kabyle law – remain to be resolved.

Pre-colonial Kabylia and the academy:
II. Towards a clarification of the debate

The morphology of Kabylia was central to the concerns of the principal nineteenth-century observers, Adolphe Hanoteau and Aristide Letourneux, joint authors of *La Kabylie et les Coutumes Kabyles*, and Émile Masqueray, author of *Formation des Cités chez les Populations Sédentaires de l'Algérie*. As these

28 Kamel Chachoua, *L'Islam Kabyle. Religion, Etat et société en Algérie. Suivi de l'Epître (Rissala) d'Ibnou Zakri (Alger 1903), Muphti de la Grande Mosquée d'Alger* (Paris: Maisonneuve & Larose, 2001). For a discussion of this book, see my review article, 'La Kabylie à la lumière tremblotante du savoir maraboutique', *Insaniyat: Revue algérienne d'anthropologie et de sciences sociales*, 16 (January–April 2002), 99–115.

29 Where Alain Mahé is Maître de Recherche and where Chachoua's doctoral thesis (on which his book is closely based), was awarded the prize for the best doctoral thesis (out of 178) for the year 2000.

authors presented it, Kabyle society was above all a society of self-governing village communities. While noting the existence of kinship groups at levels below that of the village and of forms of political organisation above this level, they did not hesitate to accord primacy to the village and to the institutional expression of its subjective existence, the village council or assembly, known by the Arabic term *jema'a* or its Kabyle equivalent *thajma'th* (plural: *thijemmu'a*). And, in describing the Kabyle *thajma'th*, they placed particular emphasis on the role of factions or 'parties' within it, the *sfûf* (singular: *saff*).[30] Thus, while assemblies and *saff* divisions existed at levels above the village – the 'tribe': *'arsh* (plural: *'aarsh*) and the supra-tribal confederation – Kabyle political life was primarily an affair of the village assembly and of the interaction of the rival *sfûf* within it.

For most of the second half of the twentieth century, this view of pre-colonial Kabylia was adhered to by – apart from the present writer – only two European authors working on the region,[31] Jean Morizot, whose remarkable books have been based upon extensive first-hand experience,[32] and Camille Lacoste-Dujardin, who carried out extensive fieldwork in maritime Kabylia. But Lacoste-Dujardin, while adhering to the view of the nineteenth-century authorities regarding Kabyle political organisation,[33] devoted her research to other questions and made no intervention of her own in the debate on the political anthropology of the region. As for Morizot, his experience was that of a colonial administrator; he had no academic standing and his writings have been largely ignored by his academic contemporaries. Neither Pierre Bourdieu[34]

---

30 The French literature on Kabylia usually transcribes this word as *çof* or *çoff*.

31 It was also adhered to by the French specialist on the Moroccan Berbers, Robert Montagne (1893–1954) and more recently by Gabriel Camps; see his *Berbères: Aux marges de l'Histoire* (Paris: Éditions des Hespérides, 1980), 309–10 and 331–3.

32 Jean Morizot, *L'Algérie kabylisée* (Paris: J. Peyronnet, 1962); *Les Kabyles: Propos d'un Témoin* (Paris: Publications du CHEAM, 1985).

33 In her introduction to *Un village algérien* (Algiers: SNED, 1976), Lacoste-Dujardin provides an elegant summary of the classical view of the village as a 'unité politique, administrative et juridique' and indicates that she subscribes to this, but her book, a sociological study of a contemporary Kabyle village, focuses on other matters. More recently, in two striking articles, 'Géographie culturelle et géopolitique en Kabylie', *Hérodote*, 103 (2001) and 'Grande Kabylie: du danger des traditions montagnardes', *Hérodote*, 107 (2002), she discusses pre-colonial Kabylia's political organisation in the course of considering how the Kabyles' democratic and egalitarian traditions informed the outlook of the rioters in 2001 and the subsequent protest movement, but without addressing the problems in the nineteenth-century view that I have raised here. The question of the contemporary significance of Kabylia's political traditions, which I have also addressed (Roberts: *Co-opting identity* (2001), and *The Battlefield* (2003), chapters 2, 18 and 19), is to be distinguished from that of the nature of the pre-colonial Kabyle polity and falls outside the scope of this book.

34 Bourdieu, *op. cit.*, 1–24; see also his *Sociologie de l'Algérie* (Paris: PUF, 1958).

nor Jeanne Favret[35] nor Ernest Gellner followed the opinions of Hanoteau and Letourneux and Masqueray. Each of them, if on different grounds, denied the earlier view of the Kabyle village and its *jemaa*.

The most coherent alternative to the nineteenth-century view is that derived from the theory of segmentarity, expounded in the case of the Berbers of the central High Atlas of Morocco by Ernest Gellner[36] and subsequently stated by him to be applicable to the Kabyle case.[37] The theory explains how tribal populations living beyond the ambit of the state and without specialised institutions of order-maintenance are nonetheless able to solve the problem of order by means of the principle 'divide that ye need not be ruled'[38] – that is, through the self-regulating interaction of the kinship groups of which they are composed at every level of social organisation. Each tribe is segmented into a number of clans, each clan into a number of lineages and each lineage into a number of households or tents, and at each level – there may be more than three – order is maintained by the 'balancing and opposition' of the various segments,[39] the theory presupposing that, at each level, the number of segments is fairly small (rarely more than seven) and that the segments are of roughly equal size and strength.

In the central High Atlas, Gellner shows how this 'ordered anarchy'[40] is dependent upon the presence of saintly lineages which are outside the system of kinship rivalries of the lay population and so available to mediate disputes and lubricate the functioning of the segmentary system. These saints, *igurramen* (singular: *agurram*), have their counterparts in Kabylia, where they are known as *imrabdhen*.[41] But it is a necessary implication of the theory that no single level of the segmentary system is more important than the others; as Gellner insists, it is the segmentary system as a whole which is the order-maintaining mechanism. This theory therefore cannot accommodate the nineteenth-century view of the primacy of the village in Kabyle political organisation, and Gellner's rejection of this view is a logical corollary of his own general theory.

Although it was only in 1985 that Gellner explicitly stated his theory to be applicable to the Kabyle case, it clearly informed the interpretations put forward by Bourdieu and Favret in the 1960s. In *Sociologie de l'Algérie* and

---

35 Jeanne Favret, 'Relations de dépendance et manipulation de la violence en Kabylie', *L'Homme*, VIII, 4 (October–December 1968), 18–43.

36 Gellner, 1969, *op. cit.*

37 Gellner, 1985, *art. cit.* and 1987, *op. cit.*, 29–46.

38 Gellner, 1969, *op. cit.*, 41 *et seq.*

39 Gellner, 1969, *op. cit.*, 42.

40 Gellner, *art. cit.*, in 1987 *op. cit.*, 34.

41 Singular: *amrabedh*, the Kabyle form of the Arabic *mrābit*, plural: *mrābtīn*.

The Algerians,[42] Bourdieu presented an analysis of Kabyle political organisation which closely resembled the segmentarist model in nearly every respect. He did not, however, adhere fully to the logic of this model, for he insisted that one level of social organisation is more important than the others. This is not the village, however, but the consanguinous clan; it is the clan, *adrum* (plural: *iderman*) which 'is the real political unit'.[43]

Bourdieu first stated his view of Kabylia in 1958, before Gellner's segmentarity model of Berber politics was in circulation,[44] and so could not take account of Gellner's forceful argument that no one level in a segmentary system can have primacy because it is the segmentary structure as a whole which is the order-maintaining mechanism. A key element of Gellner's argument here concerned 'the dynamics of fission and fusion'. Order within a group (e.g. a tribe) is a function of the fact that it is 'segmented' into sub-groups (e.g. clans) which 'balance and oppose' one another; this is the dynamic of fission. But the element of conflict inherent in these oppositions is moderated and prevented from leading to the dissolution of the larger group by that fact that the sub-groups unite to form the larger group and this higher level unity transcends the lower-level disunity whenever the solidarity of the larger group is triggered by challenges from similar groups at the same level of size (the dynamic of fusion). Because Bourdieu placed all the emphasis on the clan and dismissed the next level up, that of the village, as unimportant, he lacked any notion of how conflict between clans might be moderated by the unifying effect of their shared membership of a larger group, either in accordance with the segmentarity logic, which required the village to be a super-clan – that is, a kinship group of which the clans recognised their shared membership – or on a non-segmentary basis, which required the village to be able to moderate conflicts between kinship groups on some other principle.

Thus Bourdieu's account of Kabylia negated previous accounts without proposing a coherent alternative. The effect of his argument concerning the clan was tacitly to refute Masqueray and Hanoteau and Letourneux in respect of their view of the village. Unlike Gellner, Bourdieu did not deduce his view from a general theory. It was a generalisation from his observations in the village of Ath Hichem in central Kabylia. But this generalisation was misconceived. The political importance which Bourdieu attributed to the *adrum* is actually to be attributed to the *saff*. At Ath Hichem, as Bourdieu made clear, there are only two *iderman*; they therefore constitute the basis of the two rival *sfûf* whose interaction is the stuff of local politics. In many other villages, more than two

---

42 *The Algerians* is a translation of *Sociologie de l'Algérie* but includes additional material on Kabylia omitted from the French text.

43 Bourdieu, 1962, *op. cit.*, 18.

44 Gellner submitted his doctoral thesis, *The organization and role of a Berber zawiya*, in 1961.

iderman are to be found, such that the *sfūf* do not coincide with particular clans but are based upon or subsume more than one. In these villages, the clan as such has no particular political significance. It is only because the *sfūf* at Ath Hichem coincided with the clans that the latter functioned as 'real political units'. Bourdieu's argument for the general primacy of the clan against that of the village thus falls to the ground, for the political significance of the *sfūf* is, as we shall see, a function of their role in the village assembly. And his ancillary claim that the Kabyle village has become 'a true political unit' only since the colonial administration made it into an administrative unit with its own *amīn* ('a sort of mayor'),[45] ignores the fact that every Kabyle village in the pre-colonial period was a political unit and had its own *amīn*, as Hanoteau and Letourneux make abundantly clear.

The muddle which Bourdieu got into on this cardinal point precluded him from arriving at a lucid understanding of the *sfūf*. He initially presented them as moieties and appeared to imply that order in Kabyle society was a product of the way the *sfūf* balanced each other, without explaining either *how* order was the result of this or, indeed, *why* the *sfūf* existed in the first place. On the latter point, he subsequently suggested that they should be understood as an expression in the political sphere of a general feature of Kabyle life to which he gave unprecedented emphasis, namely the prominence in the traditional Kabyle vision of the world of archetypal binary oppositions: male/female, outside/inside, open/closed, east/west, high/low, right/left, straight/crooked, fire/water, dry/wet, etc. These oppositions were also, he observed, prominent in ritual games and he actually went so far as to claim that the logic of the *sfūf* was derived from the logic of these games (whatever this logic consisted of, a point he omitted to specify).[46] Thus, in Bourdieu's account, the *sfūf* appear to be both important and enigmatic, a mystery he could neither ignore nor elucidate.

Favret's view amounts to another variant of what may be called 'quasi-' (or 'sub-') segmentarist' theory. Unlike Gellner, she insisted on the importance of the *sfūf* and, unlike Bourdieu, she presented an elaborate, although largely abstract and speculative, picture of the logic of their interaction which systematically implicated them in the adversarial relations between kinship groups and especially the vendetta. Yet, like Gellner and Bourdieu, she too dismissed the nineteenth-century view of the Kabyle village, by describing it as merely the form of settlement corresponding to the clan ('*le patrilignage*').[47] This choice would have enabled her, unlike Bourdieu, to construct a coherent segmentarist

---

45 Bourdieu, 1962, *op. cit.*, 19.

46 Bourdieu, 'The Kabyle house or the world reversed', in Pierre Bourdieu, *Algeria 1960* (Cambridge: Cambridge University Press, 1979), 150, footnote 40.

47 Favret, 1968, *art. cit.*, 23.

explanation of Kabyle order had she wished to do so. Her claim that the village community formed a 'clan' – which logically entailed that the *iderman* were to be regarded as 'sub-clans' – made it possible to argue that the segmentarist dynamics of fission and fusion could operate, in that the conflicts between *iderman* were moderated by their unity at the village ('patrilignage') level. But her insistence on the central importance of the *sfūf* ruled out this option. At the same time, however, her claim that the Kabyle village was a kinship unit made it impossible for her to explain the significance of the *saff* system, which, as we shall see, was predicated in part upon the fact that the *thaddarth* was *not* a kinship unit, such that whatever occasional connection there may have been between *saff* mobilisation and conflicts (not to mention vendettas) between kinship groups was secondary to the main action and function of the *sfūf*, which Favret failed to grasp.

Alain Mahé's discussion of this issue locates itself 'at the intersection of the two currents' – that is, the nineteenth-century view (Hanoteau and Letourneux, Masqueray) and the segmentarist and quasi-segmentarist perspective (Gellner, Bourdieu, Favret) – and does not advance an alternative theory of its own.[48] While criticising Favret's identification of the village with a 'patrilignage' (and so agreeing on this point with my own long-held view), Mahé partly accepts Favret's view of the *sfūf* as thoroughly implicated in the logic of vendetta between rival kinship groups, and simultaneously recycles Bourdieu's view of the *sfūf* as the organised indulgence of a taste for binary oppositions rooted in a timeless and allegedly idiosyncratic collective psychology that is simply an unexplained given.

Thus it can be seen that what these twentieth- and early twenty-first-century views have had in common is the failure to understand the character, role and logic of the *sfūf* in Kabylia and the way in which these were integral and indispensable elements of the nature and conduct of the *jema'a*. As such, these accounts have all, in different ways, represented regressions from rather than advances on the understanding of the best of the nineteenth-century French observers and of Hanoteau and Letourneux and Masqueray in particular.

The only theoretically coherent alternative to the nineteenth-century interpretation is the segmentarity thesis as expounded by Gellner. Neither Bourdieu nor Favret nor Mahé has put forward a coherent analysis. While the segmentarity thesis is not applicable to Kabylia, as will become clear, it is understandable that Gellner should have put it forward, in so far as he did so in response to the failure of the nineteenth-century theorists, and Masqueray in particular, to explain fully the peculiar character of the Kabyle village. It is the lacunae in Masqueray's description of the *thaddarth* which explain the apparent inconsistencies in his account. And it is these apparent

---

48 Mahé, *op. cit.*, 119.

inconsistencies which formed the point of departure of Gellner's argument in 1985, which amounted to the claim that what Masqueray described in Kabylia and the Aurès were segmentary systems essentially similar to those Gellner found in Morocco and that Masqueray was accordingly a segmentarity theorist *avant la lettre* and despite himself.

The two perspectives

Gellner's claim that Masqueray was the true ancestor of the segmentarity theory posited a linear development of Western scholarly theory regarding Berber society from the 1880s to the 1960s. To put it schematically, the line of descent was Masqueray to Durkheim to Evans-Pritchard to Gellner. Gellner borrowed Evans-Pritchard's concept of segmentarity and the concomitant segmentarist theory of order-maintenance in stateless societies and applied it to Morocco's Berbers, but Evans-Pritchard had worked this up out of the concept of 'segmental social organisation' which Durkheim had expounded in *The Division of Labour in Society* and which Durkheim claimed was partly based on the work on the Kabyles undertaken by Masqueray and by Hanoteau and Letourneux before him, sources Durkheim acknowledged in a famous footnote.[49]

This version of the genealogy of the segmentarity theory involved several ploys. First, it emphasised the empirical element of Masqueray's work – claiming this described segmentary societies whether Masqueray realised this or not – while ignoring its theoretical and conceptual content and its actual argument, which stressed the role of institutions (the *jemaʿa* and the *sfūf*). Second, it relied heavily on Durkheim's footnote, taking this as proof that the segmentarity idea can indeed be read back into Masqueray at least if not Hanoteau and Letourneux as well. Third, it faced a big problem in the extremely important work of Robert Montagne,[50] since major elements of Montagne's analysis concerned the role of the *jemāyaʿ* and the *ilfūf*.[51] Gellner got around this by lauding the aspect of Montagne's analysis he could accept – the discussion of the relations between the Chleuh of south-western Morocco and the central power (the *Makhzen*) – while dismissing the indigestible emphasis on the *ilfūf* as a logical error, on the grounds that, since the *ilfūf* operated at only one level (or so Gellner claimed), they could

---

49   Emile Durkheim, 1893. *De la division du travail social.* Paris. English translation: *The division of labour in society* (New York: The Free Press, 1964), 177.

50   Author notably of *Les Berbères et le Makhzen dans le Sud du Maroc: Essai sur la transformation politique du groupe Chleuh* (Paris: Félix Alcan, 1930).

51   *Liff* or *Leff* (plural: *ilfūf*) is the word used in Morocco to indicate a political alliance and so the counterpart of the Algerian *saff*.

not explain the maintenance of order as whole. This tacitly presupposed that the political systems of the Chleuh were segmentary systems, for this was the unstated premise of Gellner's insistence that no one level could predominate. Thus Gellner's argument was a circular one and a false solution to the problem Montagne's work posed for his position.

I have argued elsewhere in detail that Gellner's reading of Masqueray, Durkheim's citation and reading of Hanoteau and Letourneux and of Masqueray and Gellner's account of the history of Western theories of Berber politics are all mistaken.[52] This history has not been that of a single perspective, evolving from the theoretically primitive (or confused) but empirically reliable work of Masqueray while gaining steadily in sophistication until it reached its finished form in Gellner's model. On the contrary, two quite distinct perspectives have been present in the scholarly literature but one emerged later than the other, and what has happened is that the second perspective supplanted and dispossessed the first.

The first perspective (hereafter perspective A) is that of Hanoteau and Letourneux, Masqueray and Montagne. In saying this I am not arbitrarily pigeonholing these writers, but endorsing their own view. Masqueray described himself as a disciple of Hanoteau and Letourneux[53] and Montagne equally clearly presented himself as a disciple of Masqueray.[54] That these authors had grounds for suggesting that they belonged together in the same intellectual tradition is clear from the fact that their analyses were concerned with the same features of Berber political organisation. These were:

  i. the role of the *jema'a* (council or assembly) of the village or 'canton' or tribe;
 ii. the role of the man who presides it, usually known as the *amīn* in Algeria and *moqaddem* or *amghar* in Morocco;
iii. the role of the other men who compose it, variously known as *temman* or *l-'uqqāl* in Algeria and *aït arbaïn* or *inflas* in Morocco;
 iv. the corpus of Berber law, called *qānūn* in Algeria and *qānūn* or *izirf* in Morocco;
  v. the nature and action of the parties or factions or alliances known as *sfūf* in Algeria and *ilfūf* in Morocco;
 vi. the question of what is the principal unit of government, to which the answer given by Hanoteau and Letourneux in Kabylia was the village, *thaddarth*, and that given by Montagne in Morocco was the 'canton', *taqbilt*.

---

52 Hugh Roberts, 'Perspectives on Berber politics: on Gellner and Masqueray, or Durkheim's mistake', *Journal of the Royal Anthropological Institute* (N.S.), 8, 1 (March 2002), 107–26.

53 Masqueray, 1886 (1983), *op. cit.*, 19.

54 Montagne, 1930, *op. cit.*, 8.

The second perspective (hereafter perspective B) is that of Gellner and those other authors who have taken their cue from his segmentarity theory, such as David Hart,[55] Ross E. Dunn,[56] Amal Rassam Vinogradov[57] in Morocco and Mohand Khellil and Tassadit Yacine in Algeria. This emphasises an entirely different set of features of Berber social organisation, namely

i. the kinship groups which are 'segments' of larger groups at the next level up and themselves composed of segments at the next level down and so on;

ii. the dynamics of fission and fusion by which kinship groups divide and unite;

iii. the extent to which power both within and between segments is diffused and a rough egalitarianism prevails, articulated in terms of the code of honour;

iv. the manner in which segments oppose and balance each other at the same level, illustrated in the legal register by the practice of the collective oath and in the register of violence by the feud;

v. the mediating and arbitration functions performed by the 'saints' or *baraka* (charisma)-possessing members of holy lineages, called *igurramen* in central Morocco and *mrābtīn* (or, in Berber, *imrabdhen*) in Algeria; and

vi. the *absence* of a crucial unit of government at a particular level of the social organisation.

The two perspectives evidently emphasise different things and each plays down those features emphasised by the other. Theses differences between A and B are connected with the fact that they are asking significantly different questions. A's question is: 'how do these populations – independent of the central power – contrive to govern themselves?'[58] B's question is: 'how – in the absence of specialised order-maintaining institutions – is order maintained?' But they are

55 David Hart, 'Segmentary systems and the role of "five fifths" in tribal Morocco.' *Revue de l'Occident Musulman et de la Méditerranée*, 3, 1 (1967), 65–95; 'The tribe in modern Morocco: two case studies', in Gellner and Micaud, 1972, *op. cit.*, 25–58; *The Aith Waryaghar of the Moroccan Rif: an ethnography and history* (Tucson: University of Arizona Press, 1976).

56 Ross E. Dunn, 'Berber imperialism: the Aït Atta expansion in southeast Morocco' in Gellner and Micaud, 1972, *op. cit.*, 85–107; *Resistance in the desert: Moroccan responses to French imperialism, 1881–1912* (Madison: University of Wisconsin Press, 1977).

57 Amal Rassam Vinogradov, 'The socio-political organisation of a Berber "Taraf" tribe: pre-Protectorate Morocco' in Gellner and Micaud, 1972, *op. cit.*, 67–83; *The Aït Ndhir of Morocco* (Ann Arbor: Michigan, 1974).

58 See Hanoteau and Letourneux, 1872–3, *op. cit.*: II, 1, where they remark of the Kabyles' political organisation, 'Jamais, peut-être, le système de *self-government* n'a été mis en pratique de manière plus complète et plus radicale ...' (italics in original).

also related to the difference between their respective conceptions of the political sphere. A suggests or depicts a political sphere which possesses a substantial measure of autonomy of the social structure, whereas for B the political sphere is a simple reflection – indeed, a mere aspect – of the social structure. On this point, B is very clear: the social structure, the segmentary system, *is* the order-maintaining mechanism. A, on the other hand, is both less explicit and less coherent; only Masqueray appears to have had a definite understanding of the measure of autonomy of the political sphere from the social structure in Berber society, but he failed to convey it effectively.

This dichotomy between two clear-cut perspectives does not account for all the authors who have done serious work on Berber politics. But, as I have explained elsewhere,[59] they are in fact the only two coherent perspectives, and we may as well now name them.

A is what I propose to call the *Institutional-Historical* perspective on Berber politics. It recognises and affirms the existence of political institutions amongst the populations it studies,[60] it makes these institutions the central focus of its analysis of how they govern themselves, it is generally inclined to consider how these institutions evolve and how they came into existence,[61] and accordingly tends to view the populations in question and their political life in historical perspective.[62]

B is the *Structural-Sociological* perspective. It affirms the radical absence of political institutions amongst the populations in question and it accordingly regards the social structure as the central feature of political life, both the source of the problem of order and the source of the solution to this problem. But, because it conceives of the social structure as a kinship structure which exists in virtue simply of the ties of blood which obtain within the populations in question, it is not led to look outside this structure for the secret of its existence and in particular is disinclined to engage in historical investigation; lacking political institutions, the populations in question are considered to lack any history properly so-called and to possess only legends and genealogies, which they interpret and manipulate according to the requirements of the present. So there can be no question of explaining Berber political life in terms of the

---

59 Roberts, 2002, *art. cit.*
60 Witness the title of chapter IV of the second part of Montagne's classic work (1930): '*L'organisation républicaine: les institutions politiques*'.
61 This was not really true of Hanoteau and Letourneux, preoccupied with French policy towards the Kabyles and so disinclined to consider the pre-colonial history of Kabylia, but it was certainly true of their successors, Masqueray and Montagne, and in some measure also of earlier French authors, notably Carette and Devaux.
62 As Gellner himself, rather oddly, observed, Montagne 'felt no obligation whatever to be ahistorical. On the contrary, he made ... remarkable use of history'; see 'The sociology of Robert Montagne' in Gellner, *Muslim Society* (Cambridge: Cambridge University Press, 1981), 179–93: 187.

historical chain of cause and effect and it is instead explained in terms of the static, circular or at most cyclical logic of the relationships constitutive of the structure and the functionality of the various procedures, arrangements and patterns of conduct elaborated in accordance with this logic.

The central event in the history of Western ideas about Berber society in the twentieth century was the paradigm shift whereby the second perspective supplanted the first and it did this without seriously refuting the first. It is my contention that, whatever this shift may have yielded in the way of valuable insights into Berber organisation elsewhere, it has precluded a lucid and accurate understanding of the Kabyle case and marked a regression in the academic understanding of this case. This contention is a major premise of the argument of this book, which I locate very firmly in the tradition of the institutional-historical perspective, while at the same time addressing the shortcomings of earlier work done in this tradition without departing from the perspective that constituted it.

It would be a straightforward matter to demonstrate that many of the empirical premises and postulates of the segmentarist thesis do not obtain in Kabylia. But to list these empirical differences would be tedious and they will in any case emerge from my own analysis of pre-colonial Kabylia as this is developed. There are, however, two other objections to Gellner's argument which I wish to make here.

The first concerns the inability of the segmentarist theory to take account of the ground and content of individuality in the various Berber societies of which it speaks and of the extent to which these societies may differ from one another in these respects. The ground and content of the individuality of an illiterate, tent-dwelling, transhumant sheep-herder in the remote fastnesses of the central High Atlas – a w-Abdi of the Koucer plateau, for example – are hardly the same as those of a skilled silversmith from Ath Yenni or a trader from Ath Irathen in central Kabylia, whether we are talking about the 1850s or the 1950s or the 2010s. The wholly sedentary character of the population and the large, compact and densely populated villages in which it was settled, the proximity to Algiers and the intense intercourse with urban society, the far more complex economy of the region – the prevalence, in particular, of commercial craft manufacture and the importance of the migratory tradition – combined to produce a culture in which economic calculation and enterprise, a cosmopolitan interest in the outside world and both civic virtues and political skills were far more highly developed.

To anticipate my later argument, we may briefly note two of the main factors responsible for this: first, the permanent presence and intensity of public opinion in Kabyle social and political life and, second, the variety of relationships and forms of association into which Kabyles necessarily and regularly entered, both at home and abroad. Among the Aït Abdi of Koucer, as described by Gellner, relations with others outside the kinship network are undeveloped and marginal;

all the important relationships are based on kinship, which presumably is why the segmentary structure is so important to the Aït Abdi and why they have developed such an elaborate form of it. In Kabylia, the segmentary structure is certainly, in a sense, there, but only in a rudimentary form. The kinship groups at the various levels exist – conjugal family, extended family household, lineage, clan, village, tribe and confederation (although the last three mentioned are *not* kinship groups in reality and should no longer be treated as such by anthropologists and sociologists) – but they constitute only the social background or, rather, the main invariant element of the social background to the action, which is by no means solely or even mainly determined by it. The segmentary structures are an element in the political system, but they are not to be mistaken for this system, which is not at all a segmentary one. The energy of the Kabyles has long gone into creating and sustaining other relationships over and above and outside and, sometimes, at odds with those inherent in the kinship network, instead of refining and elaborating their segmentary structures into a baroque system of stateless self-government *à la* Aït Abdi.

A general theory of Berber political organisation and behaviour which is disposed to ignore the content of individuality in Kabyle society cannot equip us to comprehend the remarkable role which the Kabyles have played in modern Algeria; it can serve only to inhibit the growth of this comprehension. This would not be so were Kabylia remarkable only for the number of accountants, businessmen, civil servants, doctors, lawyers, teachers and technicians which it has produced in recent generations; such things could be explained, at a pinch, in terms of the effect of French cultural influence on the region. But what is remarkable about Kabylia is the scale and character of its contribution to the *politics* of modern Algeria. And, *pace* Mahé, a capacity for politics is not something which can be imported into a society.

The second objection is, in a sense, a generalisation of the first. It is that Gellner's theory, as a theory of Berber politics, is reductionist in the extreme. In effect, politics is reduced to sociology and sociology to kinship. The first reduction involves dispensing with history. The society in question is conceived as entirely lacking in history: it merely possesses legends and genealogies, whose content and character are to be understood as more or less straightforward functions of present-day interests and their requirements. But it also involves the systematic denial of significance to institutions such as the *sfūf* and their Moroccan counterparts, the *ilfūf* and, above all, the *jemaʿa*, the council or assembly of the lineage, clan, village or tribe. Customs and practices, such as the way in which a tribe elects its chiefs, are very important, as is the mediating activity of the *igurramen*. But political institutions are quite unimportant; indeed, it is a presupposition of segmentarist theory that there are no political institutions at all. *Ilfūf* and *sfūf* are accordingly dismissed as at most occasional and secondary phenomena and the *jemaʿa* is explicitly denied any independent role. It is only a collective manifestation of the kinship group in question and has no purposes or prerogatives or authority of its own. The second reduction involves above all the denial of significant social stratification[63] and of forms of association or relationships which cut across kinship links. Kinship (which, of course, embraces fictive or putative as well as 'real' – that is, biological – kinship) and the *baraka* of the saints are all there is or, at any rate, all that matters.

This is a radical form of reductionism, hence its appearance of explanatory power.[64] In this respect, Gellner's model is a kind of mirror image of (a simplified version of) Marxism. Marxism sets out to explain social development and operates with the concepts of class, state and history. In Gellner's theory, the society in question has neither state nor classes nor history. Gellner can accordingly explain how this society achieves a certain kind of order, by means of a theory which, while amounting to a kind of anti-Marxism, can also be seen to be a kind of political equivalent of the 'hidden hand' theory of market equilibrium. Tribesmen engage in pugnacious assertions of mechanical solidarity and, thanks to saintly mediation, the sum total of all this is an effective and self-sustaining system of social control and order. But this theory can reach this elegant conclusion only by entertaining a static vision of the society. Occasional breakdowns are allowed for, but not evolution; conflict may throw things out of joint but they sooner or later return to square one. What this theory cannot explain or even permit itself to notice is social development (other than that precipitated by colonial intervention) amongst the populations to which it refers.

It is possible that social development among the Berbers of the central High Atlas in Morocco was conspicuous for its absence, at least until the later colonial period, and that such development as has occurred has been largely a product of external intervention. It is no part of my argument here to challenge the static vision of Berber society which Gellner put forward in the case of central Morocco. What is at issue is whether this static vision is applicable to Kabylia. It is not.

Significant social development was occurring in Kabylia well before the colonial period. The kind of order which prevailed there by the mid-nineteenth century was not that of a society without a history. And central to the history of pre-colonial Kabylia was the establishment of political institutions and a system of self-government based upon these institutions, and the development thereby of political traditions which have survived the colonial impact and with which the independent state still has to reckon.

---

63 As Abdallah Hammoudi pointed out in an early critique of Gellner's model; see his article 'Segmentarité, stratification sociale, pouvoir politique et sainteté', *Hespéris-Tamuda*, Rabat, vol. XV (1974), 147–79.

64 The complaint by Réné Gallissot and Gilbert Badia (*Marxisme et Algérie* (Paris: Union Générale d'Éditions, 1976), 238) that 'the approach through segmentarity … remains purely descriptive' is puzzling. Gellner's exposition of the theory certainly undertakes to explain the realities it describes and, in respect of central Morocco, unquestionably succeeds in doing so, if at a price.

CHAPTER 2

~

Economy and Forms of Settlement

What is the use of my describing to you a piece of ground which you ought to see, in order to judge of its nature?

(Friedrich Engels, *The Moorish War*)[1]

Leqbayel and Igawawen

The heartland of Greater Kabylia is the Jebel Jurjura and the series of parallel ridges which extend northwards from it. The inhabitants of these ridges and of the central Jurjura proper are the *Igawawen* and they are the core of the Kabyle population. It was the Igawawen whose defeat at the battle of Icherriden in 1857 is generally taken to have marked the French conquest of Greater Kabylia as a whole and it was they who provided the majority of the Kabyle element in the leadership of the nationalist movement from 1926 onwards. In so far as the revolutionary war of 1954–62 had a theorist before the fact, it was Hocine Aït Ahmed, from the Igawawen tribe of the Ath Yahia, and it was the central Jurjura which furnished the nucleus of Aït Ahmed's rebellion against Ben Bella's government in 1963–5.

The political salience of the Igawawen was evident to the colonial authorities by 1857 if not earlier and ensured that the attention of the colonial ethnographers and other observers thereafter was concentrated upon them. The works of Carette and Devaux,[2] Hanoteau and Letourneux and Masqueray abound with references to the villages and tribes of the Jurjura but display only a superficial interest in or acquaintance with the inhabitants of western

---

1   Friedrich Engels, 'The Moorish War', *New York Daily Tribune*, 17 March 1860, reprinted in Shlomo Avineri (ed.), *Karl Marx on Colonialism and Modernization* (New York: Anchor Books, Doubleday & Company, 1969), 416–21: 420.

2   Ernest Carette, *Études sur la Kabilie proprement dite* (Paris: Imprimerie Nationale, 2 vols., 1848); Charles Devaux, *Les Kebaïles du Djerdjera* (Marseilles: Camoin, and Paris: Challamel, 1859).

Figure 2.1: The south-west of the Igawawen district, with the peaks of the Jurjura behind. In the middle distance, the ridge bearing the Ath Boudrar villages of Bou Adnane, Ighil n'Tsedda and Ath Ali ou Harzoun and the Ath Wasif villages of Tassaft Waguemoun and Ath Eurbah.

and maritime Kabylia (and virtually none at all with those of Lesser Kabylia). This tendency to concentrate upon the Jurjura has also characterised the twentieth-century literature on the region.[3]

One effect of this bias has been to encourage the assumption that the society of the Jurjura is representative of Kabyle society in general, thus obscuring the important dichotomy between the Igawawen and the rest of the Kabyle population. Because of this, the remarkable political salience of the Igawawen has never been adequately explained. For it is because the society of the central

---

3   For example, the works of René Maunier, Jean Morizot, Pierre Bourdieu, Ramon Basagana and Ali Sayad and the output of the *Fichier de Documentation Berbère*. Most of the exceptions to this rule have not really been concerned with the political anthropology of Kabylia and have accordingly not influenced the debate about this, for example the ethnological studies, based on research on maritime Kabylia, of Camille Lacoste-Dujardin.

Jurjura differed in significant ways from that of the rest of Greater Kabylia that the Igawawen were able eventually to function as the core of the Kabyle population.

The same tendency to overlook the main difference within the society of Greater Kabylia has also characterised the perceptions of Arabophone Algerians. In Algerian Arabic, *Zwawa* (singular: *Zwawi*, usually written *Zouaoua*, *Zouaoui* by the French) is the term used to denote the people of Greater Kabylia in general as distinct from those of Lesser Kabylia. It is, of course, a derivative of *Igawawen*. This usage has arisen from the fact that the inhabitants of Greater Kabylia with whom the Arabic speakers of Algeria were acquainted were very predominantly from the Jurjura, where the migratory tradition was most highly developed.

This usage has not been confined to Arabophone Algerians. The Berbers of Lesser Kabylia have also been accustomed to refer to Greater Kabylia in general as *le pays zouaoua*, *bled Zwawa* or, in Berber, *thamurth Igawawen*. Jean Amrouche, the distinguished Kabyle poet, was born in Ighil Ali in Lesser Kabylia, but his mother, Fadhma Aïth Mansour Amrouche, came from Tizi Hibel, of the Ath Mahmoud tribe in Greater Kabylia, which Jean referred to in his memoir of his mother as 'the Zouaoua region'.[4] Strictly speaking, however, Fadhma Aïth Mansour Amrouche was not from the Igawawen district. The Ath Mahmoud tribe did not regard itself as an Igawawen tribe, nor was it so regarded by its neighbours or by the Igawawen tribes themselves.[5] For, within the society of Greater Kabylia, the dichotomy between Igawawen and the rest of the Kabyles (*Leqbayel*) has long been established. In the Kabyle dialect, *Igawawen* (singular: *Agawa*) denotes the people of the central Jurjura as opposed to those of the rest of the region. This is putting matters a little vaguely, however, and there has been a degree of uncertainty about the precise limits of the range of reference of the term in Kabylia itself.

According to Hanoteau and Letourneux, the term referred properly only to the four tribes of the Ath Bethroun confederation (the Ath Yenni, Ath Wasif, Ath Bou Akkach and Ath Boudrar) and the four tribes of the Ath Menguellat confederation immediately to their east (the Ath Menguellat proper, the Ath Attaf, Aqbil and Ath Bou Youcef). This is the most restricted use of the term, however. Devaux reported that two tribes to the east of the Ath Bou Youcef – the Ath Itsouragh and the Illilten – were known locally as 'the eastern Igawawen',[6]

---

4   Quoted by Dorothy Blair in her introduction to Fadhma Aïth Mansour Amrouche, *My Life Story*, English translation by Dorothy Blair (London: The Women's Press, 1988), xiii.

5   H. Genevois, *Taguemount Azouz des Beni Mahmoud*, 126. See also Mouloud Feraoun's account of the attitude of the people of the fictional village of 'Tizi' (based on his native village, Tizi Hibel) towards the population of the Jurjura in his semi-autobiographical novel *Le Fils du Pauvre* (Paris: Éditions du Seuil, 1954), 15.

6   Devaux, *op. cit.*, 273 *et seq.*

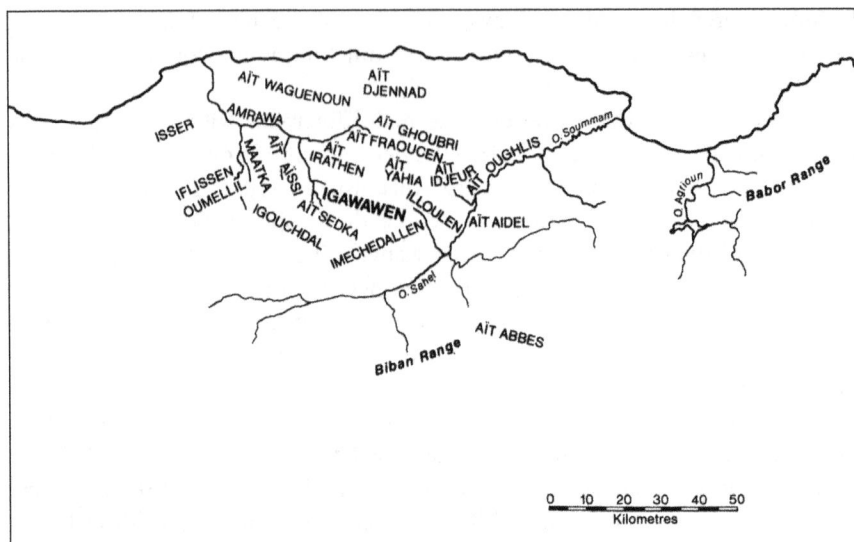

Map 2.1: Kabylia: the Igawawen and the
other main confederations and tribes.[7]

and Bourdieu states that the Ath Yahia are also considered to be an Igawawen tribe.[8] Morizot, on the other hand, uses the term 'Zouaoua' to refer, in addition to the above, to all the tribes to the north of the Ath Menguellat and the Ath Yahia up to the Sebaou valley.[9] In this usage, the five tribes of the Ath Irathen confederation and their eastern neighbours – the Ath Fraoucen, Ath Khelili and Ath Bou Chaïb – are also considered to be Igawawen.

There is a sociological warrant for this extended usage, for the tribes in question resemble their southern neighbours in most essential respects and differ in the same respects from the rest of the Kabyle population. There is also a historical warrant for Morizot's usage, for the Ath Irathen and their neighbours were referred to as 'Igawawen' by the tribes on the north side of the Sebaou

---

7   This is a modified version of a map drawn for me in 1980 by Mrs Barbara Dewing of the School of Development Studies, University of East Anglia. It does not include all tribes and confederations of the region; those absent include the Iflissen Lebahar of maritime Kabylia; the Ath Fliq, Izerkhfawen, Iazzouzen and Ighil n'Zekri of north-eastern Kabylia; the Ath Khelili and Ath Bou Chaïb to the north of the Ath Yahia; the Ath Wakour, Ath Qani and Ath Melikech of the Wad Sahel; the Aourzellaguen and Ifenayen of the Soummam valley and the Ath Mansour of Akfadou.

8   Bourdieu, 1962, *op. cit.*, 19.

9   Morizot, 1985, *op. cit.*, 62, n. 50. See also Lacoste-Dujardin, 1970, *op. cit.*, 430.

valley, notably the Ath Jennad confederation.[10] Thus Morizot's extended usage is soundly based and I shall follow it here, although it should be borne in mind that some Igawawen were definitely more Igawawen than others, and that the Ath Irathen in particular have been inclined to distinguish themselves from their fellow Igawawen to the south, a fact which has been of political significance in certain contexts, as we shall see.[11]

The fact that Kabyles from the non-Igawawen tribes of Greater Kabylia should, when abroad, refer to their native region as *thamurth Igawawen* is evidence of how far the Igawawen had succeeded in imposing their hegemony on the region as a whole. And the way in which the ordinary Kabyles of Greater Kabylia employed the terms *Agawa* and *Igawawen* within the region is in itself evidence of the unsegmentary character of Kabyle politics in the pre-colonial period.

It is an implication of the segmentarist thesis that proper names, other than those of individuals, can identify only segments of socio-political organisation – families, clans, tribes and so forth. Only one exception to this rule is allowed for, at any rate in the case of the Berbers of North Africa – that is, linguistic groupings, such as the Chleuh, Imazighen and Rifians in Morocco and the Chaouia, Mzabis and, for that matter, of course, the Kabyles themselves in Algeria. But, within the society of Greater Kabylia, 'Igawawen' is neither the name of a tribe or a confederation of tribes nor that of a distinct linguistic grouping. It denotes neither a level of segmentary organisation nor the sole admissible alternative to this. There is no comparatively uniform and distinct Igawawen variant or sub-dialect of *Thaqbaylith*[12] and the Igawawen were (and still are) divided into a number of tribes and confederations, as we have seen.

---

10 Lacoste-Dujardin, 1970, *op. cit.*, 429–31. The same view, applying the term 'Igawawen' only to 'the populations of the Larbaa n'Ath Irathen and Aïn el-Hammam districts' is taken by their western neighbours of the Ath Aïssi confederation to this day (interview with Mme Malika Aïtel of Tighzert village, Beni Douala, 13 July 2012).

11 The ambiguity and inconsistency in the use of the terms *Zwawi*, *Zwawa* etc. are vividly illustrated in the writings of an eminent Kabyle writer, Si Amar ou Saïd Boulifa (1865–1935), a native of Adeni in the Irjen tribe of the Ath Irathen confederation. In *Le Djurdjura à travers l'histoire (depuis l'Antiquité jusqu'à 1830): organisation et indépendance des Zouaoua* (Algiers: J. Bringau, 1925), he first refers to all the inhabitants of Greater Kabylia indiscriminately as 'zouaoua' (1), then implies the need for a more restrictive usage when he notes that the Ath Jennad of maritime Kabylia were not regarded locally as *Zwawa* (17) and finally refers to the Jurjura massif – as distinct from the rest of Greater Kabylia – as 'the really Zwawa district' ('pays réellement zouaoua') (41).

12 That is, *within* Greater Kabylia. The dialect of *Thaqbaylith* spoken in Greater Kabylia is often referred to by outsiders as the Igawawen dialect, in opposition to, for example, the dialect of the Wad Sahel or the Guergour and Biban mountains in Lesser Kabylia. There are local differences of speech within Greater Kabylia, but no clear distinction between the speech of the Igawawen district and that of the rest of the region, and there are even differences amongst the Igawawen, between the usages of the Ath Irathen, say, and those of the Ath Wasif or the Ath Itsouragh.

What united the Igawawen and endowed them with a particular and enduring identity which has no counterpart elsewhere in Kabylia was not kinship solidarity nor organisation nor language, but a common and distinctive culture. It is the particular culture of the Igawawen which has enabled them to function as the core of the Kabyle people. They have done so, not because they are the most ancient and long-established element of the Kabyle population, but despite the fact that they are the youngest or newest element of this population. As Jean Morizot has explained, contrary to a widespread misconception of the matter, the Jurjura was the last part of Greater Kabylia (and probably of all the several Kabylias) to be settled and its settlement began probably no earlier than the eleventh century CE.[13] The manner in which it was settled gave rise to a unique cultural development which, so far as I am aware, has no counterpart among other Berber populations in Algeria or elsewhere.

This development was that of a mountain society which was both egalitarian and unusually orderly, fiercely independent and highly integrated but also outward looking, and of an economy characterised by intensive and highly diversified commercial craft manufacture and by an equally diversified pattern of commercial and labour migration. This society was regulated by a remarkable system of self-government which achieved its final form between the early seventeenth century and the middle of the eighteenth century CE and both constituted the framework within which a complex economic life could be carried on and simultaneously gave rise to an unusually complex and sophisticated orientation to the central power.

The economy of Kabylia

Pierre Bourdieu begins his account of Kabyle society with the statement that

> settled in very heavy densities (267 inhabitants to the square kilometre in the arrondissement of Fort National) in regions of hilly, rugged terrain, the Kabyles are primarily arboriculturalists

and continues

---

13 On this point I follow Morizot's account (1985, *op. cit.*, 61) rather than the more recent suggestion by Brett and Fentress that the Jurjura was not settled until the thirteenth or even fourteenth century CE (Michael Brett and Elizabeth Fentress, *The Berbers* (Oxford: Blackwell, 1996, p/b 1997), 134), which is difficult to reconcile with Ibn Khaldun's observations on the Zwawa (see Chapter 5 below).

the economy depends mainly on two trees, the olive and the fig, together with a few complementary crops (hard wheat and barley) and some small-scale stock raising.[14]

This is a very incomplete picture.

The population density of Greater Kabylia and, above all, of the central Jurjura is certainly one of the region's most important and striking features. It has no equivalent elsewhere in the Maghrib and bears comparison with that of the Nile delta. Unlike the Nile delta, however, this superabundance of humanity is combined with an acute scarcity of arable land. It is inconceivable that this population could have been sustained had its economy depended mainly on the olive and the fig and complementary farming activities.

To ask what was the primary economic activity of pre-colonial Kabylia and what its economy mainly depended on is to ask questions which cannot be answered. The rare statistics which exist are incapable of yielding a reliable general picture.

This is partly because Greater Kabylia in the pre-colonial period was not an economy in the proper sense of the word – that is, an economic unit subject to some degree of collective accounting of resources and expenditure of the kind which generates, *inter alia*, accurate statistical records. There was no unified regional market. The units of measurement varied from one district to another and often from one tribe to another, as did the units of currency. The economic fragmentation of the region mirrored its political fragmentation.

But it is also because of the wide range of productive activities engaged in by the people of Greater Kabylia in the pre-colonial period and, in many cases, well into the twentieth century. It is extremely doubtful that any one of these was primary in the sense of being the economic mainstay of the population, such as was the case of potato cultivation in southern Ireland and rice paddy cultivation in Java. On the contrary, it would seem that the reproduction of the society depended upon its ability to engage in a wide diversity of activities rather than on any particular one of them. It would therefore be more accurate to say that the economy of pre-colonial Kabylia depended on five things – arboriculture, horticulture, craft manufacture, external trade and labour migration – and that all of these were indispensable, if in varying degrees, to the prosperity of each of the tribes and villages which composed the society.

Arboriculture and the various farming activities which complemented it were engaged in throughout the region. The olive and the fig were the principal crops, although in some districts almond, pear and cherry trees were also cultivated. The surplus production was sold on the market, especially olive oil. The importance of olive oil production can be gauged from the fact that in 1834

---

14 Bourdieu, 1962, *op. cit.*, 1.

no fewer than 358 oil mills were counted in what was later known as the *cercle* (district) of Fort Napoléon[15] (encompassing the central Jurjura and its outcrops) and 348 in that of Tizi Ouzou (encompassing the rest of central Kabylia and the western half of maritime Kabylia). In the same year, nearly one million litres of olive oil from Kabylia are estimated to have been sold on the Algiers market.[16]

The other farming activities were (and still are) stock raising and horticulture. The land in the immediate vicinity of every Kabyle village is given over to gardens which, like the orchards, are the private property of individual families. From these each household obtained most if not all of its requirements in vegetables: beans, chick peas, chili peppers, courgettes, green peppers, marrows, onions, parsnips, potatoes, tomatoes, turnips, and so on.

For most villages in the region, stock raising was a secondary activity. Most households would keep a few head of sheep and goats, the former supplying wool and meat for the rare occasions when it was consumed – that is, religious festivals and family celebrations (marriages and circumcisions) – the latter providing milk and hides. In the remoter villages of the Jurjura that had access to plentiful pasture, the flocks would be much larger and in some cases small herds of cattle would be kept. Chickens would also be kept and occasionally bees for their honey. The other animals kept (although not by all families) were mules, donkeys and oxen, the latter being bought at the start of the ploughing season and resold at its end.

Thus the people of Greater Kabylia in the pre-colonial period were self-sufficient in fruit and vegetables and (given their modest consumption) meat, poultry and eggs and produced an important surplus of olive oil for sale outside the region. With the exception of the narrow plains between Draa el-Mizan and Wadhia and between Tizi Ouzou and Azazga, however, the region produced no cereals and depended upon the Arabophone regions to the south for its supplies of the corn and barley upon which it relied for the staple elements of its diet, bread and *seksu* (cous-cous). It obtained the cereals it needed in exchange for figs and olive oil and, above all, the products of craft manufacture.

Much of Kabyle artisan production involved the exploitation of natural resources available in the region itself. Wood from the forests of the Jurjura and Akfadou and elsewhere was used in making bowls, caskets, chests, looms, paddle-wheels for water mills, ploughs, screws for olive presses, tables, tool handles and the wooden pillars, beams and doors used in house building. Much of the timber used at Algiers for boat building in the Turkish period and earlier came from

---

15 The town established by the French in the centre of the Ath Irathen territory in 1857; renamed Fort National in 1870 and Larba'a n'Ath Irathen after Independence.

16 Morizot, 1985, *op. cit.*, 74. For the description of the economic life of pre-colonial Kabylia I am indebted to Morizot, who provides a very useful summary of the findings of Hanoteau and Letourneux and the main sources since them.

Figure 2.2: Colonial-era postcard
showing an olive-oil mill in Kabylia.

the forests of Kabylia as well, as did the resin and pitch that was also required. Thus joinery and carpentry were widely practised and most villages would have a specialist or two in these crafts.

The land itself supplied other materials for craft production: stone for house building, but also for the making of small flour mills and grinders as well as the large mill-stones in use in the numerous olive-mills and water mills in the region. From the earth a wide range of pottery goods was produced including most of the vessels used in each household: bowls and dishes, the huge jars known as *ikufan* in which grain and dried vegetables and fruit would be stored, and pots of various shapes and sizes.

A great deal of Kabyle craft manufacture relied on materials obtained elsewhere, however. Woolen goods, particularly burnouses (men's cloaks) and coverlets and various types of clothing, were made from wool bought from the markets of the High Plateaux to the south. Some of the flax used in the production of linen cloths was grown locally, but much of the linen also had to be imported. The charcoal used in the manufacture of gunpowder was produced locally, but the sulphur and part of the saltpetre had to be imported from outside. The oak forests, especially in the Akfadou district, were the source of the tannin used in the preparation of leather skins.

In addition to this already impressive range of artisan production, the tribes of the central Jurjura engaged in three closely linked and highly specialised branches of craft industry: jewelry making, arms manufacture and the manufacture of counterfeit money. Of these three, only jewelry manufacture appears to have survived to this day and is almost entirely confined to certain villages of the Ath Yenni tribe, especially Ath Larba'a, and the tribe of Iwadhien (Wadhia), although the craft of gun-making appears to have survived at least until the 1940s in the village of Darna of the Ath Boudrar tribe,[17] and possibly elsewhere as well. In the pre-colonial period and probably well into the latter half of the nineteenth century, nearly all the tribes of the central Jurjura engaged in these branches of craft production, although the Ath Yenni were already pre-eminent before 1830. The weapons manufactured were rifles and pistols, sabres and daggers, as well as cutlery.[18] Counterfeit coins were the speciality above all of the village of Ath Larba'a; they were made to order and orders reputedly came from as far away as Morocco and Tunis, the Sahara and Tripoli.[19] The importance of this activity was recognised by the village, which made provision for its regulation in its local by-laws.[20]

Evidently a great deal of the craft manufacture which has been described above was not for domestic consumption but for the market and for export beyond the confines of the region. Greater Kabylia depended on a wide range of commercial exchanges with the other regions of the Algerian interior. It exported carobs, figs, fruit, grapes, olive oil, red pepper, sweet acorns, arms, jewelry, wooden utensils, clothes, leather goods of various kinds, linen cloths, pottery, soap and wax. It imported corn and barley, bullocks for ploughing and also for meat, milk cows, mules, sheep, cotton, silks, wool, copper, iron, lead and tin.

The distribution of Kabyle craft products was undertaken by the producers themselves, who would transport their goods on the backs of mules and donkeys to the markets of Algiers and the other towns but also further afield, to wherever there was a market for them. Sometimes this trade was conducted in groups; the tribes of the Ath Bethroun and Ath Menguellat confederations of the central Jurjura formed regular caravans for the merchants from their constituent villages who wished to sell their goods in the Arab interior.[21] Sometimes, however, merchants would travel alone and so approximate in appearance at least to that other characteristic figure from Greater Kabylia, the pedlar.

The Kabyle pedlar was a familiar figure in the Algerian interior in the pre-colonial period and well into the colonial period. Indeed, it is likely that, until comparatively recently, most Arabic-speaking Algerians of the countryside

17 Hocine Aït Ahmed, *Memoirs d'Un Combattant* (Paris: Sylvie Messinger, 1983), 140, n.1.
18 A notable exception to the Jurjura's near monopoly of arms manufacture was the confederation of the Iflissen Lebahr in maritime Kabylia, whose artisans were famous for the distinctive swords they made.
19 Morizot, 1985, *op. cit.*, 73.
20 Morizot, *ibid.*, n.39.
21 Hanoteau and Letourneux, *op. cit.*, vol. I, 564.

formed their opinion of the Kabyles in general from their encounters with Kabyle pedlars and this opinion was a distinctly unfavourable one. Although commercial craft manufacture was widely developed in the Jurjura, it is probable that only a minority of families engaged in it. Poorer Kabyles, unable to trade in substantial commodities of their own making, relied on long-distance peddling to supplement the meagre income from farming. They would equip themselves in Algiers or other urban centres with spices, perfumes, charms and trinkets of all sorts and then travel through the Arabophone regions and among the Chaouia of the Sud-Constantinois and act as intermediaries between these regions, re-stocking their portfolios as they went.

The pedlars were known in Kabylia as *i'attaren*, which means literally 'purveyors of perfume' (from the Arabic: *'attar*) but had perhaps already come to acquire the additional meaning that Berque notes for the word in the twentieth century, that of sellers of groceries.[22] The Kabyles distinguished between the *i'attaren ou qidhoun*, 'the pedlars with tents', and the *i'attaren ou ketsaf*, 'the pedlars with sacks'.[23] The former travelled from market to market, transporting their wares on mules and passing the night under their own tents. The latter went from door to door on foot, carrying their wares in large sheepskin knapsacks, and relied on their customers to provide them with shelter for the night.

The resort to long-distance peddling was a mass phenomenon in nineteenth-century Kabylia. Hanoteau and Letourneux noted that 'in the circle of Fort National alone, out of a population of 76,616 inhabitants, between 8,000 and 10,000 passports are issued each year to traders, of whom at least three quarters are pedlars'.[24]

The extent of Kabyle dependence upon this commercial migration was reflected in Kabyle law. For example, the third article of the *qānūn* (by-law) of the village of Koukou of the Ath Yahia tribe stipulated that 'those absent from the village who are at Constantine or Souk Ahras have two months in which to exercise the right of *shefa'a*',[25] while the second and seventh articles of the *qānūn* of the village of Taourirt Amrane of the Ath Bou Youcef tribe read as follows: 'the man who disparages an inhabitant of the eastern province pays a fine of 5 reals' and 'the man who flees the eastern province leaving debts of more than one real pays a fine of one real'.[26]

It was also noted by the French administrators of the nineteenth century. Thus we read in official reports on individual tribes that 'the Beni Bou Attaf' (i.e.

---

22 Jacques Berque, *French North Africa: the Maghrib between two world wars*, translated by Jean Stewart (London: Faber and Faber, 1967), 397.

23 Hanoteau and Letourneux, *op. cit.*, vol. I, 569–70.

24 Hanoteau and Letourneux, *op. cit.*, vol. I, 569.

25 Hanoteau and Letourneux, *op. cit.*, vol. II, 386. The right of *shefa'a* was the right of pre-emption of landed property by agnates of the vendor, subject to a specified time limit.

26 Hanoteau and Letourneux, *op. cit.*, vol. II, 429.

the Ath Attaf or Yattafen) 'devote themselves to the cultivation of the olive tree and the fig; they also engage in peddling and go periodically to trade with the populations of the interior'.[27] As for their neighbours, the 'Beni Bou Drar' (i.e. the Ath Boudrar or Iboudraren),

> the inhabitants are active and industrious. A proportion of them devote themselves to the occupation of pedlar; some exercise the profession of armourer, jewelers and turners; the rest engage in cultivation.[28]

Perhaps the best illustration of the importance of this commerce is provided by the tribe of the Ath Bou Akkach, neighbours of the Ath Boudrar on their western side, and noted for their large and extremely beautiful villages, of whom Émile Masqueray commented in 1886,

> external trade is the sole cause of this extraordinary prosperity. You will meet there, from spring to autumn, only women, old men and prodigious numbers of children. The able-bodied men are all away ... Most of them are in the province of Constantine. They stock up with goods from the Jews and Mozabites of Souk Ahras, load thin mules with spices, calico, scarves, oranges – everything which may please the Nomads and, above all, their women and head south ... One can meet them among the Nememcha and at Negrine, and even further afield ...[29]

The extent to which the Kabyle pedlars exploited the susceptibilities of their women customers in their trading ventures undoubtedly contributed to the low opinion in which they were widely held *dans le pays arabe*. As Hanoteau and Letourneux noted,

> the continual relations of the iattaren with the Arab women greatly facilitated their engagement in amorous intrigues; but these were fatal

---

27 Gouvernement-Général de l'Algérie, Direction des Affaires Indigènes, Service de la Propriété Indigène (hereafter GGA/DAI/SPI): *Minute de Rapport sur la délimitation et la répartition du territoire de la tribu des Beni Bou Attaf*, 19 March 1900 (Archives Nationales de France, Annexe d'Aix-en-Provence: Dossiers du Sénatus-Consulte des Tribus d'Algérie, series M96, dossier 244).

28 GGA/DAI/SPI, *Minute de Rapport sur la délimitation et la répartition du territoire de la tribu des Beni Bou Drar*, 19 February 1900 (M 96/242).

29 Masqueray, *op. cit.*, 100; The Nememcha mountains are to the south of Khenchela and Negrine is to the south-east of the Nememcha, near the Tunisian border, that is about 130 km from Khenchela as the crow flies and about 190 km by road – getting on for 600 km from the Jurjura.

for many of them. It is very rare that there is not, each year, occasion to record several catastrophes that have befallen pedlars who have been too gallant.[30]

If Bourdieu in his account of Kabyle society makes no mention of Kabyle craft manufacture and commercial migration, this may be because he carried out his fieldwork in the region during the war, by which time capitalist development in Algeria, linked as it was to that of the metropolis by the customs union, had largely destroyed the indigenous artisanate, not only in Kabylia but also in the towns, and the demand for cheap labour in France from 1914 onwards had brought about the reorientation of Kabyle emigration from the Algerian interior to the factories of the metropolis. While Bourdieu's picture of the Kabyle economy is understandable, then (although still misleading), it bears little relation to the situation in the pre-colonial period or, indeed, in the colonial period up to *c.* 1939.[31]

A very different understanding of the matter is suggested by the Algerian historian Mohammed Harbi. If Bourdieu's account would lead us to infer that the colonial period had seen the disappearance of Kabyle craft manufacture and commerce, Harbi implies the opposite. In seeking to explain the development of a 'Berberist' tendency within the nationalist movement in the 1940s, he remarks

> the particularism is even more pronounced in Greater Kabylia, a rural region withdrawn in a defensive posture and closed in on itself. With the advent of colonial rule, the sentiment of regional identity becomes important and acquires a new content. Thanks to the multiplication of commercial exchanges as a result of capitalist penetration, little isolated and closed universes open up to the ideas of the world outside. Sanctuary of poverty, Kabylia to survive exports its men to France and to the Algerian interior ...[32]

In other words, Greater Kabylia was a closed world, rural in character, which only opened up in response to the stimulus of colonialism. The development of Kabyle commerce and the associated migratory activities inside Algeria, instead

---

30 Hanoteau and Letourneux, *op. cit.*, vol. I, 572 (my translation).

31 As has been documented for the village of Ath Ziri of the Ath Yahia tribe (and a near neighbour of Ath Hichem, where Bourdieu did his fieldwork), Kabyle trade migration in the Algerian interior was still important up to the Second World War and fluctuated in inverse proportion to the demand for migrant labour in France; see Amrane Ben Younès, *Émigration et Société: un village de Kabylie* (Mémoire pour le Diplôme d'Études Supérieures en Sciences Politiques, Université d'Alger, Institut des Sciences Juridiques, Politiques et Administratives, June 1977), 32–3.

32 Harbi, 1980, *op. cit.*, 59–60.

of antedating colonialism, were a by-product of the capitalist development it ushered in.

Again, this picture is misleading but it is understandable that Harbi should have believed it to be true. While the people of Greater Kabylia and the Igawawen above all were not merely open to the outside world but dependent upon their intercourse with it and moved freely around it, from the point of view of an Arab Algerian (such as Harbi), the region certainly appeared to be closed to outsiders. There was no reciprocal movement of Arabic-speaking Algerians into the region to balance the outflow of merchants, pedlars and labour migrants from it, for there was no economic basis for such a movement, and the society of the Jurjura, being already overpopulated and jealous of its independence, has long evinced a predominantly suspicious and sometimes unwelcoming if not hostile attitude to strangers, wherever they may come from. But the region was closed only in this sense and in other respects was permanently interested in and oriented to the outside world.

Second, Harbi's claim that it was the colonial impact and the development of the capitalist market economy which gave rise to Kabyle migration into the Arabophone interior ignores the pre-colonial trading and migratory traditions of the Kabyles. But there is nonetheless a germ of truth in his statement. For, whereas the long-term effect of the development of colonial capitalism was to undermine traditional craft manufacture and the associated trading circuits, it is likely that, as Morizot has suggested, the initial short-term effect was to stimulate them both, in so far as the enhanced security in the Algerian interior consequent upon the establishment of the colonial order combined with the development of communications facilitated and stimulated Kabyle commerce and the artisan production associated with it.[33] Indeed, Hanoteau and Letourneux cite instances of new productive ventures developing in Kabylia in response to the European market as early as 1867 (within ten years of Icherriden), notably the cultivation of grapes on a much greater scale than before for sale to *colons* for wine-making.[34]

But, while Kabyle enterprise and commerce may well have expanded under the stimulus of the colonial impact, they were not created by it. A capacity to respond to new market opportunities when these appear is characteristic of a culture which is already oriented towards commercial and productive enterprise. Such things cannot be created or implanted in the space of a decade. And the existence of the most important kinds of Kabyle craft manufacture, notably jewelry, arms manufacture and coining, and of Kabyle migration in the Algerian interior, is well documented for the Ottoman period.

Commercial craft manufacture and long distance trade and peddling were not typical of Greater Kabylia as a whole, but only of the tribes of the

---

33 Morizot, 1985, *op. cit.*, 115–16.
34 Hanoteau and Letourneux, *op. cit.*, vol. I, 511–13.

central Jurjura, the Igawawen. Maritime and western Kabylia were less densely populated and their populations were better able to support themselves by their farming activities. These were certainly not sufficient, however, but the activity by which they were supplemented was labour, rather than commercial, migration. The main form was seasonal migration to assist the harvest in the areas of cereal cultivation. The men from western Kabylia would mostly head for the Mitija plain to the south of Algiers and to the Titteri, while those from other districts would head south to the Bouïra area and much further afield to the high plains of the Setifois, the Constantinois and the Sud-Algérois. In addition, many Kabyles, especially from maritime Kabylia, found work at Algiers or in its suburbs, as masons, navvies, gardeners, domestic servants and day-labourers. The bath attendants in Algiers were traditionally from the Ath Jennad confederation to the north of Azazga.[35]

Finally, the men of Greater Kabylia also found employment and notoriety as mercenaries. The French word *zouave*, meaning originally a native light infantryman, is a derivation of *zwawi*, but here as in so many other respects France merely took over an established tradition. In his *Annales Algériennes*, Pélissier de Reynaud noted that 'the Zouaves or Zouaoua are independent Kabyles of the province of Constantine who sell their services to the Barbary powers as do the Swiss in Europe'.[36] As Charles-André Julien has observed, the Ottoman rulers of Algeria

> soon came to realise that their authority stood in greatest danger not from their subjects, but from the janissaries. Accordingly they endeavoured to form an equally valiant but more reliable army from Kabyle, principally Zwawa, contingents.[37]

This policy, first tried under the beylerbeys in the sixteenth century, was also adopted by the penultimate Dey of Algiers, Ali Khodja, on his accession in 1817, when he quickly formed an 'honour guard' of 2,000 Zwawa 'which was charged with both guarding his person and seeing to the strict execution of his decisions'.[38] Following his death in 1818, his successor Husseïn Dey retained the services of the Zwawa contingent he had formed.[39] Ahmed, the last Bey of Constantine, followed the same policy, his infantry being composed partly of Turks and partly of Kabyles.[40]

35　Morizot, 1985, *op. cit.*, 78 and n. 54.
36　Quoted in Morizot, 1985, *op. cit.*, 78.
37　Charles-André Julien, *History of North Africa: from the Arab conquest to 1830*, translated by John Petrie (London: Routledge & Kegan Paul, 1970), 293.
38　Boulifa, *op. cit.*, 285. See also Mouloud Gaïd, *L'Algérie sous les Turcs* (Tunis: Maison Tunisienne de l'Édition, 1974), 178–9.
39　Gaïd, 1974, *op. cit.*, 205.
40　Morizot, 1962, *op. cit.*, 54.

The mercenary activities of the Zwawa were not confined to Algeria. The Ottoman rulers of Tunis also employed Zwawa, and the Tunisian case gives a striking indication of the importance of the Zwawa forces. According to L. Carl Brown, there were between 1,500 and 2,500 Zwawa in the Tunisian army, in the infantry, in the period 1837–55. (Since these figures refer only to the number actually registered, it is possible that the true number was higher.) They were drawn both from Zwawa immigrants and from the permanent Zwawa community of Tunisia, which numbered some 20,000 at this time.[41] This community had its own patron saint, Sidi Mohammed El-Bachir, who died in 1827[42] and Hussein Bey built Sidi Mohammed El-Bachir a *zāwiya* (religious lodge). As Brown remarks, 'the beys understandably courted the man (and his successors) who commanded the religious fealty of such an important part of the army.'[43]

The people of Greater Kabylia were far from being 'primarily arboriculturalists' in the pre-colonial period. They engaged in a wide range of productive and commercial activities and these activities took them in large numbers to all parts of Algeria and even further afield. There can be no doubt that it was their success in developing a skilled and diversified craft industry and in exploiting the range of commercial opportunities open to them in the interior of the country which enabled them to sustain the astonishing density of population which already characterised the region as a whole and the Jurjura in particular by the time the first French troops disembarked at Sidi Frej in 1830.

The development of this remarkable economy was uneven, however. As we have seen, the people of western and maritime Kabylia relied largely on labour migration to supplement their farming activities, whereas the Igawawen of the Jurjura relied on commercial craft manufacture and peddling and the much greater returns from these trading activities supported a correspondingly higher density of population. Thus the cultural dichotomy between the Igawawen and the inhabitants of the rest of Greater Kabylia had a clear economic content.

But if the villages of the Jurjura could not have supported their populations without the recourse to external trade and emigration on a large scale, it is also true that they could not have sustained these activities had it not been for the particular qualities of their socio-political organisation.

Morizot emphasises the role of the patriarchal family in this context.[44] Within the family there was a strict and elaborate division of labour: the first division was between those who stayed at home in the village and those who were delegated by the family to go abroad. The latter were uniquely males and a young man setting out on his first trip was obliged to marry beforehand

---

41 L. Carl Brown, *The Tunisia of Ahmed Bey, 1837–1855* (Princeton, NJ: Princeton University Press, 1974), 133–9.
42 Brown, *op. cit.*, 177.
43 Brown, *ibid.*
44 Morizot, 1985, *op. cit.*, 88.

to ensure his eventual return, the woman being on no account permitted to leave the village. In addition, the austere sexual mores of the Kabyles and the constant surveillance of each woman by her family and by village public opinion allowed her husband to remain abroad for long periods in total confidence that, on his eventual return, he would find his household as he had left it. But there are grounds for reconsidering Morizot's view of this matter, for this feature of the division of labour only developed in the colonial period, essentially from 1914 onwards, in the context of the reorientation of Kabyle labour migration to France, when it was grafted onto an underlying and far older sexual division of labour which Morizot does not discuss.

Similarly, Morizot also emphasises the significance in this context of the traditions of mutual aid and village solidarity, the extent to which Kabyle traders and pedlars in foreign parts could count on the support of fellow villagers should they ever find themselves in difficult circumstances, as not infrequently occurred.[45] Since men from a particular village tended to migrate to the same regions of the interior and of France, such solidarities would frequently be invoked. Here again, it is only one, external, aspect of the role of the village, the solidarity it engendered among its members when abroad, that is mentioned; yet this solidarity had its origin in the character of the village itself on its own ground.

The 'arsh in Kabylia

Morizot has, with reason, described Kabyle society as 'a village society' ('une société villageoise'),[46] classifying Kabylia together with, among others, the Aurès, the Mzab and the Wad Ghir in this respect, in contrast to those other regions of the Algerian countryside where dispersed settlement or transhumant pastoralism have been the rule. But it is not only a society of villages. A condition of the existence of the Kabyle village is its membership of a larger whole.

Every Kabyle village without exception belongs, or at any rate in the pre-colonial era used to belong, to a community known as an 'arsh.[47] This term is conventionally translated as 'tribu' in the French and 'tribe' in the English literature, a usage which, for brevity's sake, I have myself followed thus far. But

---

45 Morizot, *loc. cit.*, 89–90.

46 Jean Morizot, 1962, *op. cit.*, 20 *et seq.* and especially 32–68; see also Morizot, 1985, *op. cit.*

47 The only exceptions to this rule were the settlements of descendants of slaves – *abid* or *aklan* – established by the Ottoman Regency in the 1720s as advance posts in the vicinities of its forts in the lowlands (see Chapter 7). These were not true exceptions to the rule since by definition not *Kabyle* villages.

this convention encumbers the word with connotations that are out of place and misleading.[48]

The word tribe is used for populations in North Africa and the Middle East that are quite unlike those designated as 'tribes' in, for example, sub-Saharan Africa or Amazonia, where a number of salient features such as habitat, ecology, language, religion, socio-political organisation, diet and even physiognomy usually distinguish one population quite sharply from another (e.g. the Kikuyu and the Masai in Kenya) in a way and to a degree that is self-evidently untrue of the 'tribes' of North Africa and the Middle East. Such features as distinguish tribes elsewhere distinguish much larger and looser categories of population in North Africa and the Middle East – Arabs, Berbers, Kurds, Turks, Persians, Pashtun, etc. – and also, if less sharply, the regional or other historically formed identities into which these population categories may be sub-divided (e.g., for Berbers: Rifians, Imazighen, Chleuh, Kabyles, Chaouia, Mzabis, Tuareg, etc.), but not the so-called 'tribes' into which these are further sub-divided. It is, of course, widely understood that, in respect of the features (ecology, language, religion, etc.) instanced above, one Kabyle or Rifian (or Beduin or Kurdish etc.) 'tribe' is generally very like another. But, while 'tribe' does not, therefore, usually connote a distinctive and exclusive ethnic or cultural identity in the North African context, it does connote at the very least a specific kinship identity, *and this is the problem*. It is in part because it has been taken for granted that the Arab and Berber populations of the Atlas mountains and the high plateaux and deserts of the Maghrib consist of 'tribes' and that these are essentially extended kinship groups that the segmentarity thesis of Berber (but also Beduin[49]) politics possessed its initial plausibility.[50] But, in Kabylia at least, the 'arsh is not a kinship group and this fact matters.

The Arabic word 'arsh (Arabic plural: 'urūsh or 'arūsh; Berber plural: 'aarsh) is derived from the root: '-r-sh which, as a verb ('arasha), has the meaning 'to erect a trellis' and a secondary meaning of 'to roof over'.[51] One of the nouns

48 Jacques Berque has questioned the notion of tribalism in the Maghrib in his thoughtful essay 'Qu'est-ce qu'une «tribu» nord-africaine?' (in Jacques Berque, *Maghreb, histoire et sociétés* (Belgium: J. Duculot and Algiers: SNED, 1974), 22–34), but does not address the question of the 'arsh that I am examining here.

49 It should not be forgotten that the immediate source for Gellner's segmentarity thesis was E.E. Evans-Pritchard's application of the segmentary model to the Beduin of eastern Libya in his book *The Sanusi of Cyrenaïca* (Oxford: Clarendon Press, 1949). For an analysis of local level politics in Qadhafi's Libya that relies on the segmentary model, see John Davis, *Libyan Politics* (London: I.B.Tauris, 1989).

50 Indeed, in the preface to his book, *Tribesmen* (Englewood Cliffs, NJ: Prentice-Hall, 1968), *vii-viii*, Marshall D. Sahlins defines the very notion of the tribe in the terms of the segmentarity theory.

51 Hans Wehr, *A Dictionary of Modern Written Arabic*, edited by J. Milton Cowan (Wiesbaden: Otto Harrassowitz, London: George Allen and Unwin, 1971 (3rd impression)), 602.

derived from this root, *'arīsh*, has the meanings of 'arbour, bower, hut, trellis',[52] and is the name of a town in the northern Sinaï, El Arish, close to Egypt's border with Gaza. Another, which probably also subsumes the notion of a deliberately created structure, has given rise to the name of the town of Larache (*El-'arash*), at the other end of North Africa, on the Atlantic coast of northern Morocco.[53] In the Arab Mashriq, the substantive *'arsh* derived from this root means 'throne', the seat of sultans and kings, sovereign rulers. It is accordingly a mystery why this word should have come to be used in Algeria to refer to the discrete communities of which the populations of the countryside have traditionally been composed.

This mystery can been seen to be all the deeper in the light of the fact that the Arabic term translated as 'tribu/tribe' in the Moroccan case is not *'arsh* but *qabīla* (plural: *qbā'il*),[54] which is the standard term for 'tribe' in the Mashriq as well; the Beduin 'tribes' of Libya, Egypt, Sudan, Jordan and Saudi Arabia are all called *qbā'il*.[55] In addition, the word *qabīla* has certainly long been known to and employed by Algerians; as already mentioned, the standard term used by the townsfolk of pre-colonial Algeria to refer to the populations of the mountains was *el-qbā'il* – 'the tribes' – whence the derivation of the words Kabyle and Kabylia. Finally, as if this were not enough, the word *qabīla* was not only known to the Kabyles themselves but employed by them in its Berber form, *thaqbilth*, to refer to the highest level of political unity which the scholarly literature has called 'the confederation'. Why, then, should what most observers call the 'tribe' in Kabylia and, for that matter, the rest of Algeria, be known as *'arsh*?

To answer this question we should break it down into two parts. Why *'arsh* and not *qabīla*? And what is the etymological significance of *'arsh* in this context? The answer to the second question will indicate the answer to the first.

Qabīla is derived from the root *q-b-l* which, as the verb *qabila*, has the basic meaning of accepting, receiving, admitting, but the derived meanings of 'to stand exactly opposite, face, confront or counter'.[56] In Algerian Arabic and in Thaqbaylith (which has borrowed it), the adverb *qabel* can mean 'face to face', 'frontally', 'directly', 'straightforwardly', 'frankly' etc. and carries a positive value in the context of the code of honour.[57] Thus the idea at the root of the word *qabīla* is that the populations in question are divided by a number of oppositions between

---

52 *Ibid.*

53 The plural of the word *'arsh* itself gives us the name of a town in north-eastern Algeria, El-Arrouch (*El-'arūsh*).

54 David M. Hart, *Qabila: tribal profiles and tribe-state relations in Morocco and on the Afghanistan-Pakistan frontier* (Amsterdam: Het Spinhuis, 2001).

55 Madawi Al Rasheed, *Politics in an Arabian Oasis: The Rashidis of Saudi Arabia* (London, I.B.Tauris, 1991), 17.

56 Wehr, *op. cit.*, 739–40.

57 Bourdieu, 'The sense of honour' in Bourdieu, 1960, *op. cit.*, 106n, 113, 123, 128, 141, 149–50.

them, that it is the opposition between Groups A and B and between Groups C and D (and so on) that gives them their stable identities.[58] We should note that there is no reference to kinship or shared descent in this root meaning. What defines a *qabīla* is not the degree of real or putative (or entirely fictive) descent its members may (or may not) share from a distant ancestor, but its relations – primarily of facing, opposing, competing – with other similar groups. Thus it is the political aspect that is constitutive of the community. Since it is precisely my argument that it is equally the political that is constitutive of the Kabyle *'arsh*, it remains to consider why this is not, like its Moroccan (etc.) counterpart, also called a *qabīla*.

Let us rephrase this question. Why should the Arabic word for *throne* have been employed to indicate a particular kind of community in Algeria?

A throne is the seat of a sovereign ruler. What materially characterises a throne in the North African context is not merely the distinctive splendour of this item of furniture, its size and weight and the quality of the materials used to make it and so forth, but also two features which distinguish it from ordinary chairs: the fact that it has a high back and that it also, at least usually, has a kind of quasi-ceiling or canopy protruding from the top of its back above the person sitting on it that at least partially covers and protects him. Thus the idea of a throne incorporates two ideas that belong to different registers: the basic idea, intrinsic to the root *'-r-sh*, of a deliberately erected superstructure and the derived idea of a seat of sovereignty. Both of these ideas enter into the way the word *'arsh* has historically been used in Algeria to refer to a particular kind of community.[59]

The *'arsh* in Algeria in general and in Kabylia in particular was a sovereign political community collectively possessing and controlling a definite territory.[60] The community was sovereign and its territory was its seat. The territory of an *'arsh* could not be intruded upon with impunity; outsiders needed a laissez-passer, the *'anāya* (guarantee of protection) of a leading member of the *'arsh*, in order to enter and travel across this territory in safety. The leadership of the *'arsh*, whether an egalitarian assembly as in most of Kabylia or an aristocratic dynasty as obtained elsewhere, was the sovereign

---

58 Much as Mouloud Feraoun remarks, of the competing parties in a Kabyle village, 'They define themselves in opposing one another' ('Ils se définissent en s'opposant.'), *Jours de Kabylie* (Paris: Éditions du Seuil, 1954), 60.

59 I am grateful to the late David Hart for discussing and confirming his agreement with my hypothesis on this point (private correspondence, July 1990).

60 Shelagh Weir has similarly emphasised the importance of sovereignty to the populations of the Jabal Razih in north Yemen, while retaining the term 'tribe' to refer to them (Shelagh Weir, *A Tribal Order: Politics and Law in the Mountains of Yemen* (London: The British Museum Press, and Austin: The University of Texas Press, 2007)). I learned that she and I had long been working along parallel lines quite independently of one another only as recently as 2002.

government of the community, the upholder as well as partial source of the laws which regulated the social life of its inhabitants and the allocation and enjoyment of rights in its land. The territory of a Kabyle village, both its commons – pasture, woodland and watercourses – held collectively (*meshmel*) and the arable land held in individual private ownership (*lemluk*), was part of the collective territory of the 'arsh and access to it presupposed membership of the 'arsh. The collective capacity of the population of the 'arsh to defend its territory as a whole was the guarantee of the security of its constituent villages and of the integrity of their individual territories. It is here that the idea of the superstructure can be discerned, in that the 'arsh existed over and above its constituent villages and provided protection for them all.

Sovereignty was not the exclusive monopoly of the 'arsh; the latter did not have absolute authority in relation to its constituent villages, for each village also enjoyed its measure of sovereignty and so its authoritative capacity to make its own law. Rather than concentrated in a single locus, sovereignty was diffused between the two levels of 'arsh and constituent villages. But the 'arsh was normally the upper level and limit of sovereignty; while some 'aarsh might belong to a higher-level grouping, the *thaqbilth*, this was optional and many did not. In Lesser Kabylia there have never been any *thiqbilin*.

In one respect, the relationship of village and 'arsh appears to be circular. A Kabyle was a member of 'arsh X because a member of a constituent village of this 'arsh and membership of 'arsh X was simultaneously a political condition of the existence of the village in question. No village might exist outside an 'arsh. Proof of this is furnished by the perfect limiting case. There is, in Greater Kabylia, a large and well-known village that is unquestionably a Kabyle village (as distinct from an Ottoman-sponsored settlement of outsiders) and which exists in both spatial and political isolation, all on its own. This is Ighil Imoula, where the historic Proclamation of 1 November 1954 was printed. Instead of being an exception to the rule, however, Ighil Imoula confirms it, for it has been its own 'arsh: that is, Ighil Imoula is an 'arsh consisting of a single village of the same name and the sole constituent village of an 'arsh of the same name.

The notion, implicit in the root meaning of 'arsh, of a deliberately erected superstructure reflected the fact that the community in question was not constituted by kinship, by shared descent from a common ancestor, but by political agreement. While many 'aarsh in Kabylia, as elsewhere in Algeria, had names that suggested a shared kinship: Ath Yahia ('the sons of Yahia'), Ath Mahmoud ('the sons of Mahmoud') and so on, at least as many did not. Often an 'arsh name evoked the most salient feature of its territory: Ath Boudrar ('the people who possess the mountain'), Ath Wasif ('the people of the river'), Ath Oumalou ('the people of the shadow' – that is, of the north-facing slopes), Ath Ousammeur ('the people of the sunlight' – that is, of the south-facing slopes); Ighil Imoula means 'the ridge of the forest'. And where the collective name might be interpreted as implying shared descent, this was not to be taken literally. At most it commemorated an individual credited in local legend with establishing in the dim and distant past the original nucleus of the 'arsh in question in the shape of the founding settlement, around which the other constituent settlements subsequently gravitated or coalesced.

A corollary of the fact that the Kabyle 'arsh was not a kinship group, that shared kinship was not constitutive of the community even where the idiom of kinship was vaguely employed to provide a given 'arsh with its collective name, is that, for each of its villages, membership of the 'arsh was voluntary or, at any rate, the result of a political decision (whether strictly voluntary, as opposed to coerced, or not) and therefore conditional. Although most Kabyle 'aarsh have displayed impressive continuity and stability in their size and membership, it was not at all unheard of for villages to switch their allegiance to or be annexed by another 'arsh. It is well known that the villages of Tassaft Waguemoun and Ath Eurbah in the central Jurjura originally belonged to an 'arsh (now defunct) called Ath ou Belkacem before joining the Ath Wasif, as did the village of Taourirt el-Hajjaj (then called Thakhabit) before joining the Ath Yenni and the village of Ath Ali ou Harzoun before joining the Ath Boudrar. Among the Ath Mahmoud, the oral tradition records that the villages of Taguemount el-Jedid, Tala Khelil and Tighilt Mahmoud all belonged to the 'arsh before being 'surrendered' at different moments to its hostile neighbours, the Iwadhien, Ath Douala and Ath Zmenzer respectively.[61] And the remote village of Ath Waaban in the heart of the Jurjura is another case in point. Originally founded by migrants from the Ath Wakour south of the watershed, the village subsequently severed its connection with its 'arsh of origin and secured incorporation into the Ath Boudrar.[62] It is likely that other cases could be identified if the relevant research were to be conducted.

Precisely how Kabyle political organisation at the level of the 'arsh was articulated with that at village level will be considered in a later chapter. But the fact that this extended form of human settlement was – and still is – known as 'arsh, not qabīla, reflects a fundamental way in which Algeria has differed historically from Morocco and, for that matter, most other countries of North Africa and the Middle East, namely the remarkable degree of independence (if not preponderance) of the society of the mountains in relation to the towns, an independence that the Ottoman Regency struggled against with difficulty, which French colonial rule began only partially to modify and contained rather than abolished and which was subsequently reflected in the fact that the revolutionary movement which fought the war of national liberation and constituted the

---

61 Genevois, 1972, *op. cit.*, 10.

62 According to local informants at Ath Waaban, whose testimony is corroborated by French records: see Commission Administrative du Senatus-Consulte du Département d'Alger: *Rapport sur l'application du Senatus-Consulte dans la tribu du Beni Bou Drar*: sub-section 'Au sujet de la fraction d'Aït Ouabane', 14 August 1897 (M 36); see also Devaux, 1859, *op. cit.*, 236.

independent state was based overwhelmingly on the society of the countryside and of the mountains above all.[63]

To refer to the extended forms of settlement of the mountains as *el-qbā'il* is to employ the vocabulary and adopt the frame of reference of the urban population. The conception of these communities as *qbā'il*, as groups constantly opposed to and confronting one another, was the corollary of the negative conception of the society of the hillsmen 'beyond the pale of civilisation' as essentially anarchic. The existence since the ninth century CE of a comparatively stable state tradition in Morocco based on and controlling the society of the Atlantic plan and promoting the development of flourishing cities (Fès, Meknès, Marrakesh) ensured that urban conceptions of the society of the mountains have long prevailed there. But the configuration of the relationship between mountains and high plateaux on the one hand and coastal plains on the other in Algeria has been very different, and there was no tradition of continuous state formation in the lowlands until the consolidation of Ottoman power in the sixteenth and seventeenth centuries CE. A consequence of this very different history is that the hillsmen's own, essentially positive, conception of their extended forms of settlement has historically prevailed over that of the urban populations.

This conception – of sovereign communities – reflected the fact that, however forbidding it might appear to the town-dwellers, the society of the mountains was not anarchic. The territories of the *'aarsh* were governed spaces.

Thaddarth and *tūfiq*

Generalisations about the economic life of Greater Kabylia have had the effect of obscuring the dichotomy which existed between the Igawawen and the people of the rest of the region. Generalisations about Kabyle social organisation have had the same effect. This is especially true of the numerous attempts to explain that enigmatic abstraction, 'the Kabyle village'.

The *'aarsh* of Kabylia come in a wide range of sizes but they have in common the fact that they are composed of units which are conventionally referred to as 'villages'. This usage, which was established by the nineteenth-century French observers, abstracts from an important difference between the two kinds of constituent unit in question, the village proper, in the sense of a self-governing and highly integrated settlement, *thaddarth*, and the association of scattered hamlets, *tūfiq*. While most writers have noted the existence of these two forms, they have invariably taken the *thaddarth* as the standard form and based their

---

63 As one of the best known songs of the Algerian revolution, *Min Jibālina* ('From Our Mountains'), testifies.

interpretations of Kabyle social organisation upon it and have for practical purposes ignored the *tūfiq* altogether. This has been a great mistake.

In order to rectify this mistake, we must first discuss with more precision than we have needed hitherto the terms we are using. Three terms and their meanings need to be explained: *thaddarth*, *tūfiq* and *thakhelijth*.

Thaddarth, plural: *thudrin*, is a Berber word which means a place of habitation or residence. In parts of Morocco it is used to mean 'house' but it is not used in this sense in Kabylia. This is because, in Kabylia, houses as a rule are not isolated places of habitation, but parts of larger agglomerations. It is the agglomeration or settlement as a whole which is designated by the term *thaddarth*. The Kabyle word for house and, by extension, household or family, is *akhkham*.[64]

Thudrin can in principle be of any size. A *thaddarth* may consist of a few houses totalling a hundred people or even substantially less. Or it may consist of two or three hundred houses belonging to as many as twenty different lineages which in turn belong to several clans, giving a total population of a thousand or even, these days, several thousands. The Kabyle language makes no distinction between these two cases, yet they are very different in important ways. In the first, the *thaddarth* is almost invariably a kinship unit; in the second, it almost invariably is not. This important difference is connected with other differences as we shall see.

Tūfiq, plural: *tuwāfeq*, does not mean a place of residence or settlement or agglomeration. The Arabic word *tawfiq* has a number of closely related meanings, including 'adaptation, adjustment, reconciliation, arbitration, peace-making, re-establishment of relations'. In Kabylia, *tūfiq* designates a group of usually small *thudrin* which are dispersed in space but associated with one another to constitute a political unit, this association being expressed in the institution of an assembly, *jemaʿa*, of the *tūfiq* as a whole, in which each constituent *thaddarth* is represented. (It should be noted that, although the *thudrin* are dispersed in space, the territory they collectively inhabit forms a continuous whole and is inhabited by no groups outside the *tūfiq* in question.)

Thus the word *thaddarth* can refer either to a large village inhabited by numerous lineages divided into several clans which are rarely if ever descended from a common ancestor, and which is entirely autonomous subject to the conditions of its membership of the *ʿarsh*, or to a much smaller settlement, composed of closely related families, which usually forms a dependent part of a larger association of such settlements and is subject to the collective decisions of this association. In the second case, the settlement in question, although a *thaddarth* in the sense of agglomeration of houses, is more generally known as a *thakhelijth*.

---

64 *Akhkham* is used by the Berbers of the Moroccan Rif to mean a *room* of a house only; see David Hart, *The Aïth Waryaghar of the Moroccan Rif: an ethnography and history* (Tucson: University of Arizona Press, 1976), 452.

Thakhelijth, plural: *ikhelijen*,[65] is a Berber derivation from the Arabic *khalīj*, one of the meanings of which is 'canal' or 'channel'. The metaphor of a channel is employed in Kabylia to designate a social group which is a dependent part of a larger whole. (In Morocco, anatomical metaphors are often used: bones, limbs and so on.) The small *thudrin* which compose a *tūfiq* are its 'channels' in the sense that the collective life of the association and the collective decisions of its *jemaʿa* are transmitted to the individual households which form the base of the community through the intermediary of the constituent *ikhelijen*. The English word which best corresponds to this meaning (without, however, wholly doing so) is 'hamlet'.

But *thakhelijth* is *also* used to refer to the component parts of a large autonomous *thaddarth*. While this kind of *thaddarth* is composed of several clans, themselves composed of a number of lineages, it is divided spatially into a number of areas which correspond broadly to the spatial distribution of the clans, although this correspondence is not absolute. Where these areas are clearly separate from each other on the ground, they may also be referred to as *ikhelijen*. Thus the *thaddarth* of Ath Waaban is composed of two *ikhelijen*, *thakhelijth n'Ath Tighilt* and *thakhelijth n'Ath Wadda*,[66] each of which is occupied by two clans (*iderman*). The English word which conveys this meaning is 'quarter'. Thus the meaning of *thakhelijth*, like that of *thaddarth*, depends upon the context. It should be noted that there are *thudrin* which have taken the process of integration to the point where the buildings form a virtually continuous whole, such that there is no clearly visible division of the village into two or three quarters, merely narrow streets and alley-ways. At Taguemount Azouz, for instance, which is traversed by two long narrow streets (*azniq oufella*, 'the upper street', and *azniq bouadda*, 'the lower street'), the inhabitants do not speak of this or that *thakhelijth*, but of successive sections of each *azniq*, each section being associated with and bearing the name of a particular lineage – e.g. *azniq Ath Lmessaoud*, *azniq Ath Bouzid*, *azniq Ath Chemloul* – while passing their houses.[67]

Like *thaddarth* and *thakhelijth*, the term *tūfiq* also has acquired two meanings. In Kabylia, *tūfiq* is, as I have stated, an association of a number of small hamlets, roughly equal in size, at least to the extent that no one constituent settlement dominates the *tūfiq* as a whole. However, both Hanoteau and Letourneux and, following them, Masqueray apply the term *tūfiq* on a number of occasions to the very different situation where a large complex *thaddarth* possesses outlying smaller settlements. In these cases, the *tūfiq* in question is unequivocally

65 Strictly speaking, *ikhelijen* is the plural of *akhelij*, of which *thakhelijth* is the diminutive form. In my experience, only the diminutive form is used for the singular and only the standard (non-diminutive) form is used for the plural.

66 'Ath Tighilt' means 'the people of the little hill'; 'Ath Wadda', 'the people settled lower down the valley'.

67 Genevois, 1972, *op. cit.*, 9–10.

dominated by the principal *thaddarth*, and it is more appropriate to regard the social unit in question as a large *thaddarth* plus satellite settlements than as a *tūfiq* in the normal sense of the term.[68]

There are thus three main kinds of autonomous unit below the level of the *'arsh* to be found in Greater Kabylia: the small *thaddarth*, comprising often less than a hundred and rarely more than two hundred people who all belong to the same lineage or clan and which is therefore a kinship unit; the *tūfiq*, a group of small *thudrin* associated for political purposes in one unit of which they are the dependent hamlets; and the large *thaddarth*, comprising many hundreds and sometimes more than a thousand people who belong to distinct clans and do not pretend to be descended from a common ancestor, and which accordingly derives its unity from something other than kinship.

The internal political organisation of Kabyle *'aarsh* varies considerably, depending on which of these forms of settlement prevails. This can be illustrated by comparing an *'arsh* from north-western Kabylia, the Ath Slegguem, an *'arsh* from north-eastern Kabylia, the Ath Adas of the Ath Jennad confederation, and an *'arsh* from the Jurjura, the Ath Wasif of the Ath Bethroun confederation.[69]

Table 2.1: *'arsh* Ath Slegguem

19 constituent units (*thudrin*)	Population *c.* 1868
Aafir Oukoufi	154
Tala Arous	88
Tadjenant	59
Toumjaj	47
Abada	157
Alma Bouaman	80
Kennout	43
Tasirra	56
Tadhount	63
Mechchouka	132
Tala Aggach	150
Arbiai	67

68 For instance, although Hanoteau and Letourneux rightly present Ath Waaban as a *thaddarth* and not a *tūfiq*, two of its lineages, the Ath Merzouq and the Ath Saïd, inhabit hamlets situated in the valley to the south-west of the main agglomeration; these locations have enabled them to guarantee the village's access to its high pastures.

69 Data concerning villages and their populations are provided by Hanoteau and Letourneux, *op. cit.*, vol. I, 302–63.

Table 2.1 *continued*

Azib	77
Chaina	52
Bou Mati	150
Ath Bel Hizem	112
Bechali	23
Ifejdan	22
Azib et-Tolba	18
Total population	1,550
Average population per *thaddarth*	82

Table 2.2: *'arsh* Ath Adas (confederation of Ath Jennad)

6 constituent units (*tuwāfeq*)	Population *c.* 1868
Izarzen (composed of 7 *ikhelijen*)	1,576
Abizar (composed of 5 *ikhelijen*)	1,667
Ath Mameur (composed of 10 *ikhelijen*)	805
Ibedach (composed of 9 *ikhelijen*)	781
Timizar n'Sidi Mansour (composed of 2 *ikhelijen*)	813
Ath Mira (composed of 6 *ikhelijen*)	965
Total population	6,607
Average population per *tūfiq*	1,101
Average population per *thakhelijth*	169

Table 2.3: *'arsh* Ath Wasif (confederation of Ath Bethroun)

7 constituent units (*thudrin*)	Population *c.* 1868
Ath Abbas	1,272
Zoubga	348
Ath Bou Abderrahmane	1,212
Tiqidount	972
Tiqichourt	984
Ath Eurbah	384
Tassaft Waguemoun	360
Total population	5,532
Average population per *thaddarth*	790

These examples have not been chosen at random. In north-western Kabylia, the small isolated *thaddarth* prevails. In the Jurjura, the large complex *thaddarth* prevails; the *thudrin* of the Ath Wasif are on average nearly ten times larger than those of the Ath Slegguem. In north-central and north-eastern Kabylia, neither the small isolated *thaddarth* nor the large complex *thaddarth* is to be found, except occasionally; here the prevalent form is the *tūfīq*. But the *tūfīq* actually prevails in all parts of Greater Kabylia other than the western and north-western marches at one extreme and the Jurjura at the other.

Hanoteau and Letourneux provide detailed data concerning the distribution of the population in the four *cercles* (administrative sub-divisions) of Greater Kabylia c. 1868, by confederation (*thaqbilth*), tribe ('*arsh*) and village (*thaddarth* and *tūfīq*).[70] The cercles were those of Dellys (western and north-western Kabylia), Draa el Mizan (south-western Kabylia), Tizi Ouzou (northern, north-eastern and part of central Kabylia) and Fort Napoléon (renamed Fort National after 1870, covering the central and eastern Jurjura, its northern outcrops and the southern Akfadou district). If we examine this data in aggregate form in the light of our distinction between the three zones characterised by different settlement patterns, we can arrive at a rough estimate of the relative predominance of the two kinds of *thaddarth* and the *tūfīq* in the three zones in question. This is shown in Table 2.4.

Table 2.4: Regional distribution and relative significance
of *thudrin* and *tuwāfeq* in Greater Kabylia c. 1868[71]

	West and north-west Kabylia	South-west, west-central, north and north-east Kabylia	Central and eastern Jurjura and Akfadou
No. of *thudrin*	364	107	126
No. of *tuwāfeq*	17	146	62
Population resident in *thudrin*	42,843	38,352	59,350
% resident in *thudrin*	84.9	30.3	60.3
Population resident in *tuwāfeq*	7,603	88,199	39,010
% resident in *tuwāfeq*	15.1	69.7	39.7
Average population of *thudrin*	118	358	471
Average population of *tuwāfeq*	447	604	629

70 Hanoteau and Letourneux, *ibid.*

71 This table is a slightly revised version of Table 1 in my 1978 paper *Notes on relations of production, forms of property and political structures in a dissident region of Algeria: pre-colonial Kabylia.*

Thus in the central and eastern Jurjura in the second half of the nineteenth century, *thudrin* outnumbered *tuwāfeq* by two to one and accounted for 60 per cent of the population as against 40 per cent, whereas in the rest of Greater Kabylia, apart from the western and north-western marches, *tuwāfeq* outnumbered *thudrin* and accounted for over twice as much of the population – 70 per cent as against 30 per cent. Moreover, the *thaddarth* of the central Jurjura was on average four times larger than its counterpart in the western and north-western marches, and 32 per cent bigger than in the rest of Greater Kabylia. Furthermore, since, as has already been stated, Hanoteau and Letourneux classify as *tuwāfeq* many large *thudrin* in the central Jurjura possessing satellite hamlets, the above figures seriously understate the prevalence of the large *thaddarth* in the central Jurjura and the peculiarity of the central Jurjura in this respect.[72]

Twenty-one of the *thudrin* listed by Hanoteau and Letourneux were recorded by them as possessing populations of 1,000 or more *c.* 1868. Sixteen of these belonged to the *'aarsh* of the central and eastern Jurjura or its northern outcrops and these figures are also underestimates, for the same reason.

The movement in space from the western and north-western periphery of Greater Kabylia to the region's core in the central Jurjura was a movement from less integrated forms of settlement and socio-political organisation to more integrated ones. The *tūfīq* represents a higher level of integration than the isolated small settlements of the marcher tribes, and the large *thaddarth* of the central Jurjura represents a higher level of integration than the *tūfīq*. And at the same time the movement from north-west to south-east was one from populations which were broadly incorporated into the political system of the Ottoman Regency through the agency of local dynastic leaderships to populations which were intermittently dissident or, in the Jurjura heartland, permanently independent of the Regency in respect of their political arrangements and governed themselves by means of representative assemblies and so without recourse to self-perpetuating hierarchies or the dynastic principle.

There is an evident irony in the fact that the nineteenth-century French ethnographers and their successors, in concentrating their attention upon the Jurjura, took the large *thaddarth* they found there to be the typical form of settlement and the standard political unit, below the level of the *'arsh*, of Kabyle society in general. For the large and complex *thaddarth* was not at all typical of

---

72 They also slightly underestimate this for another reason, in that they include the *'aarsh* of the Akfadou district, which were not regarded as Igawawen and amongst which the large *thaddarth* only very narrowly prevailed over the *tūfīq*.

Greater Kabylia as a whole. It was typical only of the central Jurjura – that is, of the society of the Igawawen.

Morizot is himself a victim of this oversight. In stressing the role of the patriarchal family in the society of the Jurjura as one of the key factors underlying the remarkable migratory activities of the Igawawen, he emphasises an aspect of their social organisation which was not at all peculiar to them but, on the contrary, common to the whole of Kabylia. In emphasising the traditions of mutual aid and village solidarity, on the other hand, Morizot gets closer to the heart of the Igawawen enigma. There is no doubt that these traditions were enormously important to the commercial and migratory enterprise of the Igawawen. But what Morizot overlooks is the fact, which we have now unearthed, that the traditions in question here are those of a village which is all but peculiar to the Igawawen, the large and complex *thaddarth*.

The Igawawen *thaddarth*

> Pour décrire convenablement un village Kabyle des Igaouaouen …, il faudrait être peintre, poète …
>
> (Henri Genevois, *Tawrirt n'At Mangellat*)[73]

To understand the Igawawen *thaddarth* it is essential to recognise that it is not a kinship unit.

A very large number of social groups in Kabylia, from the topmost level of the confederation to the village or even the constituent hamlet of the *tūfīq* or quarter of the village, do not have genealogical names but topographical or territorial ones. This fact has been quite simply ignored by certain authors. Bourdieu, for instance, has written

> if genealogy is used in more or less arbitrary fashion every time that it is important to create or justify a social unit, it is because it allows a kind of relation of kinship to be created, through the fiction of the eponymous ancestor, between individuals joined together as a result of the operation of quite different forces; it is as if this society could not conceive of any type of relationship existing within a social body other than that which exists between relatives …[74]

---

73 H. Genevois, *Tawrirt n'At Mangellat: notes d'histoire et de folklore* (Fort National: Fichier de Documentation Berbère, 1962), A 2.

74 Bourdieu, 1962, *op. cit.*, 16–17.

Figure 2.3: Ath Lahcène, the largest of
the Ath Yenni villages, in 1920.

Bourdieu is quite right to suggest that such ancestors as are invoked are often entirely fictional and that kinship provides an idiom through which relationships resulting from 'the operation of quite different forces' may be expressed. But it is simply untrue that Kabyle society invariably employs the idiom of kinship to denote social units and cannot conceive of other types of relationship.[75] Many Kabyle tribes and villages do refer to themselves as 'the sons of X', but at least as many do not, employing names which are simply topographical or geographical expressions. Only two of the seven villages of the Ath Wasif referred to above, for example, have genealogical names (Ath Abbas and Ath Bou Abderrahmane). Similarly, only two of the seven villages of the neighbouring Ath Boudrar tribe have genealogical names (Ath Ali ou Harzoun and Bou Adnane); the names of the other villages are 'the ridge of the middle' (Ighil Bouammas), 'the ridge of the lioness' (Ighil n'Tsedda), 'the fountain of the dried figs' (Tala n'Tazart) and so on. And Ath Wasif and Ath Boudrar themselves mean only 'the people of the river' and 'the people who occupy (or possess) the mountain', as we have seen.

Of those Jurjura villages which have been investigated, all have been formed by families and lineages which had been previously unrelated and had arrived at different times and from different points of the compass, some from neighbouring *'aarsh*, some from maritime Kabylia, some from the Wad Sahel and Bouïra districts south of the Jurjura, some from Lesser Kabylia, and even

---

75   As Bourdieu himself implicitly recognises elsewhere, in his discussion of the *sfūf* in Kabylia.

some from much further afield, the Arab regions of the Constantinois and the
Sud-Algérois and the Cheliff valley. According to local traditions, the important
villages of Taguemount Azouz, of ʿarsh Ath Mahmoud, and Taourirt, of ʿarsh
Ath Menguellat, were constituted in this way.[76] So too were the villages of
Ath Lahcène, Ath Larbaʿa, Taourirt Mimoun and Agouni Ahmed of the Ath
Yenni.[77] Aucapitaine details the distant origins of many of the families of Jemaʿa
n'Saharij and of the other villages of the Ath Fraoucen.[78] And I know from my
own fieldwork that the villagers of Ath Waaban, of the Ath Boudrar, take a
similar view of their own history.

Anthropologists coming across legends which assert a common ancestry
are often rightly inclined to discount these as convenient fictions. But where
local traditions regularly assert, on the contrary, the absence of such common
ancestry, there is no reason to discount them and every reason to take them
seriously, both as factually reliable and as sociologically significant.

The extent to which the *thudrin* of the Jurjura are composed of families and
lineages of diverse origins is inconsistent with the segmentarist thesis. As such,
the constitution of these villages is to be distinguished from the more general
phenomenon of migrant or refugee families being incorporated into entirely
different kinship groups. One of the reasons why Gellner felt that this general
phenomenon did not affect his argument in the case of Moroccan Berbers is
that it was very marginal in the central High Atlas.

> Berber society of the central High Atlas may not be totally rigid – birth
> and kinship do not hold the individual in an iron vice – but it is certainly
> not very fluid … In any one village, the proportion of male immigrants
> will be under ten per cent, usually well under this ratio.[79]

In Kabylia – at any rate, in central Kabylia and in the Jurjura in particular –
the truth is the exact opposite of this. For all the villages for which evidence
is available, it is clear that those families able to claim an origin going back to
the foundation of the village are a minority and that the majority of families
are immigrants from elsewhere and, moreover, are well aware of the fact and
see no inconvenience in acknowledging it. (The only villages in the Jurjura
which are a regular exception to this rule are the exclusively saintly settlements

---

76 H. Genevois, 1972, *op. cit.*, 34–7; and 1962, *op. cit.*, A6.
77 Basagana and Sayad, 1974, *op. cit.*, 53–4; H. Genevois, *At-Yänni – Les Beni Yenni:
    Eléments historiques et folkloriques* (Fort National: Fichier de Documentation Berbère,
    1971), 5, 15–16.
78 Baron Henri Aucapitaine, 'Notice sur la tribu des Aït Fraoucen', *Revue Africaine* (1860),
    446–58.
79 Gellner, 1969, *op. cit.*, 62–3.

of the *imrabdhen*, which only rarely constitute autonomous *thudrin* and whose populations even more rarely exceed two or three hundred.)

Kabyle society may well give the appearance of a certain rigidity. 'Fluid' is not the first word which springs to mind when one gropes for adjectives to describe it. But the rigidity in question is not that of kinship structures. All the evidence suggests that pre-colonial Kabylia was the theatre of unusually intense movements of population in all directions, at any rate from the early sixteenth century onwards. The rigidity which one may observe there is the rigidity of political arrangements which were evolved in the context of this turmoil and in response to it.

The large, complex *thudrin* of the Igawawen were not invented out of thin air. The evidence suggests that the first of them were formed through the concentration of scattered hamlets previously united only loosely, if at all, in the *tūfiq* form. This is what local traditions attest for Taourirt n'Ath Menguellat and the three core villages of the Ath Yenni: Taourirt Mimoun, Ath Lahcène and Ath Larba'a. According to local traditions, the consolidation of the last three dates from the early seventeenth century and was effected under the aegis of a local *amrabedh*, Sidi Ali ou Yahia.[80] The formation of Taourirt n'Ath Menguellat is also credited to the influence of a local saint, Sidi Lhadi Bou Derbal, and occurred at the same period.[81] The same processes are likely to account for the formation of some of the large, complex *thudrin* which exist elsewhere in Kabylia, outside the Igawawen district proper. The leading village of *'arsh* Ath Mahmoud, Taguemount Azouz, for example, was formed, at an unknown date, out of 'primitive farm hamlets' situated in the immediate vicinity of the future *thaddarth*, but in this case without the prompting of a saint.[82]

I believe that further research would find that many of the other large *thudrin* of the Jurjura were formed in the same evolutionary manner. But I doubt that all of them were. It seems more likely that it was the earliest *thudrin* which developed out of *tuwāfeq* and scattered hamlets and that those formed in the second half of the seventeenth century or later were in many cases constituted from the outset as integrated villages, in imitation of a model of social and political organisation which was by that time well established locally and had demonstrated its merits. This certainly appears to be the case of Ath Waaban, for example; although no one knows precisely when it was founded, it is almost certainly the youngest of the seven Ath Boudrar villages, constituted most probably in the second half of the eighteenth century if not

---

80 Genevois, 1971, *op. cit.*, 19–32.
81 Genevois (1962, *op. cit.*, A6–8) believed this to have occurred much earlier, in the fifteenth or even the thirteenth century but this is because he has the wrong dates for the saint in question. According to one of the saint's descendants, Sidi L'Hadi Bou Derbal was in fact born in 1544 CE and died in 1637; see http://sidilhadi.vipblog.com.
82 Genevois, 1972, *op. cit.*, 34–5.

Figure 2.4: Igawawen villages today: looking north along the ridge of the Ath Bou Akkach and Ath Wasif, with the Ath Yenni villages perched on their hilltops on the horizon.

later, and there is no memory of hamlets or a *tūfiq* preceding the formation of the present village.

The development of the Igawawen *thaddarth* – that is, of a form of settlement and community which was not a kinship unit – immediately created a fundamental problem, because it meant that order could no longer be (if it ever had been) maintained on segmentarist principles. In a segmentary system, order of a kind can be preserved through the balance and opposition of the segments precisely because the segments conceive of themselves as segments – that is, as related parts of a larger whole which is itself a kinship unit at the next level of size and so unites its constituent segments at that level. But, since the large and complex *thaddarth* of the Igawawen was not a kinship unit, and its constituent clans were well aware of the fact and in no way disposed to pretend the contrary, how was its cohesion and internal order to be secured?

It may be objected that the Igawawen *thaddarth* was not unique in this respect. It is certainly true that amongst Berber populations elsewhere one also finds village settlements which are not kinship units. In southern Morocco, for instance, many villages contain lineages belonging to quite unrelated clans,

Figure 2.5: Looking beyond Taourirt
el-Hajjaj (Ath Yenni) to the south-
east of the Igawawen district, with
in the middle distance the Aqbil
villages of Beni Mahmoud and Aourir
Ouzemmour (right) and those of the
Ath Bou Youcef (left), with the Jurjura
beyond.

such that these villages also are not kinship units. But there is a fundamental
difference with the Igawawen case. For the clans in southern Moroccan villages
are rarely confined to a single village; in general, a given clan will be settled in
several villages, often at considerable distances from each other. In the internal
organisation of the large transhumant tribes, notably the Aït Atta, a virtue, if
not an obligation, was made of this territorial discontinuity and reduplication
of the clan: the fact that a clan had members in various far-flung parts of the
tribe's territory was a major factor preserving the subjective unity of the tribe,
while also affording each clan access to the various types of natural resources –
pasture, woodland, water, oases, etc. – contained within the tribe's territory.[83] In
this system, village settlements are not the main constituent units of the tribe's
political structure, the clans and, above all, the 'five fifths' (*khams khmas*)[84] into

---

83 Gellner, 1969, *op. cit.*, 58–9, 171–4; but see also David Hart, *Dadda ʿAtta and his Forty
    Grandsons: the socio-political organization of the Aït ʿAtta of southern Morocco* (Wisbech:
    Menas Press, 1981), 71–6, 99–100.
84 Hart, 1967, *art. cit.* and 1981, *op. cit.*, 29–69.

which they combine are, so the fact that a settlement is not a kinship unit does not create a significant political problem.

In the wholly sedentary society of the Jurjura, matters were very different. There is no territorial discontinuity and reduplication of the clan; a clan does not have members settled in several villages, it is invariably confined to one village.[85] And, *pace* Bourdieu, the village in Kabylia is not merely a territorial unit, a settled space, but a political unit of the first importance. Below the level of the *'arsh*, it is the village – *thaddarth* or *tūfiq* – which forms the constituent political unit, not the clan. It is the village which was and often still is the ultimate owner not only of common land (*meshmel*) but also of all cultivable land, in that land previously in the possession of a family that has left (or been banished from) the village or died out reverts to the village for the *jema'a* to reallocate, unless there are agnates of the last owner still present in the village to exercise the right of *shefa'a* in respect of it. It is the village which organises at intervals the mobilisation of collective labour for work done in the collective interest (*thashmelith*), such as the annual overhaul of the irrigation system for the village's gardens; it is in effect the village which mobilises to build a new house for a young family that has finally moved out of its earlier home in the house of the man's parents;[86] and it is the village which decides upon and organises the occasional sacrifice of cattle or sheep for a *thimshret*, in which the meat is distributed with meticulous fairness to every family, the funds for buying the animals coming from the village chest and the allocation of meat being conducted by the *temman* under the watchful eyes of the rest of the adult male population. The fact that, amongst the Igawawen, this crucial political unit was usually not a kinship unit was therefore of the greatest significance, and had no parallels elsewhere in Berber society.

The problem which arose with the constitution of the large and complex *thaddarth* was unique. Moreover, it was not merely (so to speak) an abstract problem of political order, of the principles upon which the self-government of the *thaddarth* was to be based; it involved at least one very practical problem, to which a practical solution had to be found early on, if not immediately, that of the physical proximity of unrelated clans, lineages and families.

The establishment of the original complex *thudrin* of the Jurjura was effected through the voluntary amalgamation of the constituent hamlets of the pre-

---

85 The sole exception to this rule is that of the more important of the saintly lineages (*imrabdhen*), which are sometimes to be found settled in several different villages.

86 This is formally regarded as an instance of *thiwizi*, mutual aid, and thus an affair of reciprocal exchanges between families. But the expectation that every family will participate in a house-building *thiwizi* is so strong that it amounts to a virtual mobilisation of collective labour; see René Maunier, 1926, *op. cit.*

Figure 2.6: A *thimshret* in the Jurjura at
Ath Anzar (Ath Itsouragh).

existing *tuwāfeq*. The complex *thaddarth* was a development out of the *tūfiq*
which occurred when the hamlets which composed the latter agreed to regroup
in one place – often, although not always, on the summit of a ridge – and
thereby form a single, concentrated settlement. This process of concentration
obliged clans and lineages and families which had previously dwelt in quite
distinct settlements at some distance from one another to exist henceforth
cheek by jowl. Where before a kilometre or more, plus a belt of woodland and
orchards, as well as pasture and gardens, might have separated the houses of
clan A from those of clan B, now only a narrow alley would separate them, and
perhaps nothing more than a stone wall.

This unprecedented contiguity of families recognising no common descent
introduced an entirely new element into the daily social life of the people
concerned. This change was clearest in relation to the women: whereas, in the
tūfiq, the women of a given clan could visit their gardens, collect firewood
and fetch water from the well, as well as visit one another's homes, without
once leaving the territory of the clan to which they belonged, in the complex
thaddarth they were obliged to traverse parts of the village inhabited by unrelated
clans on most of these errands and to do so, moreover, perhaps several times a

Figure 2.7: An alley in an Igawawen village: Taourirt Mimoun of the Ath Yenni.

day. In addition, many houses in a *thaddarth* overlooked the courtyards of their neighbours, so that the privacy of the women would be in jeopardy even when they were at home.

The way in which these problems were handled was through the development of a strict code of proper male behaviour, which has remained in force to this day.[87] It was not done for a man to look at a woman when passing her in the street or alley-way, unless she was a relative (in which case a brief greeting was in order); the rule was to ignore her presence entirely and so enable her to pass by as if she was invisible and so unflustered. The fountain, the women's public meeting place *par excellence*, was entirely out of bounds for the men. And for a man to post himself in a strategic spot in order to look at the women as they passed by was the ultimate in anti-social behaviour and widely condemned as such.[88] In the same way, it was not done to look out of a window into a

---

87 At any rate into the late twentieth century, as I can testify from personal observation at Ath Waaban and other villages in the Tassaft district in 1975, 1976 and 1983.

88 Witness the remarkable vehemence of the passage in which Mouloud Feraoun evokes this kind of behaviour in his novel *La Terre et le Sang* (Paris: Éditions du Seuil, 1953), 157.

neighbour's yard. In the old days, to break this rule was to risk an immediate riposte from the outraged menfolk next door, namely a bullet through one's window.[89]

More generally, this intense physical proximity of unrelated lineages was bound to provide endless occasions for friction between them which would simply have been absent from the social routine of the *tūfīq*. The preservation of the unity of the village as a whole therefore required its inhabitants to develop a degree of civic consciousness expressed in a kind of social behaviour and an array of polite manners embodying to an unusually developed degree the value of consideration (*'anāya*) for others.

Such a development would have been unlikely to occur of its own accord and in the case of the Igawawen *thaddarth* it occurred on the basis of an underlying innovation of a wholly unspontaneous and deliberate character. This innovation was a development in Kabyle law.

---

89 I was informed during fieldwork in 1983 that this element of the old code was still in force, at any rate among the Illilten, whose reputation for being absolute sticklers for the traditional code of honour is unsurpassed in Kabylia as a whole and appears, from what I have seen of them, to be soundly based.

CHAPTER 3

～

Kabyle Law

The means employed by Nature to bring about the development of all the capacities of men is their antagonism in society, so far as this is, in the end, the cause of lawful order among men …

> (Kant, *Idea For A Universal History from A Cosmopolitan Point Of View*)[1]

What our laws show is the extent and degree to which conflict has to be suppressed.

> (Alisdair MacIntyre, *After Virtue*)[2]

The *qawānīn*

The rules which regulate the social life of a Kabyle village (*thaddarth* or *tūfīq*) form a body of law known as *qānūn*, plural: *qawānīn*.[3] They are made by the assembly of the village, the *jema'a* (in Berber, *thajma'th*), although in the pre-colonial period it is possible that the *jemāya'* of some *'aarsh* made certain laws for the *'arsh* as a whole, while leaving the *jemāya'* of its constituent villages free to make their own local by-laws in all matters not dealt with at *'arsh* level.

If we examine the *qawānīn* recorded by Hanoteau and Letourneux in Greater Kabylia in the 1860s, we can see that the *qānūn* of a Kabyle village normally included the following types of law:

---

1 Immanuel Kant, *Idea For A Universal History From A Cosmopolitan Point Of View*, 1784, in *Kant On History* (USA: Liberal Arts Library, 1963), 13–23.
2 Alasdair MacIntyre, *After Virtue* (London: Duckworth, 1981, 2nd edition 1985), 254.
3 This is the Arabic word for law, rule, norm, precept, etc.; it almost certainly comes from the Greek κάνων (kanōn) either directly or via the Latin *canon*. It should not be confused with the very different word *kānūn*, which is the Arabic word for stove and is used in Kabylia to mean hearth, fireplace.

   i. laws forbidding certain acts by stipulating the penalties imposed on those who commit them;

   ii. laws regulating access to the commons, *meshmel* (especially pasture lands) and use of public utilities; these may also stipulate penalties for those who transgress them;

   iii. laws defining local variations on general social customs; for example, the locally agreed amount of the dowry, or the time within which the right of pre-emption of land (*shefa'a*) by kinsmen of the previous owner must be exercised;

   iv. laws defining certain customary obligations, the conditions of their fulfillment and the penalties for shirking them: for example, attendance at meetings of the *jema'a*, participation in collective labour service, attendance at funerals, etc;

   v. laws regulating contractual relationships, notably commercial partnerships and especially share-cropping agreements (the *khammesat*).[4]

Most of the laws belonged to the first type. The *qānūn* of the village of Agouni n'Taslent, of *'arsh* Aqbil in the Jurjura, for example, had 249 articles, 219 of which were of type (i).[5]

It is probable that, in most cases, it was only with the arrival of the French in the region and in response to their enquiries that the *qawānīn* began to be recorded in documents. Most if not all of the *qawānīn* recorded by Hanoteau and Letourneux were in fact written down at their instigation.[6] In the precolonial period, the *qawānīn* were generally not written down. Most lay Kabyles could not read or write and literacy was the preserve of the *imrabdhen*. That the *qawānīn* were unwritten did not mean that their existence was doubtful. A corollary of the fact that Kabyle culture was predominantly oral was the regular exercise given to the faculty of memory and the fact that it was possible to rely on this. The *qawānīn* would be committed to memory by the elders in each village and would be well known to the rest of the adult population.[7]

Moreover, in asking some of their informants to provide *qawānīn* of particular tribes, as distinct from villages, Hanoteau and Letourneux may well have induced what amounted to the invention of the tribal *qānūn* where this did not previously exist, at any rate in most cases,[8] an early instance of the French tendency to abstract from the diversity and complexity of social reality in the quest for the 'essence' of the matter they were examining. This consideration clearly mandates

---

4   Hanoteau and Letourneux, *op. cit.*, vol. III, 326–443.

5   These are reproduced in full in Jules Liorel, *Kabylie du Djurdjura* (Paris: Ernest Leroux, 1893), 315–34.

6   Augustin Bernard and Louis Milliot, 'Les qânoûns kabyles dans l'ouvrage de Hanoteau et Letourneux', *Revue des Études Islamiques*, 2 (1933), 1–44: 13–18.

7   Masqueray, 1983 (1886), *op. cit.*, 72–3; Bernard and Milliot, *art. cit.*, 20.

8   Bernard and Milliot, *art. cit.*, 22–4.

caution in using these particular *qawānīn* as evidence. In many if not most cases, the *qānūn* thus attributed to an entire *'arsh* was in reality merely that of its most important village.[9] It can accordingly be taken as evidence of a particular rule and practice but less surely of a whole *'arsh's* subscription to this.

Nonetheless, in publishing the *qawānīn* that were transmitted to them by their informants in the course of their fieldwork in Greater Kabylia between 1858 and 1864, Hanoteau and Letourneux made accessible to others what is probably the most extensive corpus of Berber law available.[10] Despite this wealth of evidence, the question of Kabyle law has been an immensely contested matter. Two quite different issues have been at stake in the controversy. The central issue in nineteenth-century French discussion of Kabyle law was the light it might be considered to shed on the broader questions of the relation of the Kabyles to the Islamic faith and their attitude to France. Quite different questions became central to the academic debate in the course of the twentieth century, namely the relationship between the *qawānīn* and Kabyle customs in general and the code of honour in particular.

Qānūn, 'urf and *Sharī'a*

The question of the relationship of Kabyle law to the *Sharī'a* was linked, in the views of many French commentators, to the question of whether the Kabyles were genuinely Muslims or not. The latter question reflected, in turn, the abiding preoccupation of numerous nineteenth-century authors with the problem of assimilating Muslim Algerians within the French political framework. It came to be believed that the Kabyles, unlike 'the Arabs', were very susceptible to assimilation; this belief was largely predicated on the supposition that they were not 'real' Muslims, which in turn was premised on the supposition that Kabyle

---

9 Bernard and Milliot, *art. cit.*, 4.

10 Hanoteau and Letourneux provided (*op. cit.*, vol. II, 135–552 and vol. III, 1–326) a very full digest of Kabyle law as of the 1860s; in doing so they itemised the various elements of the content of the *qawānīn* in an exposition organised in accordance with European legal categories; they then provided the raw material upon which their exposition was based in the shape of the complete *qawānīn* (in French translation) of eight *'aarsh* and 10 other villages from all over the region, plus excerpts from the *qawānīn* of 19 other *'aarsh* and 10 other villages (*op. cit*, vol. III, 327–443), followed by French translations of a number of documents recording legal decisions. Masqueray for his part provided (*op. cit.*, 263–324) a full record, again in French translation, of the *qawānīn* of nine *'aarsh* of the Wad Sahel, i.e. the Kabyle populations of the southern slopes of the Jurjura. Subsequently Bernard and Milliot published (*art. cit.*, 31–44) the text of one village *qānūn* (Ath Ali ou Harzoun), a *qānūn* of the Ath Irathen confederation and even a *qānūn* of the 'Zouaoua' in general; I regard the last two as suspect and do not rely on them.

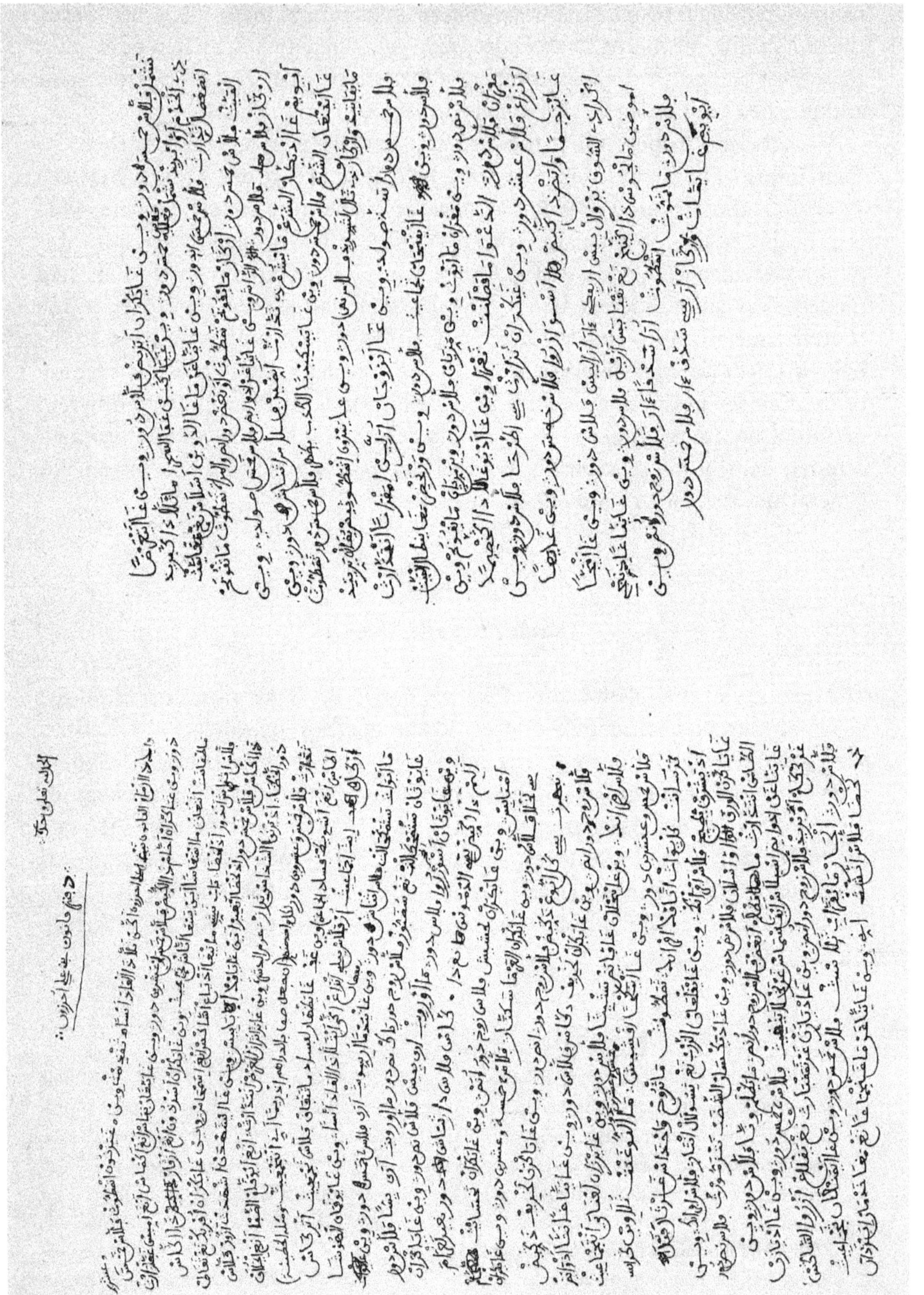

Figure 3.1: *Qānūn* of Ath Ali ou Harzoun.

law was independent of and even opposed to Islamic law. In this context, three specific aspects of the *qawānīn* were at issue: their sources, their content and their origin.

The most reasonable opinion in this matter was that put forward by Hanoteau and Letourneux. As they presented it, Kabyle law was derived from three distinct sources:

i. the Qur'ān and the *Sharī'a*, which determined the provisions of Kabyle law in matters of religious faith and hygiene;

ii. the *'āda* – general custom – of the Kabyle region, which determined Kabyle law in respect of personal status, property transactions and contracts; and

iii. *'urf* – that is to say, specific local usages arising out of modifications of general custom deliberately made by this or that village or *'arsh* in consideration of local conditions.[11]

The first alone was derived ultimately from divine revelation; the second and third were based on general consent that was an emanation of popular sovereignty.[12] Moreover, in certain respects, especially the question of inheritance, Kabyle law self-consciously differed from Islamic law, most notably in denying to women their right, guaranteed by the *Sharī'a*, to a share in the inheritance of landed property.[13]

Hanoteau and Letourneux suggested that the un-Islamic element of Kabyle law was partly a survival and partly a revival of long-standing customs and practices, due to the failure of first the Arab and subsequently the Turkish conquests of the central Maghrib to extend fully into the mountains of Kabylia.[14] They also suggested that the word *qānūn*, derived ultimately from the Greek, 'seems to have been borrowed from the terminology of our early Church'.[15] Masqueray for his part contented himself with insisting on the importance of the *qawānīn* among all three of the populations he considered in his book (Kabyles, Mzabis and Chaouia), quoting some *qawānīn* at length and remarking that their principal feature – the list specifying certain actions as forbidden by stipulating the penalties they incurred – resembled the *interdicta* of early Rome.[16]

These sober and for the most part factually accurate views of the matter subsequently gave way, however, to the far more tendentious interpretations of what became known as the *Kabylophiles*, who considered that the Kabyles were

---

11 Hanoteau and Letourneux, *op. cit.*, vol. II, 136–7.
12 Hanoteau and Letourneux, *op. cit.*, vol. II, 137.
13 Hanoteau and Letourneux, *op. cit.*, vol. II, 282 *et seq.*
14 Hanoteau and Letourneux, *op. cit.*, vol. II, 135–6.
15 Hanoteau and Letourneux, *op. cit.*, vol. II, 138.
16 Masqueray, 1983 (1886), *op. cit.*, 54–6.

highly promising material for assimilation and elevated the perceived differences between Kabyle law and Quranic law into a major opposition of enormous significance. A characteristically histrionic statement of the more extreme and fanciful view was put forward by Camille Sabatier, who declared that

> The unknown Lycurgus who dictated the Kabyle kanouns [*sic*] was neither of the family of Mohammed nor of Moses, but of that of Montesquieu and Condorcet. Even more than the skull of the Kabyle hillsmen, this work bears the mark of our race.[17]

As he also remarked,

> Among the Kabyles, religion is absent; outwardly, it is true, the Kabyles profess their adherence to Islam, in reality the Kabyle is essentially anti-clerical. His kanouns [*sic*] are the most energetic negation of the fundamental principles of the Muslim code.[18]

Numerous similar statements are to be found in the outpourings of the late nineteenth-century French *kabylophiles*;[19] exaggeration was their stock in trade.

The ideological and other reasons why many (but, it is important to note, by no means all) nineteenth-century French observers should have indulged in these far-fetched views have already been discussed in magisterial depth by Ageron and especially Patricia Lorcin and I shall not pursue that issue here. I must, however, give here my own view of the central matters in dispute.

First, the opposition these writers made between *qānūn* and Islamic law (the *Sharī'a*) by no means implied that the Kabyles were not real (that is, sincere and devout) Muslims. The latter thesis, a key tenet of Sabatier and many others, was a *non sequitur*. The five pillars of the Islamic faith, the *shahāda* (bearing witness to the oneness of God), prayer, alms-giving, fasting during Ramadan and the pilgrimage to Mecca (*hajj*) were all respected by the Kabyles, even if only a small minority were able to make the *hajj*, and the main religious festivals of the Muslim calendar – the 'Mouloud', that is *mawlid en-nabī*, the Prophet's birthday, as well as *'īd el-fitr* and *'īd el-adhā* and, curiously, the *'āshūrā*[20] – were all regularly celebrated.

17 Quoted in Charles-Robert Ageron, *Les Algériens musulmans et la France (1871–1919)* (Paris: Presses Universitaires de France, 2 vols, 1968); vol. I, chapter X: 'Le « mythe kabyle » et la politique kabyle (1871–1891)', 267–92: 275. (The English translation is mine.)

18 *Ibid.*

19 Ageron, *op. cit.*; Patricia Lorcin, *Imperial Identities: Stereotyping, prejudice and race in colonial Algeria* (London and New York: I.B.Tauris, 1995).

20 The *'āshūrā'* is primarily celebrated by Shi'ites, not Sunnis. Its celebration in Kabylia and elsewhere in Algeria may be a survival from the period when the Berbers embraced Shi'ism as a way of expressing, within Islam, their revolt against their Sunni Arab conquerors.

Second, the notion that the *qawānīn* were a relic of Kabylia's pre-Islamic (and especially Roman) past ignored the fact that the term *qānūn* had long since entered the Arabic language and that there was, accordingly, no need to postulate a direct, unmediated, derivation from the Greek or the Latin languages or the early Christian church to account for them.

Third, in so far as the Kabyle *qawānīn* enshrined as law important elements of custom, this was not in itself unusual, let alone confined to Berbers. *'urf*, meaning custom, is an Arabic word and the concept of *'urfi* law (law derived from custom) is widespread in the Arab world and a longstanding feature of tribal and especially Beduin society.[21] It is also, for that matter, found in the Arabophone regions of Algeria itself.[22] Thus the fact that they had other, customary, sources of law in addition to the *Sharī'a* did not, in itself, distinguish the Kabyles from the other populations of the Algerian countryside.

Moreover, the opposition or conflict between *Sharī'a* law and *'urfi* law posited by the purveyors of the Kabyle myth was, generally speaking, a false antithesis; the relationship between the two was mainly one of complementarity, in that *'urfi* law dealt with matters on which scripture was silent. The matter has been well explained by David Hart in his account of the role of tribal custom (known locally as *izirf*) as a source of law amongst the Berbers of south-eastern Morocco. 'The Shari'a and the *izerf* worked at different levels of society. The two were by no means diametrically opposed to each other as the French administration claimed.'[23]

Finally and above all, there was absolutely no recognition in the writings of the purveyors of the Kabyle myth that the concept of *qānūn* was a central feature of Ottoman law,[24] where it indicated laws made by the ruling authority (the Sultan) and thus man-made, as distinct from the *Sharī'a* originating in divine revelation. Moreover, as Sami Zubaida has pointed out, such 'laws issued by the ruler were known as *'urfi*' also.[25]

The existence of *qānūn* law in the Ottoman empire goes back at least as far as Mehmed II (1432–81 CE). According to Zubaida,

---

21 Al Rasheed, 1991, *op. cit.*, 89–90.
22 See a recent study of the Zardezas district of the north Constantinois by Karim Rahem, *Le Sillage de la Tribu: imaginaires politiques et histoire en Algérie (1843–1993)* (Paris: Riveneuve Éditions, 2008), 234, where Rahem records that local tribes had *'urfi* law but – unlike the Kabyles – no *qawānīn*.
23 Hart, 1981, *op. cit.*, 159. Shelagh Weir (*op. cit.*, 144–7) makes much the same point in the case of north Yemen.
24 Brett and Fentress, 1996, *op. cit.*, 184. The authors' brief account of Kabyle law is one of the very few such discussions to have included a reference to Ottoman practice.
25 Sami Zubaida, *Law and Power in the Islamic World* (London: I.B.Tauris, 2003), 103–13: 108; see also Halil İnalcık, *The Ottoman Empire: The classical period, 1300–1600*, New York, Washington: Praeger Publishers, 1973; 2nd edition, New Rochelle, New York: Orpheus Publishing Co., 1989), chapter X.

it was Mehmed II, conqueror of Constantinople, who issued the first historically recorded *qanun-name*. His first book specified taxes to be paid by the *re'aya*, Muslim and Christian; his second promulgated administrative regulations for court and government. Neither makes any reference to the *shari'a*.[26]

Thus there was nothing unusual, let alone un-Islamic, about the corpus of law governing a Muslim people including laws derived from custom rather than from the *Sharī'a*. It was established practice in the heart of the Ottoman empire before this expanded to include what is now Algeria. That the Kabyles had *qawānīn* and that these embodied precepts derived from regional and local customs as well as precepts derived from scripture did not in themselves constitute evidence at all for the notion that they were bad Muslims, let alone 'anti-clerical'.

It follows that what is to be explained is not the misconceived proposition that the Kabyles were in general heterodox or bad Muslims, but, on the contrary, the fact that, although perfectly devout Muslims in most respects, they nonetheless explicitly decided, at a definite moment in time, in the mid-eighteenth century CE, to depart from Islamic precepts in respect of their laws of inheritance. This is the 'revival' of ancient custom to which Hanoteau and Letourneux referred. It is a problem for the historian rather than the anthropologist and I shall address it in the penultimate chapter of this book.

Finally, regarding the origin of *qānūn* law in Kabylia, it seems to me to be far more likely that the Kabyles embodied their customary laws in something they called a *qānūn* in direct imitation of the observable practice of the Ottoman Regency from the mid-sixteenth century onwards, than that they did so in deference to a memory, mysteriously preserved over one and half millennia and countless generations, of the practice of the Roman empire or the early Christian church.

The code of honour and the code of law

Two further questions which arise when we consider the *qawānīn* of the Kabyles have been at issue in the twentieth-century debates. First, are they properly to be regarded as law at all? Second, are they consistent with the segmentarity thesis? Clearly the answer to the second question depends to a large extent on the answer to the first.

---

26 *Ibid. Qanun-name* means 'Book of Laws'. *Re'aya* is the Turkish form of the Arabic *ra'iya* (literally 'flocks') used to mean subjects, that is tribes or other docile populations that demonstrated loyalty (e.g. by paying taxes) to the Sultan.

Are the articles of the *qawānīn* laws? It was certainly the view of Masqueray and of Hanoteau and Letourneux that they were. Masqueray not only devoted many pages to a discussion of the 'kanoun' [*sic*] of the Mzabis, the Chaouia and the Kabyles, as we have seen, and explained at length how they resembled the early law of the Romans, but also explicitly translated the word as 'law', *loi*.[27] Hanoteau and Letourneux for their part insisted on the existence of a system of law, *droit*, among the Kabyles,[28] and their principal purpose in collecting and recording the *qawānīn* of Greater Kabylia was to facilitate the effective colonial government of the region on the basis of its own legal traditions.[29]

This clear-cut view of the matter has since gone by the board. The twentieth-century literature on Berber society conventionally distinguishes between Berber *custom* and Islamic *law* and tends very much to convey the impression that the Berbers had customs but not laws of their own. In this respect, if no other, this literature has endorsed the prejudices of the urban bourgeoisies of Algeria and Morocco. Gellner, for instance, contrasts the customs, *qā'ida* (an Arabic word), of the central High Atlas Berbers of Morocco to the *Shra'a* (i.e. *Sharī'a*, Quranic law), and employs the terms 'custom' and 'customary law' interchangeably.[30] Although Bourdieu, for his part, speaks at one point of the *qawānīn* of the Kabyles as 'the laws that are laid down by (the village) council, which differ from Islamic law and which govern daily behaviour in great detail',[31] a passage which recalls the nineteenth-century view, he subsequently refers to the *qawānīn* as merely 'a set of customs peculiar to each village' and explicitly rejects the view that they constitute 'a code of law', insisting instead that 'the group knows no other code than that of honour'.[32]

In other words, this question has become a grey area in the literature on Berber societies. The frequent employment of the term 'customary law' has allowed the issue to be evaded: is 'customary law' custom or law? While numerous scholars have been patently unclear about the matter, I shall state my own view in respect of the Kabyle case, which is that custom is one thing and law is another; that the Kabyles had both customs and laws (including laws derived from customs) and were moreover perfectly aware of the fact, even if they ultimately failed to convince latter-day European observers of it; and that the highest development of law in Kabylia occurred in the society of the Jurjura – that is, among the Igawawen.

The implication of the thesis that the Kabyles had laws is that they also had legislatures – that is specialist law-giving institutions – and courts. It is precisely

27 Masqueray, *op. cit.*, 51.
28 Hanoteau and Letourneux, *op. cit.*, vol. II, 135 *et seq.*
29 Ageron, *op. cit.*, vol. I, 281.
30 Gellner, 1969, *op. cit.*, 105–6.
31 Bourdieu, 1962, *op. cit.*, 13.
32 Bourdieu, *op. cit.*, 21.

the radical absence of such things which is one of the chief presuppositions of the
segmentarity thesis. And, if Bourdieu ultimately came down on the side of the
view that the Kabyle *qānūn* fell short of being a legal code, it is because he denied
that the Kabyles possessed law courts worthy of the name, a denial contained in
the following characteristic passage:

> In reality, the group knows no other code than that of honour, which
> demands that the crime, whether murder, insult or adultery, should
> contain within itself its own punishment; it has no court of law other
> than public opinion; each individual passes sentence on himself in
> accordance with the common and inwardly felt code of the group, and
> without interference from any power placed outside or above. It will be
> objected that the council of the clan or village acts as a court of law, that it
> promulgates 'a code of law' (qanoun) that is sometimes put in writing, that
> it sees to the preservation of law and order and has at its disposal a whole
> system of punishments, penalties, reprisals and banishment. But rather
> than a court of law in the sense of a specialized organism charged with
> pronouncing verdicts in conformity with a system of formal, rational and
> explicit norms, the assembly is in fact a council of arbitration and perhaps
> even a family council.[33]

So two quite different 'codes' existed in some sense, but only one of them – the
code of honour – had any force 'in reality'. Bourdieu thus recognised the existence
of two different codes, but regarded them not only as opposed but as mutually
exclusive, such that the contradiction between them could be resolved only by
dismissing one of them (the *qānūn*) as entirely insignificant. What this ruled out
of consideration was the possibility that both codes had substantial force in reality
and that the element of conflict in the relationship between them was not capable
of being resolved once and for all by the definitive triumph of one over the other,
but constituted a continuing problem for Kabyle society and the stuff of much of
its political life.

Second, in the same way as Bourdieu assumed that the two codes in question
were mutually exclusive, such that only one of them had any force 'in reality', he
assumed that the functions of pronouncing a verdict and those of arbitration are
also mutually exclusive, such that an institution which performs the latter cannot
be credited with discharging the former and is therefore not to be regarded as a
court of law. This assumption was entirely arbitrary and groundless, an affair of
mere (if unspecific) dogma.

Moreover, it should be noted that Bourdieu was operating with a very
demanding definition of a court of law. It is by no means only the *jema'a* of a

---

33 Bourdieu, 1962, *op. cit.*, 21–2.

Kabyle village which falls short of this definition, which was clearly derived from the legal traditions with which Bourdieu, as a Frenchman, was familiar. In the English tradition of Common Law, there is no guarantee whatever that the jury's verdict will be '*in conformity with* a system of formal, *rational* and explicit norms' (my emphasis) and, given the emphatically adversarial nature of the relationship between prosecution and defence in this tradition, the function of the jury might well be described as, at least to some extent, that of acting as arbiter of what is at issue between the two sides of the case in dispute. While one may well be inclined to admit the superiority of Continental Law, it would be an audacious French sociologist indeed who claimed that an English court was not 'in reality' a court of law in the proper sense of the term.

Above all, however, Bourdieu's argument rested on the systematic confusion between different levels of Kabyle social organisation. He did not speak specifically of the *jema'a* of the village, but of 'the council of the clan or village', and thereby tacitly denied that there was any substantive difference between the two in their constitutive principles or their prerogatives. And when he said that 'the group knows no other code than that of honour', it should not (but may easily) be forgotten that the group which Bourdieu had in mind was in fact not the village at all but the clan, which, he claimed elsewhere, was 'the real political unit'.[34]

In this way the whole question has been thoroughly muddled. For, while it is certainly the case that informal *jemāya'* of a kind exist intermittently at the level of the clan (*adrum*) and indeed at levels below this, there is no question whatever of these *jemāya'* having the function of promulgating articles of the *qānūn* or of ensuring that they are enforced and their transgression penalised. By refusing to consider the significance and status of the *qānūn* in relation explicitly and specifically to the *jema'a* of the village alone, Bourdieu succeeded in confusing the issue completely, in a way which marked not a theoretical advance on but a regression from the clarity of his nineteenth-century predecessors' treatment of these questions. The fact of the matter is that the *jema'a* of a Kabyle village, at any rate in the Jurjura, most certainly did perform the functions both of legislature and of law court, as Masqueray and also Hanoteau and Letourneux observed, and that Bourdieu's dismissal of the earlier view was unaccompanied by the slightest attempt at an empirical refutation of it.

This refusal to take seriously the earlier view may well have been prompted in part by Masqueray's unsatisfactory formulation of it.

Bourdieu's view of the relationship between the legal code of the *qānūn* on the one hand and the code of honour on the other, namely that the former was of very limited and superficial significance and the latter alone had real substance, represented an attempt to resolve theoretically the contradiction inherent in

---

34 Bourdieu, *op. cit.*, 18.

this relationship. But it was not the first such attempt. Eighty years before him Masqueray also attempted to resolve this contradiction, but in the opposite direction.

Speaking generally of 'the city among our sedentary Africans' (by which he clearly meant the peoples of the Maghrib alone) and notably of the Kabyle *thaddarth*, the Chaoui *thaqelath* [sic],[35] the Mzabi *'arsh* and the Moroccan *tireremt* [sic],[36] he insisted that these 'cities' transcend the solidarities and divisions of the kinship groups out of which they have been constituted. As he remarked in his introduction,

> ... far from being an extension of the narrow institutions of the family, they develop outside them and are even opposed to them from the first moment of their existence ... [37]

In this he was, in a sense, quite right, at least in respect of the Kabyle *thaddarth*, as we shall see presently. But he then went on to claim that 'the City'

> ... is composed only of individuals, it knows only individuals, it protects and punishes only individuals ... it has, as soon as it is formed, the character of being the expression of individual energies.[38]

It would be difficult to imagine a statement more thoroughly at odds with the segmentarist conception of Berber society in general and with Bourdieu's emphasis on the role of the clan in Kabyle society in particular. It is not surprising, then, that Gellner, in arguing that Masqueray's description of Kabylia was that of a segmentary society even if he was subjectively inhibited from recognising the fact, should call this 'a very strange passage'[39] and suggest that it 'is in conflict with [Masqueray's] own material'.[40]

---

35 That is, *thaqel'ath*, the Berber form of the Arabic *qal'a* (often pronounced and sometimes written as *guelaa* in Algeria). This word is used in the society of the Aurès mountains to refer to a most distinctive institution in the life of a Chaoui village, namely the collective storehouse, but by extension it can indicate the village as a whole and it is in this sense that Masqueray is employing the term here.

36 That is, i.e. *tighermt*, the diminutive of *igherm*, which can mean a large, fortified house, resembling a small castle, of a prominent family, such as those described by Gellner (1969, *op. cit.*, 162) at Zawiya Ahansal, but it can also mean a collective storehouse (Gellner, *op. cit.*, 167); in southern Morocco it usually refers to a fortified settlement comprising a – possibly large – number of individual households (David Hart, 1981, *op. cit.*, 5, 22, 51, 53, 138–9). In this context it is the Moroccan Berber equivalent of the Arabic *qsar*. Masqueray here is using it in this sense.

37 Masqueray, *op. cit.*, 20.

38 Masqueray, *op. cit.*, 24.

39 Gellner, 1985, *art. cit.*, in Gellner, 1987, *op. cit.*, 29–46: 35.

40 Gellner, *ibid.*

There is another way of reading Masqueray's statement which resolves the apparent conflict between it and his empirical material, as we shall see. But there is no doubt that, at first sight, Masqueray appears here to have advanced an extreme and indefensible position. It would certainly seem that, in recognising (unlike Bourdieu and Gellner) that one of the pillars of the Kabyle system of village self-government was a legal system incorporating a code of law worthy of the name, Masqueray was led to deny *all* significance to the kinship groups – families, lineages, clans – which composed the population of the village and which were the principal bearers of the ideology of honour and thus the upholders of the code of honour in opposition to the code of law.

In the light of this, Bourdieu's solution to the theoretical problem posed by the law/honour dichotomy in Kabylia appears as merely the obverse of Masqueray's earlier solution. Each of them seems to have tried to solve the problem by suppressing one of the terms of the dichotomy. Neither of them, apparently, has managed to cope theoretically with the contradiction which existed in reality.

The Kabyles coped with it politically. And the way in which they did this is embodied in the *qawānīn* themselves, in so far as the *qawānīn* recognised the code of honour and accommodated the kinship rivalries it expressed by bringing them within the sphere of law and thereby curbed their anti-social potential.

Antagonism in society

The extreme physical proximity of unrelated lineages in the Igawawen *thaddarth* furnished an unending series of occasions for friction and disputes between them. Unless this fact was compensated for, the *thaddarth* would have quickly fallen prey to these kinship conflicts, which were liable to be both more frequent and more intense than those arising within the far less integrated form of settlement of the *tūfiq*. The *thaddarth* coped with this problem in three main ways.

The first of these I have already discussed, namely the fact that the *jema'a* of the *thaddarth*, by functioning whenever necessary as a court of law, made available to all families resident in the village the means of resolving disputes by orderly litigation. The second was the way in which the *jema'a* actively encouraged all parties to proceed in this way, by penalising the recourse to violence. The third was the way in which alternative outlets for the expression of kinship solidarities and rivalries were provided by the operation of the *saff* system, a point I shall develop presently. Let us consider the second point, which is a much misunderstood matter.

Without exception, the *qawānīn* of Kabyle villages and tribes included articles which stipulated the penalties for the exchange of blows and the proffering of threats and even insults. These articles were usually very detailed, with distinct penalties – that is, fines, to be paid to the village chest, not the injured party –

for each offence, specified normally by the nature of the weapon employed or brandished (as indicating the offender's intention) rather than the nature of the injury actually inflicted, but also by other circumstances (e.g. the time and place of the offence). Hanoteau and Letourneux cite numerous *qānūn* articles from a wide range of Kabyle villages to illustrate this. Amongst those drawn from the Igawawen villages we find the following stipulations and penalties:

- The fine for a fist-fight between men is a ½ réal (Koukou);
- He who strikes with a shoe or a stone pays 5 réals (Agouni n'Taslent);
- Those who fight after sunset must each pay 2 réals (Taourirt n'Tidits);
- He who fights at the market pays the market's fine and, in addition, pays ¼ réal to the village (Taourirt Amrane);
- If two litigants fight in the presence of the *jema'a* assembled to settle their case, they each pay 10 réals fine. The man who strikes alone pays, if his adversary has not defended himself (Koukou);
- He who strikes with an iron instrument, 5 réals; if he threatens without striking, 2½ réals (Taourirt n'Tidits);
- He who threatens to fire (sc. his gun), without firing, 5 réals (Taourirt n'Tidits);
- He who fires a shot at another, 10 réals (Taourirt n'Tidits);
- He who goes out of his house with a weapon hidden under his arm pays 1 réal (Tiqichourt).[41]

The philosophy underlying the highly discriminating penal codes in force can more easily be inferred from the following articles of the *qānūn* of the Ath Wakour, a small *'arsh*, consisting of only two villages, whose 'tribal' *qānūn* was probably simply that of the larger village, Thaddarth el-Jedid:

Art.17.   He who threatens with a firearm in a dispute pays two and a half douros fine; if he fires, five douros.

18.   He who brings a sword into a dispute, but does not use it, pays three francs and six sous fine; if he strikes with it, the fine is six francs and six sous.

19.   He who threatens with a little pick-axe, but without striking, pays three francs and six sous fine; if he strikes, the fine is six francs and six sous.

---

41 Hanoteau and Letourneux, *op. cit.*, vol. III, 187–99 (my translation into English here and below). Taourirt Amrane is a village of *'arsh* Ath Bou Youcef, Koukou a village of *'arsh* Ath Yahia, Agouni n'Taslent a village of *'arsh* Aqbil; Taourirt n'Tidits (also known as Taourirt n'Ath Menguellat) is the leading village of the Ath Menguellat; Tiqichourt is a village of the Ath Wasif.

20. He who hits with a stick pays a half-douro fine.
21. He who threatens with a stone, but without striking, pays one franc and six sous fine; if he strikes, the fine is a half-douro.
22. If two men exchange abuse, each of them pays ten sous fine.
23. Whoever has violated the ʿanāya of the *jemaʿa* pays two and a half douros fine.[42]

Thus the different forms of violence were specified and a sliding scale was employed. (A douro equalled five francs; one franc equalled twenty sous or a hundred centimes.[43]) It should be noted that acts of violence or exchanges of insults which were committed in the *jemaʿa*, in the sense of public place of assembly, were deemed to violate its ʿanāya (the protection it affords in virtue of the consideration it is due) and were punished more severely in consequence. The *jemaʿa* is the domain of reason and reasonable men, and the *qānūn* afforded it special protection, as the public space *par excellence*.

It is also interesting to note that the exchange of blows and insults were punished less severely than offences against property, notably acts of theft, arson and housebreaking, for which, among the Ath Wakour, the penalties were invariably an affair of douros, not francs, ranging from three to twenty-five. The *qawānīn* of the Igawawen were, if anything, even more severe in this regard:

- He who steals in the village during the day, if an adult, 20 réals; if a minor, 5 réals (Ath Ferah);
- The adult woman who steals figs or grapes, 1 réal; the (minor) girl, ½ real (Ath Ferah);
- He who gives information enabling a villager's flocks to be stolen, 30 réals fine (Ath Saada);
- The person who breaks through a wall during the night in order to steal, 50 réals (Ath Ferah);
- He who steals in a house pays 50 réals (Tiqichourt);
- If a woman steals in a house, during the day or at night, 25 réals (Tiqichourt);
- He who steals from a house or a farm where women or children are present, either by making a hole (sc. in a wall) or by forcing the door, pays 50 réals fine: 25 to the jemaʿa, 25 to the owner (Tiqichourt);

---

42 Masqueray, *op. cit.*, Appendix, 306.
43 I have been unable to discover for certain what the exact French franc equivalence of a réal was in the mid-nineteenth century; the réal was a Spanish coin of silver or gold, and so a fine of 5 réals was a stiffer penalty than a fine of the same number of francs or douros.

- Burglary at night of an inhabited house is punished by a fine of 100 réals and reparation (sc. to the owner) of 100 réals (Taourirt n'Tidits).[44]

The evident implication of this contrast is that it was recognised that frictions and enmities and their violent expression were routine (as they are, of course, in 'modern' societies), and could not be suppressed, but could be subject to official condemnation and financial penalty. That is, the *jema'a* knew better than to try to prevent such things but could and did at least discourage them by legal means. Theft, on the other hand, of olives or figs from someone's orchard and especially of animals (mules, goats, sheep) and above all where housebreaking was involved, was taken far more seriously. The far higher fines incurred established these acts as crimes rather than misdemeanours, as acts of dishonesty, in contrast to the eminently honest business of expressing one's feelings about someone in words or blows.

The point about theft, housebreaking and so on is that they were legitimate and counted as honest acts only in the state of war, and it was a major purpose of the *jema'a* of a Kabyle village to prevent a state of war from developing between any of its constituent families, to prevent – that is to say – the feud.

Sociologists and anthropologists who subscribe to or have been influenced by the propositions of the segmentarity theory have often argued that the feud is itself an order-maintaining mechanism. And they have had no difficulty in showing that feuding in many societies, including Berber societies, has been subject to its own internal rules of a kind. The same is true, of course, or at any rate used to be true, of war between states. There have long been rules of war and there is the Geneva Convention. But, if feuding is in some sense an order-maintaining mechanism, it is a very different one from the business of political argument and negotiation, legislative enactment and judicial process. It is an alternative to them and is subversive of them. This has been recognised by Evans-Pritchard, in his remark that 'corporate life is incompatible with a state of feud'.[45]

Now, Gellner himself has acknowledged that even in the tribal society of the Central High Atlas of Morocco 'groups of about village size (300 people or so) are not "purely" segmentary but do have a corporate existence vis-à-vis individuals or sub-groups'.[46] And what holds good of small settlements among the predominantly transhumant and economically undiversified populations of the Moroccan Atlas is, *a fortiori*, very likely to be even more true of the very much larger villages of the entirely sedentary and economically more diversified

---

44 Hanoteau and Letourneux, *op. cit.*, vol. III, 240 *et seq.* Ath Saada is a large village of *'arsh* Ath Attaf of the Ath Menguellat confederation.

45 E.E. Evans-Pritchard, *The Nuer* (London: Oxford University Press, 1940), 156.

46 Gellner, 1969, *op. cit.*, 116–17, n. 2.

Kabyles. But the implications of this point have been contested by Jeanne Favret in her assertion that, in the penal sphere, the Kabyle village (which, as we have seen, she mistakenly insisted on referring to as a 'patrilignage')

> constitutes a corporation which sees to it that its moral order is not transgressed by its members, and which obliges its segments to assume their responsibilities, which is to say, to return blow for blow.
>
> The corporation referred to by British anthropologists re-establishes a necessary peace between hostile lineage segments ... The Kabyle corporation, on the contrary, precipitates violence in the case where its segments would like to remain in peace.[47]

The great difficulty with this assertion is one which Favret herself appears to recognise when she remarks, at the very end of her article, that 'it would remain to explain ... how compact villages can subsist as distinct residential units'.[48] Indeed it would, were her statement, that the Kabyle village regularly and deliberately precipitated conflict between its constituent lineages, at all accurate. It isn't.

More than any one other thing, the survival of the Kabyle *thaddarth* – and, above all, of the large and complex *thaddarth* of the Igawawen – depended upon its ability as a corporation to prevent or at least curb feuding among its constituent clans and lineages. Far from encouraging feuds, it inhibited and in some cases outlawed and punished feuding behaviour; it sought by pre-emptive measures to render recourse to it unnecessary and it afforded alternative, political, outlets to the impulses which would otherwise have expressed themselves in it.

The first two ways in which the *thaddarth* sought to prevent feuding were embodied in the *qawānīn*. The *qānūn* of the Ath Mansour tribe of the Wad Sahel had no fewer than 120 articles. The 88th read as follows:

> Whoever has committed a murder without having the right pays sixty douros, and he alone is killed, or is banished. Among us murder is expiated by direct murder. He who transgresses this rule, and, for compensation, kills one of the relatives of the murderer of his relative, exercises a personal vengeance; and it is why we have written that whoever commits a murder is alone killed, without the murder being taken out on another. If the murderer dies before having suffered vengeance, the heirs of the victim have no compensation to claim of them,[49]

'them' in this context being presumably the relatives of the deceased murderer.

---

47 Favret, 1968, *art. cit.*, 36.
48 Favret, *loc. cit.*, 43.
49 Masqueray, *op. cit.*, Appendix, 271.

So killing was not always a crime; there were cases where killing was lawful. Kabyle law recognised the 'blood debt' – that is, the right and even obligation of revenge (*reqba*[50]) up to a point – and revenge – the principle of 'an eye for a eye' – against a murderer was accordingly lawful. As the *qānūn* of Agouni n'Taslent put it, 'There is no punishment for the man who exercises vengeance following a blood debt'.[51] But indirect revenge, the killing of a relative in lieu of the murderer himself – the characteristic and fundamental act of feud – was, among the Ath Mansour, a crime.

This may, however, be an extreme case. By no means all the villages and tribes of Kabylia had *qawānīn* which were as explicit as this in outlawing the feud. Hanoteau and Letourneux cite only three instances drawn from the populations of the northern side of the Jurjura of similar restrictions being placed on the exercise of the right/obligation of *reqba*, allowing rightful revenge to be taken on the murderer alone and outlawing its exercise against his agnates. These are found in the *qānūn* of *'arsh* Ath Khelifa of the Maatqa confederation,[52] that of *'arsh* Ath Ameur ou Faïd of the Ath Aissi confederation[53] and that of Ighil Imoula of the Ath Sedqa confederation.[54] To these we can add the important village of Taourirt Amoqran, of *'arsh* Ath Ousammeur of the Ath Irathen confederation; the relevant articles of its *qānūn* read:

> When a murder is committed, it is the murderer who must die; if he dies accidentally, his successors incur the blood price.
> He who, contrary to the law, kills someone other than the murderer, pays 100 reals and incurs the death penalty.[55]

It is possible that, in much of Kabylia, the right of the family of a murder victim to take revenge on any of the murderer's adult male kin was generally uncontested in principle. But in many cases this formal recognition of the right

---

50 This is the Arabic word; in *Thaqbaylith*, the word for the right of revenge is *tsaar*; see Augustin Ibazizen, *Le Pont de Bereq'mouch ou le bond de mille ans* (Paris: Éditions de la Table Ronde, 1979), 233, 253 *et seq*. The Arabic term features more often in the *qawānīn*, because these were recorded in Arabic by the *imrabdhen*.

51 Hanoteau and Letourneux, *op. cit.*, vol. III, 62.

52 The article reads: 'When an individual kills another, he alone is subject to the blood debt' (Hanoteau and Letourneux, *op. cit.*, vol. III, 70).

53 The article reads: 'If an individual kills another, vengeance must be exercised upon the murderer and not on his kinsmen' (*ibid.*).

54 'He who exercises a reprisal for a murder must not take out his vengeance on the murderer's brother nor his uncle, nor their children, nor his (sc. the murderer's) sons, nor his father. He may exercise reprisals only on the murderer himself' (Hanoteau and Letourneux, *op. cit.*, vol. III, 336).

55 Quoted in Baron Henri Aucapitaine, 'Kanoun du village de Thaourirt Amokran chez les Aïth Irathen (Kabilie)', *Revue Africaine*, 7 (1863), 279–85: 280.

to resort to feud was tempered and partially negated by an effort to circumscribe this right by means of limiting conditions. One way this was done was by distinguishing between those homicides which entailed a right of revenge and those which did not. Thus we find *qawānīn* that explicitly stipulate that accidental homicides but also certain deliberate killings – for example, that of a burglar by a house owner defending his home – do not expose the perpetrator to the menace of *reqba* and that if the kinsmen of the victim in such cases seek revenge they are themselves committing an offence punishable by a stiff fine.[56]

More generally, the concern to pre-empt feuding was evident in many cases, in so far as certain kinds of killing were decreed to be unlawful and subject to penalties imposed by the *jema'a*, thereby obviating and in principle precluding action by the bereaved family. These penalties varied with the gravity of the offence and with the tribe or village in question, but certainly included death in some cases. For example, the 38th article of the *qānūn* of the Imecheddalen tribe, immediate neighbours to the west of the Ath Wakour, decreed that

> Whoever is convicted of having served a poisoned meal by malefice, either to a man or to a woman, or to an old man or to a child, pays five douros fine and is stoned to death.[57]

The same law existed among the *'arsh* Ath Khelifa of the Maatqa confederation[58] but the Ath Fraoucen had a different version, imposing a very stiff fine of 50 réals whether or not the victim succumbed, but apparently not presuming to execute the offender.[59]

An especially significant instance of pre-emption concerned killings of kin motivated by the desire to inherit from the victim. These were generally outlawed very explicitly and punished with severity. Among the populations of the north side of the Jurjura, the rule was that the *jema'a*, in addition to confiscating all of the offender's property (and in some cases slaughtering his flocks) or at least imposing very stiff fines, inflicted the further punishment of demolishing his house and banishing him from the village.[60] Among the Ath Boudrar, an Igawawen *'arsh* in the most restricted sense, matters were taken much further. Article 3 of the *qānūn* of the village of Ath Ali ou Harzoun states:

---

56 Hanoteau and Letourneux, *op. cit.*, vol. III, 72.

57 Masqueray, *op. cit.*, Appendix, 292.

58 'If a man or a woman poisons someone, the culprit pays 10 douros fine if death has not occurred; if death has resulted, the culprit pays 25 douros and is put to death' (Hanoteau and Letourneux, *op. cit.*, vol. III, 71).

59 Hanoteau and Letourneux, *op. cit.*, vol. III, 174.

60 Hanoteau and Letourneux, *op. cit.*, vol. III, citing the *qawānīn* of Taourirt Abdallah (of *'arsh* Iwadhien), *'arsh* Ath Bou Chaïb, *'arsh* Ath Ameur ou Faïd, Ath Ferah, Koukou, Taourirt n'Tidits and Agouni n'Taslent.

He who kills his father, his brother or his son with the intention of inheriting from him is put to death, if he is arrested; if he escapes, all his property is confiscated by the *jema'a*.[61]

A similar severity obtained among the Ath Qani of the southern side of the Jurjura; articles 15 and 16 of their *qānūn* stipulated that:

If someone kills one of his relatives in order to inherit from him, the *jema'a* puts him to death, and appropriates both the goods of the dead man and those of his murderer.
If the murderer has escaped and left the region, he cannot return.[62]

Thus treacherous killing and killing for an inherited gain were not regarded as justified by the claims of honour. Yet these were precisely the sorts of killing which would be likely to precipitate a feud if the *jema'a* did not punish them itself. Moreover, we should bear in mind that, as Favret has pointed out, an implication of the Kabyle system of land tenure, as a consequence of the right of pre-emption of real estate (*shefa'a*) accorded to agnates, was that

one can hope to acquire (land) only from one's closest agnates – in other words, one has an interest in getting them into debt in order to push them into selling; economic competition therefore exists only within the village and between agnates ...[63]

It follows that in Kabyle society there would have existed a substantial incentive to kill close agnates for material gain, were this not subject to severe penalties imposed by the community.

There is a very striking contrast with the Berbers of the Moroccan Rif on this point. For, as David Hart has amply documented for the largest of the Rifian Berber tribes, the Aïth Waryaghar, amongst whom the blood feud was a permanent fact of life for practically all families, feuding frequently occurred precisely within the family itself or the immediate lineage because motivated in many cases by the struggle over landed inheritance. The *qānūn* of the Aïth Waryaghar contains no article prohibiting such killings and the serving of poisoned food or drink was apparently an entirely legitimate tactic.[64]

Another kind of killing which was explicitly outlawed by at least some Kabyle tribes was that of a man by his wife. The Ath Aïssa tribe, southern neighbours of

---

61 Bernard and Milliot, *art. cit.*, 31.
62 Masqueray, *op. cit.*, Appendix, 310. Masqueray refers to this *'arsh* as the Beni Kani, Hanoteau and Letourneux as Aït Kani.
63 Favret, 1968, *art. cit.*, 27.
64 Hart, *op. cit.*, 335.

the Imecheddalen, stipulated in the 36th article of their *qānūn* that 'The woman who kills her husband is stoned by the notables of the *jema'a* until death ensues.'[65] In other words, the husband's household was not allowed to exact vengeance for itself. 'Vengeance is mine,' said the *jema'a*, almost certainly for the same reason as in the other cases cited. A marriage is an alliance between two families, which often belong, moreover, to different lineages and different clans and occasionally different villages. The killing of a man by his wife would not merely signal the definitive and disastrous collapse of such an alliance, it might well precipitate a feud between the families (lineages, clans, villages) in question unless the *jema'a* stepped in smartly and inflicted punishment in the interest of the community as a whole.

There can be little doubt that the outlawing in Kabylia of these various kinds of killing was intended to prevent feuding and that their punishment by the *jema'a*, by pre-empting private vengeance, had the same purpose. This purpose was probably only imperfectly realised. There is no reason to doubt that the reports of feuding in the nineteenth-century literature on Kabylia had a solid basis in fact. But these reports did not always distinguish between the kinds of killing which, as we have seen, the Kabyle *jema'a* was inclined to regard as honourable and also lawful and those which it stigmatised as neither and accordingly punished. And the fact that killings of the latter, unlawful, variety occurred does not mean that the attempts to prevent and pre-empt them were vain, any more than the incidence of murder in a modern state can be cited as proof of the vanity of the laws which define it as a crime. Murder as such cannot be entirely prevented, but many individual murders are punished and murder as such is inhibited by this fact.

There can be also little doubt that the incidence of feud killings in Kabylia was much lower than in the Moroccan Rif, where no attempt was made to deter them. Neither the *qānūn* of the Aïth Waryaghar, for example, nor those of its neighbours contain any articles outlawing or seeking to pre-empt feuding.[66] The only attempt to control feuding was the outlawing of killing on market day (and, in some cases, on the day before and the day after as well, to take account of the time some people spent travelling to and from markets).[67] And this limit was clearly motivated by the concern to preserve the functioning of the markets from violent disruption rather than the concern to inhibit feuding as such, which was evidently accepted by all and sundry as a fact of everyday adult life. (Moreover, we should note the significant fact that the stiff fines – *haqq* – imposed for transgressing this rule were shared out between the 'five fifths' – *khams khmas* – of which the tribe was composed, not deposited in

---

65 Masqueray, *op. cit.*, Appendix, 317.
66 Hart, *op. cit.*, 290 *et seq.*
67 Hart, *ibid.*

a village or tribal treasury for the benefit of the community as a whole, as in Kabylia.[68])

The *jemaʿa* of a Kabyle village did not have the moral authority to outlaw, let alone the power actually to prevent, all kinds of killing. The strong impression conveyed by the *qawānīn* of the various villages and tribes is that they condoned or, at least, did not condemn certain kinds of killing in order to be able to outlaw other kinds, in what amounted to a trade-off. The killings condoned were those judged to be rightful because honourable. Thus the code of law recognised the code of honour. But it did not subordinate itself to it, as in the Rif. On the contrary, it incorporated it and subsumed it and thereby subordinated it to itself. It accepted the practice of *reqba* as a fact of Kabyle life, but undertook to regulate it. It was for the *jemaʿa* to judge whether a killing claimed to be required by the code of honour was indeed such.

In other words, considerations of honour entered into the functioning of the Kabyle legal system as arguments in court. And, in establishing as crimes the various kinds of killing which were dishonourable either in motive (to gain an inheritance) or in spirit (the treacherous killing of a husband by his wife, from whom absolute loyalty was expected) or in method (the treacherous serving of poisoned food or drink, in violation of the honourable code of hospitality) and by stipulating the severest penalties (banishment or even death) for them, the *jemaʿa* simultaneously transformed an offence against a particular person (and, by extension, a particular kinship group) into a crime against society and pre-empted the recourse by relatives of the victim to honourable revenge, in the general interest of the community as a whole.

So Favret's claim that, in Kabylia, 'the right of the lineage prevails over the right of the village'[69] is the opposite of the truth, at any rate in the case of those populations among whom the large, complex, *thaddarth* characteristic of the Igawawen prevailed. It is in the Rif that her claim would apply. Amongst the Aïth Waryaghar and their neighbours, political life is (or at any rate used to be) extremely rudimentary by Kabyle standards and, in consequence, the old motto of the English Mosley family – '*mos legem regit*': 'custom rules the law'[70] – also holds good. The *qawānīn* of the Rifians do not outlaw or even try to pre-empt the feud at all; they merely seek to impose – in the interest of a minimum of regular commercial activity – a single limitation of time and place upon the otherwise entirely unfettered and legitimate business of killing.

In Kabylia, *lex mores regit*. The *qawānīn* neither meekly endorsed nor vainly opposed the dictates of the code of honour. They incorporated them selectively in a remarkable and entirely functional compromise between the public interest and

---

68 Hart, *op. cit.*, 294–302.
69 Favret, 1968, *art. cit.*, 19.
70 Sir Oswald Mosley, *My Life* (London: Nelson, 1968), 5–6.

the private interest. And the tendency apparent within this formal compromise was unquestionably for the code of law to prevail over, in the sense of governing the operation of, the code of honour. And what this meant in the long run was that the very conception of honourable behaviour in a Kabyle village was influenced by the conception of lawful behaviour.

I began this chapter with a quotation from Kant. It seems to me that one way in which one may express the difference between populations, including Berber-speaking populations, to which the segmentarity theory might conceivably apply and those, notably the Kabyles, to which it does not is that in the one case the antagonisms between kinship groups are not yet, or at any rate not fully, what Kant meant by 'antagonism in society', whereas in the other case they are precisely this. While in some theoretical sense of other it may be legitimate to speak of the 'society' of the Rifian Berbers, this 'society' – with its absence of villages, its population of scattered family households and the permanent and omnipresent blood-feud – resembles in certain fundamental respects Hobbes's vision of the 'State of Nature', of *'bellum omnium contra omnes'*, where there exist

> no Arts; no Letters; no Society; and which is worst of all, continuall feare, and danger of violent death; And the life of man, solitary, poore, nasty, brutish, and short.[71]

In Kabylia, and amongst the Igawawen above all, 'society' in no way resembles Hobbes's 'State of Nature', because it is in the first place a society of large, densely settled, extremely compact and strictly governed villages. Bourdieu's claim that 'up to a relatively recent date the clan *(adrum)* was the framework in which social life developed'[72] was nonsensical as well as untrue. If it were true, then there would have been no social life as such, merely family life and its extension in the life of the extended family which is the clan. Social life begins where the limits of kinship are met, and crossed. These limits were and still are met and crossed as a matter of daily routine in the Igawawen *thaddarth*.

Kant develops the fifth in the series of theses referred to above with the reflection that

> All culture, art which adorns mankind, and the finest social order are fruits of unsociableness, which forces itself to discipline itself, and so, by a contrived art, to develop the natural seeds of perfection.[73]

---

71 Thomas Hobbes, *Leviathan*, edited with an introduction by C.B. Macpherson (London: Penguin, 1968), 186.

72 Bourdieu, 1962, *op. cit.*, 12.

73 Immanuel Kant, *op. cit.*, 17.

The unsociableness of the Aïth Waryaghar did not force itself to discipline itself, other than in the most rudimentary and marginal way, but that of the Igawawen did precisely this, by inserting politics, the quintessence of sociableness, into its own core. The disciplining of Igawawen unsociableness was precisely a matter of 'a contrived art' – the political art, the empirical and innovative art of contriving arrangements by which to govern vital social forces – by means of which it ensured that the particular interests which divided the inhabitants of an Igawawen village expressed themselves as antagonisms *in society* and not as antagonisms which precluded society or subverted it.

The principal arenas in which these antagonisms expressed themselves were the *jemāya'*.

CHAPTER 4

~

The Kabyle Polity

Ce que nous voyons dans l'Afrique n'est ni merveilleux ni rare; … la 'Politique' d'Aristote ne convient pas moins à ses bourgs de moëllon et de boue qu'aux cités éclatantes du monde grec.

Emile Masqueray, *Formation des Cités chez les Populations Sédentaires de l'Algérie*[1]

Of all the odd forms of government, the oddest really is government by a public meeting.

Walter Bagehot, *The English Constitution*[2]

The *thijemmu'a* of Kabylia

The *jema'a* in the sense of occasional assembly or council is found in all Berber societies, including that of the Rifians. It is not peculiar to the Berbers, however. The Arabic-speaking tribes of Algeria and Morocco (at least) certainly had – and in many cases still have – their *jemāya'*. In Kabylia, *jemāya'* of a kind are found at every level: an *ad hoc* 'council' of the adult males of a single family or lineage will be called a *jema'a*, although a wholly makeshift affair. But these improvised and occasional *jemāya'*, so characteristic of Maghribi tribesmen in general, are not *characteristic* of the Kabyles. They are incidental rather than fundamental to their political organisation.

There are two kinds of *jema'a* which are characteristic of Kabyle society and fundamental to its political organisation, one of them a special body, the other a special place. Both of them are institutions. (The same word, *jema'a* or, in Berber, *thajma'th*, is used in the two cases; there are different kinds of *jema'a*, but no constant difference of meaning between the variant forms of the word.)

---

1   Masqueray, *op. cit.*, 49–50.
2   Walter Bagehot, *The English Constitution* (Glasgow: Fontana, 1963, 11th impression 1975), 155.

Figure 4.1: *Thajma'th* at Taourirt
Mimoun, Ath Yenni.

The first kind of *jema'a* characteristic of Kabylia is the one I have already been discussing, the deliberative assembly which is both the sovereign legislature and law court of the village. The literature on Kabylia suggests that this does not function in a wholly uniform manner throughout the region, but the principal authors, in presenting descriptions which differ from one another, have apparently been unconscious of this diversity and each has conveyed the impression that his or her account of the matter is generally valid.

If it were the case that in all the many hundreds of villages in Greater and Lesser Kabylia the *jemāya'* functioned in an identical manner in all essential respects, this would strongly suggest that the political organisation of Kabyle villages was the product of a general sociological law rather than the historically evolved artifice of sovereign communities. In fact, however, there is a discernible variety in the functioning of the *jema'a* from one village to another. Beyond minor matters of detail, this variety concerns the way in which the Kabyles handled the distinction universally observed between ordinary adult males in general and those few senior figures possessing especial influence – the 'sages', *l-'uqqāl*.[3]

---

3   From the Arabic *'āqil*, plural: *'uqqāl*: 'understanding, reasonable, discerning, judicious, wise'.

There are, or were, three main variants. In some cases, the full assembly of adult males is a frequent and regular event, taking place every week or every fortnight and dealing with all matters which may arise, but its deliberations are dominated by the *'uqqāl*, the others speaking only (i) very occasionally and at many meetings not at all, (ii) when especially concerned by an item under discussion and (iii) after such *'uqqāl* as wish to speak have had their say. In this case, there are some grounds for saying that, within the form of an egalitarian and democratic assembly, the substance of government is an oligarchy of the wise. This is the variant described by Mohand Khellil[4] and his account may well be valid for much of Kabylia outside the Jurjura.

In other cases, the body which meets regularly is quite explicitly the assembly or council of the sages, *thajma'th l-'uqqāl*, who sit together in the limited space of the village *thajma'th* (which in this case is a small rectangular building with a roof and stone seats along the inside walls, very like a much enlarged porch or covered gateway, and usually open at either end) and discuss the business of the village, while the rest of the men of the village stand or sit around the *thajma'th* and listen to the discussion without taking part in it. This procedure, which is that described by Masqueray,[5] is oligarchic in form as well as substance, but not more oligarchic than a representative assembly in a modern state, in that the lineages and clans are represented among the *'uqqāl*, each by a spokesman, *tamen* (plural: *temman*). This form may well be the tradition of some Jurjura villages, as Masqueray suggests, but it is not that of all of them. For there is a third variant, which is also evoked by Masqueray[6] and alluded to by Basagana and Sayad in their monograph on the village of Ath Larba'a of the Ath Yenni,[7] which should be distinguished from the two already mentioned. In this case, there are two distinct bodies, the council of the sages (*thajma'th l-'uqqāl*) on the one hand, which consists of the officers of the *jema'a* – *amīn* (president), *wakīl* (secretary/treasurer), *aberrah* (public crier) and the *temman* – and a few 'elder statesmen' of the village in addition to these and meets regularly and frequently and, on the other hand, the full assembly of all adult males, which meets on particular occasions in the annual calendar and also whenever convoked for a particular reason by the *thajma'th l-'uqqāl*. It happens to be the variant which has obtained at Ath Waaban and a description of the procedure followed there may serve to convey the spirit and flavour of the thing.

At Ath Waaban, the *thajma'th l-'uqqāl* meets every week, on a mid-week evening, when the men have come in from work. It considers the current affairs

---

4 Mohand Khellil, *La Kabylie ou l'Ancêtre Sacrifié* (Paris: L'Harmattan, 1984), 61–6.
5 Masqueray, *op. cit.*, 81–2.
6 Masqueray, *op. cit.*, 45–8.
7 Basagana and Sayad, 1974, *op. cit.*, 51.

Figure 4.2: *Thajma'th Oufella* at Jema'a
n'Saharij in use during an arts festival,
July 2012.

of the village, receives reports and hears complaints and then proceeds to take the
necessary decisions. Since Ath Waaban does not possess a building for its *jema'a*,
unlike many other villages, the *thajma'th l-'uqqāl* meets in the 'old schoolhouse',
which dates from the late colonial period and is no longer used as a school (the
village now possesses newer schools). The meetings are not attended by the rest
of the men of the village; the only non-members of the *thajma'th l-'uqqāl* who
attend are those who have significant news or complaints to lay before it; these
are free to attend the entire meeting or to appear only for their own item on the
agenda, as they prefer. The prerogatives of this council are quite limited.[8] For all
important or controversial matters, such as the promulgation of a new article
of the *qānūn* or the building of a new public facility (road, bridge, mosque,
schoolhouse, telephone box, etc.) or a question of the village's external political
relations, it will summon a meeting of all the men of the village. This plenary
session of the village *jema'a* is known as *aberrah*, which may be translated as
'convocation' or 'summoning'. Thus the men of honour of Ath Waaban resemble
the dons of Oxford University in at least this respect, having both a hebdomadal
council and a convocation.

8   Contrary to what Masqueray suggests (*op. cit.*, 47–8).

Figure 4.3: Ath Waaban today, seen
from the east end of its high valley in
the Jurjura. The village was the HQ
of the ALN's *Wilāya* III from May to
December 1957, when it was destroyed
by the French. It was rebuilt after
independence.

At Ath Waaban (and doubtless elsewhere), the *aberrah* is held on a Friday, the Muslim day of rest and prayer, in the open air on the site designated as the place of assembly and in the morning, starting promptly at 8 o'clock. The village crier (also known as *aberrah*, i.e. 'the man who summons') announces the *aberrah* from a convenient place in the village centre at sunset the previous evening, at first light the following morning and again at 7.30 a.m. The roll call is taken at about 7.55 a.m. and anyone who is late is fined. A second roll call is taken after the meeting has been in progress for half an hour and anyone who is still unjustifiably absent is subject to a second, much stiffer, fine. (In 1983, the rates for these two fines at Ath Waaban were ten and fifty dinars respectively – about £1.50 and £7.50 at the official rate of exchange.)

The *aberrah* is not dominated by the *'uqqāl*. It is certainly the case that men who have acquired particular influence and personal authority are called to speak first, and that the assembly shows them the respect due to their experience and proven judgment. But this is an unwritten rule which is entirely of a kind with the unwritten rules which tacitly regulate the functioning of many a democratic assembly in modern states. In the *aberrah* at Ath Waaban, every man has the right to speak and this right is widely and frequently exercised as a matter of course.

The villagers of Ath Waaban do not consider this extremely democratic system to be a recent innovation. They affirm that this is how they have always conducted their affairs. And, since their village is one of the remotest in the Jurjura and in many respects one of the most traditional in the region as a whole, I know of no reason to doubt them on this point. They appear, moreover, to take it for granted that their practice is shared by their neighbours in the central Jurjura, as it very probably is. The physical proximity of and social intercourse between neighbouring villages in Kabylia are such that, were Ath Waaban's political procedures significantly different from those of their neighbours, the people of Ath Waaban would certainly be aware of the fact and self-conscious about it. This is not the case. Indeed, my principal informants there were surprised and intrigued when I pointed out to them that the political arrangements of villages in certain other districts of Kabylia differed from their own.

These political arrangements have survived at Ath Waaban to this day.[9] If there has been any change in recent times, it is that less importance than previously is attached to the sheer fact of age. In the old days, young men attending the *aberrah* would rarely, if ever, speak in the presence of their father or another older male of their family. This traditional inhibition, which, like the deference shown to the *'uqqāl*, is a particular instance of the general respect shown to one's elders,[10] is still in force, but the deference in question is displayed with less punctiliousness than previously; the inhibition is undoubtedly weaker than it used to be, although probably still stronger at Ath Waaban than in many of the less remote, more 'evolved', villages to its north.

These are the three main variants of political organisation at village level in Greater Kabylia.[11] In all cases, it cannot be seriously disputed that the village *jemaʿa* (whether a single body or one differentiated into a limited council plus plenary assembly, the former functioning as the executive of the latter) possesses

---

9   Telephone interview with Salah Oumohand of Ath Waaban, 4 November 2012.

10 It applies only to senior members of one's own family or lineage, however, in this context; a young man would not be inhibited from speaking in the presence of older men of other lineages.

11 There may be further variants in the Soummam valley and the Biban, Guergour and Babor mountains of Lesser Kabylia; the political organisation of the populations of these districts has been almost entirely ignored in the ethnographic and sociological literature and remains to be seriously investigated. The same is true of the western and north-eastern fringes of Greater Kabylia.

the basic attributes of a political institution. Its meetings are conducted in accordance with a clear procedure known to all and are convened at regular and frequent intervals, it has its own officers and procedures for determining them, and it has its own site and usually its own building. Above all, as we have seen in our consideration of the *qawānīn*, it has authority to make and enforce law, which in the old days extended to the power of life and death in certain cases, and it unquestionably has a corporate existence independent of the social groups represented within it, illustrated by its right to compel attendance and punish unwarranted absence, among its other, comparable, powers and prerogatives.

So much for the first kind of *jema'a*. The second kind of *jema'a* is not an assembly in the sense of a political institution, but a *place* of assembly, a forum for public life in general rather than the venue of particular political or judicial proceedings. While the *jema'a* or *thajma'th* in the first sense is the council of the village as a whole, the *jema'a* or *thajma'th* in the sense of public place is found in each of the principal quarters, *ikhelijen*, of which the *thaddarth* is composed. Thus, at Ath Waaban, both the *thakhelijth* of the Ath Tighilt and that of the Ath Wadda have their own *thijemmu'a*, one apiece. But, although a *thajma'th* in this sense will invariably be associated (and sometimes, but not always, identified by name) with a particular quarter and so, by extension, with a particular clan or group of clans or lineages, it will not belong to this quarter alone, but to the *thaddarth* as a whole: any man, from any quarter or clan, has the right to sit in any *thajma'th* and will be made welcome there, with great courtesy, whatever his kinship or political relationship with his 'hosts' and whatever their private feelings towards him.[12] For each of the *thijemmu'a* of a given *thaddarth* forms part of the common property of the *thaddarth*, the land in question – like that on which the mosque, schoolhouse, etc. stand – belongs to the *thaddarth* as a whole and, while the men of a given quarter enjoy *de facto* possession of 'their' *thajma'th* and feel at home there, this possession falls short of proprietorship since it confers no right to exclude the men of the other quarters.

Most of the *thijemmu'a* of this kind in Kabylia do not perform political functions directly. At Ath Waaban, for example, the *aberrah* is held in neither *thajma'th n'Ath Tighilt* nor *thajma'th n'Ath Wadda*, but in a third spot on the borderline between the two quarters in the heart of the village. This place, the only one used for meetings of the village's plenary assembly,[13] is used for nothing

---

12 Mouloud Feraoun suggests that this courteous welcome would be merely ironic, intended to emphasise the fact that members of other quarters were not *'chez eux'* and therefore not really welcome (*Jours de Kabylie*, 27). But at Ath Waaban I have seen men from Ath Tighilt engaged in lengthy conversations in the *jema'a* of the Ath Wadda and have been assured that there is nothing unusual or new about this.

13 Apart from the shrine of the village's patron saint, Sidi M'Hand ou Amrane, where the men assemble at the start of the summer before embarking on the collective work (*thashmelith*) of repairing the village's irrigation system.

else. Its only virtue is that it is neutral ground, so to speak. It is not a place where men gather informally to pass the time of day, whereas the *thijemmu'a* of the two quarters are precisely that. Nonetheless, while not the site of collective decision-making, the latter have a fundamental importance in the political life of the village.

The *jema'a* of the quarter is the place where men meet, exchange news and discuss current affairs informally. While courtesy is *de rigueur*, rivalries and enmities are discreetly expressed and monitored by onlookers, since conversations can be overheard and comportments witnessed by all. The fact that two men exchange no more than the minimum greeting politeness demands before warmly saluting others and engaging them in animated conversations, for example, conveys to others present the state of relations between two families or lineages. The *jema'a* is the stage on which public announcements can be made, by implication and gesture and nothing more, as often as not. (The Ath A and the Ath B are reconciled; relations between the Ath C and the Ath D are as bad as ever, and so on.) It is also the place where news from the village's immediate environment is registered; the news itself is gathered at the market and reported by villagers on their return, who invariably make the *jema'a* their first stop if they have interesting information to transmit. In various ways, then, the *jema'a* is the forum within which public opinion informs itself and ripens. It is correspondingly essential for every Kabyle man to spend some time there every day and a man who fails to do so will soon be the object of adverse comment. Why does So-and-So no longer come to the *jema'a*? Is he unwell? If not, what is wrong? Do the affairs of the village no longer concern him? Does he no longer feel the need to know the opinions of his fellow villagers? Who does he think he is? (I have witnessed conversations of this kind at Ath Waaban.)

The point is that, in Kabylia, the very idea of being a man is bound up with the idea of being a citizen – that is, a member of a political community. The *jema'a* of the quarter is the civic forum and, while in most villages there will always be one or two individuals who, for some reason or other (to do with dramatic incidents in the past as often as not) emphatically stay aloof from routine village affairs, men with no such generally understood motive will not be allowed to shirk their civic role and public pressure on them to assume their responsibilities will eventually take the form of a questioning of their manhood. To stay at home is what the women do. A man must show himself, must play his part in public life, must keep the company of his peers, take the risk of confronting them and expose himself to the claims and challenges of other men.[14]

The place where public opinion forms, where the man acts the citizen, the *jema'a* is also and consequently the arena in which boys and young men are socialised into the public life of the village and undergo a major part of their

---

14 Feraoun, *ibid.*; Bourdieu, 'The Sense of Honour', in Bourdieu, 1979, *op. cit.*, 123.

apprenticeship of manhood, by listening to the conversations and arguments and observing the public comportments of their elders.[15] It is also the collective memory of the village and its window on the world. During the summer, the young men will stay at the *jema'a* long into the night, listening to recollections of past events, arguing the *pro* and *contra* of long decided disputes. (In 1975 and 1976, I heard the most remarkable conversations about the political and military history of the Revolution in the *jema'a* of the Ath Wadda at Ath Waaban.) And every traveller returning from foreign parts – France, Morocco, Tunisia, or the other regions of Algeria – will be expected to recount his experiences at the *jema'a* and will look forward to doing so. (These days, the news may be of Canada and England, the United States, Germany and Sweden, or even Australia.) In this way, the minds of young Kabyle men are trained in public affairs and simultaneously oriented to and informed about the outside world from an early age and their curiosity about other countries and societies stimulated.

The *jema'a* of the quarter has been performing this complex role and having these remarkable effects in virtually all the villages of Kabylia and, above all, the villages of the central Jurjura for generations.

Among the Berbers of the Rif or the Central High Atlas, the *jema'a* in this sense does not exist, or is only very rarely found.[16] Apart from mosques, law courts, *mahākim*, dependent on the central power, and markets, there is no public place, merely private territories on the one hand and the no-man's-land of the occasional township or military outpost and the roads which lead to them on the other. But the *thijemmu'a* of a Kabyle *thaddarth* are not no-man's-land. They each have their own *horma* (honour) and *'anāya* (the consideration they are owed and the protection they consequently afford).[17] No-man's-land has neither *horma* nor *'anāya*. It is the realm of shamelessness and *sauve-qui-peut* precisely because it belongs to no man. But, as Mouloud Feraoun has put it so well, 'la djemaa est à tout le monde en général et à chacun en particulier.'[18]

The complex character of the *thajma'th*, the public space *par excellence*, as public property which is in the virtual private possession of a particular quarter, a private possession which is qualified and controlled by the ability of men from other quarters to exercise their right to make use of the space in question as public space in the certainty that this right will be admitted, directly reflected the third way in which the Kabyles coped politically with the contradiction between the code of law and the code of honour, which was also the way in which a Kabyle *thaddarth* afforded alternative modes of expression

---

15 Feraoun, *op. cit.*, 28.

16 Neither Hart (1976, *op. cit.*) nor Gellner (1969, *op. cit.*) make any mention of this kind of *jema'a*.

17 Detailed discussions of *horma* and *'anāya* are provided by Masqueray, *op. cit.*, 32–4 and especially by Bourdieu, *art. cit.*, in 1979, *op. cit.*, 117 *et seq.*

18 Feraoun, *op. cit.*, 22.

to the feuding impulses of its constituent families. This was by building into
the political system which underlay and informed the functioning of the
village council a major element of representation of kinship groups, but on
terms which, while satisfying the latter, underwrote and consolidated the
supremacy over them of the former. This was done in two ways, through the
agency of the *temman* and through the medium of the *sfūf.*

The *temman*

The position of the *tamen* has not been adequately explained in the literature
on Kabylia. On this, as on so many other questions, an examination of this
literature reveals a striking, if hitherto unremarked, diversity of interpretation.

Favret refers to the *temman* as 'the leaders of lineages'.[19] It is possible that the
thajma'th in some of the remoter parts of Kabylia is, in effect, a mere assembly
of lineage heads, which is what it appears to be in the Central High Atlas of
Morocco. But this is not the position in the heartland of Greater Kabylia, and
least of all among the Igawawen. Here the *tamen* is by no means necessarily
the leader of his lineage; the informal functions of lineage leadership and the
formal functions of the *tamen* are distinct, and neither set of functions implies or
presupposes the other.

Khellil refers to the *tamen* as a 'representative' or 'delegate' or 'proxy'
(*mandataire*), presumably employing these terms as synonyms. He does so in the
course of presenting a picture of the *thajma'th* which resembles that required by
the segmentarity theory, in which power emanates from below and the *thajma'th*
itself is essentially an assembly of heads of segments without institutional
authority of its own:

> Each entity within the village delegates its representative in the tajmaat,
> the village assembly. Axxam will send to the assembly the head of the
> household (bab bbwexxam); for adrum, it will be ṭṭamen, so that finally
> the village designates its chief, lamin, among the latter ...[20]

Elsewhere, however, he speaks of the *temman* as 'the assistants' of the *amīn* and
notes that the *amīn* may delegate his powers to one of them on occasion. But

---

19 Favret, 1968, *art. cit.*, 23.
20 Khellil, 1979, *op. cit.*, 62; see also his glossary, 192. I have here kept Khellil's spelling of
    Kabyle words, which is that of the alphabet now in vogue in Berberist circles. Thus, for
    tajmaat, axxam, bab bbwexxam and *ttamen* read *thajma'th, akhkham, bab bu akhkham* and
    tamen; lamin is *amīn* with the definite article attached, as is common practice in the Berber
    language.

this is presented by him as only a slight qualification of the *temman*'s primary role as defenders of 'the particular interests of their respective fractions within the assembly', which, he reminds us, 'is a meeting of families'.[21]

It is quite possible that this interpretation is valid for the Ath Fliq, the 'arsh to which Khellil belongs and on which he has based his analysis of Kabyle society in general. If so, it probably also holds good for the neighbours of the Ath Fliq – that is to say, the 'aarsh of maritime Kabylia to the north of Azazga. But it is not valid for the 'aarsh of the central Jurjura and thus, if accurate, actually confirms the distinction which I have already drawn on other counts between the Igawawen and the rest of Kabyle society.

Tamen does not mean representative or delegate or proxy or lineage head or even assistant of the *amīn* (although the *temman* are, in practice, the assistants of the *amīn*). The word is the Kabyle form of the Arabic *dhamīn*, meaning 'responsible, answerable or liable for; bondsman, guarantor, surety'. The *tamen* does not represent his lineage[22] so much as *answer for it*. He gives undertakings on its behalf, he vouches for it. This was understood by Masqueray and by Hanoteau and Letourneux, who translated it by the French words *caution* and *répondant*, which have precisely the principal meanings of *dhamīn*.[23]

The *tamen* answers for his lineage in two main contexts, in the regular meetings of the *jemaa* or *thajma'th l-'uqqāl* and on the intermittent occasions of the sharing of meat for public feasts (*thimshret*), when it is the *tamen* who receives on his lineage's behalf the meat which falls to its share. In the *jemaa*, the *tamen* answers for his lineage in numerous different ways: when a decision has been taken, he answers for his lineage's willingness to respect this decision and accept it; if the decision involves some demand upon the various lineages – a mobilisation of labour, the provision of fighting men, the raising of money to finance a communal project and so on, he is the guarantor of his lineage's willingness to furnish its quota. Above all, he answers to the *jemaa* and so, through the *jemaa*, to the village as a whole for the behaviour of the people of his lineage; it is the *tamen* who pays the fines imposed on individual members of his lineage for whatever transgressions they may have committed.

In some villages, the *temman* will also be the prosecutors of individual misbehaviour, in that complaints will be made to them in the first instance,

---

21 Khellil, 1984, *op. cit.*, 70.

22 In most of the villages for which I have information, the kinship group answered for by the *tamen* in the *jemaa* is the lineage, called variously *kharruba*, *akharrub*, *thakharrubth* or, in the high Jurjura, *afrag*. But in certain villages it is the clan, *adrum*, which is answered for, such that the number of *temman* is much reduced, perhaps to no more than four. This is the practice at the Ath Yenni village of Tigzirt, for instance, according to local informants, and is now the practice at Taguemount Azouz of the Ath Mahmoud, according to Genevois (1972, *op. cit.*, 41–2).

23 Masqueray, *op. cit.*, 46; Hanoteau and Letourneux, *op. cit.*, vol. II, 9.

which they will then transmit to the *jema'a* or the *thajma'th l-'uqqāl* for judgment. But it is in their capacity as members of the *thajma'th l-'uqqāl* and thus as officers of the *jema'a* as a whole, rather than that of 'answerers' for their respective lineages, that they perform this prosecuting role. That there may be a very real element of ambiguity in this is evident: in bringing a charge against a member of another lineage, is a given *tamen* acting on behalf of the village as a whole by upholding the village law, or is he acting on his own lineage's behalf and scoring off a rival lineage?

It is probable that the political danger inherent in this ambiguity will have remained latent, as a possibility only rarely realised in practice, in most Kabyle villages. In the *tuwāfeq*, the physical separateness of the constituent lineages, each residing in its own hamlet, would limit the occasions for complaints arising between them. In the smaller *thudrin*, the presence of a public opinion that is permanently well informed about all the goings-on would be likely to deter any *tamen* from bringing other than well-founded charges against members of hostile lineages. The problem, then, is most likely to have arisen in the unusually large *thudrin* of the Igawawen, where the sheer size of the village and its population would be likely to reduce appreciably the effect of public opinion in this particular context, since, having to remain abreast of events in a larger community, it would be less likely to be completely *au fait* of the details of every little incident. If this reasoning is sound, it would explain the fact that it is in the Jurjura that a most interesting variation on the position of the *tamen* is to be found.

At Ath Waaban, which, I have argued, is likely to be broadly representative of its Igawawen neighbours in these matters, there are two, quite distinct, kinds of *tamen*: the man who answers for his lineage in the *jema'a*, known as *tamen bu afrag*,[24] and the man who reports infractions of the *qānūn* to the *jema'a* and proposes the appropriate penalty. The latter is known as *tamen n'lakhda*, 'the tamen of fining'.[25] Whereas each lineage has its *tamen bu afrag*, such that there

---

24　In the villages of the high Jurjura such as Ath Waaban and its neighbours, *afrag* (plural: *iferguen*), literally 'enclosure', is used to refer to the lineage (the social group intermediate between the family household, *akhkham*, and the clan, *adrum*). It also means 'lineage' in the Biban mountains (Tassadit Yacine, *Poésie berbère et identité: Qasi Udifella, héraut des At Sidi Braham* (Paris: Éditions de la Maison des Sciences de l'Homme, 1987), 35) but is used to mean 'clan' in the Mansourah district east of the Biban (Ouitis, 1977, *op. cit.*, 21).

25　The standard Kabyle word for fine is *lakhtia* (given as *lexṭeyya* in J.M. Dallet, *Dictionnaire Kabyle-Français: Parler des At Mangellat* (Paris: SELAF, 1982), 911). But *lakhda* (*lexḍa*, with an emphatic 'ḍ' in place of the occlusive 'ṭ'), is found in the central high Jurjura, among not only the Ath Boudrar but also other *'aarsh* of the district, notably the Ath Menguellat (private communication from a correspondent from *'arsh* Ath Menguellat, October 2012). At Ath Waaban, both terms are used; the distinction between them is that between the fine as penalty, *lakhtia*, and the action of penalising with a fine, *lakhda*. At Ath Waaban, the *tamen n'lakhda* reports infractions and proposes fines not to the weekly *thajma'th l-'uqqal*, but uniquely to the *aberrah*, at which the accused has the right to defend himself.

Figure 4.4: A classic *thajma'th* at the
Igawawen village of Thirwal, Ath Bou
Akkach.

Figure 4.5: A *thajma'th* at Guenzet
n'Ath Abbas in Lesser Kabylia.

are 23 *temman bu afrag* in all at Ath Waaban,[26] there are only four or five *temman n'lakhda*, and they are not chosen on grounds of kinship representation at all. For example, the lineages at Ath Waaban are broadly grouped in four *iderman*, but the *temman n'lakhda* are not chosen on this basis, one per *adrum*. They are designated by an *aberrah* of the full assembly of adult males on the basis of their personal qualities, irrespective of their lineage and clan backgrounds. The qualities sought are integrity and decisiveness.

In other words, the Igawawen village had *policemen*. This is clearly inconsistent with Gellner's claim – a generalisation from the case of the Central High Atlas in Morocco – that Berber society everywhere lacked specialist agents or institutions of order-maintenance. It also puts further in question some of the premises of Durkheim's social theory,[27] for the existence of policemen in the Igawawen

---

26 I am using the historic present here; this was the position over the period of my fieldwork, 1975–83. It may have changed slightly since then.

27 In addition to my criticism of his misuse of Masqueray and Hanoteau and Letourneux as sources for his notion of 'segmental social organisation'; see Roberts, 2002, *art. cit.*

villages has clearly been the fruit of the development of the social division of labour among them, necessity being the mother of invention.

But, in all villages, the *temman*, whether combining these two functions or distinguished by their responsibility for only one or the other, exemplify the primacy of the village collectivity as a whole, articulated by the *jema'a*, over the lineages and clans of which the whole is composed. To say that the *tamen bu afrag* or *tamen bu akherrub* 'represents' his lineage is thus misleading. The entire spirit of his title and function is that he represents the *jema'a* to his lineage and answers for his lineage to the *jema'a*. This is more or less the opposite of the role of a representative politician in a modern liberal democracy.

In this way did the *jema'a* of a Kabyle village assert its primacy over the centrifugal forces of kinship solidarities and antagonisms, while taking care to knit the kinship groupings into its own functioning via the agency of the *temman*. But it was not the only way in which this was done. The second way was through the action of the *sfuf*.

The *sfuf*

Saff (generally pronounced *seff* in Kabylia) is an Arabic word (plural: *sfuf*) meaning 'row, array, alignment'. It is conventionally regarded by anthropologists as the Algerian counterpart of the Moroccan term *liff* or *leff* (plural: *ilfuf*), which is also derived from an Arabic word, *laff*, with the rather different primary meanings of 'circumambience, circumvention, subterfuge'.[28] *Liff* is usually translated as 'alliance', but alliance can, of course, mean many different things, from an informal agreement between two politicians to a formal electoral pact between two or more political parties (e.g. the Alliance of the Liberal and Social Democratic Parties in Great Britain 1982–7) or a highly institutionalised system of collective military security composed of sovereign states (e.g. NATO, 'the Western Alliance').

The *liff* systems in south-western Morocco as described by Robert Montagne were collective security systems of a kind, in which tribes adhered to one or the other of two regional alliances. The tribes of the Nfis valley in the Western High Atlas belonged to the *liff* of the Aït Iraten or that of the Aït Atman; their neighbours to the west belonged to the *liff* of the Indghertit or that of the Imsifern, while those of the Anti-Atlas belonged to the *liff* of the Igezulen or the *liff* of the Isouktan.[29] These alliances may have maintained a kind of order or security at the regional level but in Gellner's view they cannot be credited

---

28 Hart, *op. cit.*, 313.
29 Robert Montagne, 1930, *op. cit.*, 182–216.

with having maintained order at other levels because they were not implicated in the way in which the constituent tribes and sub-tribal communities were governed.[30]

In the Rif, a very different system of *liff* alliances has obtained. Hart has argued that there were two types, the permanent (or relatively permanent) *ilfūf* at the upper levels of the social structure and the lower-level temporary *ilfūf*.[31] These alliances or, rather, in this context, factions existed within each tribe, their components being clans or, in some cases, sub-clans, but the factional alignments would sometimes cut across kinship links and a given *liff* in tribe A would often include a neighbouring clan or sub-clan of tribe B. It is clear from Hart's account that the system of *liff* alliances took precedence over segmentary kinship links in what one may call political life in the Rifian tribes,[32] but also that the activity of the *ilfūf* was secondary to the blood-feud and that factional conflict did not tend to sublimate and contain feuding impulses but to correspond to and reinforce them.[33]

Whatever may be the truth of the matter amongst the Rifians or the Chleuh, the *saff* systems of the Kabyles cannot be grasped by means of putative analogies with Moroccan *ilfūf*. It is possible that elsewhere in Algeria, amongst the Chaouia of the Aurès, for instance, or the pastoralist tribes of the High Plateaux and the Sahara, the *sfūf* approximated to the *ilfūf* of the Chleuh or the Rifians. But, in Greater Kabylia, the *sfūf* were not alliances in the sense of collective security blocs nor factions that corresponded to opposed feuding groups. Nor were they, as Bourdieu has claimed, moieties which maintained order through the equilibrium they created in opposition to each other in a kind of 'dualist organisation' which 'guarantees a balance of forces through strange processes of weighing, a stalemate resulting from the crisis itself'.[34] As Favret, reiterating Hanoteau and Letourneux, has pointed out, the *sfūf* were not of equal but of manifestly unequal strength.[35] Order was not, therefore, achieved through some 'strange process of weighing' because there was no such process. Nor, we may add, was there any stalemate.

Unfortunately, Favret does not follow up her pertinent observation about the inequality of the *sfūf* into a coherent explanation of their nature and functioning. Although she frequently cites the nineteenth-century observers against their twentieth-century successors, by rendering '*sfūf*' as 'leagues' she

30 Gellner, 1969, *op. cit.*, 66–7.
31 Hart, *op. cit.*, 313–14 *et seq.*
32 Hart, *op. cit.*, 316–17.
33 Hart, *op. cit.*, 322.
34 Bourdieu, 1962, *op. cit.*, 16.
35 Favret, *art. cit.*, 30; Hanoteau and Letourneux, *op. cit.*, vol. II, 13–14.

departs from the most important insight of the former's accounts. For, as Hanoteau and Letourneux realised, the *sfūf* of Greater Kabylia were *parties*.[36]

The basis of the Kabyle *saff* systems as systems of party division and competition was the combination of four facts: first, the fact that the system of self-government of the Kabyle village rested on the authority of the *jema'a* and thus upon the primacy of the legislature; second, the fact that every Kabyle village was part of an *'arsh* comprising a number of villages and possessing its own *jema'a* in which all the constituent villages were 'answered for'; third, the fact that, notwithstanding the formal equality of status of all Kabyle men, the accidents of birth and fortune and enterprise entailed that, within any one village, certain families would be larger, more prosperous and more influential than others and would often succeed in preserving their influence and prestige over successive generations; and, fourth, the fact that the population of each village consisted of a number of lineages divided into different clans.

The existence of several clans was not itself the starting point. Had it been, one would expect the number of *sfūf* in each village to correspond to the number of clans. This was not usually the case. At Ath Hichem, where Bourdieu carried out his fieldwork, there are only two *iderman* and the two *sfūf* do indeed correspond to them. But the multiplication of *iderman* beyond the number two did not usually entail the multiplication of the *sfūf*. The important village of Taourirt n'Ath Menguellat, about three miles west of Ath Hichem, has four *iderman*; two form one *saff*, the other two the other *saff*.[37] At Ath Waaban there are also four *iderman* grouped politically in the same fashion, two in each *saff*. The *saff* system was essentially a binary system.

Undoubtedly there were exceptions to this rule, notably where the clans in a given village totaled that most awkward of numbers, three. In this case, internal village politics would sometimes be a three-handed game, a situation evoked by Mouloud Feraoun.[38] But the *saff* systems in Greater Kabylia were not limited to the village but extended well beyond it, and at all levels above the village these systems were invariably two-party systems. It is for this reason that I believe that it is a mistake to try to explain the existence of *saff* divisions by the prior existence of clans.

The starting point for the existence of the *sfūf* was the fact that each Kabyle village and, for that matter, each Kabyle *'arsh* governed itself through its *jema'a* – that is, *by a public meeting*. Government by public meeting presupposes the existence of parties. It is impossible to sustain in their absence.

Those observers of Kabyle political organisation such as Masqueray who have tried to make sense of it without travestying it have often been driven

---

36   Hanoteau and Letourneux, *op. cit.*, vol. II, 11.

37   Genevois, 1962, *op. cit.*, 11.

38   Feraoun, *Jours de Kabylie*, 21 and *Le Fils du Pauvre* (Paris: Éditions du Seuil, 1954), 14.

to resort to the analogy with the city states of classical antiquity, Athenian democracy or republican Rome. This analogy they have invoked rather than explored and justified in depth, however, and there has been another analogy available to them which they have never used. This is the analogy with the one democratic state in the modern era of which it has been true to say, since its constitution, that it has been governed by a public meeting. For, *mutatis mutandis*, the intrinsic logic of this form of government is the same in whatever conditions it develops.

The logic of the British example of this form of government was described four years before Hanoteau and Letourneux published their study of Kabylia, by Walter Bagehot:

> ... we are ruled by the House of Commons; we are, indeed, so used to be so ruled, that it does not seem to be at all strange. But of all the odd forms of government, the oddest really is government by a public meeting ... Nobody will understand Parliament government who fancies it an easy thing, a natural thing, a thing not needing explanation ... It is a saying in England, 'a big meeting never does anything'; and yet we are governed by the House of Commons – by 'a big meeting' ... The House of Commons can do work which the quarter-sessions or clubs cannot do, because it is an organised body, while quarter-sessions and clubs are unorganised ... At present the majority of Parliament obey certain leaders; what those leaders propose they support, what those leaders reject they reject ... [T]he principle of Parliament is obedience to leaders ... If everybody does what he thinks right, there will be 657 amendments to every motion, and none of them will be carried or the motion either ... The House of Commons lives in a state of perpetual potential choice; at any moment it can choose a ruler and dismiss a ruler. And therefore party is inherent in it, is bone of its bone, and breath of its breath.[39]

There is no question of the Kabyle *jema'a* being generally analogous to the British House of Commons.[40] Where the *jema'a* was an assembly of all adult males, it evidently differed from the House of Commons in being a form of direct,

---

39 Bagehot, *op. cit.*, 155–8.

40 There can be little doubt that pre-colonial Kabylia had more in common with the city states of the ancient world than with contemporary or even eighteenth-century England. But the usefulness of the classical analogy is vitiated by the fact that the interpretation of the constitutions of the classical city states is controversial and the reader's knowledge of these constitutions cannot be assumed. To sustain this analogy, it would therefore be necessary to engage in a discussion of ancient Greece and Rome. But the British constitution as elucidated by Bagehot is still with us, at least in some degree, so the British analogy, if less complete, is more serviceable in the context of the present discussion.

not representative, democracy. And, where the representative element obtained, through the agency of the *temman*, the conception of representation which was operative in the Kabyle case was, as I have already insisted, very different from that traditionally underlying the position of a British MP. Moreover, a Kabyle *jemaʿa* was not primarily an elective body. The emphasis which Bagehot placed upon the elective functions of the House of Commons has little application to the Kabyle case in the pre-colonial period. The *jemaʿa* did, it is true, elect the *amīn* and the other officers, but the powers delegated to them were very modest compared with those entrusted by MPs to ministers.

But in one cardinal aspect at least the analogy holds. In both cases it is the deliberative assembly which is supreme within the form of government in question.[41] And for it to preserve this supremacy, it needs to be organised. The diversity of points of view which obtain within it has to be controlled and transcended by the existence within it of organised political followings, few in number, practising obedience to their leaders, by means of which coalitions of interests can be constructed which enable debate to focus on a limited range of options, if not, as often enough is the case, no more than two, *pro* and *contra*. Only in this way can minds be concentrated sufficiently for debate to give rise to the necessary decisions. A 'public meeting', even one which styles itself the National Assembly, which is in reality no more than a talking shop because the business of governing is being tended to elsewhere, need have no limit on the number of 'parties' it contains. But a 'public meeting' which governs must take decisions and often hard decisions at that and will therefore tend to reduce the number of parties it contains to two. It is in this sense that the logic of the Kabyle *jemaʿa* and that of the British Parliament in its historic hey-day are the same. In each case, 'party is inherent in it, is bone of its bone, and breath of its breath'. And in each case the party system is essentially a two-party system.[42]

It says much for the broad-mindedness and clarity of vision of the nineteenth-century French ethnographers that they recognised the Kabyle *sfūf* for what they were, for they were parties very unlike those with which most Frenchmen would have been familiar.[43] They most certainly did not embody and canvass opposed visions of society or mutually exclusive constitutional conceptions, as French political parties had done for most of the time since 1789. Like the

---

41 It may be argued that this is no longer the case in the United Kingdom today. But, while the authority of Parliament has certainly been gravely weakened over the last 30 years, the fact of Parliament's previous longstanding supremacy is not in serious dispute. It is the constitutionally supreme British Parliament of the nineteenth and most of the twentieth centuries that is the subject of the analogy I am drawing.

42 The collapse of the Social Democratic Party-Liberal Party Alliance and the electoral recovery of the Labour Party in the 1990s clearly demonstrated the essentially binary character of the British system.

43 As Hanoteau and Letourneux explicitly recognised, *op. cit.*, vol. II, 11.

English parties from the Hanoverian succession in 1714 to the 1832 Reform Act, they took the general constitutional framework of politics for granted, as their common ground, and the structure of society as given and immutable. And, like them, they articulated differences of interest and opinion within one and the same class, not a division between classes.

What the nineteenth-century ethnographers were disposed to refer to as the 'democratic republics' of Kabylia were based on very different principles from the democratic republics of the world of nation-states. It is in part for this reason that the nineteenth-century view of the matter was abandoned by Bourdieu and others. Kabyle political organisation was not based on the philosophy of the Rights of Man, or the abstract democratic principle of universal suffrage, or even universal adult male suffrage. In addition to women (who were answered for by their menfolk), two categories of the population were excluded from participation and representation within the *jema'a*: the hereditary saintly lineages (*imrabdhen*) and the *aklan*, literally 'the blacks' – that is, those families which gained their livelihoods from practising despised specialist occupations (butchers, grain-measurers, musicians) and whose disreputable professions and consequent status were conceived as the product of slave descent.

Neither the *imrabdhen* nor the *aklan* were regarded as *leqbayel*. A Kabyle was, by definition, a man of honour and a man of honour was by definition a man who owned land, carried arms and was, in contrast to both religious and profane specialists, a rounded man of parts, *argaz lkamel*, 'the accomplished man',[44] able to turn his hand to a wide variety of tasks, ploughing, house-building, trade, war and politics.

Because the maraboutic and *aklan* elements of the population were a very small minority, Kabyle political organisation had the appearance of democracy: the enfranchised population was the vast majority of the adult male population as a whole. But the *jema'a* was, nonetheless, an assembly of land-owners who bore arms. The division within a Kabyle *jema'a* between rival *sfūf* was, therefore, not the political form of a class division. Like the British parliament before 1832, only the landed interest was represented in it. (In neither case did the franchise exclude all commercial and manufacturing interests, but it did exclude commercial and manufacturing interests disconnected from landed property.) The basis of the opposition between the *sfūf* was therefore not ideology nor class conflict, but the rivalry between the leading families in each village, a rivalry which, whenever the interests of these families inclined them to favour opposed courses of action, expressed itself in differences over *policy*.

What gave these differences a stable and enduring form of expression in the *saff* system was the fact that each Kabyle village included a number of clans inhabiting, at least originally, distinct parts (quarters) of the village. The

---

44 Bourdieu, *art. cit.*, in 1979, *op. cit.*, 100.

constituent unit of a Kabyle *saff* is therefore a quarter, *thakhelijth*, of a village, whether this is occupied by a single clan or by several. The clan division is politicised where there are only two or three clans in the village. Where there are four or more clans, the clan division is not politicised but transcended by the politicisation of the division of the village into *ikhelijen*. The stable basis of allegiance to a village *saff* is therefore not kinship but residence, not *adrum* but *thakhelijth*.

This state of affairs gave the system of *saff* competition at village level both a measure of stability and a measure of fluidity or uncertainty. Because the base of a *saff* is identified with a particular quarter of a village, it has a stable existence over time, so that the replacement of a leader from one of its families by another from a different family will not normally disrupt the lines of *saff* allegiance and division within the village. On the other hand, the fact that allegiance to a given *saff* is, for many families, primarily a function of mere residence means that within each *saff* there will be a potentially floating element: the stable core of the *saff* will be composed of a minority of leading families and their close kinship relations, but other lineages in the quarter only loosely related, if at all, to those which make up this core will be susceptible on occasion to overtures from the other *saff*. Within the Igawawen *thaddarth*, then, there is a floating vote and it was this which enabled *saff* X to gain the ascendancy at one moment and *saff* Y to gain it at another.

It is this which explains the fact, reported by Devaux and confirmed by Hanoteau and Letourneux,[45] that at any one time the *sfûf* were manifestly unequal in strength. It is true is that this inequality at any one moment can be said to have masked an underlying equality over time: the minority *saff* at one point could usually expect to be able to become the majority *saff* at some future point. But the fact of inequality mattered politically: the deliberations of the village *jemaʿa* on controversial matters of policy would be dominated by the majority *saff* of the moment.

That this was the way things worked was obscured by the fact that all decisions of the *jemaʿa* were formally agreed by all present. But it is a mistake to suppose that a Kabyle *jemaʿa* was subject to a requirement of real unanimity. This was a matter of form rather than substance.

The *sjem* (parliament) of the Polish *szlachta* (nobles) in the seventeenth century was subject to a real unanimity requirement. Every deputy possessed what was known as the *liberum veto* (the freedom to forbid) and this was a real veto. A deputy exercised it by the simple device of uttering, in respect of any piece of legislation he disliked, the words '*nie pozwalam*' ('I do not allow'), and that was that. The spirit of liberty was kept alive by such means and successive

---

45 Devaux, *op. cit.*, 266, 272; Hanoteau and Letourneux, *op. cit.*, vol. II, 13.

attempts to make the Poland of the nobles into a governable and defendable state got nowhere.[46]

Any Kabyle man could object to a proposal in the *jema'a*. And there was no question of a majority riding roughshod over the minority with impunity, as happens as a matter of course in modern parliaments. But there was also no question of a measure or a course of action upon which a large majority was agreed being prevented by an obstinate handful (which is exactly what used to happen in Poland). No one had a veto. An objection was not the end of the matter. It simply prolonged the discussion or caused it to be deferred while the necessary negotiations went on in the Kabyles' equivalent of the 'corridors of power'. There was therefore no requirement of true unanimity, of all being of one *mind*. What was required was that the minority *accept* the decision even though they had disagreed with it. The customary form of general acceptance therefore masked the political fact that one point of view had prevailed over another. This formal requirement gave the advocates of the majority point of view an interest in moderating their own proposals in order to secure the minority's consent. When the majority failed to do so, the conflict between the two parties would rapidly burst the bounds of the village, with possibly calamitous consequences.

The danger that the majority party in the British Parliament may abuse its power is warded off by the rule that the composition of the House of Commons must be renewed at regular intervals by general elections in which the positions of majority and minority are liable to be reversed. Liberty in the British system, freedom from arbitrary rule, is (in principle) safeguarded by the fact that the result of every election is uncertain.[47] But the *jema'a* of a Kabyle village is not an elected body. There is no mechanism to ensure that the balance of forces within it may change at regular intervals. The solution which the Kabyles found to this problem, the defence they possessed against the danger of the despotism of the majority, lay in the fact that the *saff* division within each village was not self-contained but part of a far wider *saff* division embracing the *'arsh*, the confederation (where this existed) and beyond. This has been simply overlooked by Bourdieu and Favret, who both suggest, quite mistakenly, that *saff* divisions obtained only 'at all levels below the tribe'.[48] But it was recognised by Hanoteau

---

46 Brendan Clifford, *James Connolly: The Polish Aspect* (Belfast: Athol Books, 1985), 13–17.

47 The British Conservative Party's third successive election victory in 1987 prompted alarm within the British intelligentsia, articulated notably by the *Charter '88* group, over the implications for civil liberties of the prospect of an endless succession of Conservative governments. The subsequent electoral recovery of the Labour Party equally promptly took the wind out of the sails of *Charter '88*'s agitation. With New Labour's successive victories in 1997, 2002 and 2005, however, a fresh discernible threat to civil liberties accordingly developed.

48 Favret, *loc. cit.*, 27; Bourdieu, 1962, *op. cit.*, 13.

and Letourneux, who, while noting the existence of a formal unanimity requirement,[49] also observed that:

> each village, with very few exceptions, is divided into two *sfūf*, which are rarely equal in number or in means ... The weaker party, if it was abandoned to itself, would be incessantly prey to the law of the stronger or obliged to forsake the region ... To counter these dangers, it is naturally led to seek the alliance of one of the *sfūf* of the neighbouring villages. The range of the *saff* expands in this way from one place to the next, extends to the tribe, to the confederation and even to outside tribes, in a vast radius.[50]

This observation is true in part and in part very misleading. The misleading element concerns the dynamics of *saff* politics on the extended stage. Hanoteau and Letourneux offer a bottom-up view of these dynamics: each *saff* at village level is motivated by fear of its rival at this level and therefore looks for support in neighbouring villages; thus are the *sfūf* constituted at *'arsh* level and thus are they constituted at levels above the *'arsh*. I believe this to be the opposite of the truth and that the *sfūf* were constituted from the top down. A village *saff* was certainly linked to the *sfūf* of other villages and such linkages certainly provided its main defence against the despotic impulses of its local rival. But it did not effect this linkage for itself, of its own volition; it was linked to other *sfūf* by a force outside and above itself. This can be seen if we consider the *saff* division at the first level above that of the village, that of the *'arsh*.

The *sfūf* and the *'arsh*

At the level of the *'arsh*, as at all other levels above the village, the *sfūf* were invariably two in number and were often identified by names which appeared to have no political content whatsoever, names which were geographical or topographical terms employed apparently as mere metaphors to express the fact of binary opposition. The *sfūf* of the Ath Wasif were known as *Isherqien* ('the easterners') and *Igherbien* ('the westerners'), while those of the neighbouring Ath Boudrar were known as *Ilemmasen* ('those of the centre') and *Iqarnien* ('those of the edges').[51] In other *'aarsh*, the two parties were sometimes called after their current leaders. According to Hanoteau and Letourneux, this was the case in *'arsh* Iwadhien of the Ath Sedqa confederation, where the two *sfūf*

---

49   Hanoteau and Letourneux, *op. cit.*, vol. II, 22.
50   Hanoteau and Letourneux, *loc. cit.*, 13–14 (my translation).
51   Hanoteau and Letourneux, *loc. cit.*, 11. I have amended the spelling of these names slightly.

were known (*c.* 1870, at any rate) as *saff El Hadj Boudjema'a* and *saff Ameur n'Ath Amara*.[52]

A fourth possibility was and still is exemplified by the Ath Yenni, who are divided into the *Ath Yahia* and the *Aâruren*, the two *sfûf* being represented in each of the six lay villages of the *'arsh*, incorporating one or another of the *ikhelijen* of each village, as follows:

Table 4.1: *Saff* divisions of the Ath Yenni

Village	*Ikhelijen* belonging to *Saff n'Ath Yahia*	*Ikhelijen* belonging to *Saff n'Aâruren*
Taourirt Mimoun	Ath Yahia ou M'Hammed	Aâruren
Ath Larba'a	Ath Qayed	Ath Ali ou M'Hammed
Ath Lahcène	Ath Teglits & Ath Aâzza	Ath Tama Oufella
Agouni Ahmed	Ath Slimane	Ath Anter
Taourirt el-Hajjaj	Ath Chikker	Ath Tighilt
Tigzirt	Ath Adwan	Iboudraren
Tensaout	(*Imrabdhen* outside *saff* division of lay population)	

Source: Basagana and Sayad, *op. cit.*, 102

We can see from this that the *saff* division within the *'arsh* is an extension of the *saff* division within the village of Taourirt Mimoun. This is explained by the fact that Taourirt Mimoun has long been considered the 'capital' or centre of the Ath Yenni, the seat of many of its oldest and proudest families.[53] It was a party division between the *ikhelijen* of this leading village which organised the pre-existing divisions in the five other lay villages into a stable two-party division at *'arsh* level (inducing the three *ikhelijen* of Ath Lahcène to align themselves on a binary basis in the process, incidentally). It did this through the medium of the *jema'a* of the *'arsh*.

When considering the role of the *jema'a* in Kabylia, it is easy to concentrate exclusively upon the *thijemmu'a* of the village and to forget that in the pre-colonial period, each *'arsh* also had its *jema'a*, composed of the *umanā'* (plural of *amīn*) of its constituent villages and sometimes one or two other *'uqqāl* per village in addition.[54] Since we possess not one description of a *jema'a* of an *'arsh* in session, we do not know for certain what business it transacted. We

---

52 Hanoteau and Letourneux, *ibid.*
53 Genevois, 1971, *op. cit.*, 14–15, 19 *et seq.*
54 Hanoteau and Letourneux, *op. cit.*, vol. II, 66.

do not even know how often such *jemāya'* met, or where. But we know that markets in Kabylia were almost invariably attached to particular *'aarsh*, so that the organisation and safeguarding of these markets is likely to have been an issue of regular business for the *jema'a* of an *'arsh* to consider. The safeguarding and promotion of trade outside Kabylia and the protection of members of the *'arsh* when away from home, in Algiers or when trading or peddling or engaging in seasonal labour in the Algerian interior, are also likely to have been matters for discussion and collective decision at *'arsh* level in at least some cases. Above all, the question of relations with neighbouring *'aarsh* is likely to have been a perennial item on the agenda (in part because it would often have been intimately connected with the question of safeguarding the local market). It is probably the last of these issues which tended to generate the most controversy within a Kabyle *'arsh*.

Every Kabyle *'arsh* has at least two, often four and sometimes five or more *'aarsh* for its immediate neighbours. The Ath Yenni share boundaries with six: the Ath Ousammeur and the Aouggacha of the Ath Irathen confederation to the north and north-east, the Ath Menguellat of the confederation of the same name to the south-east, the Ath Wasif of the Ath Bethroun confederation (to which the Ath Yenni also belonged) to the south, the Aouqdal of the Ath Sedqa confederation to the south-west and the Ath Mahmoud of the Ath Aïssi confederation to the north-west: six *'aarsh* as neighbours, belonging to and so implicating five different confederations. The Ath Menguellat share boundaries with seven other *'aarsh*: Aouggacha, Ath Yenni, Ath Wasif, Ath Attaf, Aqbil, Ath Bou Youcef and Ath Yahia. The Ath Boudrar share boundaries with eight: the Ath Bou Akkach, Ath Wasif, Ath Attaf, Aqbil, Ath Bou Youcef and, south of the Jurjura watershed, the Imecheddalen, Ath Wakour and Ath Qani.

It follows that the question of relations with one neighbour often if not invariably raised the question of relations with other neighbours and there can be little doubt that those who supported good relations with neighbour X would on occasion find themselves at loggerheads with those who had a vested interest in good relations with neighbour Y (or Z, etc.), whenever the two were mutually exclusive, which was not infrequently the case. It seems likely, then, that it was arguments of this kind which constituted the staple subject matter of *saff* politics at the level of the *'arsh* and that, where one village was accustomed to provide the political leadership of the *'arsh* as a whole, the division of opinion within this village on such matters was the factor organising the *saff* division within the *'arsh* as a whole.

For the pre-eminent position of Taourirt Mimoun amongst the Ath Yenni was not at all unusual. In many other *'aarsh*, one village held a similar ascendancy. Among the Ath Mahmoud, it was Taguemount Azouz; among the Ath Boudrar, Ighil Bouammas; among the Ath Menguellat, Taourirt n'Tidits; among the Illilten, Tifilkout; among the Ath Fraoucen, Jema'a n'Saharij; among the Ath Yahia, Taqa; and so on.

So, among the Ath Yenni, the names of the *sfūf* are not mere arbitrary conventions. They reflect the constant political fact of Taourirt Mimoun's pre-eminence within the *'arsh* and the historical fact that *saff* politics in the Ath Yenni originated in and radiated out from this pre-eminent village. It is probable that comparable, if different, facts are similarly reflected by the names of the *sfūf* in other *'aarsh*.

Why should *saff* politics among the Ath Wasif have been an affair of 'easterners' and 'westerners'? Let us consider the evidence from a map of the area (see Map 4.1). The Ath Wasif are settled in seven villages on two parallel ridges running north from the main Jurjura range (see bottom left hand corner of Map 4.1). Five villages are situated on the western ridge, the other two on the eastern ridge. The western villages (Ath Abbas, Zoubga, Ath Bou Abderrahmane, Tiqidount, Tiqichourt) share their ridge with three villages of the *'arsh* Ath Bou Akkach (Zaknoun, Ath Sidi Athmane and Tiguemounin), which are located to the south and higher up, closer to the main ridge of the Jurjura. Moreover, the local market, Souq el-Arba'a n'Ath Wasif, is located in the valley at the *western* foot of the western ridge (to the south-west of Tiqichourt), and is the point of contact for the Ath Wasif, the Ath Bou Akkach and the *'aarsh* of the Ath Sedqa confederation immediately to their west. The two villages of the eastern ridge, Ath Eurbah and Tassaft Waguemoun, share this with three Ath Boudrar villages (Ath Ali ou Harzoun, Ighil n'Tsedda and Bou Adnane) which are similarly located higher up the ridge to the south, while to the north of Ath Eurbah the ridge terminates in the large mountain outcrop on which the Ath Yenni villages are situated. Ath Eurbah and Tassaft are some way from Souq el-Arba'a and their inhabitants are much more inclined to frequent Souq el-Jema'a, the market of *arsh* Aqbil in the valley immediately to their east, traditionally the main commercial point of contact for the Aqbil, Ath Boudrar, Ath Attaf and Ath Menguellat.

The facts of geography suggest that Ath Eurbah and Tassaft Waguemoun needed to live on terms of good neighbourliness with the Ath Yenni and the Ath Boudrar, while the five other Ath Wasif villages were less concerned about this and more concerned with their relations with the Ath Bou Akkach and the *'aarsh* of the Ath Sedqa confederation and could afford to indulge in occasional hostilities with the Ath Yenni. And in fact the oral traditions of the Ath Yenni are studded with references to hostilities with the Ath Wasif and especially with the village of Ath Abbas,[55] which faces the Ath Yenni across the intervening Asif n'Tleta valley.[56] We can therefore see how the eastern and western villages of the

---

55 Genevois, 1971, *op. cit.*, 23–30, 50–65.
56 That this valley was a dangerous frontier is suggested by the placement by the Ath Yenni of the maraboutic village of Tensaout (misnamed Ten n'Saoud on the map) in the line of march of the Ath Abbas in the event of their attacking.

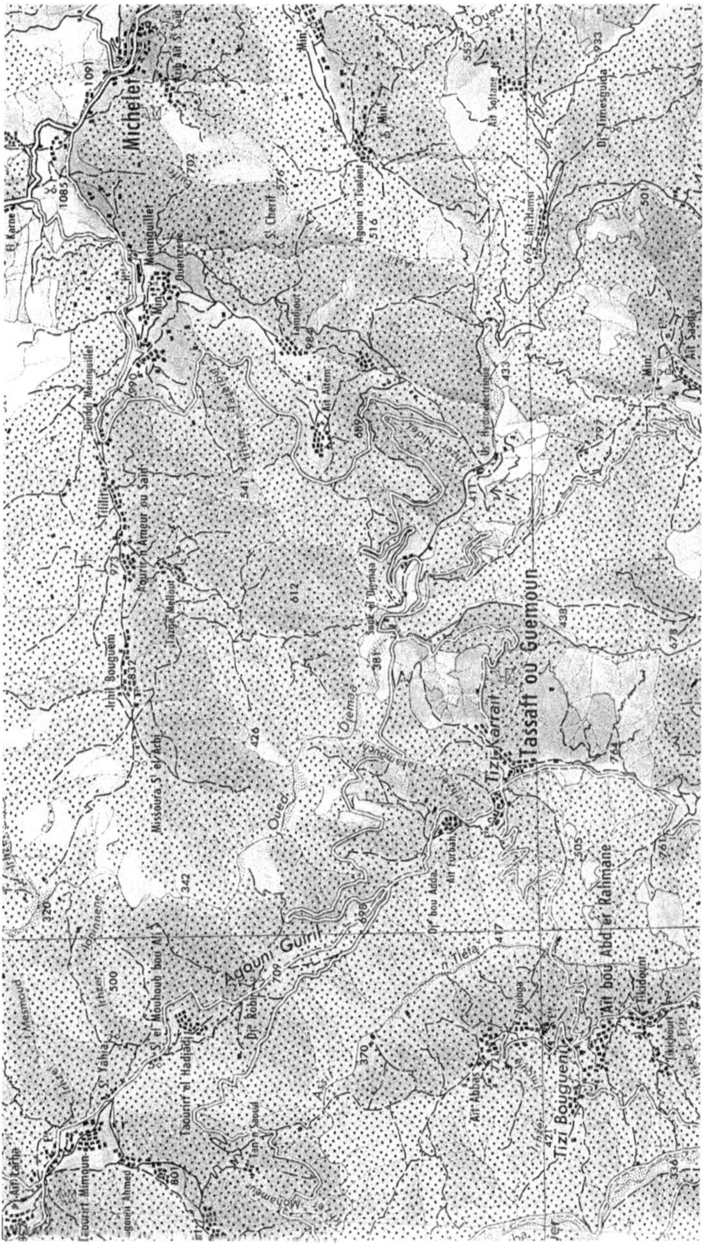

Map 4.1: The Ath Wasif villages.[57]

---

57 This is a section of the French 1:50000 map of the Fort National (now Larba'a n'Ath Irathen) district, which included the Michelet (now Aïn el-Hammam) district. The spelling of some place names differs slightly from mine.

Ath Wasif would have had different and potentially conflicting priorities in their external relations. Moreover, the eastern villages were latecomers to the 'arsh; Ath Eurbah and Tassaft Waguemoun originally belonged to another 'arsh, the Ath ou Belkacem, which disintegrated or was dismembered by its neighbours at some point in the mid-eighteenth century.[58] (The other villages of this 'arsh, Takhabit and Ath Ali ou Harzoun, were incorporated into the Ath Yenni and the Ath Boudrar respectively at the same time that Ath Eurbah and Tassaft Waguemoun were incorporated into the Ath Wasif; in this process, Takhabit moved closer to the rest of the Ath Yenni and changed its name to Taourirt el-Hajjaj.[59]) It seems likely that the incorporation of the two new villages from the eastern ridge transformed the internal politics of the Ath Wasif and precipitated a new line of *saff* cleavage.

There are accordingly strong grounds for thinking that the names of the *sfūf* of the Ath Wasif were not at all mere conventions, borrowed arbitrarily from topography in order to express an abstract impulse to binary opposition bereft of moorings in material circumstances and historical events. They directly expressed the substance of what was (or, at a critical period, had been) at issue in the main disputes within the 'arsh.

The same is very probably true of the Ath Boudrar. Here the *saff* division was between 'those of the centre', Ilemmasen, and 'those of the edges', Iqarnien. Once again, this may sound like a purely arbitrary choice of topographical terms employed in order to express an abstract and unexplained impulse to dualistic organisation. But, if we take the trouble to look at the geography and history of the Ath Boudrar, we shall see the matter in a very different light.

Map 4.2 shows the geographical situation of the seven Ath Boudrar villages and their immediate neighbours. The core villages of the 'arsh are Ighil Bouammas[60] and Tala n'Tazart, situated on the central ridge, and Bou Adnane and Ighil n'Tsedda (which was originally part of Bou Adnane) on the western ridge. The other villages of the 'arsh were all incorporated later than these four. To the north, Ath Ali ou Harzoun was added from the defunct Ath ou Belkacem. To the south-east, Darna originally belonged to the Ath Attaf,[61] whose two remaining and unusually large villages, Ath Saada and Ath Daoud,[62] dominate the ridge on which Darna is situated. As for Ath Waaban, located in a large valley even further to the south-east, this was founded by migrants from

---

58   Hanoteau and Letourneux, *op. cit.*, vol. II, 67.

59   Genevois, 1971, *op. cit.*, 50–6.

60   The map's spelling of place names differs from mine; for Irhil read Ighil: e.g. Ighil Bouammas, Ighil n'Tsedda.

61   Devaux, *op. cit.*, 263.

62   Of the other settlements on this ridge shown by the map, Ath Moussa was historically part of Ath Daoud; 'Taous Relfa' is the French army map-maker's oddly mistaken rendering of Tazaghart, also a satellite hamlet of Ath Daoud.

Map 4.2: The villages of the Ath
Boudrar and their western and eastern
neighbours.[63]

---

63 This is a section of the French army's map of the Tazmalt district, which covers the highest
part of the northern side as well as the whole of the southern side of the central Jurjura.

the 'arsh Ath Wakour south of the watershed and was almost certainly the last village to be incorporated into the Ath Boudrar.[64]

Now, Ighil Bouammas, whose name means 'the ridge of the centre', has long been regarded as the leading village of the Ath Boudrar. It has been extremely important in the modern era,[65] but there is nothing new about this. In 1852, the French recognised as Bachagha of the Jurjura a certain Sid El-Djoudi, a marabout from Ighil Bouammas,[66] on whom they initially relied in their dealings with the Igawawen prior to the military conquest of what the colonial cartographers called 'la Kabilie indépendante' in 1857.[67] As for Ath Ali ou Harzoun, it was the largest village of the 'arsh c. 1868, with 1,400 inhabitants to Ighil Bouammas's 1,344 according to Hanoteau and Letourneux, and far more than either Darna (618 inhabitants at that date) or Ath Waaban (400).[68] And there is evidence from several sources that it was far from enthusiastic about being incorporated into the Ath Boudrar.

The first serious investigation of the Jurjura after the military conquest of 1857 was undertaken by Devaux, who reported in 1859 that

the Aïth Ali-Ouarzoun [sic] have always made a show of staying aloof from the new tribe which events had forced them to adopt. Very often they have protested, arms in hand, against the measures taken by the Aïth Boudrar.[69]

Moreover, he observed, the ikhelijen of Ath Ali ou Harzoun, whatever their differences amongst themselves, all belonged to the same saff within the 'arsh, which was most unusual.[70] This information was noted by the French

64 Commission Administrative du Sénatus-Consulte du Département d'Alger: *Rapport sur l'application du Sénatus-Consulte dans la tribu des Beni Bou Drar: au sujet de la fraction d'Aït Ouabane*, 14 August 1897 (M 36). This document does not support the earlier suggestion of Devaux (*ibid.*) that Ath Waaban once belonged to the Aqbil.

65 The mayors of the commune of Tassaft in 1962–5 and 1967–75 were both men from Ighil Bouammas, which is also the native village of Belaïd Abdesselam (minister of industry and energy 1965–77, head of the government 1992–3) and the celebrated singer-poet Lounis Aït Menguellet.

66 A detailed but most unflattering biographical portrait of Sid El-Djoudi is provided by A. Hanoteau in the Notes appended to his *Poésies Populaires de la Kabylie du Djurdjura* (Paris: Imprimérie Impériale eds, 1867), 451–3.

67 See the fascinating maps of L. Bouffard in *Atlas de l'Algérie* (Paris and Algiers: Librairie de la Hachette, 1847), reproduced in Charles-André Julien, *Histoire de l'Algérie Contemporaine* (Paris: PUF, 1964).

68 Hanoteau and Letourneux, *op. cit.*, vol. I, 306.

69 Devaux, *op. cit.*, 262 (my translation).

70 Devaux, *op. cit.*, 266–7.

authorities. With the generalisation of the *douar* as the basic unit of the colonial administration of the Muslim population in the Algerian countryside in the 1870s,[71] the *'arsh* Ath Boudrar became the *'douar* Beni Bou Drar' (or *'douar* Iboudraren'). The *qā'id* of the *douar* was invariably from the Aït Kaci family of Ath Ali ou Harzoun.[72] In other words, having played the Ighil Bouammas card before 1857, the French decided to play the Ath Ali ou Harzoun card thereafter, these being the two main options available to them in the *douar* in question.

The evidence strongly suggests that the incorporation of Ath Ali ou Harzoun into the Ath Boudrar following the disintegration of the Ath ou Belkacem set up a new basis for *saff* conflict within the *'arsh*, and that Ath Ali ou Harzoun was the headquarters of the *saff* of 'the edges', while the *saff* of 'the centre' had its headquarters in Ighil Bouammas. The political history of the Ath Boudrar since the middle of the eighteenth century was, in its foundations, an affair of 'core' and 'periphery', just as that of the Ath Wasif was an affair of 'westerners' and 'easterners'. The *saff* division among the Ath Boudrar came to be based on this fact and the names of the two *sfūf* bore witness to it.

The existence of *sfūf* at the level of the *'arsh* was not at all the product of an abstract imperative impelling Kabyles to equip themselves with some kind of 'dualistic organisation' as the unexplained emanation of an idiosyncratic psychology.[73] It was the product of the entirely material and straightforward fact that Kabyle *'aarsh* decided their policy in public meetings, which necessarily engendered a two-party division, and of the particular and equally material facts of geography and history of each *'arsh*, which determined the particular ground and character of the party division in each case. The ground of the *saff* division varied from one *'arsh* to another, but in each case had its source in the particular history of the *'arsh* concerned.

---

71 Among the Beduin of southern Algeria, *douar* (literally 'circle') indicated a circle of tents and thus a fraction of the tribe whose families were accustomed to camp together because related. The term was generalised by the French to the rest of Algeria as the basic unit of native administration in the countryside. In Greater Kabylia, it was simply a change of nomenclature, as former *'arsh* X became *douar* X in the discourse of the colonial authorities.

72 The first 'President' of the *jema'a* of the *'douar* Beni Bou Drar' when this was reconstituted under French auspices in 1890 was Ramdane Naït Kaci, who already held the position of *Adjoint Indigène*, i.e. *qā'id* (Arrêté of 28 June 1890, M 213, Dossier 125); his successor was Hadj Belkacem Ben Mohammed Aït Kaci, who signed a letter to the Governor-General of Algeria from 'the President and members of the *jema'a* of the *douar* Beni Bou Drar' on the latter's behalf, 2 July 1895 (M 36); Naït Kaci and Aït Kaci are merely variant renderings of the same family name, as is clear from the *Procès-Verbal de Délimitation du Douar Iboudrarène* of 24 December 1897 (M 36), which gives the name of the *adjoint indigène* and president of the *jema'a* of 'la tribu Beni Bou Drar' (= *douar* Iboudrarène) as 'Si Elhadj Belkacem naït Kaci'. The continuing reliance of the French on the Aït Kaci family in the later colonial period is attested by local informants from the Ath Boudrar.

73 Which is what Bourdieu has suggested, 1962, *op. cit.*, 16.

The *saff* division at the level of the *ʿarsh* was a factor in the stable government of the constituent villages, because it was what constituted the *ikhelijen* into parties. I have suggested that the *ikhelijen were* the *sfūf*, at village level. This formulation of the matter, employed for brevity's sake, simplifies the actual reality. The villagers at Ath Waaban, for instance, do not refer to the Ath Tighilt and the Ath Wadda as *'sfūf'*. They refer to them merely as *'ikhelijen'*. They do so while freely admitting that village politics is essentially grounded on the long-standing opposition of the two. What makes a *thakhelijth* into a *saff* or into a component part of a *saff* is the fact that it is aligned with the *ikhelijen* of other villages in a wider arena of political activity.

This usage is not universal. The exact opposite of it is also encountered in Kabylia. According to Genevois, the village of Taourirt n'Ath Menguellat consists of four *iderman* grouped in two *'sfūf'*.[74] While the people of Ath Waaban refrain from describing their *ikhelijen* as *sfūf*, their counterparts at Taourirt do not bother to describe their *'sfūf'* as *ikhelijen*.

Part of the explanation of this variation in usage lies in the fact that, whereas Ath Waaban has historically been a marginal village of the Ath Boudrar, Taourirt has historically been the leading village of the Ath Menguellat.[75] The division between the *ikhelijen* at Ath Waaban has been fully politicised only when the *saff* division at the level of the *ʿarsh* has been galvanised by some fresh controversy.[76] But, in the leading village of an *ʿarsh*, the *saff* division would be permanently alive, if only simmering for much of the time. While the quarters of Ath Waaban are only potential and occasional *sfūf*, those of Taourirt are permanently conscious of their partisan character because they are leading components of the two *sfūf* at *ʿarsh* level.[77]

The two usages, however contradictory in appearance, are therefore consistent with and reflect the fact that it was the *saff* division at the level of the *ʿarsh* which organised the *saff* division at the level of the village. And in this we can see one of the major respects in which the *ʿarsh* was necessary to its constituent villages. It provided a wider political framework which was conducive to stable government at village level, because, by organising the *saff* division, it facilitated the provision of political outlets to the feuding impulses of the clans in each village. Its ability to do this was grounded in the common interest which its constituent villages had in the *ʿarsh*, in that the *ʿaarsh* not only guaranteed the territorial integrity of their respective villages but also were the crucial agents in the system of distribution and exchange of goods within the region,

---

74 Genevois, 1972, *op. cit.*, 42.

75 *Ibid.*

76 The same logic applies to the Ath Yenni village of Ath Larbaʿa, according to Basagana and Sayad, *op. cit.*, 57.

77 Genevois, 1972, *op. cit.*, 3–4, 10.

as the organisers and guarantors of markets. Among the Igawawen, the *'aarsh* also organised caravans for external trade and *'arsh* solidarity underpinned the ventures of individual merchants and pedlars *dans le pays arabe.*[78]

Were it not for the *'arsh*, there would have been no *sfūf* in the proper sense of the term. And were it not for the *sfūf*, politics in a Kabyle village would have been mere clan politics – that is, the primitive politics of kinship antagonisms – and the large, complex, *thaddarth* of the Igawawen would have been ungovernable and would not exist. And the political history of modern Algeria would be other than it is.

But while the *'arsh* level was, arguably, the crucial level for the constitution of *saff* divisions, these divisions also existed at levels beyond the *'arsh*.

The *saff* systems

As we have seen, Hanoteau and Letourneux reported that the range of a *saff* extended 'to the confederation and even to outside tribes, in a vast radius.' The failure of subsequent writers to pay attention to this observation is not the least remarkable aspect of the literature on Kabylia over the last 140 years.

The confederation, *thaqbilth*, does not seem to have been an important level in itself in *saff* politics. The *raison d'être* of a *thaqbilth* was essentially defensive: a group of adjacent *'aarsh* having formed a confederation for purposes of collective security in the military sphere, the only decisions taken at *thaqbilth* level would be those of war and peace and the *thaqbilth* did not normally possess a regular *jema'a* like that of the *'arsh* or the village. Moreover, it should be remembered that many Kabyle *'aarsh* did not belong to a *thaqbilth* but were entirely independent. By and large, those *'aarsh* which were linked to others in a *thaqbilth* either were fairly small or inhabited territory which could not be easily defended, or both. The institutionalised link with their neighbours thus furnished indispensable guarantees for their strategic position. This was clearly the case of the *'aarsh* of the Ath Bethroun confederation, but also of those of the Ath Irathen, the Ath Ijjeur and the Ath Jennad confederations. Larger *'aarsh*, such as the Ath Fraoucen or the Ath Ghoubri, or those inhabiting an extensive or easily defended territory, such as the Illilten and the Ath Itsouragh, had no need to belong to a *thaqbilth* and did not do so.

This modest estimate of the political significance of the *thaqbilth* admits of two exceptions. The confederations of the Ath Irathen and the Ath Bethroun

---

78 Hanoteau and Letourneux, *op. cit.*, vol. I, 564; Masqueray (*op. cit.*, 97–101) provides an excellent discussion of the way in which the migratory activities of the Kabyles developed the sentiment of *'arsh* identity and solidarity.

appear to have possessed considerably more political cohesion than any of their counterparts, for they proved capable of collectively addressing and dealing with a major issue of a non-military character. At some point after 1737 but before 1749, the Ath Irathen decided to abrogate Quranic law in the matter of female inheritance. They resolved that henceforth the right of females to inherit landed property, enshrined in the *Sharī'a*, would no longer be recognised and that landed property, as distinct from movable goods, could only be inherited by male heirs. In 1749, the Ath Bethroun followed suit.[79] There are no recorded instances of other confederations taking similar decisions; the Ath Irathen and the Ath Bethroun appear to have been exceptional.

Devaux was aware of the remarkable nature of the Ath Bethroun. He reported that they considered themselves the heart or core of the Igawawen ('le coeur des Igawawen') and that their *qawānīn* were 'very severe' and observed 'with a rigour without equal among their neighbours'.[80] He also gave details of the *saff* division among them.[81] According to him, this was a division between 'sof Cheraga (de l'est) et sof R'raba (de l'ouest)' and obtained not only amongst the Ath Bethroun but also amongst the other Igawawen to their east (which he presented as independent tribes, but which Hanoteau and Letourneux reported as forming the *thaqbilth* of the Ath Menguellat, a usage I have followed in Table 4.2).

Table 4.2: *Saff* divisions of the Igawawen
(mid-nineteenth century), after Devaux

Thaqbilth	*'arsh*	*'Sof Cheraga'* (no. of rifles)	*'Sof R'raba'* (no. of rifles)
Ath Bethroun	Ath Yenni	825	500
	Ath Wasif	730	490
	Ath Bou Akkash	475	290
	Ath Boudrar	700	525
Ath Menguellat	Ath Menguellat	900	450
	Ath Attaf	120	420
	Aqbil	685	300
	Ath Bou Youcef	200	450

79 This episode is discussed in detail in Chapter 7 below.
80 Devaux, *op. cit.*, 255.
81 Devaux, *op. cit.*, 266 and 272.

If we substitute the Kabyle versions of these terms, properly spelt, we have *saff Isherqien* and *saff Igherbien*. It is possible, then, that the *saff* division among the Ath Bethroun was an extrapolation of that of the Ath Wasif. The fact that the decision of 1749 was taken at an assembly held in the territory of the Ath Wasif [82] lends support to this hypothesis. And if the *saff* division at the level of the *thaqbilth* Ath Bethroun originated in this way from that of one of its constituent *'aarsh*, it seems equally possible that the *saff* division amongst the other Igawawen *'aarsh* listed above originated in the same manner, as an extension of the *saff* division within the Ath Bethroun, a probability which would lend serious credence to the latter's claim, reported by Devaux, that they were 'the heart of the Igawawen'.

And this brings us to what is in many ways the most remarkable aspect of *saff* politics in pre-colonial Kabylia. For much more important than the existence of *saff* divisions at the level of the *thaqbilth* was the fact that the *saff* divisions within the constituent *'aarsh* of each *thaqbilth* linked up with those of other *'aarsh* outside the confederation in question. They did this in a manner which has never been properly described or explained.

According to Hanoteau and Letourneux, the *'aarsh* and confederations of Greater Kabylia – less its western-most districts, where the population had been at least partially incorporated into the political system of the Ottoman Regency – were divided into four groups by the operation of *saff* politics. These were:

  i.   the group centred on the Ath Irathen confederation;
  ii. the group of the southern Igawawen – that is, the *'aarsh* inhabiting the highest part of the central Jurjura;
  iii. the group of the eastern Jurjura and Akfadou district;
  iv. the group of maritime Kabylia to the north of the Sebaou river.

Within each of these four groups, the *sfūf* of each *'arsh* or confederation were said to 'enter reciprocally into' the *sfūf* of all the others.[83]

There were thus four distinct and mutually exclusive *saff* systems. It should be clearly understood that these were *saff* systems, not *sfūf*. The four groups did not function as parties opposed to one another. There was no general Igawawen *saff* opposed to the Ath Irathen *saff*, for example. There were four distinct political systems, each of which was a framework within which wide-ranging *but not boundless* party conflicts were conducted.

---

82 At Souq el-Sebt n'Ath Wasif – the Saturday market of the Ath Wasif – according to the text of the decision (Hanoteau and Letourneux, *op. cit.*, vol. III, 451); this market no longer exists.

83 Hanoteau and Letourneux, *op. cit.*, vol. II, 14.

Hanoteau and Letourneux list the membership of these groups by *'arsh*.[84] If we add the figures they also provide for the population of Greater Kabylia, by *'arsh* and village, as of 1868,[85] we can get an idea of the relative size and importance of the four systems.

Table 4.3: The Ath Irathen *saff* system

Thaqbilth (confederation)	*'arsh* (tribe)	No. of villages	Population 1868
Ath Irathen	Irjen	7	4,390
Ath Irathen	Ath Akerma	12	5,444
Ath Irathen	Ath Ousammeur	4	3,848
Ath Irathen	Ath Oumalou	8	3,088
Ath Irathen	Aouggacha	7	2,728
Ath Bethroun	Ath Yenni	6	5,139
Ath Aïssi	Ath Ameur ou Faïd	2	1,611
Ath Aïssi	Ath Douala	10	2,917
Ath Aïssi	Ath Mahmoud	6	5,248
Maatqa	Maatqa	15	7,027
–	Ath Yahia	9	5,410
–	Ath Bou Chaïb	5	3,945
–	Ath Khelili	11	3,098
–	Ath Fraoucen	15	7,023
–	Ath Ghoubri	15	5,732
–	Part of Iamrawien Oufella	2	1,358

Note: Total population *c.* 1868: 68,006

84 Hanoteau and Letourneux, *ibid.*

85 Hanoteau and Letourneux, *op. cit.*, vol. I, 302–63. The Igawawen and eastern Jurjura-Akfadou *saff* systems included *'aarsh* from the southern side of the Jurjura, which Hanoteau and Letourneux omitted from their list of the tribes of Greater Kabylia and for which population statistics for *c.* 1868 are accordingly unavailable; I have estimated the number of villages in each of these *'aarsh* from my knowledge of some of them and from large scale maps of the region. According to Hanoteau's son, the authors completed their manuscript by September 1868 (Général Maurice Hanoteau, 'Quelques souvenirs sur les collaborateurs de *La Kabylie et les coutumes kabyles*', *Revue Africaine* (1923), 134–49: 147).

Table 4.4: The *saff* system of the southern Igawawen

Thaqbilth (confederation)	*'arsh* (tribe)	No. of villages	Population 1868
Ath Bethroun	Ath Wasif	7	5,532
Ath Bethroun	Ath Bou Akkach	4	3,120
Ath Bethroun	Ath Boudrar	6	5,958
Ath Menguellat	Ath Menguellat	7	4,730
Ath Menguellat	Ath Attaf	2	2,395
Ath Menguellat	Aqbil	5	3,939
Ath Menguellat	Ath Bou Youcef	5	3,348
–	Ath Itsouragh	18	4,797
–	Ath Wakour	2	?
–	Imecheddalen	*c.* 15	?

Note: Total population *c.* 1868: in excess of 33,809

Table 4.5: The eastern Jurjura and Akfadou *saff* system

Thaqbilth (confederation)	*'arsh* (tribe)	No. of villages	Population 1868
-	Illilten	11	3,030
-	Illoulen Oumalou	11	3,299
-	Ath Ziki	6	490
-	Illoulen Ousammeur	*c.* 15	?
-	Ath Melikech	*c.* 8	?
Ath Ijjeur	Imesdourar	6	1,695
Ath Ijjeur	El Jeur Alemmas	6	1,975
Ath Ijjeur	Ath H'antela	5	1,744
Ath Ijjeur	Tifrit n'Ath ou Malek	2	500

Note: Total population *c.* 1868: in excess of 12,733

Table 4.6: The *saff* system of maritime Kabylia

Thaqbilth (confederation)	*'arsh* (tribe)	No. of villages	Population 1868
Ath Jennad	Ath Kodhea	5	6,258
Ath Jennad	Ath Adas	6	6,607
Ath Jennad	Ath Ighzer	5	2,956
-	Ath Fliq	10	3,168
-	Iazzouzen	6	2,487
-	Izerkhfawen	5	6,787
Iflissen Lebahr	Ath Zouaou	13	1,010
Iflissen Lebahr	Ath Aïhmed	11	792
Iflissen Lebahr	Ath Zerara	12	1,233
Iflissen Lebahr	Tifra	4	866
Ath Waguenoun	Ath Aïssa ou Mimoun	6	3,320
Ath Waguenoun	Aâfir	2	1,751
Ath Waguenoun	Attouch	18	2,134
Ath Waguenoun	Ath Sidi Hamza	7	531
Ath Waguenoun	Ath Saïd	11	1,243
Ath Waguenoun	Iaskaren	4	515
Ath Waguenoun	Ath Mesellem	8	1,175
Ath Waguenoun	Istiten	4	550
Ath Waguenoun	Cheurfa	7	374
-	Rest of Iamrawien Oufella	4	2,987

Note: Total population *c.* 1868: 46,744

From this data we can see that the boundaries of the four systems coincided with those of *'aarsh* or confederations in almost all cases. The only definite exceptions were the case of the Iamrawien and that of the Ath Yenni.[86] In the former case, the Iamrawien Oufella (the Iamrawien villages settled higher up the Sebaou valley) were partly in the Ath Irathen *saff* system and partly in the *saff* system of maritime Kabylia, while the Iamrawien Bouadda ('the Iamrawien lower down the valley') were in neither. In the latter case, the Ath Yenni was the only *'arsh* of the Ath Bethroun confederation not to enter into the *saff* system of the Igawawen, preferring to participate in that of the Ath Irathen instead. These

---

86 The Ath Aïssi may also be an exception, since only three of their seven *'aarsh* are listed as belonging to the Ath Irathen *saff* system.

exceptions to the rule can be explained by the exceptional circumstances of the populations in question.

The Iamrawien or Amrawa[87] were composed originally of both Kabyle migrants from other districts and Arabic-speaking immigrants who settled in the central Sebaou valley and whom the Ottoman Regency eventually constituted into a *makhzen* tribe to control the lowlands on behalf of the central power. In the course of time, the Iamrawien were almost entirely Berberised and have long since been considered Kabyle. But the Iamrawien Bouadda, like the other *'aarsh* of western and north-western Kabylia, remained politically in the ambit of Algiers and outside the *saff* systems of *'la Kabilie indépendante'*. The more easterly Iamrawien Oufella, on the other hand, came under the influence of the independent *'aarsh* to their north and south. Those of its villages on the right (north) bank of the Sebaou, on the edge of the Ath Waguenoun's territory, Timizar Laghbar, Tikobaïn, Tala Athman and Tamda, were drawn into the *saff* system of maritime Kabylia, while its villages on the left (south) bank of the Sebaou, Isikhen ou Meddour and Mekla, being in the vicinity of the Ath Irathen, came under the latter's political influence and were drawn into the Ath Irathen's *saff* system.[88]

As for the Ath Yenni, there is no doubting the fact that they belonged to the *thaqbilth* of the Ath Bethroun and were an Igawawen *'arsh* in the strictest meaning of the term. Yet, according to Hanoteau and Letourneux, they did not belong to the Igawawen *saff* system like the other Ath Bethroun *'aarsh*, but to that of the Ath Irathen. On this point, Hanoteau and Letourneux directly contradict Devaux who, as we have seen, gave details of the Igawawen *saff* system in 1859 and reported that the Ath Yenni belonged to it. Hanoteau and Letourneux do not allude to Devaux's report, however, and give no evidence in support of their own account. If we assume that Hanoteau and Letourneux were right and Devaux simply wrong, how might we explain the Ath Yenni's exceptional position?

The Ath Yenni are the most northerly of the Ath Bethroun *'aarsh*, and most of the north-eastern boundary of their territory abuts that of the Ath Irathen *'aarsh* of Ath Ousammeur and Aouggacha, while part of the western boundary abuts the territory of the Ath Mahmoud, one of the three *'aarsh* of the Ath Aïssi confederation which were in the Ath Irathen *saff* system. In addition, it is possible that the nature of the Ath Yenni's manufacturing and commercial activities gave them an interest in Ath Irathen politics.

---

87 The name means 'those who populated [sc. the country]', 'the settlers'.
88 Hanoteau and Letourneux do not specify which of the Iamrawien Oufella's villages belonged to which *saff* system. My allocation of villages to *saff* systems is an inference from the disposition of the villages on the ground.

There is no way of telling precisely how important the manufacture of counterfeit money was to the material prosperity of the Ath Yenni.[89] But they were the only *'arsh* to engage in this production and it was sufficiently important to attract orders from far away, as we have seen, and to arouse the wrath of the Ottoman authorities in Algiers, who made the trade in this commodity a capital crime. The Ath Yenni did not themselves handle the circulation of their output in Algiers and the other urban centres (Constantine, Setif, Bona, etc.); according to Hanoteau and Letourneux, they somehow managed to induce men of other *'aarsh* and especially of the Ath Bou Youcef and Aqbil to act as their intermediaries.[90] But the Ottoman authorities were well aware that the Ath Yenni were the source of this commerce and were certainly concerned to inhibit it.[91] Apart from putting to death the purveyors of this commodity whenever it got its hands on them in Algiers and elsewhere, however, the Regency could do nothing short of mounting a punitive expedition into the heart of Kabylia.

Now, there was no way the forces of the Regency could reach the Ath Yenni over the Jurjura passes. The Ath Bou Youcef, controlling most of the northern approach to the Tirourda pass, and the other Igawawen *'aarsh*, controlling the passes of Tizi Boussouil, Tizi n'Kouilal and Tizi n'Ath Waaban, could be counted upon to block the advance of any force from the south. That left an attack from the north, by a force coming from the Sebaou valley and up the valley of its tributary, the Wad Aïssi. The *'aarsh* controlling this valley were those of the Ath Irathen confederation on the eastern side and those of the Ath Aïssi on the western side. Between them, these two confederations controlled the whole of the northern approaches to the territory of the Ath Yenni. In addition, the total population (and so the number of fighting men capable of being mustered) involved in the Ath Irathen *saff* system, even without counting the Ath Yenni, was almost double that of the Igawawen *saff* system. So it is not difficult to conceive why the Ath Yenni may have considered that they had more to gain from influencing the policy debates within the Ath Irathen *saff* system to their north than those in the *saff* system of the Igawawen to their south.

It is possible, then, to construct a plausible explanation for the Ath Yenni's membership of the Ath Irathen *saff* system. But a plausible explanation is not the same thing as evidence. And the one incontrovertible piece of evidence available to us is inconsistent with Hanoteau and Letourneux's view of the matter. This is the fact that the Ath Yenni did not fight alongside the Ath Irathen in resisting Randon's forces in 1857 and did not capitulate when the Ath Irathen capitulated. Their attitude to the French was not determined by that of the *'aarsh* of the Ath Irathen *saff* system. They fought on after the surrender of the latter, both in

89 That it was lucrative is affirmed by Hanoteau and Letourneux, *op. cit.*, vol. III, 120–1; for a
    general review of the Ath Yenni's manufacturing activities, see Genevois, 1971, *op. cit.*, 7–13.
90 Hanoteau and Letourneux, *op. cit.*, vol. I, 543.
91 Genevois, 1971, *op. cit.*, 8–9.

defending their own villages and in supporting the Ath Menguellat in the battle at Icherriden[92] and their own eventual surrender was the signal for the surrender of the rest of the Igawawen. All this strongly supports Devaux's contention that they were part of the Igawawen *saff* system in 1857.

But it does not follow that Hanoteau and Letourneux were simply wrong. It is not impossible that the Ath Yenni had been part of the Igawawen *saff* system when Devaux investigated them in 1857–9, but had switched to the Ath Irathen group by the time Hanoteau and Letourneux investigated them a decade later. This would be plausible only if one could identify a sufficient motive for such a change. As it happens, there is one.

The nature of the Ath Yenni's commercial activities gave them a highly developed orientation towards the central power. It brought them into conflict with this power and obliged them always to conduct themselves with an eye on the likely reactions of this power, to an extent which distinguished them from their neighbours. Until 1830 this power had been the Ottoman Regency. The overthrow of the Regency by the French threw the broader political environment within which the Ath Yenni operated into flux. This flux continued until 1857. It was possible for the Ath Yenni to consider that the French conquest had not established a stable political settlement before that date. But 1857 marked the definitive establishment of the French state as the central power in Algeria so far as the Kabyles were concerned. And this central power differed from its Ottoman predecessor in a most palpable way, in that it possessed the ambition and the resources to establish and maintain a permanent and authoritative presence in the heart of Greater Kabylia. There was to be a French administration in the Jurjura, where there had never been an Ottoman administration. The building by the French, in the centre of the Ath Irathen's territory, of the garrison township of Fort Napoléon (renamed Fort National after 1870) immediately after the defeat of the Ath Irathen in 1857, to be the centre of the French presence in upland Kabylia, testified to French intentions in the most unmistakable way.

There is evidence that this was very clearly understood by the leading families of the Ath Yenni and that they realised that the trade in counterfeit money had no future, that substitutes for it had to be found, that, more generally, they had to come to terms with the French state and that, at the local level, this meant getting on terms with the French presence at Fort Napoléon.[93] It is likely that they decided to develop closer relations with the Ath Irathen tribes, by entering their system of *saff* politics, in order to be able to obtain

---

92 See for instance the evocation by Augustin Ibazizen, a native of the Ath Yenni village of Ath Larba'a, of the role of his grandfather in the battle of Icherriden, in Ibazizen 1979, *op. cit.*, 39–64.

93 This pragmatic change in outlook in the immediate wake of the 1857 defeat was precisely that of Augustin Ibazizen's grandfather (*op. cit.*, 48–9).

and thereafter safeguard easy access to the new colonial administration and to exploit whatever business and other opportunities the new French township was likely to offer. (The Ath Yenni are nothing if not entrepreneurs.)

It is most probable, then, that the Ath Yenni broke away from the rest of the *thaqbilth* of the Ath Bethroun in the matter of *saff* systems only once the *thaqbilth*, as a military alliance, had been rendered obsolete by the conquest. The *thaqbilth* was to have a last hurrah fourteen years later, in the rebellion of 1871.[94] But this could not have been anticipated in 1857 or the years immediately following this. The 1871 rising embraced and mobilised the Igawawen but it was not launched by them and it was precipitated by a number of circumstances, including most notably the defeat of France in the Franco-Prussian war of 1870, which no one in France, let alone Kabylia, foresaw. There is every reason to suppose that the Ath Yenni took the obsolescence of their military alliance with the other 'aarsh of the Ath Bethroun in the aftermath of 1857 as definitive and adjusted their external relations accordingly. It follows that, in the Ottoman period, the Ath Yenni almost certainly belonged to the same *saff* system as the rest of the Ath Bethroun and that membership of a *saff* system did not conflict with membership of a *thaqbilth*, but invariably complemented it.

What enabled a *saff* division in a given 'arsh or confederation to dovetail with the *saff* divisions of surrounding 'aarsh was the fact that the overall population in question had a common interest. This interest, being that of a population which was independent of, and often at odds with, the Ottoman Regency, was primarily strategic.

If we look at the four *saff* systems we have described, we can see that they dominated key stretches of terrain. The 'aarsh of the Ath Irathen system controlled the south side of the central Sebaou valley and the western side of the upper Sebaou (where it is known locally as the Wad Boubehir) up to and including the Ath Yahia,[95] plus the northern part of the east side of the upper Sebaou (i.e. the Ath Ghoubri's territory), as well as the whole of the Wad Aïssi valley. The 'aarsh of the Igawawen system controlled the whole of the central Jurjura, from the eastern side of the approach to Tizi Boussouil, past Tizi n'Kouilal and Tizi n'Ath Waaban to the western side of the northern and southern approaches to Tizi n'Tirourda. The 'aarsh of the eastern Jurjura and Akfadou system controlled the eastern side of the northern and southern approaches to the Tirourda pass and all passes east and north-east of there –

---

94 On the 1871 rebellion, see Charles-André Julien, *Histoire de l'Algérie contemporaine: la conquête et les débuts de la colonisation, 1827–1871* (Paris: Presses Universitaires de France, 1964), chapter IX.

95 It is possible that the Ath Yahia's membership of the Ath Irathen *saff* system was as recent as the Ath Yenni's and that it too had formerly belonged to the Igawawen system, since it fought with the tribes of the latter in 1857 (v. infra).

Tizi n'Ichelladen, Tizi n'Ath Ziki, Tizi Wakfadou and Tizi Tiouririne – as well as the southern part of the east side of the upper Sebaou/Wad Boubehir valley. The *'aarsh* of the maritime Kabylia system controlled the coast from west of Tigzirt to east of Azeffoun and the right bank of the central Sebaou from level with Tizi Ouzou to just before Azazga.

Each *saff* system controlled a specific and extensive piece of strategic terrain and naturally implicated the *sfuf* of all those *'aarsh* with a stake in this terrain.

Hanoteau and Letourneux speak of the four *saff* systems which I have just described in a brief passage, almost in parenthesis. Their failure to provide a more developed discussion of these systems probably explains why later students of Kabylia, starting with Masqueray, have paid no attention to the matter. It may therefore be thought that my own elaboration of this point has been fanciful and that my thesis – that these four systems were immensely important to the political life of pre-colonial Kabylia and that the involvement of the *'aarsh* of *'la Kabilie indépendante'* in one or another of them was the very opposite of a superficial affair – is not soundly based. But my view of the matter is supported by a very substantial piece of evidence from the colonial period which, as far as I am aware, has also been universally overlooked.

The new colonial order in Kabylia, as elsewhere in Algeria, employed two different kinds of administrative unit. Where a significant European settler community was established, as at Fort National among the Ath Irathen and at Mekla, previously an Iamrawien village, in the vicinity of the Ath Fraoucen, the administrative unit was known as a *commune de plein exercice* because the European population enjoyed more or less the same political rights as their counterparts in the communes of metropolitan France. A few Kabyle *'aarsh* – relabelled *douars* by the French – were incorporated into these communes, while remaining excluded, for lack of French citizenship, from participation in the affairs of the commune. But, for the vast majority, the administrative unit was the euphemistically named *commune mixte*, which was run in an authoritarian fashion by a French administrator, assisted by a 'native deputy' – the *adjoint indigène*, popularly known as the *qā'id* – in each *douar*. In the central and eastern districts of Greater Kabylia, the *communes mixtes* corresponded almost exactly to the way in which the populations of these districts had previously been grouped through their participation in the *saff* systems. This correspondence is shown in Table 4.7.

It will be seen that in only five – out of fifty – cases (Ath Ghoubri, Maatqa, Ath Yahıa, Illilten and Ath Kodhea) did an *'arsh* end up in a commune other than that indicated by its previous *saff* system membership and in every case the *'arsh* in question had been located on the margin of its *saff* system. In only one case did the boundaries of the *communes mixtes* deviate substantially rather than marginally from those of the *saff* systems, where the populations that participated in the *saff* system of maritime Kabylia were divided between the *communes mixtes* of Azeffoun and the

Mizrana. In this case, the line of demarcation corresponded exactly to that separating the territory of the *thaqbilth* Ath Jennad from that of the *thaqbilth* Ath Waguenoun.[96] Apart from this one exception, the basic divisions of the population into *saff* systems in the pre-colonial era survived into the colonial era as divisions into *communes mixtes*.

My thesis concerning the crucial importance of these four *saff* systems is also borne out by a fact of which Hanoteau and Letourneux and Masqueray should have been well aware, one to which I have already alluded and which explains how and why the *saff* systems should have made such an impression on the French at the time of the conquest that they subsequently took them into account in elaborating their own scheme for the government of the region.

Table 4.7: Pre-colonial *saff* systems and colonial administrative divisions in Greater Kabylia[97]

'arsh	Thaqbilth	Saff system	Colonial commune (mixte or de plein exercice)
Ath Ghoubri	-	Ath Irathen	CM du Haut Sebaou
Maatqa	Maatqa	Ath Irathen	CM de Tizi Ouzou
Ath Ameur ou Faïd	Ath Aïssi	Ath Irathen	CM de Fort National
Ath Douala	Ath Aïssi	Ath Irathen	CM de Fort National
Ath Mahmoud	Ath Aïssi	Ath Irathen	CM de Fort National
Irjen	Ath Irathen	Ath Irathen	CM de Fort National
Ath Akerma	Ath Irathen	Ath Irathen	CM & CPE de Fort National
Ath Ousammeur	Ath Irathen	Ath Irathen	CPE de Fort National
Ath Oumalou	Ath Irathen	Ath Irathen	CM de Fort National
Aouggacha	Ath Irathen	Ath Irathen	CM de Fort National
Ath Bou Chaïb	-	Ath Irathen	CM de Fort National
Ath Khelili	-	Ath Irathen	CM de Fort National
Ath Fraoucen	-	Ath Irathen	CPE de Mekla
Part of Iamrawien Oufella	-	Ath Irathen	CPE de Mekla

96 In only one case was an *'arsh* separated both from the rest of its *thaqbilth* and its former *saff* system, that of the Ath Kodhea of the *thaqbilth* Ath Jennad, which was incorporated in the *commune mixte* du Haut Sebaou as the *douar Beni Djennad Cheurg* ('the eastern Beni Djennad') and later renamed the *douar* Tamgout after the mountain of that name. I have not come across an explanation of this unique treatment.

97 This table omits those *'aarsh* of the southern side of the Jurjura which were not included in the *arrondissement* of Tizi Ouzou in the colonial period, namely the Imecheddalen and the Ath Wakour, which belonged to the Igawawen *saff* system, and the Ath Melikech and the Illoulen Ousammeur, which belonged to the eastern Jurjura/Akfadou system.

Table 4.7 *continued*

Ath Yenni	Ath Bethroun	Ath Irathen	CM de Fort National
Ath Yahia	-	Ath Irathen	CM du Jurjura
Ath Wasif	Ath Bethroun	Igawawen	CM du Jurjura
Ath Bou Akkach	Ath Bethroun	Igawawen	CM du Jurjura
Ath Boudrar	Ath Bethroun	Igawawen	CM du Jurjura
Ath Menguellat	Ath Menguellat	Igawawen	CM du Jurjura
Ath Attaf	Ath Menguellat	Igawawen	CM du Jurjura
Aqbil	Ath Menguellat	Igawawen	CM du Jurjura
Ath Bou Youcef	Ath Menguellat	Igawawen	CM du Jurjura
Ath Itsouragh	-	Igawawen	CM du Jurjura
Illilten	-	E. Jurjura/Akfadou	CM du Jurjura
Illoulen Oumalou	-	E. Jurjura/Akfadou	CM du Haut Sebaou
Ath Ziki	-	E. Jurjura/Akfadou	CM du Haut Sebaou
Imesdourar	Ath Ijjeur	E. Jurjura/Akfadou	CM du Haut Sebaou
El Jeur Alemmas	Ath Ijjeur	E. Jurjura/Akfadou	CM du Haut Sebaou
Aït Hantala	Ath Ijjeur	E. Jurjura/Akfadou	CM du Haut Sebaou
Tifrit n'Ath ou Malek	Ath Ijjeur	E. Jurjura/Akfadou	CM du Haut Sebaou
Ath Kodhea	Ath Jennad	Maritime Kabylia	CM du Haut Sebaou
Ath Adas	Ath Jennad	Maritime Kabylia	CM d'Azeffoun
Ath Ighzer	Ath Jennad	Maritime Kabylia	CM d'Azeffoun
Ath Fliq	-	Maritime Kabylia	CM d'Azeffoun
Iazzouzen	-	Maritime Kabylia	CM d'Azeffoun
Izerkhfaouen	-	Maritime Kabylia	CM d'Azeffoun
Ath Zouaou	Iflissen Lebahr	Maritime Kabylia	CM d'Azeffoun
Ath Aïhmed	Iflissen Lebahr	Maritime Kabylia	CM d'Azeffoun
Ath Zerara	Iflissen Lebahr	Maritime Kabylia	CM d'Azeffoun
Tifra	Iflissen Lebahr	Maritime Kabylia	CM d'Azeffoun
Rest of Iamrawien Oufella	-	Maritime Kabylia	CM du Mizrana
Ath Aïssa ou Mimoun	Ath Waguenoun	Maritime Kabylia	CM du Mizrana
Aafir	Ath Waguenoun	Maritime Kabylia	CM du Mizrana
Attouch	Ath Waguenoun	Maritime Kabylia	CM du Mizrana
Ath Sidi Hamza	Ath Waguenoun	Maritime Kabylia	CM du Mzrana
Ath Saïd	Ath Waguenoun	Maritime Kabylia	CM du Mizrana
Iaskaren	Ath Waguenoun	Maritime Kabylia	CM du Mizrana
Ath Mesellem	Ath Waguenoun	Maritime Kabylia	CM du Mizrana
Istiten	Ath Waguenoun	Maritime Kabylia	CM du Mizrana
Cheurfa	Ath Waguenoun	Maritime Kabylia	CM du Mizrana

The military conquest of Greater Kabylia in 1857 is conventionally recorded as having occurred at the battle of Icherriden. This is not exactly the case. The populations of independent Kabylia did not pit themselves against the invader in one great battle. There were three if not four separate engagements.

In the first, the French forces attacked the Ath Irathen, approaching them from the north-west and the north-east and fighting their way up the mountainsides until they had gained the small plateau in the centre of their territory on which stood their Wednesday market, Souq el-Arba'a n'Ath Irathen. At this point, the Ath Irathen admitted defeat and asked for terms.[98] Their capitulation immediately entailed the capitulation of the Ath Fraoucen, Ath Khelili, Ath Bou Chaïb, Ath Ghoubri, Ath Douala, Ath Mahmoud and the 'aarsh of the Ath Sedqa confederation.[99] With the exception of these last, all these 'aarsh are listed by Hanoteau and Letourneux as belonging to the Ath Irathen *saff* system (and the omission of the Ath Sedqa may well have been an oversight, moreover).

The French then beseiged the Ath Yenni in their mountain redoubt on the one hand and engaged the Ath Menguellat, who were supported by the main body of the Ath Yenni's fighting men, in the vicinity of Icherriden and Aguemoun Izem on the other hand.[100] The capture of the Ath Yenni's villages immediately led to the capitulation of the Ath Wasif and the Ath Boudrar,[101] while the surrender of the Ath Menguellat after the defeat at Icherriden and Aguemoun Izem prompted the capitulation of the Aqbil, Ath Attaf, Ath Bou Youcef and Ath Yahia.[102] In other words, these two engagements decided the attitude of the 'aarsh belonging to the Igawawen *saff* system.

This left the 'aarsh to the south-east unconquered, however. The French accordingly invaded the territory of the Illilten from the north while simultaneously attacking the Illoulen Oumalou from the south via Tizi n'Ichelladen.[103] The capture of the celebrated holy woman Lalla Fadhma n'Soumeur in the Illilten village of Thakhelijth n'Ath Atsou marked the end of this resistance[104] and immediately prompted the capitulation of the four 'aarsh of the Ath Ijjeur confederation, which had taken no part in the hostilities themselves.[105]

---

98 Émile Carrey, *Récit de Kabylie (Campagne de 1857)* (Paris: Michel Lévy Frères, 1857; republished Algiers: Epigraphe, 1994 (all references to this edition)), 61–7.

99 Carrey, *op. cit.*, 69–70.

100 Carrey, *op. cit.*, 98–132.

101 Carrey, *op. cit.*, 166–70.

102 Carrey, *op. cit.*, 170–1. Carrey included the 'Zaoua' and the 'Aït Agache' in this list, but there are no such 'aarsh. If by the latter he meant the Ath Bou Akkach, it was an error, for they did not belong with the other 'aarsh listed, but with their neighbours, the Ath Wasif and the Ath Boudrar, and would certainly have capitulated with them.

103 Carrey, *op. cit.*, 174–9, 187–211.

104 Carrey, *op. cit.*, 213–35, gives a detailed account of this event.

105 Carrey, *op. cit.*, 236–40.

The behaviour of the Ath Ijjeur, like that of the Ath Ghoubri, Ath Sedqa, Ath Boudrar, Ath Attaf etc. before them, was dictated by the logic of membership of a *saff* system.[106] The Illilten and the Illoulen Oumalou were the leading *'aarsh* of the eastern Jurjura *saff* system, as the Ath Irathen were of the Ath Irathen *saff* system and the Ath Yenni and the Ath Menguellat were of the Igawawen *saff* system. When the leading *'aarsh* decided to surrender, this decision quickly prevailed among the other *'aarsh* of the *saff* system as a whole in each case. The French in Morocco conquered the Berber populations of the Atlas tribe by tribe. In Algeria, they conquered the populations of the heartland of Greater Kabylia *saff* system by *saff* system.

The vindication of Masqueray

Man is a political animal. The assumption of the fashionable lines of academic thought since the triumph of economic determinism in British and more generally western universities in the 1960s is that politics is merely an epiphenomenal expression in the 'superstructure' of the economic essence in the 'base'. This book is not being written on that assumption, nor is it being written on the assumption of sociological reductionism (economic determinism's *frère ennemi* if not *alter ego*) that politics is merely a reflection of the social structure. The assumption on which it is being written is Aristotle's, that politics is the framework and precondition of everything else, of all regular and orderly social activity, including economic activity. It is also being taken for granted that the practice of politics is an art and that economic determinism and sociological reductionism cannot make good sense of politics in general or Algerian and Kabyle politics in particular.

The regular reproduction of Kabyle society depended on the possibility of Kabyles engaging in a wide range of economic activities. This possibility itself depended on the innovative construction and thereafter the conservation of remarkable political arrangements. Once these arrangements had been devised, the political energies of the Kabyles went into preserving them. They had to be preserved, first, from disruption by the ineradicable tendencies to 'unsociableness' within each Kabyle village; second, from the destructive effects

---

106 Two earlier incidents bear witness to this same logic. According to Boulifa, when the French, before tackling the Jurjura, attacked the confederations of the Ath Jennad and the Iflissen Lebahr in the campaigns of 1854 and 1856, the Ath Irathen and their neighbours the Ath Fraoucen conspicuously failed to come to their aid (Boulifa, *Le Djurdjura à travers l'Histoire*, 19). As we have seen, the Ath Jennad and the Iflissen Lebahr both belonged to the *saff* system of maritime Kabylia and not to that centred on the Ath Irathen, to which the Ath Fraoucen also belonged.

of civil disorders within one village or *'arsh* spilling over into others or creating power vacuums likely to precipitate military conflicts whose outcomes might be catastrophic and, third, from interference by the Ottoman rulers of Algiers. The *saff* division within each village and *'arsh* was a crucial element of the solution to the first problem, but raised the possibility of the second. The generalisation of *saff* politics on the wider stage of the four regional *saff* systems was the pragmatic solution to the second problem and was a functional solution precisely because it was grounded in the common interest of all and sundry in coping with the third.

The *saff* systems were not *sfūf* – that is, they were not parties or alliances – nor were they units of government. They were discrete arenas of party-political activity, with clear boundaries but no structure of power that was the object of political competition. In regard to matters of government, they had no authority; government was the business of the *jemāya'* of the *'aarsh* of which they were composed and primarily of the *jemāya'* of the constituent villages of these *'aarsh*. But they had a tacit authority in respect of relations with the central power. The relations of each *'arsh* with the central power were mediated by the *saff* system to which it belonged, they were affected by movements in public opinion within the other *'aarsh* of the system in question and were unaffected by the attitudes and behaviour of *'aarsh* which belonged to other *saff* systems.

The *saff* systems were the largest units of effective public opinion in pre-colonial Kabylia. Their existence was made possible by the fact that public opinion was already being structured, informed and developed – at the level of the *thaqbilth*, the *'arsh*, the *thaddarth* and the *tufiq* and the *thakhelijth* – by the activity of the *sfūf* – that is, by parties which were not based on, or expressions of, kinship solidarities but subsumed these solidarities at the lowest level, that of the village, and transcended them at all other levels.

In the previous chapter I quoted Masqueray's assertion, à propos of the 'cities' of the Kabyles, the Chaouia and the Mzabis, that '… far from being an extension of the narrow institutions of the family, they develop outside them and are even opposed to them from the first moment of their existence'. It should now be clear that Masqueray was right about this, at any rate in the Kabyle case, and that his only error lay in his failure to explain how the Kabyle 'city' overcame the centrifugal and unsociable potential of 'the narrow institutions of the family' (by which he clearly meant the lineage and the clan and so forth in addition to the family in the most limited sense of the word) by implicating them in a system of government and party politics which expressed and upheld the primacy of the general interest over the dictates of particular interests and the code of honour. What may be less clear is the validity of his further assertion that 'the City'

> … is composed only of individuals, it knows only individuals, it protects and punishes only individuals … it has, as soon as it is formed, the character of being the expression of individual energies.

Unless this is made clear, Gellner's remark that this assertion is in conflict with Masqueray's own material must go unanswered.

Masqueray's material documents the existence of kinship divisions and antagonisms in Kabyle society, particularly but not only at the level of the village. If by 'the City' Masqueray simply means 'the village' – that is, the discrete residential units within which Kabyle society subsisted, his assertion is clearly a remarkable piece of inconsistency. But it seems to me that he is evidently not using the term 'the City' in this sense at all.

Masqueray's assertion becomes immediately intelligible as soon as we realise that he is not referring to the actual, tangible, units of collective residence such as the village and the hamlet, or even the units of collective social existence and land proprietorship above this level, the *ʿaarsh*, but that he is referring to *the political community, the polity and its constitution*. The City he is speaking of 'is in the heart of all the free men which compose it'.[107]

There is nothing unusual in a polity failing to mirror accurately the society to which it belongs. It is not the function of the polity to mirror society but to enable it to be governed. A political framework which directly reflected the main cleavages which existed in society would not facilitate the good government of the society, it would preclude it. It would merely articulate and institutionalise (and thereby reinforce) the social forces which it is the business of government to contain. A polity, if it is to endure, must embody the principles upon which government can be based, not those which give rise to unsociableness and disorder.

The Kabyle polity expressed itself most unambiguously in its laws, the *qawānīn*. These take no account whatsoever of the corporate kinship groups which made up the society. Virtually all of the *qawānīn* speak explicitly of the individual alone, 'he who does such and such ...'. It was necessary for the stable government of the Kabyle *thaddarth* that the *jemaʿa* curb the anti-social potential of the lineages and the clans. In dealing with anti-social behaviour, it held the individual responsible for his acts. It refused to delegate the business of law enforcement to the sources of the routine impulse to anti-social behaviour, the lineages and clans themselves. Fines and other penalties were explicitly imposed by the *jemaʿa* on individuals. And by stipulating that the public payment of fines to the *jemaʿa* be made in each case on the offender's behalf by the *tamen* of the offender's lineage, the *jemaʿa* of the village obtained public recognition by each lineage of the justness of the penalties imposed by the *jemaʿa* on its errant members. In this way did the *jemaʿa* implicate the lineages in the business of law-enforcement against individual law-breakers and thereby pre-empt recourse to the mobilisation of kinship solidarity to shield an individual from the penalty for his anti-social behaviour.

---

107 Masqueray, *op. cit.*, 80.

The element of movement within the Kabyle polity was provided by the *sfūf*. 'Rien de mobile comme un çof Kabyle', as Hanoteau and Letourneux observed.[108] The men of a given quarter might all belong to the same *saff* and certainly the vast majority of them would do so, but, while there was a social tendency to do so, there was nothing automatic or compulsory about this: a man was free to change *sfūf*, and enough people did so often enough to enable the pendulum to swing at frequent intervals.[109] Membership of a *saff* was a matter of choice, just as membership of a political party in a modern democracy is, whatever social factors may be held to influence such choices.

Gellner's objection to Montagne's theory that the *ilfūf* were the order-maintaining mechanisms in south-western Morocco was that they existed only at one level in the hierarchy of nested kinship groups and therefore could not be credited with maintaining order at other levels. However cogent this objection may be in the context of south-western Morocco, it has no force in the Kabyle case. For, as has been seen, a Kabyle *saff* existed *simultaneously at several levels* – the village, the *'arsh*, the confederation and even beyond.

The *sfūf* were not themselves order-maintaining mechanisms in any simple sense. But their existence and activity was indispensable to the orderly and effective self-government of the Kabyles. Through their functioning public opinion at every level was structured in such a way as to enable the *jemāya'* to conduct their business and to enable public opinion to address questions of policy in a manner which was not circumscribed by the narrow interests of lineages and clans. Because they subsumed and channelled the antagonisms of the latter, they were the instruments by means of which Kabyle unsociableness disciplined itself. And in so far as they mobilised and articulated elements of public opinion in a way which went beyond and transcended kinship relations, they tended to emancipate the Kabyles from the narrow ties of blood and so constitute them into individuals in the public sphere.

But the nature of individuality in pre-colonial Kabylia was not at all the individuality imagined by Jeremy Bentham and Francis Place and subsequently promoted by Margaret Thatcher. It was not an individuality which existed at the expense of, or in disconnection from, the wider community. The economistic and narrowly egotistical conception of individuality which has been carrying all before it in British politics since 1979 is one which has as its corollary (if not its premise) the notion that 'there is no such thing as society'.[110] Such an idea would have been incomprehensible to the people of pre-colonial Kabylia. As one of their most celebrated sayings has it, '*irgazen s-yergazen, Rebbi waḥd-es*': 'men exist through other men, only the Lord is sufficient unto Himself'. In pre-

---

108 Hanoteau and Letourneux, *op. cit.*, vol. II, 12.

109 Hanoteau and Letourneux, *ibid.*

110 Margaret Thatcher, then prime minister, in an interview on 23 September 1987, published in *Women's Own* magazine, 31 October 1987.

colonial Kabylia, the individual existed in virtue of his membership of a wider society, a dependence reflected in another Kabyle saying: *'tajmaat aṭṭeynu yiwen, yiwen ur iyennu tajmaat'*: 'the assembly enriches a man, but one man does not enrich the assembly'.

But this society existed within the framework of its politics, which transcended the ties of blood. The Kabyle was an individual in virtue of being a citizen – that is, an enfranchised member of a political community. However incomplete Masqueray's explanation of this fact may have been, he saw it and understood it clearly enough.

What remain to be explained are the place of religion and the role of the Ottomans in the development and reproduction of this state of affairs.

CHAPTER 5

~

Pre-colonial Kabylia and the Regency

Religion and Political Development, 1509–1639

Introduction

The ability of the Kabyles to govern themselves through deliberative assemblies structured by a binary system of party politics was predicated in part on the fact that there was at all times a great deal of common ground between the parties in contention. Ideological differences were radically absent from political disputes. The character of Kabyle society and the constitutive principles of its system of government were taken for granted by all and never at issue. There was no basis in pre-colonial Kabylia for the conflict between reformist (let alone radical) and conservative (let alone reactionary) tendencies. Ideologically, the Kabyles were all of one party, which is to say conservative.

This unanimous conservatism in respect of the social structure and the political system was paralleled by an equal unanimity in respect of religious belief. The fact that the Kabyles were all Sunni Muslims of the Maliki rite meant that there was no basis for political conflict in formal religious difference. Religion was a fundamental part of the common ground on which political conflict about other matters could be conducted. It was because religion united the Kabyles that they could indulge their disagreements over other matters without this threatening to disrupt the political order. That they were members of the same community of religious belief was a point recalled to all and sundry at the meetings of the *jema'a* itself, which invariably began with the *amīn* calling on the *amrabedh* to recite the *Fātiha* (the first sura of the *Qur'ān*), before the *jema'a* got down to business.

Misconceptions of the relationship of religion to politics in Kabylia were central to 'the Kabyle myth' as we have already noted.[1] The nineteenth- and

---

1 Ageron, 1968, *op. cit.*; Lorcin, *op. cit.* Concerning the way in which the Kabyle 'myth' influenced the formation of French policy in Morocco after 1912, see Edmund Burke III, 'The image of the Moroccan state in French ethnological literature; a new look at the origin of Lyautey's Berber policy', in Gellner and Micaud (eds), *op. cit.*, 175–99.

early twentieth-century French purveyors of this myth regularly insisted that the Kabyles were especially conspicuous for their lack of religious fanaticism[2] and that as such they were possibly susceptible to religious conversion[3] and certainly promising material for cultural assimilation into the French national community.[4] In particular, it was suggested that the Kabyles were only superficially – that is, not 'really' – Muslim,[5] and some observers even went so far as to claim that the constitutive principles of the Kabyle 'republics' were close to those proclaimed in France in 1789 and that the Kabyle polity was more or less secular in the French sense.[6] These notions were hallucinations.

Fanaticism is not a belief. It is the particular form – vehement and intolerant – that assertion or defence of a belief may assume in particular contexts, especially when that belief or the community which identifies itself in terms of it is under attack. The Kabyles certainly had it in them to become fanatical, in reaction to the colonial conquest, notably in the great rebellion of 1871. But because their beliefs as Muslims and their way of life were under no pressure from non-Muslims after the recapture of Bejaia from the Spanish in 1555, there was no basis for fanaticism in Kabyle society throughout the rest of the Ottoman period. The absence of fanaticism was evidence not of a merely superficial adherence to the Muslim faith but of the fact that this adherence was general and unchallenged.

The relationship of religion to politics in the Kabyle polity was quite different from that which has obtained in France since the establishment of the secular state. The separation of church and state in modern France entails (in principle) the reduction of religious belief and observance to a private matter and the emancipation of the category of citizen from that of believer. A Frenchman may believe in whatever God he chooses, or in none at all, and belong to whatever religious congregation he likes, or none at all, without this (in principle) affecting his rights as a citizen in the slightest. There was no analogy with this state of affairs in pre-colonial Kabylia.

The Kabyle polity was a Muslim polity. Membership of the political community was exclusively an affair of Muslims. Adherence to the Muslim faith and thus membership of the general Muslim community of the faithful, the *umma*, was a precondition of membership of the particular political community

2   The supposed 'fanaticism' of the Muslims of Algeria in general was a central theme of French discourse in the period of the conquest (Ageron, *op. cit.*, 293–5); to this, numerous French authors opposed the alleged 'lukewarmness' – *tiédeur* – of the Kabyles (in supposed contrast to 'the Arabs') in matters of religion (Ageron, *op. cit.*, 268 *et seq.* and 295, and Lorcin, *op. cit.*, 15, 61). A preoccupation with 'fanaticism' was also a feature of early French observers of Morocco (Burke III, *art. cit.*, 186).
3   Ageron, *op. cit.*, 271; Lorcin, *op. cit.*, 3, 62; Colonna, 1975, *op. cit.*, 112, n.29.
4   Ageron, *op. cit.*, 269–70; Lorcin, *op. cit.*, 2, 23, 39, 44, 47, 73–4, 158, 162.
5   Ageron, *op. cit.*, 268–70; Lorcin, *op. cit.*, 23, 59, 61, 157, 160–1.
6   Ageron, *op. cit.*, 271; Lorcin, *op. cit.*, 3, 73.

of this or that *'arsh* or village. That this condition was not subject to emphatic assertion was entirely due to the fact that it could be taken almost entirely for granted.[7] But this meant that religious belief was the very opposite of a private matter. It was a public matter *par excellence*, as a condition of citizenship.

Because this condition was universally (and one might say effortlessly) fulfilled, it was never at issue. And because it was never at issue, religion itself was never at issue and was correspondingly depoliticised in the sense that political disputes were never about religious belief or affiliation or doctrine or observance. There accordingly developed an important degree of *de facto* separation between religious activity and political activity, but this separation was quite different in nature from that enjoined by French secularism. (If one wants at all costs to find a modern analogy for it, one must look once again to England, which has never been a secular state but one where political enfranchisement was long predicated not merely on adherence to the Protestant faith but on membership of the Church of England and this state of affairs, far from confusing religious and political activity, tended rather to separate them, by facilitating the development of party-political divisions over other matters.)

There is, however, another reason why there was no tendency for religion to be politicised in pre-colonial Kabylia, which is simultaneously another reason for the perceptible lack of fanaticism of the Kabyles. Fanaticism is not only the expression of a defensive reaction to external pressure; it may also develop where a community which identifies itself in terms of religious belief goes onto the offensive. The Islamic conquests of North Africa and Spain may be said to have had their fanatical side. And, within populations wholly or at least overwhelmingly composed of Muslims – indeed, Sunni Muslims of the same, Maliki, rite – Islamic revivalist movements have provided occasions for the development of fanaticism, in that religious revivalism has pitted itself against what it has conceived as decadence or unbelief or heresy, with which no compromise is envisaged.

The *locus classicus* of this phenomenon is, of course, Morocco, where the rise of successive dynasties (the Almoravids, the Almohads, the Sa'adians, etc.) was regularly accompanied by the assertion of a revivalist Islam. It is not for nothing that Gellner's elaboration of the segmentarity theory of Berber political organisation in the Moroccan context should have taken as one of the elements of its point of departure the cyclical theory of Maghribi history developed by Ibn Khaldun. In this schema, which posits a fundamental antithesis between urban life and the life of the tribes (*'umrān hadarī* and *'umrān badawī*), religion – and the religion of Berber populations on the margins of the

---

7   The only non-Muslims to be found in Kabylia in the pre-colonial period would have been Jews, but these were mostly occasional visitors; their presence in Kabylia (unlike the Berber areas of southern Morocco) was almost negligible.

Moroccan state in particular – was regularly politicised, as the 'wolves' at the periphery rose against the central power and, when successful, installed a new dynasty legitimated in terms of a strict Malikism[8] before this dynasty, in turn, succumbed to the fleshpots of city life and provoked its own nemesis in a fresh coalition of hungry tribesmen mobilised in the name of religion.

It follows that the uniformity of religious belief of the Kabyles was not a sufficient condition of their perceptible lack of fanaticism in the later pre-colonial period. It was the internal condition of this state of affairs, but the latter required an external condition as well. The external condition was that the Khaldunian schema did not apply to Algeria.

Ibn Khaldun and the Kabyles

Ibn Khaldun (1332–1406 CE) not only wrote about the inhabitants of what has long since been known as Kabylia, he knew them at first hand. In March 1365 CE he was appointed prime minister by the Hafsid ruler of Bejaia, Abu Abdallah, and retained this post until Abu Abdallah's fall. From the vantage point of high office in Bejaia he was in an excellent position to observe the populations of Greater Kabylia, to whom he referred indiscriminately as 'the Zawawa'. What he wrote about them has often been quoted by French and occasionally other writers on the Kabyles. But the inadequacies in Ibn Khaldun's account have never been commented upon.

> According to the Berber genealogists, the Zawawa are divided into several branches, such as the Medjesta, the Melikech, the Beni Koufi, the Mecheddala, the Beni Zericof, the Beni Gouzit, the Keresfina, the Ouzeldjia, the Moudja, the Zeglaoua and the Beni Merana. Some people say, and perhaps rightly, that the Melikech belong to the Sanhadja race.
>
> In our time, the most outstanding Zawawa tribes are the Beni Idjer, the Beni Menguellat, the Beni Itroun, the Beni Yanni, the Beni Bou Ghardan, the Beni Itouregh, the Beni Bou Youçof, the Beni Chaïb, the Beni Eïci, the Beni Sedca, the Beni Ghobrin and the Beni Guechtola.
>
> The territory of the Zawawa is situated in the province of Bejaia and separates the country of the Ketama from that of the Sanhadja. They live

---

8   The exception to this is the Almohad empire (*c.* 1121–1269), which was inspired by a complex of doctrines, including borrowings from Shi'ism, that expressed *inter alia* a local reaction against Maliki dogmatism. But Malikism enjoyed a revival from the early thirteenth century onwards and none of the politico-religious movements which succeeded the Almohads as the founders of states in Morocco have departed from Malikism as their preferred variant of Sunni legal doctrine.

among precipices formed by mountains so high that the view is dazzled by them, and so thickly wooded that the traveller could not find his way. Thus it is that the Beni Ghobrin inhabit the Ziz, a mountain also called Djebel Ez-Zan on account of the large quantity of cork oaks which cover it, and that the Beni Fraoucen and the Beni Iraten occupy that which is situated between Bejaia and Tedellis. This latter mountain is one of the most difficult of their refuges to approach and one of the easiest to defend. From there, they defy the power of the government and pay tax only when it suits them to do so.

Nowadays, they hold fast to this elevated summit and defy the forces of the Sultan, although, however, they recognise his authority. Their name is even enscribed on the registers of the administration as that of a tribe which submits to the tax (*kharadj*).[9]

It is worth noting that most of the 'tribes' mentioned in the first paragraph quoted above have long since ceased to exist and there is, to my knowledge, no record of where they may have been located. But three of these, the Melikech, the Beni Koufi and the Mecheddala (*sic*), had not only not disappeared when Ibn Khaldun wrote, but have survived to the present day, as have all the others cited in the rest of the above passage.[10] Thus the passage attests both to political

---

9 Ibn Khaldun, *Histoire des Berbères*, trans. Baron de Slane (Paris: Imprimerie Nationale, 4 volumes, 1925 ff.), vol. 1, 256; English translation by the author.

10 The names given by Ibn Khaldun correspond to the following 'aarsh and confederations as listed by Hanoteau and Letourneux:

Melikech	Ath Melikech ('arsh)
Beni Koufi	Ath Koufi ('arsh of the Igouchdal confederation)
Mecheddala	Imecheddalen ('arsh)
Beni Idjer	Ath Ijjeur (confederation)
Beni Menguellat	Ath Menguellat (leading 'arsh of the confederation of the same name)
Beni Itroun	Ath Bethroun (confederation)
Beni Yanni	Ath Yenni ('arsh of the Ath Bethroun confederation)
Beni Bou Ghardan	Ath Bou Gherdane ('arsh of the Igouchdal confederation)
Beni Itouregh	Ath Itsouragh ('arsh)
Beni Bou Youçof	Ath Bou Youcef ('arsh of the Ath Menguellat confederation)
Beni Chaïb	Ath Bou Chaïb ('arsh)
Beni Eïci	Ath Aïssi (confederation)
Beni Sedca	Ath Sedqa (confederation)
Beni Ghobrin	Ath Ghoubri ('arsh)
Beni Guechtola	Igouchdal (confederation)
Beni Fraoucen	Ath Fraoucen ('arsh)
Beni Iraten	Ath Irathen (confederation)

This list thus includes some overlaps (e.g., mentioning a confederation and then one or two of its constituent 'aarsh) but also, more interestingly, omits a number of well-known 'aarsh,

upheavals which are likely to have occurred at some point in the distant past and to the impressive degree of subsequent stability in the political map of Greater Kabylia.

But what is most striking about this passage is that Ibn Khaldun makes no mention of the Zwawa's most remarkable features, their unusually large villages, their elaborate mode of self-government and their highly developed commercial aptitudes and traditions. Yet, had these existed in the fourteenth century CE, they would certainly have been well known in Bejaia where he lived at the time, and he goes on to show detailed knowledge of the Ath Irathen. It is likely, then, that he did not note these remarkable features of Zwawa socio-political organisation because they did not yet exist. The Zwawa existed; they were the populations of the Jurjura and they were known about in Bejaia because they defied its Sultan's power and sometimes refused to pay taxes, unlike the populations of Lower Kabylia; they therefore merited a mention. But they are spoken of in the same way that the Ketama of Lesser Kabylia (specifically, the Babor and Ferjiwa districts) were spoken of, turbulent populations with inaccessible mountain refuges, awkward customers to watch on the periphery of the state, but nothing more.

The Ketama have disappeared. But the Zwawa are still there, because of the remarkable economic and political development which occurred among them after Ibn Khaldun's time, from the arrival of the Turks onwards.

The Ottoman revolution

Modern Algeria is the heir of the Ottoman Regency. In much of the French literature, Algeria is presented as substantially a French creation, with independent Algeria the offspring, if by caesarean section, of *l'Algérie française*. But French power in Algeria was itself the successor by conquest of the Ottoman state and, while disrupting much of the political and cultural life of the country, established a structure of colonial rule which preserved and built on certain fundamental features of the Regency. These included not only aspects of the administrative

---

notably the Ath Khelili, Ath Yahia, Illilten and Illoulen, and two important confederations, the Maatqa and Iflissen Oumellil, as well as all the *'aarsh* and confederations of maritime Kabylia. In referring to all the populations that he mentions as Zwawa, Ibn Khaldun is using an extended definition of the term; as we have seen in Chapter 2, by the nineteenth century the range of reference of the term no longer covered the *'aarsh* of the Ath Aïssi, Ath Ijjeur, Igouchdal and Ath Sedqa confederations, nor those of the southern side of the Jurjura (Ath Melikech and Imecheddalen), nor the Ath Ghoubri of the Azazga district.

legacy of Ottoman rule – notably the country's eastern and western frontiers and its internal division into three main provinces – but also aspects of the Regency's political legacy and its Kabyle policy in particular.

Prior to the establishment of Ottoman power in the central Maghrib, the region we now know as Greater Kabylia had been located for generations on or near the frontier between rival states. With the break-up of the Almohad empire, which had briefly unified the entire Maghrib, what is now Algeria was divided between the Hafsids, who controlled Ifriqiyya (Tunisia) and eastern Algeria, and the Abd el-Wadids (also known as the Ziyanids), who from their capital at Tlemcen dominated western and, intermittently, central Algeria. On the coast, the western outpost of Hafsid power was Bejaia and the frontier between the two states ran south from Bejaia[11] – or, at most, from around Azeffoun,[12] some 50 miles further west along the coast – to the edge of the Sahara and beyond. It thus corresponded, in its northern section, to the subsequent line of demarcation between Greater and Lesser Kabylia.[13] The populations of the Soummam valley and the mountains to the east of this were firmly within the Hafsid territory, but the Igawawen of the Jurjura and the population of the maritime districts of Greater Kabylia were on the edge of this and their political orientation was unstable. Culturally and economically, however, the populations of Greater Kabylia were oriented towards Bejaia as the most important urban centre in their vicinity.

Ottoman rule changed this radically. The rapid rise of Algiers as the capital of the Regency[14] precipitated Bejaia, previously by far the more important city, into irreversible decline[15] and led to a reorientation of the society of Greater Kabylia and the Igawawen above all to Algiers. The growing prosperity of the city in the course of the sixteenth century attracted migrants from Kabylia and encouraged the development of a substantial Kabyle element in the city's population, while Algiers became an important source of goods which Kabylia did not produce and an outlet for Kabyle commodities (notably olive oil). In addition, Ottoman Algiers was the first state in the history of the central Maghrib to have possessed and to have relied heavily upon a substantial navy. As we have already seen, the

11 Salhi, 1979, *op. cit.*, 56 fn. 2.

12 Boulifa, 1925 (*c.* 2000), *op. cit.*, 62–3 (40–1). Forays into Abd el-Wadid territory intermittently extended Hafsid power west of this point into central Algeria and even as far as the Cheliff valley.

13 The widely received notion that the French arbitrarily conceived and imposed their distinction between Greater and Lesser Kabylia *ex nihilo* is entirely mistaken.

14 Between 1500 and 1580 the population of Algiers tripled, from some 20,000 to 61,000; see Andrew C. Hess, *The Forgotten Frontier: A history of the sixteenth-century Ibero-African frontier* (Chicago and London: University of Chicago Press, 1978); p/b 2010, 164.

15 Laurent-Charles Féraud, *Histoire de Bougie* (republication of *Histoire des Villes de la Province de Constantine: Bougie* (Constantine: Imprimerie L. Arnolet, 1869)), with an introduction by Nedjma Abdelfettah Lalmi (Algiers: Éditions Bouchène, 2001), 115.

maintenance of this navy was facilitated by the availability of vital raw materials – timber, resin and pitch – in the wooded districts of Kabylia, especially the Jebel Ez-Zeen and the Akfadou forest.

There accordingly developed a degree of complementarity and reciprocity in the economic sphere between Ottoman Algiers and Greater Kabylia that was quite unlike the asymmetrical economic relationship between *'umrān hadarī* and *'umrān badawī* described by Ibn Khaldun. But, while the degree of their economic dependence upon Kabylia was likely to have been a factor in the calculations of the Ottoman rulers, it was probably secondary to strictly political factors in determining the development of relations between Kabylia and the Regency and the consequent impact of this relationship on the political organisation of the Jurjura.

The stereotype of Berber tribesmen stoutly defying the central power from the remote fastnesses of the Atlas or the desert on the distant periphery of the *bled el-makhzen* is impossible to reconcile with the actual facts of the history as well as the geography of the relationship between Greater Kabylia and Ottoman Algiers. This relationship was an intense and intimate one and it produced identifiable effects on both parties. The population of Greater Kabylia was instrumental in the original establishment of Ottoman power in Algeria and played a significant role in the evolution of the Ottoman regime thereafter. For their part, the Ottomans were instrumental in the consolidation of the sultanate or kingdom of Koukou, which endured for over a century, in the upper Sebaou valley in Greater Kabylia, and also in precipitating its eventual decline. In addition, following the fall of Koukou, Ottoman power intervened directly in the political life of Greater Kabylia and acted to refashion it in several ways.

The net effect of this complex interaction between the population of Greater Kabylia and the Ottoman Regency was the crystallisation of a new socio-political order in the Jurjura predicated upon a novel relationship to the central power. Neither of these developments had been anticipated by Ibn Khaldun and their combination implied the obsolescence of his analysis in respect of Algeria's subsequent history and its dynamics.

The Ottoman Regency and the nature of Kabyle opposition

Ibn Khaldun identified two main ways in which, in the arid zone of the Muslim world, a new state might be established at the expense of a previous one. One way

> is for provincial governors to gain control over remote regions when [the dynasty] loses its influence there. Each one of them founds a new dynasty for his people and a realm to be perpetuated in his family. His children or clients inherit it from him. Gradually, they have a flourishing realm …

This way of forming a new dynasty avoids the possibility of war between the [new rulers] and the ruling dynasty … The latter is affected by senility, and its shadow recedes from the remote regions of the realm and can no longer reach them.

The other way is for some rebel from among the neighbouring nations and tribes to revolt against the dynasty. He either makes propaganda for some particular cause to which he intends to win the people, or he possesses great power and great group feeling among his people. His power is already flourishing among them, and now he aspires with the help of [his people] to gain royal authority. They are convinced that they will obtain it, because they feel that they are superior to the ruling dynasty, which is affected by senility …[16]

The first way fits the advent of Hafsid rule in the eastern Maghrib very well. It also works for the rise of the Abd el-Wadid state at Tlemcen. Both dynasties took over fragments of the Almohad empire, promoting themselves from provincial governors to sovereign rulers in the process, as the shadow of Almohad power receded. But this is not how the Ottoman Regency of Algiers was established and it was not established in the second manner either.

The foundation of the Regency of Algiers was a major event in the protracted conflict between the Ottoman empire and Spain over what Andrew Hess has called 'the Ibero-African frontier'[17] in the sixteenth century. But, if it was the decision of the Sublime Porte to invest in this venture that secured its success, it did not itself instigate this venture, which no more resembled the Ottoman empire's expansion into the Arab lands of the Levant and Egypt than it conformed to Ibn Khaldun's description of the revolutionary foundation of states in an earlier period of North Africa's history.

The founders of the Regency, Aruj and his brother Kheireddine, were neither officers of an empire nor provincial governors on the make nor leaders of rebellions. They were sea-faring opportunist adventurers, freebooters as Hess aptly terms them, whose attitude to and conduct along the Barbary coast resembled nothing so much as that of the more enterprising British buccaneers on the Spanish Main 140 years later. Between 1516 and 1529, Aruj and Kheireddine secured Algiers for the Sublime Porte at Spain's expense much as in the 1660s Sir Henry Morgan secured parts of the West Indies for the British Crown at Spain's expense. But, while their bold initiatives made this possible, they would not have succeeded had it not been for the practical assistance of the Ottoman empire.

---

16 Ibn Khaldun, *The Muqaddimah: An Introduction to History*, translated from the Arabic by Franz Rosenthal, edited and abridged by N.J. Dawood (London: Routledge & Kegan Paul, 1967), 252–3.

17 Hess, *op. cit.*

Initially, Aruj and Kheireddine acted under Hafsid sponsorship. It was the Hafsid sultan of Tunis, Mulay Mohamed Ben El-Hassan, who allowed them to conduct their corsairing ventures out of Gouletta from 1504 and to establish a second base on the island of Jerba in 1510. It was at the Hafsids' request that Aruj and Kheireddine tried in 1512 to recapture Bejaia from the Spaniards who had seized it two and a half years earlier; it was to Tunis that they withdrew when the attempt failed, and, after their capture of Jijel from the Genovese in 1514, it was with a degree of Hafsid assistance that they mounted a second unsuccessful attack on Bejaia the following year. Up to this point, Aruj and Kheireddine had not been acting against the Hafsids, but as their cats-paws against the Spanish. Nor had they been acting on behalf of a substantial element of the indigenous population, let alone as the leaders of a revolt. The only significant support they received inside what we now call Algeria came from Kabylia, where a certain Ahmed ou l-Qadi (or Ben el-Qadi) had raised important forces in support of the second unsuccessful assault on Bejaia and for the subsequent expedition to Algiers in 1516. But, while this support was mustered in the name of Islam and in the spirit of the jihad, it was not directed against Hafsid power, but mobilised in its name against the Spanish. It was therefore not entirely surprising that Ou l-Qadi's forces should reportedly have let Aruj down when he went on from Algiers to seize Tlemcen, where the Spanish based in Oran promptly beseiged him before managing, after he had fled the city, to kill him at Rio Salado in early 1518.

The way the Kabyle forces seemingly abandoned Aruj to his fate was apparently resented by Kheireddine, who had immediately assumed military command of Algiers, and led to a sharp conflict between him and Ou l-Qadi, which Ou l-Qadi initially won. Having successfully repulsed a Spanish assault under Hugo de Moncada on Algiers in early 1519, Kheireddine was forced to abandon Algiers and withdraw to Jijel, where he made his base for the next six years. Boulifa claims that, having defeated de Moncada, Kheireddine mounted a punitive expedition against Ou l-Qadi in Kabylia, but that Kheireddine's forces were defeated by Ou l-Qadi's army, which had been reinforced by contingents sent from Tunis, and which then went on to occupy Algiers in late 1519 or early 1520.[18]

The behaviour of Ou l-Qadi's Kabyles is described as simple perfidy by Kheireddine's Ottoman chronicler[19] and by most subsequent historians. Abun-

---

18 Charles-André Julien, 1970, *op. cit.*, 280–1; Jamil M. Abun-Nasr, *A History of the Maghrib in the Islamic Period* (Cambridge: Cambridge University Press, 1987), 150; Boulifa, *op. cit.*, 83–5.

19 That is, the anonymous author (alleged to be a certain Sinān-Chaouch) of the celebratory work known as *Gazavati-Hayreddin Paşa*, translated into Arabic as *Kitab Ghazawāt Aruj wa Khayr ed-Din* and subsequently translated into French by Jean-Michel Venture de Paradis. (*Ghazā*, plural: *ghazawāt*, means military expedition, campaign, raid; raiding along the frontier with the Christian powers was an honourable tradition in the Ottoman empire.)

Nasr, for example, remarks that 'the treachery of (Kheireddine's) Kabyle warriors enabled the Hafsids to seize Algiers from him'.[20] But the hypothesis of treachery is superfluous and unfair; what had occurred was an entirely understandable recomposition of alliances.

According to Boulifa, Ahmed ou l-Qadi was the Hafsid governor of Bona[21] in 1513 when he was instructed by Mulay Mohamed Ben El-Hassan to raise the populations of his native Kabylia and assist Aruj in delivering Bejaia.[22] Robin records that he was a lesser official, merely a *qādi* (Muslim judge) in the Hafsid administration in Bejaia.[23] In either event, his primary loyalty was to the Hafsids.[24] These had had no interest in Aruj's expansion into western Algeria, especially since the Spanish remained to be dislodged from Bejaia as well as from the *Peñón* of Algiers (the small island just opposite the city that the Spanish had seized and fortified in 1510), and they had every reason to view with alarm the brothers' various moves to build up Algiers into a political capital as the expression of independent ambitions at odds with Hafsid interests. Moreover, Ou l-Qadi had his own reasons to view the trend of his allies' project with concern. He had raised Kabylia to support the liberation of Bejaia, not to conquer Tlemcen, in which neither he nor the Hafsids had a stake, and, while Aruj and Kheireddine were extending their power west of Algiers and leaving Bejaia alone, the Spanish ensconced there were developing an understanding with the rulers of Qal'a n'Ath Abbas in the northern Biban mountains, which threatened to undermine Ou l-Qadi's position in Kabylia. Both Ou l-Qadi and Mulay Mohamed had grounds

---

I have consulted the standard edition of the French text, recently republished in Algiers: Sinān-Chaouch, *Fondation de la Régence d'Alger: Histoire des Frères Barberousse*, translated by Jean-Michel Venture de Paradis, edited by Sander Rang and Ferdinand Denis (Paris: J. Angé, 1837); republished with a preface and additional notes by Abderrahmane Rebahi (Algiers: Grand Alger Livres, 2006). For brevity I shall refer to it as *Ghazawāt*. It explicitly accuses Ou l-Qadi of treachery not in relation to Aruj's death but against Kheireddine later on (*Ghazawāt*, 110–13).

20 Jamil M. Abun-Nasr, *A History of the Maghrib* (Cambridge: Cambridge University Press, 1971, 2nd edition, 1975), 164; Julien, 1970, *op. cit.*, 281, also recycles the questionable 'betrayal' thesis.
21 Bône during the colonial period, now Annaba.
22 Boulifa, *op. cit.*, 96 (62).
23 Joseph Nil Robin, 'Note sur l'organisation militaire et administrative des Turcs dans la Grande Kabylie', *Revue Africaine* (1873), 132–40 and 196–207: 132 (republished in book form as *La Grande Kabylie sous le régime turc* (Algiers: Éditions Bouchène, 1998): 39).
24 The Hafsid interest was itself less than coherent by this point, as conflicts between the rulers of Tunis, Bejaia and Constantine came into play under the pressure of the Spanish incursion. The relevance of these rivalries to our understanding of the Ath l-Qadi is discussed in Chapter 6. The *Ghazawāt* makes no mention of Ou l-Qadi's previous links to Tunis or of his role in aiding Aruj and Kheireddine in their attempts on Bejaia and establishment at Algiers and his presence as a lieutenant of Kheireddine is not explained when belatedly mentioned (*Ghazawāt*, 93).

for considering that it was Aruj and Kheireddine who had departed from the terms of the original alliance,[25] not themselves.

Evidence of this emerging conflict of interests and *arrière-pensées* may already have been suggested by the presence of Turkish janissaries in Aruj's and Kheireddine's forces in 1516,[26] and was certainly provided by Kheireddine's behaviour after withdrawing to Jijel, since he set about expanding his control of the coast as far east as Bona and of the interior as far as Constantine,[27] thereby emphatically trespassing on Hafsid territory. But it appears to have been their ambition to make themselves the rulers of Algiers that had been the Rubicon so far as Aruj and Kheireddine were concerned, since they did not do this in the name of the Hafsid sultan. At some point in 1519–20 Kheireddine resolved to contract a clear political relationship with Istanbul[28] and it was with Ottoman support, including troops – '2,000 men equipped with artillery, followed by 4,000 volunteers having the privileges of janissaries'[29] – that he conducted his subsequent expansion in eastern Algeria before eventually defeating Ou l-Qadi's forces on the edge of Kabylia in 1525[30] and retaking Algiers in the Ottoman sultan's name.

The state power which was established at Algiers in this fashion and consolidated over the succeeding decades by Ottoman military and diplomatic support was unlike anything described by Ibn Khaldun. It was not a dynasty, but a *Regency*. It was not based on a coalition of tribes recruited from the remoter parts of the interior of the country in support of a particular family's ambitions, animated by a powerful 'group feeling' (*'asabiyya*) and cemented and legitimated by a vigorous revivalist Islam which simultaneously delegitimated the 'senile' *ancien régime*. It was essentially a foreign creation, the accomplishment of a political project led by a pair of remarkable outsiders who had built up a private navy and then secured the support of the distant empire of which they were subjects and whose strategic interests their project served, and it was consolidated with the deployment of regular troops furnished by this empire.

25 According to de Grammont, the Hafsid sultan of Tunis had by this stage come to regard Aruj and Kheireddine as 'des vassaux révoltés' ('vassals in revolt'); see Henri-Delmas de Grammont, *Histoire d'Alger sous la Domination Turque 1515–1830* (1887), reissued with an introduction by Lemnouar Merouche (Algiers: Éditions Bouchène, 2002), 49.
26 de Grammont, 1887 (2002), *op. cit.*, 42.
27 Julien, *op. cit.*, 281.
28 *Ghazawāt*, 95–99; Julien, *op. cit.*, 280–1.
29 Julien, *op. cit.*, 281.
30 Boulifa, *op. cit.*, 128–31, 147 (85–7, 99) claims Ou l-Qadi held Algiers till 1527, a claim accepted by Younès Adli, *La Kabylie à l'épreuve des invasions: des Phéniciens à 1900* (Algiers: Zyriab Éditions, 2004), 48, but neither author cites any source for this.

Ottoman rule at Algiers was not dynastic; it was rule in the name of a dynasty, but it was itself military-bureaucratic in character. Kheireddine behaved as a dutiful officer of the empire and founded no dynasty of his own; after his recall to Istanbul in 1533 to command the Ottoman navy, his successors in Algiers were never able to build up a solid and durable family interest in the political power they held only temporarily and the dynamics of intra-dynasty dissension could not come into play. As for the janissaries, their *esprit de corps* was founded on their privileged status as Turks, career soldiers and servants of the Sultan – that is, their position as an imperial and colonialist military elite, not on tribal or kinship ties – and because their strength was regularly renewed by fresh drafts from the central provinces of the empire they evinced no tendency to go 'soft' and succumb to sedentary decadence.

The specific character of the regime as a regency had another implication; far from the rulers having a tendency to rely on ostentatiousness, pomp and luxury as instruments of rule, they had a marked tendency to the opposite. The image left by the Regency was more that of barracks-room severity than an inclination to self-indulgence; its vice was harshness rather than debauchery. This was partly because the absence of the kind of court characteristic of dynastic rule meant that the dynamics of courtly rivalries expressed, *inter alia*, in competitive ostentatiousness and the entertaining of demanding clientèles were also absent or at least muted, but it was also because the revenues from corsairing were often barely enough to pay the Ojaq's wages,[31] let alone fund splendid living. Moreover, the dependence of the Regency on external sources of revenue meant that, whatever degree of comparative luxury it rulers might attain and exhibit, this was, at least until the eighteenth century, not derived for the most part from the exploitation of the indigenous population through taxation and therefore did not tend to excite popular resentment and fuel subversive propaganda, whether couched in Islamic or other terms. And since incorporation into the Ottoman empire facilitated the repulsing of the Spaniards, kept the territory and its populations within *Dār el-Islam* and appeared to guarantee this state of affairs indefinitely, the Regency had no difficulty in securing religious legitimacy and conserving it.

The state power which took shape in the central Maghrib in the course of the sixteenth century was not one which it was a simple matter to challenge. Its inner cohesion was not liable to fray within three generations, nor was it liable to become decadent in anything like that time. The divisions which later developed within the Ottoman regime, while acute, were divisions between the conflicting interests vested in the respective prerogatives of different components of the military-naval-administrative apparatus, not divisions between contending branches of the same ruling family condemned

---

31 The Ojaq was the corps of janissaries, the main element of the land army of the Regency.

to the enduring as well as profound rivalries of zero-sum games played over extended periods. And because they were divisions between members of the Ottoman ruling caste, it was difficult if not impossible for indigenous political forces to get any purchase on them and turn them to account. In consequence, while often resolved brutally, with an impressive number of rulers meeting violent ends, these divisions were clearly not fatal or even very dangerous to the cohesion of the Regency as a whole. At the same time, its ability to rely upon external sources of legitimation and extra-territorial sources of revenue as well as troops tended to insulate it from internal challenges. None of this meant that the Regency was insured against revolt and numerous revolts occurred throughout its history. It meant rather that these revolts were of a particular character and fell short of threatening the overthrow of the state.

The Regency had to face three main kinds of challenge to its control of the central Maghrib. First, there was the challenge of regional power holders derived from or linked to pre-existing dynasties, notably the Ziyanids or Abd el-Wadids at Tlemcen and what was left of Hafsid power in the east; these challenges were essentially centrifugal and separatist in nature. Second, there was the threat from the European powers, above all Spain, whose concerns were geo-political; this challenged not so much the regime in Algiers in itself as its relationship with Istanbul. Finally, there was the challenge of local power holders disposed to resist Ottoman suzerainty or, at least, to seek to negotiate the conditions of their recognition of it, notably the lords of Koukou and Qalʿa in Greater and Lesser Kabylia, but also several Saharan principalities which defied the Turks and resisted their southern expansion (Ouargla, Touggourt). The new Algerine state was really vulnerable only where these various kinds of opposition combined against them, as when the Spanish in Oran successfully intrigued to get their preferred Ziyanid candidate on the throne in Tlemcen, or encouraged either Koukou or Qalʿa to rebel against Algiers.

In the superficially bewildering events of the sixteenth and early seventeenth centuries, virtually all the political actors seem to have taken it for granted that internal opposition to the new Regency could get somewhere only in alliance with foreign powers. At no point do the various internal forces appear to have contemplated, let alone effected, an alliance of their own spanning the country and not one of them appears to have considered for a moment that it might be able to raise the country as a whole to its banner. It is as if the manner in which the Regency was established with powerful external support was taken as the template of purposeful political action by all parties thereafter. But this state of affairs testified above all to the fact that the central Maghrib at this time – in fundamental contrast to Morocco – did not constitute a unified political field in which the power at the centre was the principal stake at the highest level of the political game. It would eventually tend to do so only in so far as the expanding Ottoman power integrated the various regions into a single polity, and this took time. Of the various internal forces with which the Ottomans had to reckon, only the Kabyles can be said to have had a significant interest in the central power, over and above an interest in preserving a regional power by resisting the political pretensions of Algiers in alliance with an outside (Spanish, Moroccan, Tunisian, etc.) force. This interest induced the Ath l-Qadi to intrigue with the Spanish at the time of the Emperor Charles V's ultimately disastrous expedition against Algiers in 1541.[32] But at no point thereafter did the Kabyles seriously seek to overthrow or replace the Ottoman Regency.[33]

Between 1527 and 1574, Kheireddine and his successors acted very energetically to simplify the political problems they faced. In 1529 the *Peñón* was recaptured and the Spanish sent packing; in 1541, Charles V's massive combined land-sea assault on Algiers was decisively repulsed; in 1551 Ottoman power was finally established over most of western Algeria when the last Ziyanid sultan of Tlemcen, having played the Spanish card, was forced to flee to his patrons in Oran and replaced by a Turkish governor, and in 1555 Bejaia was at last retaken by a Turkish force under Salah Ra'is. This left the Spanish ensconced at Oran (which they retained until 1792), but with little purchase on the interior; although they continued intermittently to intrigue with both the Sa'adians in Fès and the rulers of Koukou and Qal'a in Kabylia for some time, the crisis was past. As for the Hafsids, the retaking of Bejaia and the consolidation of Ottoman authority in eastern Algeria with the installation of the first bey at Constantine in 1567–8 was the writing on the wall; in 1574 Eulj Ali and Sinān Pasha conquered Tunisia and put an end to Hafsid power for good.

Thus the particular constitution of the new state and its command of its relations with the other internal forces in the political field it was transforming in the process of establishing itself meant that the Khaldunian schema was ceasing to apply. But there was another reason for this, and this was the particular character of the second major exotic intervention in the political life of the central Maghrib at this time, the maraboutic movement.

---

32 This provoked a punitive expedition into Kabylia by an Ottoman force led by Hassan Agha. (Boulifa, *op. cit.*, 141–5 (95–7); Adli, *op. cit.*, 50); but as Boulifa explains (*ibid.*) the intrigue was a manœuvre by the Ath l-Qadi and is unlikely to have engaged Kabyle opinion.

33 As Pierre Boyer shows, the Ath l-Qadi's intrigues with Spain between 1594 and 1608 were in the nature of a flirtation, designed to impress Kabyle opinion on the one hand and secure better terms from Algiers on the other, rather than a serious bid to overthrow the Regency; see Boyer, 'Espagne et Kouko. Les Négociations de 1598 et 1610', *Revue de l'Occident Musulman et de la Méditerranée*, No. 8 (2nd quarter, 1970), 25–40: 37–8.

The second coming of maraboutism in Kabylia

Between the beginning of the sixteenth century and the end of the seventeenth century, a large number of maraboutic communities and *zawāyā* (religious 'lodges') were established in Kabylia and in Greater Kabylia in particular and this development ultimately modified the political environment in important ways. This social and religious movement was not the first to reach the region, for an earlier wave of maraboutic missionary activity and settlement occurred in the twelfth and thirteenth centuries, and certain maraboutic communities which were later to attain considerable influence appear to date from the fourteenth and fifteenth centuries and thus from the interlude between the two main waves. Nor was the second wave of religious activism the last: beginning in the late eighteenth century, Kabylia witnessed the development of a third wave with the spread of Sufi brotherhoods or religious orders, the *turuq* (sing. *tarīqa*), which assumed spectacular proportions in the nineteenth century in the context of the Algerian reaction to the colonial conquest. While it is important to distinguish the *turuq* from the maraboutic lineages, since they are social phenomena of different kinds, there is no doubt that the two interacted very intensively and that the activity of the *turuq* was itself a stimulus to a further development of Kabyle maraboutism in the nineteenth and early twentieth centuries. But it was the impact of the second wave that was historically decisive for the political development of Kabylia.

In Greater Kabylia the first wave of maraboutic activity and settlement can be linked to three developments: first, the spread of the Almoravid empire,[34] which reached the borders of Kabylia when Ibn Tashfin besieged Algiers in 1082; second, the foundation of the city of Bejaia by the Hammadid dynasty in 1062–3[35] and the subsequent decision by the Hammadid Sultan Al-Mansour, in response to pressure from the invading Hilalians,[36] to move from the dynasty's initial base at Qal'a Beni Hammad in the Hodna mountains and make Bejaia its capital in 1090; third, the capture of Algiers and Bejaia by the Almohads, the successors to the Almoravids, in 1151[37] and the installation of an Almohad governor in Bejaia the following year. The turmoil in the central Maghrib at this time undoubtedly contributed to the peopling of the mountains of Greater Kabylia, in large part by refugees from the disputed lowlands, and the religious dimension of the successive empires undoubtedly

---

34 'Almoravid' is a corruption of the Arabic *al-murābitūn*, singular: *murābit*, whence the French word *marabout*.

35 Or in 1067–8 according to Robert Brunschvig, *La Berbérie orientale sous les Hafsides, des origines à la fin du XVe siècle*, tome 1 (Paris: Adrien Maisonneuve, 1940), 377.

36 Brunschvig, *ibid.*

37 Or 1152 according to Brunschvig, *ibid.*

lay behind the initial wave of maraboutic activity and settlement. There is no real reason to doubt that the first marabouts in Kabylia were an offshoot of the zealous missionary activity associated with the Almoravids and their successors, and that the local significance of the terms (as pronounced in Algerian colloquial Arabic) *mrābit*, plural: *mrābtīn*, and their Berber forms – *amrabedh, imrabdhen* – dates from this era.

In the process of settling the region, however, the first wave of *mrābtīn* mutated; the initial missionary activity gave way to a process of adaptation to the religious life and social structures of the society they were settling in. The *mrābtīn* ended up compromising with the numerous survivals of pre-Islamic belief and practice, allowed the project of converting insufficiently pious tribesmen to Islam to evolve into the less ambitious one of embodying and representing Islam while marrying it with pre-Islamic traditions and providing the latter with a veneer of Islamic legitimacy, and were themselves absorbed into the pre-existing social structure as a new set of lineages, albeit lineages distinguished by their saintly descent and the special status which they derived from this. Thus the maraboutic movement should, as Salhi and others have noted,[38] be understood in terms of two main phases, the active and reforming phase of Islamic proselytising, and the subsequent conservative phase where the *mrābit* changes from missionary – *da'i* – to 'saint' – *sālih* or *walī* – and merges with the characteristic holy man of the pre-Islamic era, the tribal thaumaturge, performing miracles, mediating relations between groups, articulating the common interest, arbitrating disputes and providing moral and spiritual protection for the particular wider community to which he and his descendants are attached.

The second wave of maraboutic activity and settlement in Greater Kabylia dates from the late fifteenth and early sixteenth centuries. The evidence suggests that it was stimulated by the turmoil into which the Maghrib as a whole was precipitated by the *reconquista* in Andalusia, the aggressive incursions of the European powers, especially Portugal and Spain, and the various social and political crises which accompanied the decline of the three dynasties which between them had imposed a degree of order on the Maghrib since the Almohad era – the Merinids in Morocco, the Abd El-Wadids or Ziyanids in western and central Algeria and the Hafsids in eastern Algeria and Tunisia. The locus of origin and centre of gravity of the second wave, as of the first, was Morocco, and it is not for nothing that historians of Morocco speak of the protracted 'Maraboutic crisis' of the period stretching from the fifteenth to the seventeenth century as a defining era in the shaping of the Moroccan state.[39]

---

38 Salhi, 1979, *op. cit.*, 54, 61.

39 Dale Eickelman, *Moroccan Islam: tradition and society in a pilgrimage center* (Austin: University of Texas Press, 1976), chapter 2: 'Morocco, Islam and the Maraboutic Crisis'.

As a movement with ideas to realise or at least promote in its first, ascendant and missionary phase, the second wave of maraboutism appears to have been concerned above all with the need to mobilise against the Christian threat, and the need to assure a degree of order within Muslim communities in the political vacuum that was opening up with the decline of the central power. However, as Salhi has remarked,

> The maraboutic reaction took two forms. Unitary in Morocco, it gave birth to the sherifian (Saadian, Alawite) dynasties. In Algeria it was divided, and the Ottoman intervention substituted itself for it as the leadership of the counter-offensive against the attacks on and occupations of the Algerian coastal towns.[40]

Thus it was that the movement in Morocco tended to have two decisive effects in the political sphere. Ultimately, it engendered new dynasties legitimated in terms of a revivalist Islam which were able to restore the central power (the Sa'adians, 1510–1603; the Alawis, 1668 to present); in the shorter term, the movement threw up a number of 'maraboutic states' (Dila, Ahansal, Boujad) which established a degree of political order in the regions under their control. In Algeria, however, the movement, while inspired by the Moroccan example and a prolongation of it, did neither of these things. Not only was there to be no Algerian equivalent of the new sherifian dynasties, but there was no Algerian Boujad or Dila or Ahansal either. In effect, the intervention of the Ottomans pre-empted and diverted the maraboutic movement and conditioned its political impact by subordinating it to their project.

In trying to assess this impact in Kabylia, we are, it must be admitted, working to some extent in the dark. But such evidence as is available concerning some of the most significant maraboutic groupings and *zawāyā* in Greater Kabylia suggests a number of hypotheses. Table 5.1 lists a number of such groupings and *zawāyā* from both the first and second waves of maraboutic settlement by location, group origin (where known) and approximate date of settlement in Kabylia. It leaves out many maraboutic lineages and settlements in the region and merely includes all those for which information concerning their date of establishment is to be found in the published sources. But, while the evidence it contains must be used with caution, certain points stand out.

It will be seen that settlements explicitly claiming sherifian descent belong exclusively to the second wave. It is only in the context of the second wave

---

40 Salhi, *op. cit.*, 56–7 (my translation).

Table 5.1: Distribution of major saintly lineages and *zawāyā* in Greater Kabylia, by location, date of establishment and point of origin (where known)[41]

'arsh	Twelfth–fourteenth century	Fifteenth–seventeenth century
Ath Abdelmoumen	Igherbien (Seguiet el-Hamra)	
Ath Douala	Sidi Ahmed ou el-Allal (Seguiet el-Hamra)	Akal Aberkane, Ath Bou Yahia (Ath Yahia)
Ath Mahmoud	Sidi Bou Ali, Taguemount Azouz (S el-Hamra)	
Ath Mahmoud		Ath Hamouda, Tizi Hibel (Tunisia)
Ath Mahmoud		Tagragra (Morocco)
Ath Zmenzer		Itnaanen/Ath Anan (Ech-Chlef)
Ath Zmenzer		Sidi Smaïl, Bou Assem (Seguiet el Hamra)
Iferdiwen	Ath Haggoun (Syria)	
Ath Aïssi (*thaqbilth*)	**4**	**5**
Ibethrounen	Ikemouden (Seguiet el-Hamra)	
Ath Khelifa	Tirmitine (Seguiet el-Hamra)	
Maatqa	Sidi Ali ou Moussa (Kabylia)	
Maatqa		Chorfa Thajiweth (Seguiet el-Hamra)
Maatqa		Chorfa El Bachir (Morocco)
Maatqa (*thaqbilth*)	**3**	**2**
Ath Adas	Igherbien (Seguiet el-Hamra)	
Ath Kodhea	Ath el Adeur (Qairwan and Tripoli)	
Ath Kodhea		Timizar n'Sidi Mansour (El Golea)
Ath Jennad (*thaqbilth*)	**2**	**1**

---

41 Sources: Salhi, *op. cit.*, 64 (table), 210, 218–22; Youssef Nacib, *Chants Religieux du Djurdjura* (Paris: Sindbad, 1988), 20, 40, 42–3; Hanoteau and Letourneux, *op. cit.*, vol. II, 83–94; Genevois, 1971, *op. cit.*, 19–20; Mohamed Akli Hadibi, *Wedris, une totale plénitude* (Algiers: Éditions Zyriab, 2005).

Table 5.1 *continued*

Ath Ghoubri		Chorfa m'Bahloul (Sous, Morocco)
Tifrit n'Ath ou Malek		Sidi M'Hand ou Malek (Lesser Kabylia)
El Jeur Alemmas		Sidi Amar ou el Hadj (?)
Illoulen Oumalou		Sidi Abderrahmane (Illoulen Oumalou)
Illoulen Oumalou	Sidi Ahmed Wedris (Bejaia)	
Akfadou & Wad Boubehir district	**1**	**4**
Irjen		Ath Amar, Adeni (Turkey)
Irjen		Ath Ameur, Tamazirt (Turkey)
Ath Akerma		Tasherahit (Mashreq)
Ath Oumalou		Arous (?)
Ath Irathen (*thaqbilth*)	**0**	**4**
Ath Bou Youcef		Ath Sidi Ahmed (Morocco)
Ath Itsouragh		Sidi Mohand ou Malek (?)
Ath Yahia		Sidi Ali ou Taleb (?)
Ath Menguellat		Ath Sidi Saïd (Seguiet el-Hamra)
Ath Yenni		Sidi Ali ou Yahia (Seguiet el-Hamra)
Jurjura district	**0**	**5**
TOTAL	**10**	**21**

that the link is established between maraboutic status and descent from the prophet, and the existence of such sherifian settlements from this era is evidence of the Moroccan connections of the extraneous element of the second wave of maraboutism in Kabylia. But the most striking thing to emerge from this table is the almost total absence of maraboutic establishments dating from the first wave in the eastern and southernmost districts of the region.

The first wave of maraboutic activity affected only the populations of the west-central massif (the *'aarsh* of the Maatqa and Ath Aïssi confederations) and maritime Kabylia (Ath Jennad); it left virtually no trace of its activity in the Akfadou/Wad Boubehir district or in the Jurjura proper. The only saint of note to have established himself here at this time was Sidi Ahmed Wedris, a scholar of Bejaia who took up residence among the Illoulen Oumalou – midway between Akfadou and the eastern Jurjura – at some point in the mid-fourteenth century.[42] As for the second wave, while it reinforced the established tissue of maraboutic establishments in the central and northern districts, it appears to have been canvassing a vacuum in the east and south and to have had a pioneering role among the populations of these districts.[43]

This role enabled the *mrābtīn* of Greater Kabylia eventually to exercise an important influence in the political sphere. But they did not do this as wholly independent actors operating exclusively with political agendas and ambitions of their own. They did so in conjunction with the Ottoman state in Algiers on the one hand and the lay political leaderships of the region on the other, in the context of the decline, fall and aftermath of the regional power known to history as the kingdom of Koukou.

---

42 Mohand Akli Hadibi, *Wedris, une totale plénitude* (Algiers: Éditions Zyriab, 2005), 95–110.

43 Information available for *zawāyā* in Lesser Kabylia supports these findings. Thus the well-known *zāwiya* of Chellata in *'arsh* Illoulen Ousammeur was founded in 1700 by a *mrābit* of Moroccan sherifian descent (Salhi, *op. cit.*, 149).

CHAPTER 6

∼

The Rise and Fall of the Lords of Koukou

The 'kingdom' of Koukou: the enigma

The 'kingdom' of Koukou that was established by the Ath l-Qadi[1] dynasty and lasted for over a century (*c.* 1515–1632 or 1638 CE), dominating the political life of Greater Kabylia throughout this period, is something of an enigma and has presented difficulties for political historians and political anthropologists alike. The problem for the historian is to explain its rise and fall and how the 'kingdom' fits into the long-term political development of Kabylia. The problem for the anthropologist is to reconcile the particular truth about Koukou with general theories concerning the dynamics of Berber political life and the political role of saintly lineages. Comparable difficulties are posed by Koukou's rival in Lesser Kabylia, the 'kingdom' of 'Labez'[2] – that is, the regional power established by the lords of Qal'a n'Ath Abbas in the northern Biban mountains.

One of the central questions thrown up by the way the historical and anthropological issues interconnect is indicated by the judgment of Brett and Fentress that

> the 'king' of Kouko [*sic*] and the Banū 'Abbās … will have emerged out of their tribal society in the manner described by Masqueray in the nineteenth century, by an accumulation of riches, respect and success in warfare, to the point at which they possessed their own armies and fortresses, and ruled over their feuding peoples with a mixture of patronage, diplomacy and force.[3]

This is not at all a controversial view. But were these kingdoms political constructions that 'emerged out of their tribal society'? It has been natural for scholars to see things in this light for as long as the political history of pre-

---

1   In Arabic: Ben el-Qadi. Variants of the Arabic form of the name include Belqadi, Belkadi or Belkadhi.
2   As Spanish documents of the time refer to it; also written as 'Labès', the word is a deformation of 'El-Abbas', the name of the founder of the dynasty that ruled at Qal'a n'Ath Abbas.
3   Brett and Fentress, *op. cit.*, 158.

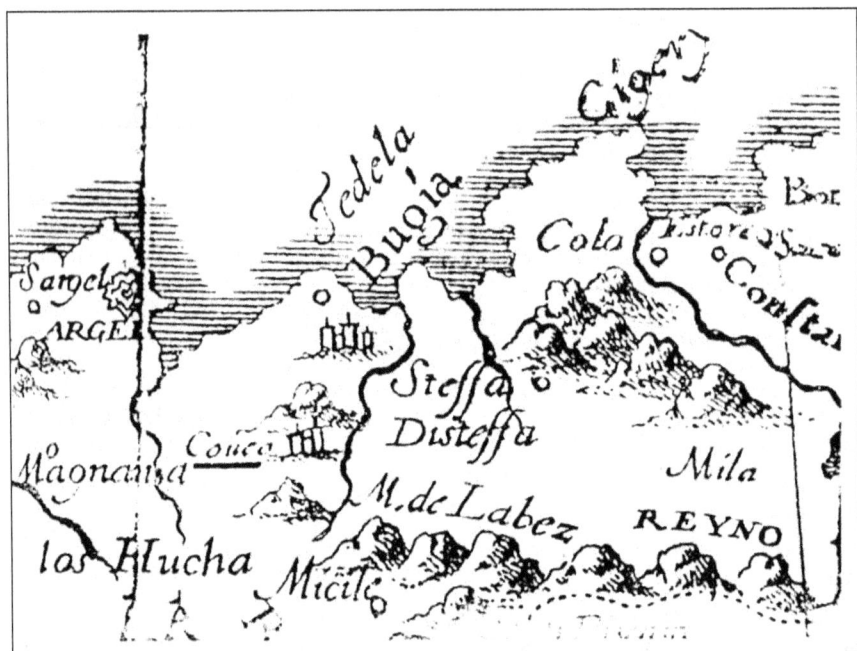

Map 6.1: Fragment of an eighteenth-
century Spanish map of north-eastern
Algeria.[4]

colonial Kabylia has been a largely unmapped terrain and the role of forces
external to the region generally discounted for the period up to 1830. When we
begin to take account of these forces, however, it becomes possible to see things
very differently. For, although its capital was an Igawawen village, the 'kingdom'
of Koukou was by no means an emanation of the society of the central Jurjura,
but an exotic graft or imposition upon that society. And a recent study shows
in detail that, contrary to previously received views, the Ath Abbas did not
exist prior to the foundation of the Qal'a shortly after the fall of Bejaia in
1509 and the founders of Qal'a were refugee Hafsid princes from Bejaia who
constituted an entirely new *'arsh* around themselves.[5] The relation of cause

---

4   This shows very approximately the locations of Algiers ('Argel'), Koukou ('Couco'), Bejaia
     ('Bugia') and Qal'a n'Ath Abbas ('Labez'). Source: H. Genevois, *Légende des Rois de Koukou*
     (Fort National: Le Fichier Périodique, 1974).

and effect was thus, in both cases, the reverse of what Brett and Fentress (and others) have suggested.

At least six specific questions require clarification: the date of the foundation of the 'kingdom of Koukou', the basis of the Ath l-Qadi's power, the logic of their decision to make Koukou their capital, their relations with the Ottoman Regency, their relationship to the Igawawen of the Jurjura and their relationship to the maraboutic movement. These questions both subsume other, more intricate questions (especially the nature of the family's Hafsid connections) and are themselves intimately linked, indeed entangled with one another.

The question of the character and genesis of the 'kingdom' of Koukou is naturally connected to the question of the date of its foundation. Certain authors have suggested that it already existed before the fall of Bejaia and the advent of the Barbarossa brothers,[6] but they are unable to cite any evidence for this. And, given the evidence that the Ath l-Qadi were trusted servants of the Hafsid rulers of Tunis and Bejaia, it is impossible to explain how the latter should have tolerated the constitution by members of this family of an independent 'kingdom' within the territory they themselves claimed to rule. It is equally difficult to explain why this 'kingdom', if founded before the fall of Bejaia in 1509,[7] should have been based at Koukou in the Ath Yahia's territory in the light of the evidence, which is generally accepted, that the Ath l-Qadi's own

---

5   Youssef Benoudjit, *La Kalaa des Beni Abbès au XVIe Siècle* (Algiers: Éditions Dahlab, 1997), 13, 15, 18, 26, 75–94. Benoudjit dates the fall of Bejaia to 1510, however; see note 7. That the lords of Qal'a n'Ath Abbas descended from the Hafsid princes of Bejaia had already been recognised by Mouloud Gaïd, previously an influential purveyor of the earlier mistaken view, in his book *Les Beni Yala* (Algiers: Office des Publications Universitaires, 1990), 24. (The Beni or Ath – or Ith – Yala of the Guergour district are the immediate neighbours of the Ath Abbas on the latter's eastern side.)

6   Robin (1873, *op. cit.*, 132 (1998 *op. cit.*, 39)) suggests that Ath l-Qadi already dominated Greater Kabylia from Koukou in 1512; this is probably a simple confusion of the fact that Ahmed ou l-Qadi demonstrably had some standing in the region by that time and the fact that, soon afterwards, he established a capital there. In his introduction to Robin (1998, *op. cit.*, 33–4), however, Alain Mahé appears to suggest that the family held power in the Sebaou valley from their stronghold of Koukou from as early as the end of the fourteenth century CE. If this is what he means to say, he adduces no evidence for this hypothesis. Abun-Nasr (1987, *op. cit.*, 163) recycles Robin's erroneous view.

7   Many historians, including Julien (1970, *op. cit.*, 276) and Hess (*op. cit.*, 42) give 1510 as the date of the Spanish capture of Bejaia but the matter is unclear. In 1862 a neglected work by a French historian insisted that 1509 was the correct date (Louis Piesse, *Itinéraire historique et descriptive de l'Algérie, comprenant le Tell et le Sahara* (Paris: Hachette, 1862, 2nd edition 1881), 9 and 403). Six years later, a copy of a remarkable document, *Unwān el-Akhbār fimā marra ala Bijāya* ('Exposé of the events which took place at Bejaia'), by an obscure Algerian author, Abu Ali Ibrahim El-Merini, having been obtained from 'a taleb of the Beni Yala', L. Charles Féraud published this in French translation ('Conquête de Bougie par les Espagnols d'après un manuscrit arabe', *Revue Africaine* (1868), 245–56 and 337–49).

roots were not in this 'arsh. Special circumstances are required to explain this remarkable fact and these circumstances obtained only after the fall of Bejaia, as we shall see.

The Ath l-Qadi were successively allies, lieutenants, rivals and then alternately vassals and adversaries of the Ottoman rulers of Algiers. This complexity in the trajectory of their political relations with the Ottomans is, if anything, exceeded by the complexity of the connections which formed the background to and premises of their rise to political prominence. The Ath l-Qadi were *imrabdhen* – that is, a saintly lineage. They were connected with the Ath Ghoubri, an 'arsh of the Upper Sebaou/Boubehir valley on the western edge of the Akfadou district, but also, subsequently, with an Igawawen 'arsh, the Ath Yahia, to which the village of Koukou belongs. Last but certainly not least, they had a crucial connection to the Hafsids, who ruled not only Ifriqiya (i.e. modern-day Tunisia) from their capital, Tunis, but also eastern Algeria from regional seats of government in Bejaia, Bona (Annaba) and Constantine.

The Ath l-Qadi's maraboutic lineage is generally acknowledged. Boulifa takes it for granted and claims that the founder of the dynasty 'made use of his maraboutic prestige' in building his political power,[8] but adduces no evidence of this. Féraud attributes a Moroccan and sherifian (indeed, Idrissi) ancestry to the founder of the dynasty, Ahmed ou l-Qadi;[9] Robin attributes a Moroccan, Fassi, ancestry but not an explicitly sherifian one.[10] A local tradition among the Ath Ghoubri claims the family's founding ancestor came from the Seguiet el-Hamra, a point of origin conventionally attributed to or claimed by maraboutic lineages in Kabylia.[11]

While neither Féraud nor Robin mention the connection to the Ath Ghoubri, Boulifa claims that the Ath l-Qadi originated in the village of Aourir n'Ath Ghoubri and were descended from one Abu Abbas El-Ghoubrini, an eminent *qâdi* at Bejaia in the late thirteenth century who was the victim of court intrigues and was put to death in 1304–5 CE (or possibly later, in 1314 CE)

This supports Piesse's view, since El-Merini dates the fall of Bejaia with precision as 'the 5th day of the month of Safar of the year 915[AH]' corresponding to 25 May 1509. This seems too early, however, given that the Spanish took Oran only eight days beforehand. However, I know of no convincing evidence for the date of 1510 and a Latin inscription on a wall in the Casbah of Bejaia affirms that the city was taken in 1509; see 'Note Critique IV' by Rang and Denis to their edition of the French translation of the *Ghazawât* (*op. cit.*, 283–8: 287), in which they try to explain this inscription away.

8 Boulifa, *op. cit.*, 113 (74).

9 Laurent-Charles Féraud, 'Histoire des Villes de la Province de Constantine: Gigell', *Recueil des Notices et Mémoires de la Société Archéologique de la Province de Constantine*, XIV (1870), 121, n. 1, quoted in Genevois, 1974, *op. cit.*, 3.

10 Robin, 1873, *op. cit.*, 132 and fn 1 (1998, *op. cit.*, 39).

11 Genevois, 1974, *op. cit.*, 31.

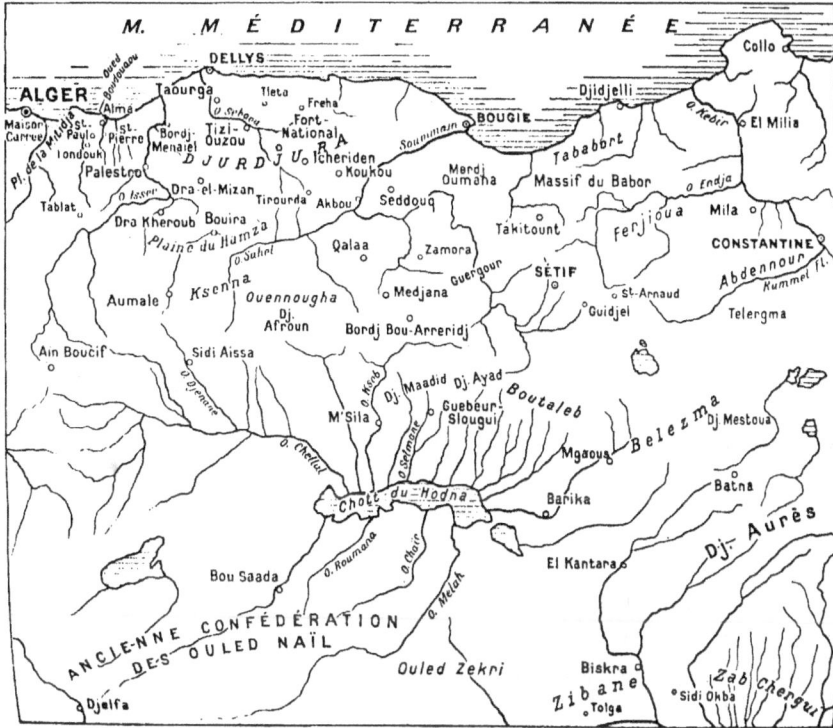

Map 6.2: Greater and Lesser Kabylia
and their hinterlands.[12]

on the orders of the Hafsid sultan,[13] an episode related by Ibn Khaldun.[14] The *nisba* (sobriquet denoting origin) 'El-Ghoubrini' indicated the *qādī*'s roots in the Ath Ghoubri. Boulifa's account is accepted by Boyer and the family's origins in the Ath Ghoubri have also been affirmed by Salem Chaker and his

12 Although from the French period, this map shows the rough positions of Koukou and Qal'a n'Ath Abbas; (source: Mohamed Seghir Feredj, *Histoire de Tizi Ouzou des origines à 1954* (Algiers: ENAP, 1990), Appendix 13, 257).

13 Boulifa, *op. cit.*, 117–18 (76–8). A well documented account of Abu Abbas El-Ghoubrini, including a discussion of his book *'unwān al-Dirāya fī man 'urifa min al-'ulamā' fī mi'āt al-sābi'a fī Bijāya* ('Sign of Knowledge of the Scholars of the Seventh Century [sc. of the Hegira] at Bejaia') is provided by Dj. Aissani in Salem Chaker (ed.), *Hommes et Femmes de la Kabylie*, tome 1 (Paris: INALCO and Aix-en-Provence: Édisud, 2001), 132–5; this places the *qādī*'s execution in 1314 CE instead of Ibn Khaldun's earlier date.

14 Boulifa, *ibid.*, citing Ibn Khaldun, *Histoire des Berbères*, trans. de Slane, vol. II, 418–19.

colleagues.[15] Stronger evidence of this connection exists in extant shrines to two members of the dynasty located near the Ath Ghoubri villages of Achallam (the source of the tradition cited above) and Tabbourt,[16] both of which are a short walk from Aourir.

As for the Hafsid connection, this is not only stressed by Boulifa but affirmed by Robin as well and corroborated in part by both Julien and Abun-Nasr; it is also affirmed by Boyer, at least mentioned by Mouloud Gaïd and Mahfoud Kaddache and emphasised by Younès Adli.[17]

What are we to make of this complexity? Several authors have not hesitated to stress one of these connections while ignoring the others. Mercier, for example, explains the rise of Ahmed ou l-Qadi as that of 'a major religious chief' ('un grand chef religieux').[18] Abun-Nasr recycles this opinion with his reference to the 'Banu al-Qadi' as being 'among the most prominent maraboutic leaders in eastern Algeria at the time of the Ottoman occupation'.[19] More recently, Chaker *et al.* have claimed that the dynasty was 'religious in origin, for founded around a *zāwiya*'.[20] These opinions contradict the earlier assessment of Carette, one of the first French ethnologists to undertake a serious study of Kabylia, who observed of both the Ath Abbas and Koukou that 'authority was hereditary, but nothing leads us to believe that it rested on a religious basis'.[21] This assessment has been ignored but never refuted.

Thus the problem with Mercier's view and that of Chaker *et al.* is that there is no evidence that Ahmed ou l-Qadi was a religious leader before he emerged as a key ally of the Barbarossa brothers in their military campaign against the Spanish in Bejaia and no *zāwiya* associated with the lineage has been identified

---

15 Boyer, 1970, *art. cit.*, 26; Salem Chaker (ed.), *op. cit.*, 74–90.

16 H. Genevois, 1974 *op. cit.*, 62. Achallam is also the native village of the poet Ahmed Hadj-Saïd, more widely known as Sheikh Hand Ouchallam, who belonged to a maraboutic lineage which claimed descent from the Ath l-Qadi; see the biographical notice in Chaker (ed.), 2001 *op. cit.*, 196–9.

17 Julien, *op. cit.*, 281; Abun-Nasr 1987 *op. cit.*, 150. Boyer, *ibid.*; Mouloud Gaïd, *Les Berbers dans l'Histoire*, tome III: *Lutte contre le colonialisme* (Algiers, Éditions Mimouni, n.d. but *c.* 1990), 9; Mahfoud Kaddache, *L'Algérie Durant la Période Ottomane* (Algiers: Office des Publications Universitaires, 1998), 5, 11; Adli, 2004, *op. cit.*, 45ff.

18 Ernest Mercier, *Histoire de l'Afrique Septentrionale depuis les temps les plus reculés jusqu'à la conquête française* (Paris: E. Leroux, 3 tomes, 1881–91); t. II (1888), 427.

19 Abun-Nasr, 1987, *op. cit.*, 163. Earlier Abun-Nasr hedges his bets by speaking of 'the religio-tribal leader of Kuku' (*op. cit.*, 150).

20 Chaker (ed.), *op. cit.*, 74. This appears simply to recycle Gaïd's claim that, at the time of the Spanish capture of Bejaia, 'La Kabylie du Djurdjura était sous la dépendance ou l'influence de la zaouia des Belkadi de Koukou (village des Aït Yahia)' (Gaïd, 1974, *op. cit.*, 23); this claim is undocumented and unreliable.

21 Carette, 1848, *op. cit.*, quoted by Masqueray, 1983 (1886), *op. cit.*, 139.

or located.[22] In both Mercier's original version and Chaker's more recent one, the thesis of a religious origin is an unwarranted inference from the single fact that the family was of maraboutic descent. But this descent by no means signified that Ahmed ou l-Qadi owed his political influence to his own prior performance of a religious role. The absence of any known *zāwiya* associated with the family suggests that the Ath l-Qadi were a minor lineage as Kabyle *imrabdhen* go. The fact that they were known as 'Ath *l-Qādi*' and not as 'Ath *Sidi X*' – that the lineage identified itself by the claimed descent from a Muslim judge (whether this was actually Abu Abbas El-Ghoubrini or not) rather than from a founding saint reputed for his *baraka* and religious role and dignified with the title of *Sīdī* ('my lord') – is also significant. Either the *qādi* in question was not himself of maraboutic birth or, if he was, his saintly ancestor was not important enough for his descendants to commemorate him in their lineage name. Thus all the evidence points to the conclusion that the Ath l-Qadi's standing and religious influence were parochial and modest at best and quite insufficient to explain their subsequent rise to political power.

As for their links with the Ath Ghoubri and the Ath Yahia, scarcely any author has sought to explain the family's political success as a function of these connections, although a passing remark by Boulifa, referring to Ahmed ou l-Qadi as 'the chief of the Ath Ghoubri' ('l'amghar des Aït Ghoubri'),[23] may have implied such a thesis, in that Boulifa's claim might be taken to suggest that Ou l-Qadi's position as chief of his *'arsh* was the springboard for his rise to regional power. But there is no reason to believe that Ahmed ou l-Qadi was ever the chief of the Ath Ghoubri. While reliance on evidence from a later period is open to the charge of anachronistic reasoning, it is striking that all the evidence from the mid-nineteenth century onwards is that most Kabyle *'aarsh* did not have chiefs as such, simply the man – *amīn el-umanā'* (the *amīn* of the *amīns*) – who presided the occasional meetings of the *jema'a* of the *'arsh* and who was usually of a lay, non-saintly, family. Those *'aarsh* which did exhibit strong (usually dynastic) leadership, such as the Iflissen Oumellil and Beni Thour in western Kabylia, the Iamrawien of the middle Sebaou valley and the Ath Abbas in the Biban, were the exception; and such chiefly families were usually *ajwād*, not *imrabdhen* or *shurafā'* – that is, of the lay, warrior, rather than religious, aristocracy.

Even if we discount such evidence, however, the hypothesis that Ahmed ou l-Qadi was the chief of the Ath Ghoubri is difficult to reconcile with his subsequent move to Koukou. Above all, it leaves entirely unexplained his earliest

---

22 There are no remains or memory of an Ath l-Qadi *zāwiya* at Koukou, merely the traces of the foundations of a tomb, *taqorrabt bou el-qadi*, believed to be of a member of the family. The only extant shrine at Koukou commemorates Sidi Ali ou Taleb, a saint of a maraboutic lineage unrelated to the Ath l-Qadi; see Genevois, 1974, *op. cit.*, 24–6, 61.

23 Boulifa, *op. cit.*, 113 (74); *amghar* is the Berber equivalent of *sheikh*.

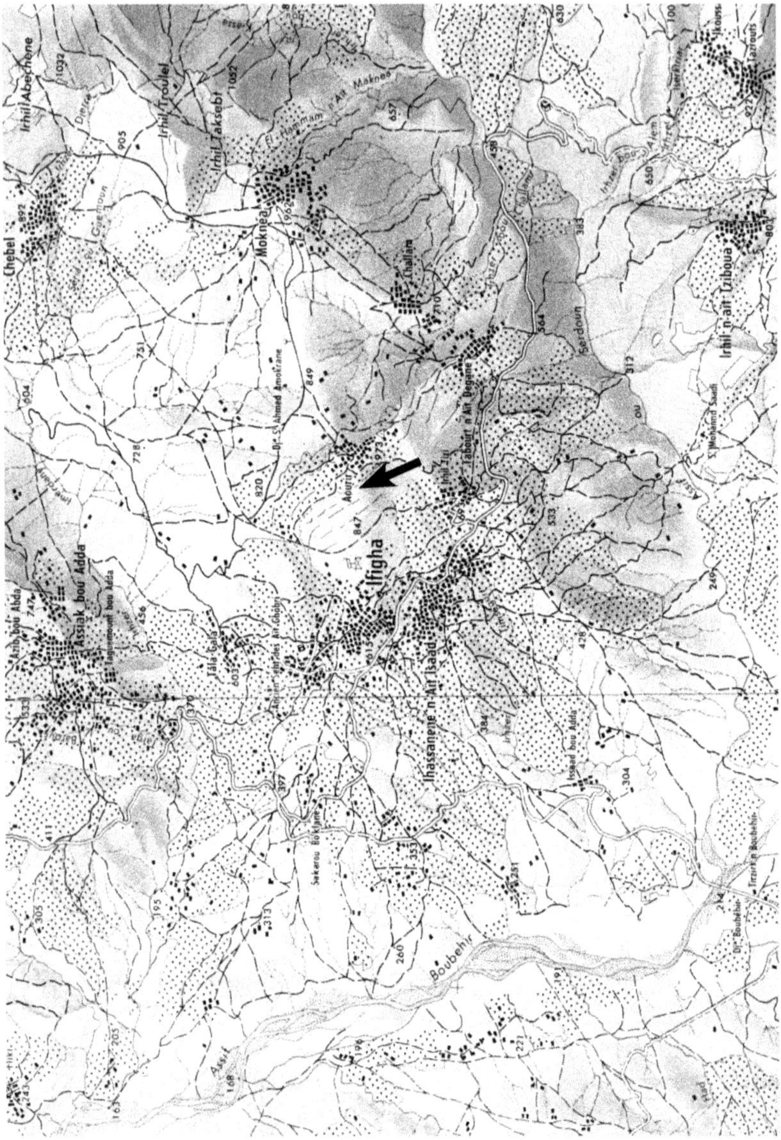

Map 6.3: The Asif (Wad) Boubehir
and the southern Ath Ghoubri, with
Aourir, indicated by an arrow, near the
centre and Achallam and Tabbourt
(both names slightly misspelled) to the
south-east of Aourir.[24]

---

24 This is a small section of the French 1/50,000 scale map (updated 1961) of Fort National and
    district, covering most of the central and eastern parts of Greater Kabylia.

exploits in raising the populations of Lesser Kabylia in support of the Barbarossa brothers' campaign to retake Bejaia, since there is no reason to believe that the chief of an *'arsh* in Greater Kabylia would have had any influence with those of the Babor and the Ferjiwa some 100 km to the east. But Ou l-Qadi had.

In his discussion of *'Les grands chefs en Kabylie'*,[25] Masqueray sketched a general theory of how a lay political leader emerges in Kabyle society. He first acquires influence in the *jema'a* of his village, then becomes the head of his *saff* at village level, then *saff* leader at the level of the *'arsh* and subsequently becomes the indispensable architect of the political unity of the *thaqbilth* in time of war. None of this applied to Ahmed ou l-Qadi and Masqueray did not pretend that it did, citing him rather as a possible instance of the second route to political leadership, that of the influential marabout, although he was, with good reason, far from categorical about this. Nor was the Ou l-Qadi case at all analogous to those of the leaders who rose to regional power amongst the Berbers of Morocco in the second half of the nineteenth century and the first three decades of the twentieth. In Robert Montagne's classic exposition of the dynamics of these cases, the leader in question invariably made sure of his own clan and tribal power base first (eliminating rivals and suppressing *liff* divisions within it) before going on to expand his power in ever widening (but increasingly fragile) concentric circles. The *grands caïds* of the western High Atlas – El-Gontafi, El-Mtuggi and El-Glawi – and the Emir Abdelkrim in the Rif all seized power in their own tribes first before subordinating neighbouring tribes to their rule. The case of Koukou is thus not an illustration of Montagne's model, but an exception to it.[26] Nor is it an instance of the ideal-typical maraboutic route to political power as Masqueray described this,[27] for the evidence of a pre-existing saintly influence in this case is lacking as we have seen.

Given the weakness of both the maraboutic aspect and the tribal aspect as explanatory factors and the corresponding difficulty of accepting the view of Brett and Fentress and others concerning the 'emergence' of Koukou, how, then, are we to understand it? I wish to put forward an explanation which takes account of all the evidence but pieces it together in a new way and recognises first and foremost that the rise to power of the Ath l-Qadi was intimately dependent on their Hafsid connections on the one hand and the context of the jihad against the Spanish on the other hand.

---

25 The penultimate section of his chapter on Kabylia in Masqueray 1983 (1886), *op. cit.*, 116–36.

26 Montagne acknowledged that his model did not apply everywhere, suggesting that in Kabylia the *saff* system was 'an obstacle to the unification of the canton (or arsh) under the control of a single leader' (Robert Montagne, *The Berbers: their social and political organization*, translated and with an introduction by David Seddon (London: Frank Cass, 1973), 62).

27 Masqueray, *op. cit.*, 121–36.

The Ath l-Qadi and the foundation of Koukou

The political fortunes of the Ath l-Qadi were built initially on the Hafsid connection. Their relations with the Ottomans varied dramatically but their relations with the Hafsids were relatively constant, if tending to increasing complexity over time. It was this connection which gave Ahmed ou l-Qadi the authority to mobilise popular enthusiasm in north-eastern Algeria and Kabylia for the attempt by Aruj and Kheireddine to retake Bejaia from the infidel. It was his connection to the Hafsid interest which enabled him to weather the consequences of letting down Aruj in western Algeria and falling out with Kheireddine, for it was this connection which furnished the troops with which he defeated Kheireddine and seized power in Algiers in 1520. Finally, it was the destruction of Hafsid power with the Ottomans' capture of Tunis in 1574 that spelled eventual doom for the dynasty and it was to Tunis that the widow of Ameur ou l-Qadi, the last but one ruler of Koukou, fled when her husband was assassinated in 1618.

The position of the Hafsids in eastern Algeria in the first decade of the sixteenth century CE was not a coherent one. The Hafsid sultan of Bejaia, Abu El-Abbas Abdelaziz, was at odds with the Hafsid ruler of Constantine, his own brother Abu Bakr, who tried repeatedly to overthrow him,[28] and both were inclined to act independently of their father, Mulay Mohamed Ben El-Hassan in Tunis.[29] In 1508, Abdelaziz finally lost patience with his brother, marched on Constantine and captured it, forcing Abu Bakr to flee south to the Belezma mountains, from where he would plot his come-back. These divisions would influence the calculations and actions of Aruj and Kheireddine on the one hand and the Ath l-Qadi on the other.

When Bejaia was taken by the Spanish in 1509, two of Abdelaziz's sons were killed in the attempt to defend the city,[30] but his two other sons, the Emirs (Princes) Abderrahmane and El-Abbas, escaped and took refuge in the hinterland of Bejaia (i.e. the Berberophone districts of Lesser Kabylia), established their base in the northern Biban mountains and negotiated a *modus vivendi* with the Spanish, embodied in a treaty in late 1511 or early 1512, whereby the Spanish, whose ambitions were confined to the littoral, recognised the princes' authority over the interior.[31] The stronghold they founded, in a virtually impregnable position, was initially known as the Qal'a (citadel) of the Wennougha,[32] taking its name from the district in question; it subsequently became known as Qal'a

---

28 Laurent-Charles Féraud, *Histoire de Bougie*, 83–4; Benoudjit, *op. cit.*, 38, 43–7.

29 Benoudjit, *op. cit.*, 37–8.

30 Féraud, *Histoire de Bougie*, 95.

31 For the Spanish capture of Bejaia and its political aftermath, I follow here the account provided by Benoudjit, in *op. cit.*, especially chapters 5–11.

32 Féraud, *Histoire de Bougie*, 100–1; Benoudjit, *op. cit.*, 67–9. In fact, Qal'a is situated on at best the extreme north-eastern edge of the Wennougha district properly so-called.

n'Ath Abbas, taking this name from the second son, El-Abbas, since it was his descendants who succeeded him as rulers there.

In the meantime, seeing a fresh chance to assert himself against both his brother and his nephews, Abu Bakr reproached Abdelaziz for failing to save Bejaia and set himself up as the leader of a jihad to take the city.[33] When Abdelaziz tried to stop him, their respective forces clashed, Abdelaziz was captured and put to death[34] and Abu Bakr retook possession of Constantine. Thereafter his designs on Bejaia led him to confront the dead sultan's heirs, Abderrahmane and El-Abbas,[35] whom he reproached for treating with the enemy. In 1512, however, having failed to make headway in his campaign to retake Bejaia by mounting expeditions over land, Abu Bakr engaged Aruj and Kheireddine, then based in Jerba, to lead an expedition against Bejaia by sea.[36] Thus the Barbarossa brothers' initial foray into the central Maghrib was not at the behest of the Hafsid rulers of either Tunis or Bejaia, but of the Hafsid ruler of Constantine, motivated by a personal ambition.

Shortly after their recruitment by Abou Bakr in 1512, the brothers mounted their first attack on Bejaia with a squadron of twelve ships,[37] supported by Abu Bakr's forces on land, but the attack was easily repulsed and Aruj (who lost an arm in the battle) and Kheireddine withdrew to Tunis. The following year, a Genovese force led by Andrea Doria captured Jijel and installed a garrison there but, in the spring of 1514, Aruj and Kheireddine recaptured Jijel without difficulty.[38] It was approximately at this point that Ahmed ou l-Qadi entered the picture.

The Ath l-Qadi were an established family at Bejaia. The significance of their maraboutic status was not that they exercised any notable religious leadership but simply that, unlike lay Kabyles of that epoch, they were literate and educated to a degree that qualified them for state employment as judges and civil servants. They had long served the Hafsids in various capacities and prospered accordingly. At the time of the Spanish capture of Bejaia, Bona was governed by Ahmed ou l-Qadi,[39] who had been appointed to this position by

---

33 Féraud, *ibid.*; Benoudjit, *op. cit.*, 97, 102, 112–13.

34 Féraud, *op. cit.*, 100; See also El-Merini, in Féraud's translation, *Revue Africaine* (1868), 338. According to these authors, the engagement took place at 'Takerkat', somewhere between Bejaia and Setif; like Féraud, I have not found a more precise indication of this location.

35 Benoudjit, *op. cit.*, 117–18, 123–4,

36 El-Merini, in Féraud, 1868, *art. cit.* 348; Mercier, *op. cit.*, t. II, 247; Féraud, *Histoire de Bougie*, 102–3.

37 El-Merini, in Féraud, 1868, *art. cit.*, 348. The dating of the brothers' two assaults on Bejaia is controversial. Some authors give 1512 for the first attempt (Boulifa, *op. cit.*, 59, Gaïd, 1974, *op. cit.*, 34; Julien, *op. cit.*, 278) and August 1514 for the second (de Haedo, *Histoire*, 28; Boulifa, 64; Gaïd, 1974, *op. cit.*, 36); Hess gives 'the summer of 1514' for the first (*op. cit.*, 61) and August 1515 for the second (*op. cit.*, 62–3). El-Merini also places the second attack (as 'three years later') in 1515 (in Féraud, *art. cit.*, 348).

38 Gaïd, *op. cit.*, 36.

39 Boulifa, *op. cit.*, 96 (61–2).

Mulay Mohamed Ben El-Hassan, and rewarded for his service with the grant of estates situated between Bona and El-Qalʻa.[40] When, in 1511, the Spanish entered into negotiations with the Emirs Abderrahmane and El-Abbas, a certain ʻAbu Mohamed Abdallah Ben Ahmed Ben el-Qadi El-Ghoubriniʼ acted as the go-between.[41] Benoudjit speculates that this person was one and the same as Ahmed ou l-Qadi, the governor of Bona, but the full name given suggests that he was Ahmedʼs son.[42] It is, besides, unlikely that the governor of Bona would have agreed to play this modest go-between role, but entirely probable that a junior member of the same respected family should have been asked to do so and, furthermore, that he did so with the approval of the governor of Bona (whether this was his father or not), since this meant that the Ath l-Qadi family was staying abreast of the overall situation and placing several irons in the fire.

It is not clear whether Ahmed ou l-Qadi entered into contact with Aruj and Kheireddine before they recaptured Jijel or only after this. Some accounts suggest the brothers retook Jijel unaided as well as on their own initiative.[43] Others claim that not only were they responding to appeals from the local population but that they were materially assisted by a force under Ou l-Qadiʼs command.[44] Boulifa suggests, plausibly, that, in contacting them, Ou l-Qadi was acting on the instructions of Mulay Mohamed Ben El-Hassan in Tunis.[45] The latter had proved unable to arbitrate the quarrel between his two sons, Abdelaziz in Bejaia and Abu Bakr in Constantine. But, following Abdelazizʼs death, he had clearly acted against Abu Bakr in sending troops into eastern Algeria to protect Bona on the coast and seize Tebessa in the south-east[46] and he appears thereafter to have consistently sided with his grandsons, Abderrahmane and El-Abbas, the legitimate heirs to the sultanate in Bejaia, in the conflict which pitted them against his unruly son, their uncle Abu Bakr. In enlisting Aruj and Kheireddine for his own campaign to retake Bejaia, Abu Bakr had at least temporarily suborned them from their previous allegiance to his father in Tunis. Although

40 Louis-Adrien Berbrugger, *Les époques militaires de la Grande Kabylie* (Algiers: Bastide, 1857), 58; Eugène Vaysettes, *Histoire de Constantine sous la domination turque de 1517 à 1837* (Paris: Challamel, 1869), republished with an introduction by Ouarda Siari-Tengour (Éditions Bouchène, 2002) (all references to this edition): 41–2. El-Qalʻa here refers to the coastal town near the Tunisian border, known in the colonial period as La Calle and since 1962 as El-Kala and not to be confused with Qalʻa nʼAth Abbas. Vaysettes (*op. cit.*, 42) recycles the statement in the *Ghazawāt* (115–16) that the estates in question were already in the familyʼs possession before Ahmed ou l-Qadi acquired them, by inheritance from his father, which suggests that he may not have been the first Ou l-Qadi to serve in the Hafsid administration at Bona.
41 El-Merini, *op. cit.*, 342.
42 Benoudjit, *op. cit.*, 133.
43 *Ghazawāt*, 59; Benoudjit, *op. cit.*, 160.
44 Boulifa, *op. cit.*, 96 (62).
45 *Ibid.*
46 Benoudjit, *op. cit.*, 190–1, citing El-Merini in Féraud 1868, *art. cit.*, 115 and 343.

Abu Bakr's campaigns had been ineffectual, he stood to benefit from the seizure of Jijel by the Genovese, since this event inflamed local opinion in the vicinity of Jijel and promised to furnish him with fresh support, unless this prospect was nipped in the bud in some way.

It appears that this was precisely the object of the mission entrusted to Ahmed ou l-Qadi by Mulay Mohamed Ben El-Hassan: to co-opt the inflamed sentiments of the populations of the hinterland of Jijel (the Babors, the Ferjiwa and the Collo),[47] to organise them in a jihad in the name of the Hafsid Sultan in Tunis before Abu Bakr could do this for his own account, and to offer this military support on land to Aruj and Kheireddine as the dowry of an alliance by means of which they might be detached from Abu Bakr and brought back into allegiance to Tunis.

In behaving in this way, Mulay Mohamed was almost certainly prompted by his concern to thwart Abu Bakr, but he was arguably acting against the collective Hafsid interest in the long term, for there was little prospect that Aruj and Kheireddine could be brought back into a genuine allegiance to his own authority in Tunis. They had their own reasons for taking Jijel, not only for its convenient location as an anchorage for their corsairing ventures but also to settle a score with Andrea Doria, who had attacked their squadron at Gouletta (the port of Tunis) the previous year and captured several of their ships,[48] and in expelling the Genovese they effectively established themselves as an independent force on the Maghrib coast. Had they taken Jijel in alliance with Abu Bakr, the town might have reverted to Hafsid rule by becoming an extension of Abu Bakr's jurisdiction in Constantine. But Ahmed ou l-Qadi, though loyal to Tunis, was not himself a member of the Hafsid line and so – unlike Abu Bakr – had no title to rule in Jijel in his own right.[49]

It is in this context that we may situate a detail that has puzzled several authors, namely the tradition that, at some point, Ahmed ou l-Qadi was invested with the title of *Khalīfa* for all the territory between Jijel and the Sahara. Robin suggests that he already held this title as of 1510, a view recycled by Chevallier.[50] This conflicts with the tradition that Ou l-Qadi was governor of Bona at this juncture. In fact, however, there is no evidence that he held the post of *khalīfa* for the territory in question as early as 1510 and it would make far more sense

47 According to the *Ghazawāt*, '20,000 Berbers led by their marabouts' rallied to Aruj and Kheireddine after their capture of Jijel (*op. cit.*, 59).

48 Diego de Haedo, *Histoire des Rois d'Alger*, translated and edited by Henri-Delmas de Grammont (Algiers: Jourdan, 1881) republished with an introduction by Jocelyne Dakhlia (Saint-Denis: Éditions Bouchène, 1998), 27.

49 Benoudjit, *op. cit.*, 42.

50 Robin, 1873 *op. cit.*, 132 (1998, 39); Corinne Chevallier, *Les Trente Premières Années de l'État d'Alger* (Algiers: Office des Publications Universitaires, 1988), 14, 102, cited by Benoudjit, *op. cit.*, 169.

to link this investiture either to the seizure of Jijel by Doria in 1513 or to its recapture by Aruj and Kheireddine in 1514. In either case, he is most likely to have been invested with this title by Mulay Mohamed,[51] with, once again, the purpose of pre-empting Abu Bakr and reaffirming, through Ou l-Qadi, the claim of the Hafsid sultanate in Tunis to the allegiance of the population of the hinterland of Jijel and south from there, whoever held power in Jijel itself.

Following their success at Jijel, Aruj and Kheireddine were free agents pursuing their own political (and not merely corsairing) agenda and controlling an important coastal town and harbour in their own name. The complicating factor was their alliance with Ou l-Qadi, who now found himself in command of a substantial jihadi army drawn from the north-eastern districts of Lesser Kabylia, a position he initially owed to his status as the representative of the Hafsid sultan, but who must have begun to realise that Tunis had no intention of furthering the Barbarossa brothers' ventures. That this was the reality of the matter was soon made clear by the failure of Tunis to provide any forces in support of the renewed campaign to retake Bejaia. When Aruj and Kheireddine made their fresh attempt to recapture the city in August 1515, they were strongly backed by Ou l-Qadi's forces, but neither Mulay Mohamed nor the Emirs Abderrahmane and El-Abbas provided any support for this, the latter choosing to honour the terms of their 1512 treaty with the Spanish rather than rally to a venture commanded by others. Abu Bakr appears to have contributed some forces in order to stay in the game but, as the assault on Bejaia gave way to a siege, these withdrew with the arrival of the autumn rains and the start of the ploughing season in September.[52]

It is likely that it was in the course of the campaign to retake Bejaia that Ou l-Qadi extended the range of his influence to Greater Kabylia. The fact that Abderrahmane and El-Abbas were staying out of the fray almost certainly ensured that most of the populations of the Soummam, Wad Sahel, Biban and Guergour districts proved deaf to the call to jihad. But Bejaia prior to the rise of Algiers was the principal urban focus for the populations of Greater Kabylia too and there is no reason to suppose that Abderrahmane and El-Abbas had influence over these. Taken together, the absence of support from the western districts of Lesser Kabylia and the competing presence of Abu Bakr's forces gave Ou l-Qadi a strong motive to enlist support from Greater Kabylia, to compensate for the one and to counterbalance and neutralise the other, and his

---

51 The term *khalīfa* (plural: *khulafā'*) is a title bestowed by a Muslim ruler claiming legitimate sovereignty. It is unlikely that Aruj presumed to appoint *khulafā'* at this stage. While the position he and Kheireddine had assumed by seizing Jijel implied their independence of Tunis, they were not yet in open conflict with the Hafsid interest.

52 De Haedo, *Histoire*, 29.

own family roots in the important 'arsh Ath Ghoubri[53] gave him an initial base in the region from which to undertake this. It is also possible that contingents from Greater Kabylia joined the campaign on their own initiative, as they had earlier mustered for the defence of Bejaia in 1509.[54] In either case, whether arriving spontaneously or deliberately enlisted, the presence of these forces will have given Ou l-Qadi, in his capacity as Mulay Mohamed's representative commanding the main body of indigenous forces in alliance with the Barbarossa brothers, the opportunity to establish political connections with local leaders from Greater Kabylia. The populations likely to have responded to the call to join the assault on Bejaia will have been primarily those of the eastern parts of Greater Kabylia such as the Ath Ghoubri and their neighbours of the Akfadou district, but they are also likely to have included some of the eastern Igawawen such as the Ath Yahia. That Ou l-Qadi should have made contact with leaders of the Ath Yahia, including those of the village of Koukou, in his capacity as authoritative commander of the land forces engaged in the jihad to retake Bejaia would furnish part of the explanation of his subsequent choice of Koukou as his political headquarters in the region.

In establishing his position in Greater Kabylia, Ou l-Qadi is unlikely to have remained for long at Aourir n'Ath Ghoubri, even if it was the village of his ancestors. A small village situated roughly in the centre of the southern part of the Ath Ghoubri territory, Aourir had no geopolitical or strategic significance in itself, commanding neither the Upper Sebaou/Boubehir valley on the 'arsh's western flank nor the main route to Bejaia via the Tagma and Tagdinnt passes on its northern flank nor the routes into the Soummam valley over the passes of Tizi Wakfadou and Tizi n'Tiouririne. Moreover, had he made Aourir his political base, his authority would have tended to eclipse that of the established leadership of the Ath Ghoubri and so upset its internal political equilibrium, quite possibly splitting the 'arsh into supporters and opponents of his leadership, while simultaneously tending to reduce his own role in the perception of wider regional opinion to that of a mere 'arsh leader instead of that of the representative of the Hafsid sultan in Tunis and commander of a jihad to which all the 'aarsh of the region were inclined to rally. It is accordingly likely that he stayed at Aourir only long enough to renew his local connections and assure himself of the Ath Ghoubri's collective support before establishing his headquarters elsewhere. It is entirely possible that, in view of his authority and prestige, he received invitations

---

53 Pierre Boyer refers to this condescendingly as a little tribe – 'la petitè trìbu des Ait Ghobri [*sic*]' (Boyer, *art. cit.*, 260). In fact, it was in the 1860s one of the larger 'aarsh in Kabylia, with a population of 5,732 inhabitants, some 15 villages (Hanoteau and Letourneux, *op. cit.*, vol. I, 332–3) and an extensive territory. It has preserved these dimensions to this day. In view of Ibn Khaldun's respectful mention of it in the fourteenth century, there is no reason to assume that it was significantly less important in the sixteenth century than it was in the nineteenth.

54 El-Merini, in Féraud 1868, *art. cit.*, 253, 337.

from more than one village or *'arsh*, for he would almost certainly have been considered an exceptional guest whose presence brought great honour to his hosts. And so there can be little doubt that the decision to move to Koukou reflected a free and studied choice.

The village of Koukou is the leading village of the smallest of the three 'fractions' of the Ath Yahia, that known as *Imessouhal*, which means 'those who inhabit the lower ground' or 'the lowlanders', by opposition to the fraction known as *Imesdourar*: 'the highlanders'. These terms are of course relative. According to Hanoteau and Letourneux, the Imessouhal in the mid-nineteenth century consisted of the *tūfiq* of Koukou, composed of the *thaddarth* of Koukou proper plus five satellite hamlets, and five other hamlets, four of which were grouped in the *tūfiq* of Tagounits and the fifth, Takenna, subsisting in isolation.[55] The Imessouhal settlements are clustered on the southern, eastern and northern slopes of a ridge which extends in a north-easterly direction from the main body of the Ath Yahia towards the Wad Boubehir and culminates in a high outcrop, on the slope of which the village of Koukou proper is perched, at an altitude of some 950 metres. Koukou thus controls the culminating height of the ridge and commands a view embracing nearly all of the Wad Boubehir. Its own satellite hamlets – Ath Haroun, Bouguettoui, Ath Bali, Taguemount and Ighil Hafedh – are situated on the south-facing slopes below it, facing the northernmost villages of the Ath Itsouragh (Ighil Igoulmimen and Iguer Lakhrar) across a narrow valley watered by a tributary of the Wad Boubehir. The rest of the Imessouhal settlements are situated on the other slopes below Koukou proper and those occupying the north-facing slope are close to the southernmost settlements of the Ath Bou Chaïb (Iguer Guedmimen, Ath Ahamiden and Igoufaf) located on the opposite side of another tributary of the Boubehir.

This position meant that Koukou was virtually impregnable and ideally situated for the purpose of controlling the Boubehir valley. Any attacking force would either have to fight their way along the Imessouhal ridge or fight their way up from the valley floor. The first possibility was in reality non-existent: the villages of the other Ath Yahia fractions – Imesdourar and Taqa – covered the south-western approach to Koukou very thoroughly (and any force attacking the main body of the Ath Yahia would first of all have to fight its way across the territory of the Ath Yahia's other neighbours: the Ath Menguellat to the west, the Ath Irathen to the north-west, the Ath Fraoucen, Ath Khelili and Ath Bou Chaïb to the north or the Ath Bou Youcef to the south). Any force attacking Koukou from below would first of all have to penetrate the Upper Sebaou/Boubehir valley, but the northern half of the east side of the valley was controlled by the Ath Ghoubri, whose loyalty to the Ath l-Qadi was assured. As for the west side of the valley, most of this is controlled by the Ath Bou Chaïb to the north and

---

55 Hanoteau and Letourneux, *op. cit.*, vol. I, 312.

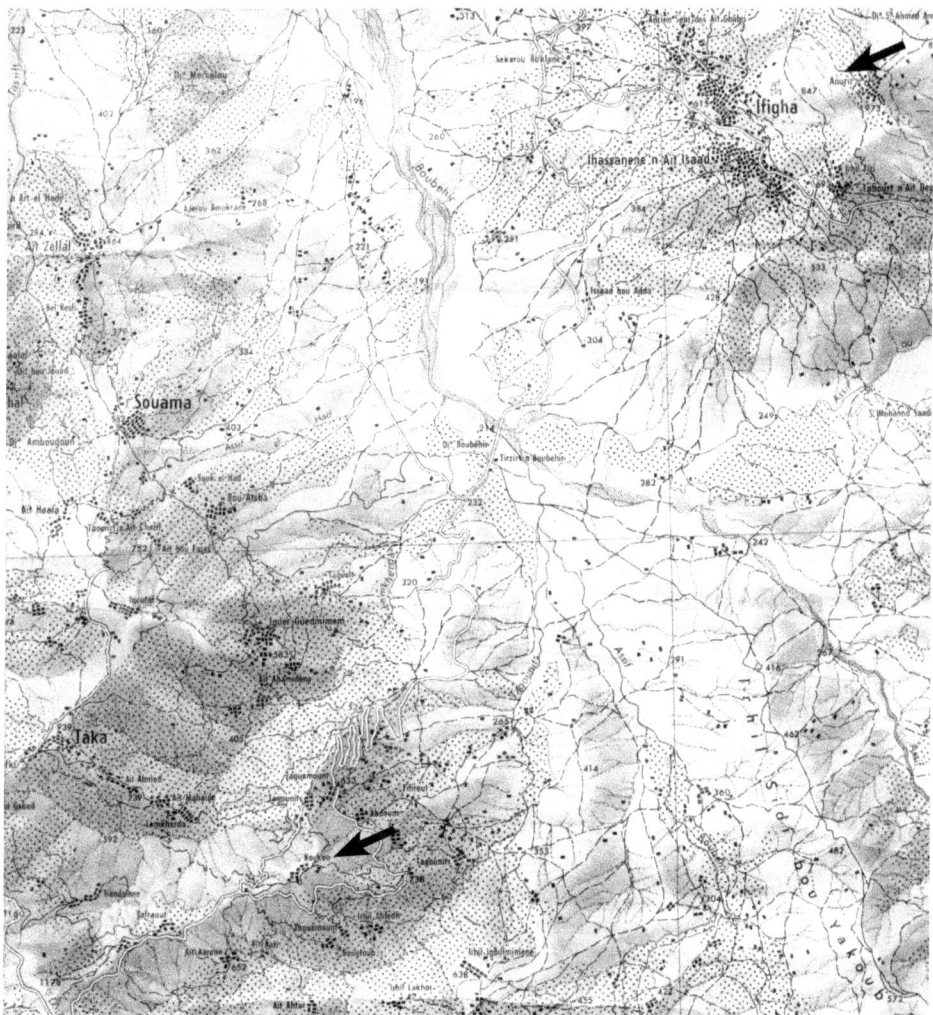

Map 6.4: Koukou, the Wad Boubehir
and Aourir n'Ath Ghoubri. Bottom left,
Koukou (indicated by an arrow) and the
Imessouhal ridge of the Ath Yahia, with the
Ath Bou Chaïb villages to the north and
the northernmost Ath Itsouragh villages to
the south-east; top centre to bottom right,
the Boubehir valley and, top right, the Ath
Ghoubri, with Aourir (indicated by an
arrow), to the north-east.[56]

---

56 This is part of the French map (which misspells many place names) of the Fort National
    district; see note 24 above.

the Ath Itsouragh to the south. The Imessouhal ridge extends, like a tongue between two rows of teeth, to separate the villages of the Ath Yahia's north-eastern neighbour (the Ath Bou Chaïb) from those of its south-eastern one (the Ath Itsouragh). Thus Koukou was the perfect position from which to negotiate the unity of all the *'aarsh* of the west side of the valley; no other village had these geo-political advantages.

Control of the Wad Boubehir and Upper Sebaou did not confer economic benefits directly, nor did it give Ou l-Qadi political control over the rest of Greater Kabylia.[57] Its significance is liable to be missed unless we situate the choice of Koukou in its historical context. At the time Ou l-Qadi made Koukou his headquarters, *c.* 1515,[58] the political orientation of the population of Greater Kabylia continued to be towards the Hafsid powers and Bejaia. The rise of Algiers as national capital, let alone that of Tizi Ouzou as regional capital, were far in the future. Having narrowly failed to assure, in alliance with Aruj and Kheireddine, the recapture of Bejaia in 1515, there was every reason for Ou l-Qadi to expect or at least hope that a renewed campaign would soon recover the city from the Spanish and no reason to assume – and no way that he could know – that this would not in fact happen until 1555, long after his own death. There is accordingly every reason to suppose that his ambition was to obtain an enhanced position for himself and his family in the new dispensation in Bejaia once Muslim rule (whether Hafsid or not) was re-established there and that he sought to guarantee this by staking out his position in Greater Kabylia. By securing control of the Wad Boubehir from his base at Koukou, with the Ath Ghoubri in reliable support and the other populations of the district (Ath Bou Chaïb, Ath Itsouragh, Illilten, Illoulen Oumalou and Ath Ijjeur) accepting his leadership, Ou l-Qadi was simultaneously making himself master of every single land route between Greater Kabylia and Bejaia: the northern route via the Tagma and Tagdinnt passes, the central routes across the Akfadou district into the Soummam valley via Tizi n'Tiouririne and Tizi Wakfadou and the southern routes into the upper Soummam valley and the Wad Sahel via Tizi Berber, Tizi n'Ichelladen and Tizi n'Tirourda, positioning himself as the indispensable guarantor of access to Greater Kabylia by, and of the loyalty of the region towards, whoever emerged as the ruler of a liberated Bejaia.

---

57 The Ath l-Qadi were to extend their control in the lowlands at a later stage, when they established a series of positions in the middle Sebaou valley from which they could maintain a watch on it, thereby making themselves masters of the main route between the region and Algiers, and encouraged settlement around these positions with grants of land. This is the origin of the *'arsh* Iamrawien or Amrawa (Feredj, *op. cit.*, 32).

58 My hypothesis is that he made Koukou his headquarters after the unsuccessful attempt to retake Bejaia in August–September 1515 and before the expedition to Algiers in 1516. Interestingly, Masqueray also situates the establishment of Ou l-Qadi at Koukou 'around 1515' ('vers 1515') (*op. cit.*, 132) without, however, explaining his reasoning.

The reluctance of Aruj and Kheireddine to renew the attempt to recapture Bejaia at this juncture accordingly posed a considerable problem for Ou l-Qadi. Unlike the brothers, whose control of Jijel gave them a harbour and a base from which they could keep their squadron of ships in business, Ou l-Qadi depended for his position on his role as the leader of a land army mustered for a jihad. A jihad is the mobilisation of religious enthusiasm for military action on behalf of the community of believers. An army mustered for jihad cannot be kept standing idle indefinitely. It was accordingly vital for Ou l-Qadi to maintain the mobilisation of his following in Kabylia in a fresh campaign against the Spanish presence and, if a third assault on Bejaia was ruled out for the moment, an alternative had to be found. It is this which explains the decision to undertake an expedition to Algiers.

Algiers at the beginning of the sixteenth century CE was a small coastal city that the decline of Hafsid power to the east and Abd el-Wadid power to the west had rendered virtually independent despite itself. This independence was significantly qualified, however, by the influence of the powerful Thaaliba tribe of the Mitija plain immediately to the south. With the advent of the Spanish threat along the coast of the central Maghrib, the Thaaliba established an informal protectorate over the city and their chief, Salim El-Toumi, became its *de facto* ruler. In 1510, following his seizure of Oran and Bejaia, Pedro de Navarre had Algiers in his sights. He was not interested in conquering the city, however, and contented himself with what the British later would call 'gunboat diplomacy', forcing the city to sign a treaty of allegiance to the Spanish crown and occupying the largest of the four islets immediately offshore, from which Algiers derived its name (*El Jazā'ir*: 'the islands'), where he constructed what came to be known as *El Peñón de Argel*, a fortification defended by a force of 200 soldiers and equipped with a powerful artillery battery aimed at the city to guarantee its allegiance and discourage the corsairing activities of its fleet.

In January 1516, King Ferdinand of Spain died. This event was invoked by elements of the Algiers population to argue for repudiating the treaty signed under duress in 1510 and an agitation developed pressing Salim El-Toumi to secure the Barbarossa brothers' aid to deliver the city from the Spaniards' intimidating presence. It is entirely possible that Kabyles in Algiers were the main source of this agitation[59] and that agents of Ou l-Qadi had had a hand in instigating it. At all events, El-Toumi's envoys received a positive response from Aruj and Kheireddine in Jijel.

The possibility that Aruj and Kheireddine were in reality less than enthusiastic about the expedition to Algiers has been obscured by our knowledge that Kheireddine subsequently made Algiers his capital and in doing so founded the Ottoman Regency of Algiers. It has been easy to assume that this outcome was

---

59 Boulifa, *op. cit.*, 100 (65).

already part, if not the central element, of the brothers' purpose in 1516. But a moment's reflection suggests how unlikely this is. Algiers had never been a major political capital before and its comparatively poor anchorage precluded any pretension to being a port of much significance. Neither the Hafsids in Tunis nor the Abd el-Wadids in Tlemcen had accorded it strategic significance and, as we have seen, the Spanish followed suit in this respect. Why, then, should Aruj and Kheireddine have, at this point, nourished any greater ambition for the place than all their predecessors? There is no hard evidence that they did. And the alacrity with which Aruj sought to exploit the opportunity to seize power in Tlemcen in 1518 supports the view that they continued instead to see the central Maghrib in traditional terms, as boasting only two capitals of significance and thus only two prizes of real value, Bejaia and Tlemcen, assigning at most secondary, tactical, importance to Algiers. It is likely, then, that they were put on the spot by El-Toumi's emissaries – they had their reputation along the Maghrib coast, as champions of Islam, to maintain – and, probably, by pressure from Ou l-Qadi as well and decided to show willing and go along with the idea, accepting (or pretending to accept) the suggestion that the *Peñón* offered an easy target – certainly far easier than Bejaia – and thus the prospect of an easy victory for the Muslim cause.

That they had mental reservations about the expedition to Algiers is suggested by their subsequent behaviour. Having sailed their squadron westward from Jijel, they put into port at Dellys on the Kabyle coast and then sailed past Algiers to Cherchell, where they deposed the Muslim ruler, Kara Hassan, another Ottoman adventurer like themselves, and imposed their own rule.[60] It was only then that they put into Algiers. Here, after a perfunctory attempt to reduce the *Peñón* with an artillery barrage, they abandoned the plan to dislodge the Spanish and instead assassinated Salim El-Toumi and seized power for themselves. The following year, while Kheireddine stayed behind to consolidate the brothers' control, Aruj set off on his ill-fated expedition to Tlemcen, in the course of which he met his death, in which Ou l-Qadi was in some degree complicit.

In so far as Ou l-Qadi's behaviour in the Tlemcen expedition requires explanation, the key to it undoubtedly lies in what transpired in Algiers in 1516–17. Why did Aruj and Kheireddine abandon the attack on the *Peñón*? And why did they kill Salim El-Toumi? The standard accounts report that the attacking force was simply outgunned, that their cannons could make no impression on the *Peñón*'s walls while the Spanish guns were able to wreak havoc on the town centre opposite.[61] This may be true, but it still leaves unanswered why, with Ou l-Qadi's force of some 3,000 troops[62] mustered for the campaign, no attempt was

60 Boulifa, *op. cit.*, 67; Hess, *op. cit.*, 63.

61 Gaïd, 1974, *op. cit.*, 37.

62 Gaïd, *ibid.*

made to take the *Peñón* by storm, especially in view of the fact that this is how it was ultimately taken thirteen years later;[63] a possibly crucial difference is that in 1529 it was Turkish forces under Kheireddine's command which stormed the *Peñón*. The evidence suggests that Aruj and Kheireddine were determined to reduce the *Peñón* themselves and, having failed to do so, refused to allow Ou l-Qadi's Kabyle forces to do the honours and take the credit for this, which in turn suggests that, underlying the formal alliance between the brothers and Ou l-Qadi, an undeclared struggle for power was in reality already taking place. At the very least, the failure to make any headway and the decision to abandon the attempt must have been an extremely embarrassing setback for Ou l-Qadi personally as well as demoralising for the forces he had mobilised.[64]

The Barbarossa brothers' motive for killing El-Toumi has never been clearly established. A tribal chieftain of merely local standing, he cannot on his own have been considered a serious rival to the brothers at the regional level in terms of military power and prestige. In view of the fact that El-Toumi (unlike Kara Hassan in Cherchell) had actively solicited the brothers' aid against the Spanish and had welcomed them with every honour on their arrival at Algiers,[65] there can be no doubt that his murder was a shocking affair at the time. An explanation advanced by certain authors is that, following the failure of their attempt to reduce the *Peñón* and in view of the arrogant and insulting behaviour of their Turkish troops towards the townspeople, Aruj and Kheireddine became extremely unpopular and El-Toumi eventually placed himself at the head of this current of local feeling seeking to induce them to leave.[66] A variant of this version is that El-Toumi went so far as to intrigue with the Spanish to secure this objective, although no hard evidence for this has been adduced.

Another way of understanding this event is suggested by Masqueray's claim that Ou l-Qadi and El-Toumi were kinsmen. This claim was advanced by Masqueray to explain Ou l-Qadi's falling out with Aruj and Kheireddine and thus, by implication, his subsequent 'betrayal' of Aruj in western Algeria as the belated settling of a personal score for the murder of El-Toumi.[67] The

---

63 'La Prise du Pegnon' in Mahfoud Kaddache, 1998, *op. cit.*, 16; see also Moulay Belhamissi, *Histoire de la marine algérienne (1516–1830)* (Algiers: ENAL, 1983), 113.

64 It could even have tended to discredit Ou l-Qadi's own credentials by association, since the failure to deal decisively with the *Peñón* had nearly disastrous consequences in the military sphere: in late September/early October 1516, a Spanish expeditionary force commanded by Diego de Vera transported by a fleet of some 30 vessels came to the support of the beleaguered garrison on the *Peñón* by mounting a concerted attack on Algiers, only to be routed by a fierce counter-attack led by Aruj, supported by Ou l-Qadi's forces; this engagement, which could well have gone the other way, might never have happened had the Spanish presence on the *Peñón* been dealt with decisively beforehand.

65 Kaddache, 1998, *op. cit.*, 8.

66 Gaïd, 1974, *op. cit.*, 37–8.

67 Masqueray, 1983 (1886), *op. cit.*, 132.

difficulty with this story is that it is extremely unlikely that there would have been any pre-existing tie of kinship between the sheikh of an Arab tribe of the Mitija and a notable of Bejaia, of Kabyle maraboutic descent, serving the Hafsid government in Bona 260 miles to the east. But something else is entirely possible – namely that, following Ou l-Qadi's arrival in Algiers, he and El-Toumi formed a political alliance as an insurance against the disquieting behaviour of Aruj and Kheireddine and sealed this in the customary way by arranging a marriage of their children, thus reinforcing the political connection with a family tie. In view of the summary overthrow of Kara Hassan at Cherchell, it is entirely plausible that El-Toumi should have sought such an alliance as a protection against a similar fate. For his part, Ou l-Qadi was dependent upon El-Toumi's cooperation for the quartering of his troops in Algiers and so may have felt he had to agree to such an alliance; moreover, he too may well have been disconcerted by the Barbarossa brothers' behaviour and the self-aggrandising agenda that was more and more clearly motivating it, and possibly interested in renegotiating the terms of his relationship with the brothers from a position of strength. An inherently plausible development in itself, whatever the precise calculations that prompted it on either side, this alliance, if such it was, appears to have been taken as an intolerable threat or challenge by Aruj and Kheireddine. Their response – to eliminate El-Toumi at once – can be seen as a ruthless counterstroke that, by depriving Ou l-Qadi of his new ally, brought him brutally to heel as the brothers' junior partner. At the same time, it committed the brothers to taking political responsibility for Algiers in the teeth of hostile local opinion, an undertaking which in turn soon prompted them to embark on the entirely novel business of subduing the hinterland through campaigns against the Hadjout tribe in the western Mitija, then the towns of Tenès, Miliana and Medea,[68] in the course of which they initially relied heavily on Ou l-Qadi's troops, which had the advantage of getting these out of Algiers but also the effect of reducing them to an instrument of repression rather than an army of jihad.

Ou l-Qadi presumably decided that he had no option but to go along with this agenda at first. The alternative was to allow his army to dissolve, leaving him with nothing. But there can be little doubt that he considered that he had been taken advantage of, slighted and humiliated by the Barbarossa brothers. His original prestige and authority both as representative of the Hafsid sultan and as leader of a jihadi army mobilised to fight the Spaniards had been seriously diminished. It is in this light that we can understand his own eventual 'betrayal' of Aruj near Tlemcen, which amounted to nothing more than his failure to come to the rescue when a counterattacking Spanish force out of Oran first beseiged Aruj in the Mechouar and then finally intercepted and killed him as he tried

---

68 Gaïd, 1974, *op. cit.*, 40.

to make his escape. In letting Aruj down in this way, Ou l-Qadi was arguably following the logic of the brothers' own attitude in reducing him to a subaltern auxiliary at the head of what was in effect a mercenary force. Since Aruj had clearly overreached himself in the Tlemcen campaign and this had turned into a disaster, there was nothing in it for his mercenary auxiliaries who accordingly had every reason to disengage and withdraw in good order while they could, leaving Aruj to pay the price for a strategic error that was his alone. This was at worst a desertion rather than a betrayal and moreover a desertion Aruj had done much to provoke. That Kheireddine considered it an act of extreme disloyalty reflected the fact that the turn of events had marked a decisive change in the relationship. From ally and then (more or less loyal or at least acquiescent) lieutenant, Ou l-Qadi had in effect declared his independence of the Barbarossa brothers and recovered his freedom of action, which made him a rebel and an enemy in Kheireddine's eyes.

That Ou l-Qadi saw things in this light is suggested by his decision, on leading his troops back to Kabylia, to continue his own journey to the east. Instead of stopping in Koukou, he continued on to Bona, from where he renewed contact with the Hafsids in Tunis.[69] Some accounts suggest he was obeying a summons from Tunis but this is not certain. It is as likely that he understood that he could not fully count on Kabyle support at this delicate juncture. The people of Koukou had welcomed him as a leader of jihad and they and the population of Greater Kabylia in general had been mobilised to fight the Spaniards in alliance with Aruj and Kheireddine, widely seen at that point as heroic champions of Islam. It was thus quite another matter to mobilise them for war *against* Kheireddine, especially since the ins and outs of the power struggle that had been going on would have been known only to Ou l-Qadi's inner circle. Once Ou l-Qadi had Hafsid troops in his support, however, this was enough to win over public opinion in Greater Kabylia and persuade it to back him, as both an authorised representative of the (still positively viewed) Hafsid interest and as a likely winner in the duel with Kheireddine.

The events of late 1518 to late 1519 have the character of a race. Kheireddine, having lost his brother and his most important native supporters, having yet to consolidate his authority in Algiers and with at best a tenuous hold over the hinterland, would soon decide to declare his allegiance to the Ottoman Sultan in order to secure the external support he needed to compensate for his loss of internal support. Thus the rivalry between Ou l-Qadi and Kheireddine quickly implicated the Ottoman as well as Hafsid empires. The latter, although in severe decline, was quicker off the mark and it was with the Hafsid troops that Tunis had promptly provided that Ou l-Qadi was able to defeat Kheireddine's forces in western Kabylia and then seize Algiers, forcing Kheireddine to withdraw to Jijel.

---

69 Benoudjit, *op. cit.*, 186.

For the next five or possibly seven years,[70] Ahmed ou l-Qadi was not merely the 'king of Koukou' but in effect the king of Algiers. (A souvenir of this period is the name of a district, on the heights of Algiers, known as 'Jebel Koukou' to this day.) The mystery in which this period is veiled is not the least striking aspect of the entire enigma. All the evidence available in the secondary literature concerns Kheireddine's eventual success in making his come-back. We know almost nothing about what transpired in Algiers and how Ou l-Qadi governed the city during this period, beyond undocumented reports that his rule eventually alienated the sympathies of part of the population. Aside from the modalities of Ou l-Qadi's rule, the main mystery concerns the failure of the Hafsids to consolidate the position of their client in Algiers.

Between 1520 and 1525, Kheireddine was able to reinforce and extend his position in eastern Algeria, not merely holding his own at Jijel but also seizing Collo (1520) and Bona (1522) along the coast and even striking inland to take Constantine in 1521. These moves clearly made it difficult for Mulay Mohamed in Tunis to send fresh forces either by sea or by land to the aid of Ou l-Qadi when Kheireddine finally moved against Algiers, but the fact that Kheireddine was able to make these inroads into Hafsid territory and that Mulay Mohamed did not counterattack, let alone preempt them by destroying Kheireddine's position at Jijel in good time, strongly suggests that the dynasty in Tunis lacked the vigour and decisiveness of its opponent, whose bold moves repeatedly threw into relief its own weakness and inertia.

But it is likely that a key consideration for Tunis was the fact that Kheireddine had also, in the meantime, rallied the rulers of Qal'a n'Ath Abbas to his cause, in return for backing them against their uncle Abu Bakr, who was finally overthrown and definitively eliminated by Kheireddine's seizure of Constantine.[71] By this stroke, Kheireddine effectively neutralised Tunis. For, while Ou l-Qadi had enjoyed Mulay Mohamed's favour as a servant of the Hafsid interest, the Emirs Abderrahmane and El-Abbas *were* Hafsids themselves; there could be no question of backing Ou l-Qadi against *them*. And so Ou l-Qadi was on his own in facing Kheireddine's forces when they eventually approached Algiers for the final showdown. What would have happened had he not been mysteriously assassinated on the eve of battle we cannot know, but it is difficult to avoid the conclusion that his inability to sustain Tunis's interest in his venture was fatal. Equally, it is important to grasp the implication of this, that the counterpart of this failure was his inability to

---

70 Most authors give 1520–5 as the period of Ou l-Qadi's rule in Algiers, accepting that Kheireddine retook Algiers in 1525 (Hess, *op. cit.*, 67) but Boulifa insists (*op. cit.*, 128–31, 147 (85–7, 99)) that Ou l-Qadi ruled till 1527, although he fails to document this. Adli in his recent book (*op. cit.*, 48) follows Boulifa's view.

71 Abu Bakr's fate has never been elucidated but he disappears from history at this time (Benoudjit, *op. cit.*, 189–98).

build, around his core support in Greater Kabylia and the Kabyles of Algiers, a broader, Arab as well as Kabyle, internal basis for an Algerian state founded on the indigenous population and commanded by its own leaders.

Vassals and the temptation of disloyalty

The death of Ahmed ou l-Qadi and the loss of Algiers to Kheireddine by no means signified the end of the dynasty's career. Under Ahmed's brother, El Hussein, and his successors, the Ath l-Qadi retained power in Greater Kabylia and for the next 90 years may seem simply to have oscillated in an opportunistic fashion between two main alliances to this end, with the Turks against the Spanish, with the Spanish against the Turks. In addition to the Ottomans and the Spanish, a third element in the equation was, until 1574, Hafsid rule in Tunis.

How are we to understand this confusing period of the history of Algeria and of Kabylia in particular? Boyer and, following him, Chaker *et al.* speak of the 'chassée-croisée' ('comings and goings') between the various players[72] and most authors have presented the dealings between Algiers, Koukou, Qal'a and Spain as a kind of political kaleidoscope in which all and sundry were mainly, if not merely, reacting to one another's moves in an almost automatic and predominantly cynical manner. This does less than justice to the conduct and motives of the actors concerned, each of which had its constancy.

In particular, the behaviour of the lords of Koukou was reasonably consistent. A preliminary understanding was reached in 1529 with Kheireddine, who, having driven the Ath l-Qadi out of Algiers, prudently made a point of coming to terms with them before taking on the Spanish again over the *Peñón*.[73] This understanding took the form of a treaty which ended the state of war between the Ottomans and the lords of Koukou while recognising the latter's autonomy; a similar treaty was signed at the same time with the lords of Qal'a. Significantly, in neither case did the treaty affirm Algiers's right to raise taxes in the region.[74] Thereafter, the Ath l-Qadi were actively in conflict with the Regency only twice. On both occasions this involved their intriguing with the Spanish. The first instance of this represented the abrogation by the Ath l-Qadi of the treaty of 1529 – and thus the breaking off of an alliance rather than a rebellion or an act of disloyalty properly so-called – and underlying this was their prior long-standing loyalty to the Hafsids in Tunis. The second instance was indeed

---

72 Boyer, *art. cit.*, 27; Chaker *et al.*, *op. cit.*, 75.
73 Boulifa, *op. cit.*, 88–9.
74 Boulifa (*ibid.*) claims that the treaty formally obliged the Ath l-Qadi to pay an annual tribute but he does not specify the nature or value of this and in any case observes that this clause remained a dead letter, the Ottomans making no attempt to enforce it.

a matter of disloyalty, but it owed much to the behaviour of the Regency itself towards Kabylia.

In 1533 Kheireddine was appointed Kapudan-Pasha (Admiral) of the Ottoman fleet and, while retaining his title and authority as *beylerbey*, delegated the business of government in Algiers to a *khalīfa* (lieutenant) in the person of his adopted son Hassan Agha, who ruled from 1533 to 1543. Soon afterwards, Kheireddine embarked on an expedition against Tunis at the head of a flotilla of 84 ships. According to Hess he did this at the behest of the Ottoman sultan, determined to strengthen the empire's position in North Africa;[75] some accounts claim he was responding to the invitation of circles in Tunis hostile to the new Hafsid sultan,[76] Mulay Hassan, who had succeeded to the throne in 1526. Another possibility is that his decision was connected to unrest at Constantine in 1533,[77] which may have been instigated by pro-Hafsid elements, and that Kheireddine intended to destroy this problem at the root. At all events, the Ottoman force easily overcame the Hafsids' defences and Mulay Hassan fled to the south of the country. This success, which seemed to have added Tunisia to the Ottoman empire as a new province, was short-lived, however. In desperation, Mulay Hassan sought the support of Spain; thus had the wheel come full circle since 1512. Concerned above all to check Ottoman power in the Mediterranean, the Spanish under Charles V were happy to restore Mulay Hassan to his throne as their protégé and did so in July 1535, while at the same time inducing the Ziyanid ruler of Tlemcen, the Sultan Mohamed, to accept a treaty by which he recognised Spanish sovereignty and agreed to trade only through Oran and not through Algiers.[78] Spanish diplomacy then sought to capitalise on these successes on Algiers's eastern and western flanks by trying to detach Kheireddine from the Ottoman connection, reportedly offering to recognise him as ruler of not only the central Maghrib but also Tunisia into the bargain if he would give allegiance to the Spanish crown.[79] When this ploy failed, the Spanish tried once more to overthrow the Regency by force.[80]

It was in this context, when everyone else was doing it, that the Ath l-Qadi themselves engaged in discussions with the Spanish and agreed to take part in the attempt on Algiers by providing troops, both cavalry and infantry, in support of Charles V's expeditionary force. Given that Spain apparently intended to commit her full might to destroying Ottoman power in Algiers and that, in any case, following Kheireddine's departure, there was no reason

75 Hess, *op. cit.*, 72.
76 De Haedo, *Histoire*, 60, 76.
77 De Grammont, *op. cit.*, 52–3.
78 Abun-Nasr, 1987, *op. cit.*, 154.
79 E. Watbled and Dr Monnereau, 'Négociations entre Charles-Quint et Kheir-Ed-Din (1538–1540)', *Revue Africaine* (1869), 139–48.
80 De Grammont, *op. cit.*, 67; Abun-Nasr, 1987, *op. cit.*, 154; Hess, *op. cit.*, 73–4.

to assume that the Ottoman presence would necessarily endure, it is likely that sheer prudence dictated some investment in the Spanish scheme by the Ath l-Qadi. When we bear in mind the changed relations between the Spanish and the Hafsids, we can see that this engagement with the Spanish, while evidently contrary to the idea of jihad, was consistent with the Ath l-Qadi's original loyalties. But it could not anticipate the weather. Charles V's expedition, comprising over 500 ships, arrived off Algiers on 23 October 1541, but when a massive storm blew up and wrecked over a quarter of the fleet,[81] the attack on Algiers disintegrated into chaos. On learning of the disaster that had overtaken the Spanish, Ou l-Qadi ordered his troops about before they had fired a shot and took them home again, contenting himself with formally honouring his promise of support by sending some provisions to his unlucky and accordingly ephemeral allies.[82]

The decisive development in Koukou's relationship to Algiers occurred in the wake of these events. Having seen off the Spanish, Hassan Agha mounted a heavily armed punitive expedition into Kabylia in April 1542. Confronted with the prospect of defeat and overthrow, El-Hussein Ou l-Qadi opted to submit to the Ottomans on terms which went far beyond the 1529 treaty with Kheireddine, paying a large fine in money and kind, accepting the obligation of an annual tribute thereafter and even surrendering his son, Sidi Ahmed, as a hostage to the Turks and guarantee of good behaviour.[83] Thus were the Ath l-Qadi reduced at last to avowed vassals of the Regency.

From that point on, their ambition was limited to the regional level, where it clashed with that of the rulers of Qal'a n'Ath Abbas, who no doubt considered their entitlement to pre-eminence in Kabylia, founded as it was on their Hafsid blood, to have far outweighed that of the upstart *qādi*'s descendants. For a while the Ath l-Qadi triumphed, in part because relations had already broken down between the lord of Qal'a, Abdelaziz, and the new Ottoman ruler Salah Ra'is, for other reasons. When Salah Ra'is took Bejaia from the Spanish in 1555, it was to the Ath l-Qadi that he entrusted the administration of Bejaia's hinterland,[84] from where they organised, among other things, the exploitation of the forests of the Jebel Ez-Zeen to provide timber to the Ottoman navy. The Ottoman capture of Bejaia and the promotion of the Ath l-Qadi meant that the Ath Abbas's hope of regaining their old kingdom in Bejaia was destroyed. Four years later, Hassan Pasha (Kheireddine's son), who had been appointed to a

---

81 Hess, *op. cit.*, 74.

82 Another version suggests that Koukou offered munitions and troops to the Spanish but that Charles V refused this help, accepting only the supply of food from Ou l-Qadi; see Daniel Nordman, *Tempête sur Alger: L'expédition de Charles Quint sur Alger* (Éditions Bouchène, 2011), 229.

83 De Haedo, *Histoire*, 79.

84 Boulifa, *op. cit.*, 156.

second term as pasha in 1557,[85] had two forts built on the northern edge of the plains to the south and east of the Ath Abbas territory (Borj Mejana and Borj Zemoura).[86] These intensely galling developments eventually provoked the Ath Abbas to rebel, which they did in 1559 by attacking and destroying the forts in question. In response, Hassan Pasha led a combined Algiers-Koukou force to attack the Qal'a, whose ruler, Abdelaziz,[87] had recently received reinforcements of 1,000 troops from the Spanish and was extending his influence in eastern Algeria.[88] However, although Abdelaziz was killed in battle in October 1559,[89] the campaign eventually ended with a peace accord between Algiers and the Ath Abbas, now ruled by Abdelaziz's brother, Amoqran. These developments thus inaugurated a period of good relations between the Regency and both of the regional powers in Kabylia. The following year, Hassan Pasha put the seal on the good relations with Koukou by not only marrying one of Ou l-Qadi's daughters himself but also inducing Hassan Griego, the son of his close friend and trusted lieutenant, Eulj Ali, to marry his bride's older sister.[90]

The relationship between Algiers and Koukou that was thus inaugurated in 1542, consolidated in 1555 and consummated in 1561 enabled the lords of Koukou to preserve their power in Greater Kabylia for at least another 90 years (from 1542 to 1632 or, most probably, to 1638) and, for the first 52 of these, from 1542 to 1594, the Ath l-Qadi gave no sign of disloyalty whatever but, on the contrary, displayed a reliable consistency in their dealings with the Regency. But it also gave rise to a conflict over policy within the Ottoman Regency. For no sooner had Hassan Pasha settled matters in Kabylia than he was faced with a concerted revolt of the janissaries in Algiers, deposed, accused of high treason and sent in chains to Constantinople.

This startling reversal of fortune for Kheireddine's son brought into the open the division of opinion that had emerged within the Ottoman ruling caste over the policy to be followed in its relations with the Kabyles. The outcome of this controversy was to prove fateful for Kabylia's subsequent relations with the Regency. It was in part the failure of successive rulers in Algiers to sustain Hassan Pasha's original policy that eventually induced the Ath l-Qadi to renew their contacts with the Spanish and to engage in a fresh and unprecedentedly

---

85 Hassan Pasha (*c.* 1516–70) was Kheireddine's own son and not to be confused with his adopted son, Hassan Agha. Hassan Pasha was appointed to three terms as governor (*Pasha*) in Algiers: 1545–51, 1557–61, 1562–7.

86 Adli, *op. cit.*, 55–6; Benoudjit, *op. cit.*, 258.

87 Abdelaziz was the son of El-Abbas; as Benoudjit persuasively argues, it was probably at this time that the Qal'a became known as Qal'a n'Ath Abbas (*op. cit.*, 244) and that its ruler, Abdelaziz, took the title of *sultan*, since he could no longer aspire to regain the title of sultan of Bejaia (*op. cit.*, 223).

88 Gaïd, 1974, *op. cit.*, 79.

89 De Haedo, *op. cit.*, 130–1; Benoudjit, *op. cit.*, 260.

90 De Haedo, *op. cit.*, 131; Benoudjit, *op. cit.*, 261.

protracted intrigue, from 1598 to 1610, at a time when Spain was once more considering an assault on Algiers. Although nothing much came of this intrigue in practical terms, it bore witness to the extent of the alienation of the Ath l-Qadi from the Regency by the end of the sixteenth century and thus to the eventual breakdown of the *modus vivendi* that had been established in mid-century and to which they had long adhered. This breakdown owed more to the way in which the controversy within the Ottoman ruling caste was resolved than to anything the Ath l-Qadi did.

Ottoman policy between the Kabyles and the Ojaq

The consolidation of Ottoman power by the mid-sixteenth century CE obliged the Regency to deal with the Kabyles in several contexts and on several levels simultaneously. But the development of the apparatuses of the Regency in the period following Kheireddine's departure from Algiers in 1533–6 revealed a fundamental problem at the heart of the form of government of the Regency itself, namely the difficulty of governing with the Ojaq (the elite corps of the janissaries) and the impossibility of governing against it. These two problems, the problem of the Ottoman rulers' relations with the Kabyles and the problem of their relations with their own army, intersected to create an exceptionally acute dilemma.

The growth of Algiers attracted migrants from the region who swelled the already longstanding Kabyle presence in the city's population. Precisely how important this already was by the 1560s is unclear, but a Spanish Benedictine, Diego de Haedo, gives us a graphic idea of the position as he observed it a little later, during his sojourn in Algiers from 1578 to 1581. Informing his readers that, at Algiers, the 'Moors' – the indigenous inhabitants of the country – are 'of four kinds' and that the first kind are the '*Baldis*' (literally 'townsfolk'), meaning those belonging to established families of the city, he goes on to speak of the Kabyles as 'the second type of Moor', the third being 'the Arabs who continually come to Algiers from their douars where they live in the open under their tents' and the fourth being the refugees from Andalusia.[91] Of the Kabyles, 'who come from their mountains to live in Algiers', de Haedo comments:

> These are the ancient Africans properly so-called, born and raised from the beginning in these parts of Africa. They are all brown in colour, either more or less; some of them, natives of the high mountains of Cuco or of

---

91 De Haedo, *Topographie*, 55–60.

Labès, where the snow stays the year round, are almost entirely white and fairly well proportioned. They are all poor folk whom necessity brings to live in Algiers in shacks or rented rooms. Some of them earn their living working for the Turks or for rich Moors, others in working as gardeners or tending vines. There are also those who row in the galleys and brigs for wages ... Finally there are the sellers of fodder, fruit, coal, oil, butter, eggs, etc.

Among these Kabyles there are also certain individuals designated by the name of *Azuagos* (Zouaoua), natives of the kingdom of Koukou ... and of the kingdom of Beni el-Abbas ... The Turks frequently make use of the Zouaoua in warfare, because they are not at all bad soldiers ... There may be as many as a hundred Zouaoua households; the rest [sc. of the Zouaoua] consist of bachelors who live in barracks like the janissaries, amounting to some two or three hundred and sometimes more. There are about six hundred houses of the other Kabyles.[92]

Source of an increasingly important element of the population of Algiers itself, Kabylia also became of increasing importance in geo-political terms as the Ottoman regime extended its control across the eastern half of the country. Having expelled the Spanish and secured Bejaia in 1555 and reached an understanding with the Ath Abbas in 1560, the Regency moved to consolidate its control over the Constantinois. In 1567, Hassan Pasha's successor, Eulj Ali, appointed the first Bey of the 'Eastern province' who took up residence in Constantine. From then on Algiers's overland communications with Constantine became a major preoccupation. According to Robin, it was at this point that the Ottomans began to think of constructing a series of forts along the Algiers-Constantine route to guarantee its security.[93] But, for much the greater part of the route, the principal threats to its security came from the Kabyles of Greater and Lesser Kabylia. A major benefit of preserving good relations with both Koukou and Qal'a, therefore, was that it forestalled this threat and so obviated the need to invest in the laborious business of building, garrisoning and supplying forts over an extended distance.

But the Kabyles did not matter only in Algiers and in Kabylia itself. They also mattered for another reason, which was the extent to which the Regency continued to depend on Kabyle troops. In 1542, within months (if not weeks) of the Ath l-Qadi's submission to Hassan Agha, Kabyle troops were part of the forces sent to the south-east to extend Ottoman power to the Hodna and the Zab and, in the west, to Tlemcen and even as far as Fès in a thrust against the Moroccan sultan.[94] In 1550, when Hassan Corso mounted an expedition against

---

92 De Haedo, *Topographie*, 56–9 (my translation).
93 Robin, *op. cit.*, 41.
94 Boulifa, *op. cit.*, 101.

Mostaganem, his 10,000-strong force included 2,000 troops from Lesser Kabylia commanded by Abdelaziz, the lord of Qal'a, in person;[95] moreover, following the capture of Mostaganem, these forces engaged and routed a Moroccan army near Tlemcen.[96] In 1552, Salah Ra'is's expedition to the Sahara to secure the submission of the rulers of Touggourt and Ouargla relied on native troops, Arabs, Kouloughlis and Kabyles, for three quarters of its forces. 'The latter, commanded by Abdelaziz, were the most numerous and had up until then given proof of their bravery and loyalty.'[97] In 1555, a large force from Greater Kabylia under Ou l-Qadi's command took part in Salah Ra'is's campaign to retake Bejaia.[98] When Salah Ra'is promptly announced his plan to follow up the recapture of Bejaia with an expedition to retake Oran from the Spanish, there were 6,000 'Algerian volunteers', many of whom would have been Kabyles.[99] The same year, there were 2,000 Kabyles in the force led by Dragut Ra'is in his expedition to Tunisia to try (without success) to retake Mahdia from the Spanish.[100] In 1559, Ou l-Qadi contributed Zwawa troops to Hassan Pasha's campaign against Qal'a n'Ath Abbas.[101] In 1562, no fewer than 'twelve thousand Kabyles', according to de Grammont, 'of the Zwawa and the Beni Abbes' were mustered by Hassan Pasha for his expedition against Oran and Mers el-Kebir.[102] In addition, Kabyle forces saw action under the Ottoman colours even further afield. When in 1565 Hassan Pasha contributed 5,000 troops to the Ottoman combined forces' assault on the island of Malta, only 2,000 of these were Turkish janissaries; the remaining 3,000 were 'Moors and Kabyles'.[103] And when Eulj Ali mounted his determined expedition to Tunis to overthrow the Hafsid sultan once again, he recruited large numbers of native volunteers en route. As de Haedo tells the story, Eulj Ali 'started out in October 1569', but

> he did not send a fleet, but set off over land with five thousand Turks and renegade musketeers. While passing via Bona and Constantine, he recruited three hundred more, and all along the way he secured in addition six thousand Moorish cavalry, dependents of the king of Koukou, of the king of Labès and of certain other chiefs.[104]

---

95 Gaïd, 1974, *op. cit.*, 66.
96 Gaïd, 1974, *op. cit.*, 67.
97 Gaïd, 1974, *op. cit.*, 69.
98 Boulifa, *op. cit.*, 103; the Kabyle contingent numbered 3,000 according to de Grammont, *op. cit.*, 84.
99 Gaïd, 1974, *op. cit.*, 73.
100 Gaïd, 1974, *op. cit.*, 75.
101 Gaïd, 1974, *op. cit.*, 79.
102 De Grammont, *op. cit.*, 95.
103 Gaïd, 1974, *op. cit.*, 84.
104 De Haedo, *Histoire*, 152 (my translation). See also Ferdinand Braudel, *The Mediterranean and the Mediterranean World in the Age of Philip II* (London: Collins, 1972), vol. II, 1067–8, and de Grammont, who speaks (*op. cit.*, 104) of 'six thousand Kabyles'.

That the Regency should have finally induced the Ath l-Qadi to take sides against their old Hafsid patron in this way suggests that, as a consequence of the policy of Hassan Pasha and especially the marriage alliances that had been contracted, the Ath l-Qadi had indeed committed themselves to a new loyalty.[105] This sense of having a stake in the Ottoman dispensation must also in part explain the willingness of the Kabyles – in contrast to their attitude in 1518 – to take part in Ottoman expeditions in western Algeria and even Morocco. For when, in late 1575 and early 1576, Ramadan Pasha (Eulj Ali's successor) mounted an expedition to Fès to depose the Moroccan sultan, Mulay Mohamed, and reinstate his predecessor, Mulay Malek, Ramadan's forces included 1,000 Zwawa from Koukou who, together with 300 janissaries, remained in Fès once Mulay Malek had recovered his throne to form the latter's honour guard at his request.[106]

Indispensable to the offensive operations that secured the expansion of Ottoman power in Algeria and beyond it, then, the Kabyles were also relied on for the defensive role of garrisoning the towns. How far matters had gone in this respect by the late 1570s was also noted by de Haedo, who recorded that

> in the garrisons that they have all over this kingdom, such as at Tlemcen, Mostaganem, Biskra, Constantine, Bona or other places, and at Algiers itself, a third of the soldiers, often more than this, consists of *Azuagos*. They are also to be found in the camps or detachments when, as is the custom, sorties are made several times a year to go and collect taxes at the point of a gun from the Arabs and the Moors. These Zouaoua auxiliaries have their own officers, their platoon leaders, with an *agha* or a colonel who is their commanding officer, just like the Turkish soldiers, except that this *agha* is subordinate in rank to the *agha* of the janissaries.[107]

It is in this context that Hassan Pasha's policy can be understood. What he seems to have proposed was the formation of native regiments of Kabyles and Kouloughlis, to be part of the standing army of the Regency in addition to the janissaries and the troops formed by renegades from Europe. But he aimed to regularise the position of the native forces, and of the Kabyles forces in particular, not only in order to ensure the Kouloughlis' loyalty and that of Koukou and Qal'a, but also in order to provide a counterweight to the janissaries. It is probable that this was perfectly understood by the Ojaq and, taken together with the

---

105 The Regency also, of course, induced the Ath Abbas to side against their Hafsid cousins in Tunis. It is possible that the Ath l-Qadi and Ath Abbas both behaved in this way with *arrière-pensées*, namely to seek, by participating, to be in a position to attenuate the fate of the Tunisian Hafsids in the event of their overthrow by guaranteeing their personal security at least.

106 Boulifa, *op. cit.*, 123; De Haedo, *Histoire*, 171–2.

107 De Haedo, *Topographie*, 58 (my translation).

disconcerting sight (which brought matters to a head) of large numbers of armed Kabyles swaggering around Algiers,[108] would explain its violent reaction.

The Ojaq, the corps of janissaries,[109] was a privileged, self-serving, and extremely turbulent element in the power structure of the Regency. Consisting primarily of recruits from the Anatolian heartland of the empire, it regarded itself as indispensable to the maintenance of Ottoman power in Algeria and displayed a routinely demanding if not frankly insubordinate attitude towards the beylerbeys who had overall responsibility for governing the Regency and the triennial pashas who succeeded them, and was particularly disposed to engage in open mutiny or revolt whenever its pay was late or deemed insufficient. Even Kheireddine himself, whose role in establishing the Regency and subsequent eminence as Kapudan-Pasha of the imperial navy gave him a degree of authority over the janissaries that none of his successors could emulate, found himself faced with such a mutiny during the occupation of Tunis in 1533 and initially felt obliged to humour the janissaries before eventually acting firmly towards them, executing a number of the ringleaders, when they mutinied a second time.[110]

At the same time, the Ojaq exuded a contemptuous and hostile attitude to the indigenous population; among its privileges were provisions that sought to guarantee the latter's permanent respect, including the extremely intimidating rules that any native who struck a janissary, even if provoked, would have his hand cut off and anyone who killed a janissary, even in self-defence, would be burned alive or impaled or smashed to death with a sledgehammer.[111] This intensely elitist *esprit de corps* was not founded on a simple proto-national pride in the Turkish identity. The Ojaq was willing – or at any rate agreed eventually[112] – to admit non-Turks into its ranks; renegades – that is, individuals of European extraction who, following capture, opted to convert to Islam and swear loyalty to the Ottoman sultan – might, if possessing military aptitudes, be allowed to become janissaries on the same basis as the 'oxen from Anatolia' who formed the Ojaq's core. But the janissaries were adamant that no natives, whether Arab or Kabyle, could ever be admitted to their number and this prohibition extended to the Kouloughlis – that is, the sons of Turkish fathers by native women – clear proof that the fundamental element of their outlook was an explicitly colonialist, rather than a tacitly national or racist, one. No one with any kinship ties to the

---

108 De Haedo, *Histoire*, 132.

109 The Turkish word *ojaq* (Arabic: *wujāq*) literally means hearth, fireplace, cooking stove or, by extension, kitchen and, as John Ruedy has explained, 'originally designated a platoon-sized unit of men who ate, lived and maneuvered together. It was subsequently applied to the whole body of Janissaries' (John Ruedy, *Modern Algeria: the origins and development of a nation* (Bloomington: Indiana University Press, 1992, 2nd edition 2005), 17).

110 De Grammont, *op. cit.*, 53.

111 De Haedo, *Topographie*, 86–7.

112 De Haedo (*Topographie*, 71) dates this change to 1568.

native population was to be admitted to the Ojaq; that was the iron rule. It represented a doctrinaire application in the Algerian context of a crucial aspect of the established Ottoman practice known as the *devşirme*.

The *devşirme* (literally: 'gathering', 'harvest') was the levy, made roughly every three to seven years, of male children of Christian families in the Ottoman empire's European territories (Greece, Albania, Bulgaria, Serbia, Hungary) and southern Russia who were then brought up as Muslims and trained to serve the empire in one of four capacities: at the sultan's court, in the state administration of religion, as officials of the bureaucracy or as soldiers. The original idea was to establish and maintain bodies of trained servants whose loyalty to the sultan could be guaranteed because of their Christian family backgrounds. The early Ottoman sultans were above all concerned not to have to rely on the support of the Turkish noble families since these were potential sources of challenges to the Osmanli dynasty or of local resistance to its authority; the loyalty to the sultan of troops or other state personnel with ties to this nobility could never be unqualified and wholly dependable. But the loyalty of the products of the *devşirme* could be: their backgrounds meant that they had no connections whatever with the Turkish nobles, while their conversion to Islam detached them radically from their original family and local ties. Disloyalty to the sultan was thus not an option, whereas they had every reason to be loyal, since this anchored their otherwise problematic identities, and everything was done to encourage a loyalty of the most fervent and zealous kind.[113]

It is far from clear how many genuine products of the *devşirme* served in the Ojaq in Algeria. Most sources stress the Anatolian origins of the core of the janissaries in Algeria; according to de Haedo, it was Kheireddine who proposed and got the Ottoman Sultan to agree that any Turk who was not a janissary or a son of Christian but who wished to emigrate from Anatolia to Algiers would be entitled to belong to the corps of the janissaries and enjoy all the rights and privileges of this status. Moreover, de Haedo observed, 'for many years it could be observed at Algiers that no corsair or renegade could be a janissary if he was not himself Turkish'.[114] And of course the original purpose of the *devşirme* was to supply loyal servants to the Sultan in Istanbul, not to staff the most far-flung provinces of the empire. But what seems clear is that the Ojaq in Algiers insisted that one of the key rules of the *devşirme* – that no Muslims native to the country might be recruited – should apply regardless, despite the fact that what one might call the Algerian nobility by no means posed the sort of threat to the Osmanli sultan's position that the Turkish nobility in Anatolia might well have been considered to pose.

That there was something perverse about this in the case of both the Ath l-Qadi and the Ath Abbas should be clear. The rulers of Qal'a had been part

---

113 İnalcık, 1989, *op. cit.*, 78–80.
114 De Haedo, *Topographie*, 70.

of the Hafsid dynasty; the Ath l-Qadi a respected family enjoying political favour and high office. Far from having any interest in challenging let alone supplanting the Osmanli dynasty in the imperial heartland, they were seeking to retrieve or find acceptable surrogates for their former positions as pillars of the state in the central Maghrib; they both had much to offer the new Ottoman state and by 1561 if not earlier their ambitions did not go beyond this. It was the inability of the Regency to accommodate them for long, notwithstanding their willingness to be accommodated, that made them into rebels and threats to Ottoman rule and it was the dogmatic and self-serving refusal of the Ojaq to accept such an accommodation that underlay the Regency's failure in this regard.

All this appears to have been well understood by Hassan Pasha. Hassan's mother was a 'Moorish woman from Algiers'[115] and his wife was Kabyle and, furthermore, an Ath l-Qadi princess, the daughter of the ruler of Koukou. Above all he was his father's son. Kheireddine and Aruj were not wholly Turks, but the sons of a Turkish (or possibly Albanian) Muslim father and a Greek Christian mother from the island of Mytilene, and Kheireddine had appealed to Istanbul for help only when his plans were on the brink of total disaster. He can accordingly be seen to have had an instrumental rather than sentimental attitude to both the Ottoman connection and the role of the janissaries. While his loyalty to the Sublime Porte after 1518 was never in doubt, it can be seen to have been essentially political – that is, conditional – in origin. And there is no reason to suppose he shared the outlook of either the 'oxen from Anatolia' or the renegades or the products of the *devşirme* who composed the Ojaq, in their exaggerated loyalism towards the sultan or their arrogance towards the 'Moors'.

The attitude of the Sublime Porte to this vexed issue was not at all a simple one and there was some sympathy for Hassan Pasha's position. Kheireddine had become an immensely respected figure at Istanbul and his influence had played its part in securing the appointment of his son as *pasha* in 1545. After Kheireddine's death in 1546, Hassan continued to benefit from the support of powerful courtiers who had been friends of his father, notably the Grand Vizier Rostan, and this influence informed the decision to appoint him pasha for the second time in 1557.[116] Above all, however impressed by the 'loyalism' of the Ojaq and concerned to conserve it, Istanbul could not casually tolerate mutinies and revolts by the janissaries against its own senior appointees. Indeed, the immediate reason for Hassan Pasha's own appointment to a second term in June 1557 had been the pressing need for a safe pair of hands to restore order in

---

115 De Haedo, *Histoire*, 75; Gaïd (1974, *op. cit.*, 77) claims she was Kabyle; though possible there is no evidence for it.

116 I follow De Grammont, *op. cit.*, 89, rather than De Haedo and, following him, Gaïd on this point. The death of Rostan in 1561 may have influenced the timing of the Ojaq's coup d'état against Hassan as well.

Algiers after a period of turmoil and faction fighting since the death (from the plague) of Salah Ra'is in May 1556.[117] For these reasons, the Porte took a dim view of the Ojaq's actions, dismissed the treason charges against Hassan, had the ringleaders of the Ojaq's rebellion beheaded, and sent Hassan back to Algiers to resume his office as Pasha.

This by no means resolved the underlying policy dispute. The Porte had punished a rebellion and vindicated its choice of pasha, not endorsed Hassan's policy towards the Kouloughlis and the Kabyles, and for the rest of his time in office (1562–7) Hassan prudently abstained from forcing the issue while maintaining good relations with Koukou and Qal'a in other respects. These good relations lasted, under Hassan's successors, until the 1590s, when they broke down badly.

Ottoman policy and the end of Koukou

By this stage, the rule of the beylerbeys had given way to that of the so-called 'triennial bashaws', pashas appointed by Istanbul for fixed three-year terms, and it was the third of these, Kheder Pasha, who precipitated the breakdown in relations by setting aside the agreement with the Ath Abbas that had held since 1560. Why he should have done this is unclear but he probably hoped that this would strengthen his position in Algiers. Intended to guarantee Istanbul's authority, the change to triennial pashas did the opposite, for the pashas lacked real power, which resided in the *dīwān*, the council of state, dominated by the representatives of the Ojaq. In these circumstances, there developed a tendency for newly appointed pashas to engage in dramatic military initiatives, in part to occupy the Ojaq, in part to gain its support and thereby authority over the *dīwān*. Such considerations may explain, at least in part, the decision of Kheder Pasha in 1590 to mount a military campaign against the Qal'a. Another important consideration is likely to have been the case for bringing the Ath Abbas to heel in order to assert Ottoman control over the road linking Algiers to Constantine, since the central section of this, from the Wad Sahel to Setif, ran along the south-western and southern edges of the Ath Abbas territory; the Regency's dire financial straits at the time[118] may also have tempted Algiers to try to impose taxes on the populations of Lesser Kabylia.

---

117 In 1556 the Ojaq's favourite to succeed Salah Ra'is, Hassan Corso, was arrested and cruelly executed by the Porte's nominee, Teckerli, who was then killed by Hassan's lieutenant, Yussuf, to avenge his chief. Yussuf ruled only a few days before also succumbing to plague and was succeeded by the sagacious Yahia, who ruled for six months before gracefully making way for Hassan Pasha in June 1557.

118 Hess, *op. cit.*, 109–10.

Kheder's campaign against Qalʿa ended in negotiations, a cease-fire and eventually an agreement by which the Ath Abbas submitted in principle to Ottoman authority and paid a substantial sum of money.[119] Thus the era when the territory ruled from Qalʿa enjoyed the attributes of a sovereign realm was over and the Ath Abbas were now, formally, on the same footing as the Ath l-Qadi since the latter's submission to Ottoman authority in 1542. But matters did not end there; the long period of peaceful relations inaugurated with the Ath l-Qadi in 1542 found no equivalent in Algiers's relations with the Ath Abbas in the 1590s. Kheder came under violent attack from the Ojaq, ostensibly on grounds of illicit enrichment but most probably for having called off the military campaign against the Ath Abbas and come to terms with them, and was recalled to Istanbul. In 1595, under Chabane Pasha or his *khalīfa*, Mustapha, hostilities with the Ath Abbas suddenly resumed. That the Ojaq was behind this is suggested by Kheder's behavior, following his return to office in December of that year, which was to take on the Ojaq in an unprecedented trial of strength, arming the Kouloughlis[120] and mobilising their support in a ferocious and overt faction fight verging on a civil war, which lasted several months, in 1596. His recall to Istanbul signalled the Porte's refusal to give effective backing to such efforts to tame the Ojaq, which seems to have persisted in its attitude.

In the context of renewed conflict between Algiers and both Qalʿa and Koukou, the Regency eventually committed itself to a quite different policy towards Kabylia from that originally envisaged by Hassan Pasha. This was a policy of containment and incremental conquest and it was pursued at the expense of both the Ath Abbas connection and the Ath l-Qadi connection. For it was at this point that Algiers, under the rule of Kheder's successor and bitter rival, Mustapha Pasha, began to insulate its communications with Constantine from the harassment of the Ath Abbas by establishing a second, more southerly route to the eastern province via Sour el-Ghozlane and the Hodna.[121] According to Robin, it was also at this time that the Ottomans established forts at Borj Menaiel on the north-western marches of Greater Kabylia and at Borj Hamza (Bouïra) on its south-western marches.[122]

---

119 Benoudjit, *op. cit.*, 281.

120 The resentment of the Kouloughlis at the ban on their becoming janissaries had become acute by this time; see Hess, *op. cit.*, 110. It is not clear that Kheder actively mobilised Kabyle support as well; the Kouloughlis reportedly enjoyed the spontaneous support of the 'Moors' of Algiers, who will have included Kabyles, but the balance of evidence suggests that matters did not go further than this.

121 Robin (*op. cit.*, 41) dates the foundation of Sour el-Ghozlane to 1594 but De Grammont (*op. cit.*, 130) attributes it to Mustapha, who ruled as Chabane Pasha's *khalīfa* from July to December 1595; this gives us a fairly precise date for this development; Boyer (*op. cit.*, 28) follows De Grammont on this point.

122 *Ibid.*

The conflict between Algiers and the Ath Abbas reached its climax in 1598 when the latter went onto the offensive, an entirely unprecedented event, descending from their mountains and mounting an expedition of their own against Algiers, which they besieged for eleven days before withdrawing.[123] It was in this context, characterised by acute instability within the Regency, the repeated failure of pashas and the Porte alike to curb the Ojaq and the latter's evident commitment to an aggressive policy towards Kabylia, that the Ath l-Qadi renewed contact with the Spanish in June 1598[124] and engaged in discussions with them that continued on and off for the next twelve years.

Boyer, who has provided the fullest account of these dealings, concludes that the Ath l-Qadi did not seriously envisage helping the Spanish to destroy the Ottoman state, but were, in effect, seeking Spanish attention and recognition in order to strengthen their position at home which, he suggests was menaced more by the resurgent maraboutic movement than by the Ottomans. A difficulty with this analysis is that treating with the Christian Spanish, the traditional enemy of *Dar el-Islam*, was hardly a convincing way of seeing off challenges from a resurgent maraboutic movement; rather than restore lost prestige it would tend to aggravate the problem of the dynasty's popular standing by making it vulnerable to attack on religious grounds and allowing its maraboutic critics to wield a monopoly of the jihadi discourse against it. Moreover, the evidence is that the Ath l-Qadi had good reason to feel threatened by the Ottomans' aggressive initiatives[125] and thus ample motive for seeking an alliance with the Spanish as a defensive move or at least as a bargaining counter in their dealings with Algiers. It is probable therefore that the Ath l-Qadi still saw the Regency as the main threat and they may have been taken by surprise by the agitation, led by certain *mrābtīn*, that subsequently developed in parts of Kabylia.

What is certain is that the Ath l-Qadi lost a lot of ground during the affair. When in June 1603 the Spanish tried to land a force at Azeffoun, troops supplied by Ameur ou l-Qadi to protect the landing defected to the Regency and the Spanish were massacred.[126] When in March 1604 Spanish vessels tried to land supplies for the Ath l-Qadi, this too went awry because the Regency had got wind of the plot and its troops were on hand to foil it.[127] This second incident is evidence of the Ottomans' success in penetrating maritime Kabylia

---

123 De Grammont, *op. cit.*, 131.

124 An earlier attempt to make contact in 1594 had led nowhere (Boyer, *op. cit.*, 33–4).

125 Boyer's belief that the Ath l-Qadi were, on the contrary, in a strong position vis-à-vis the Regency relies on the supposition that the Kabyle siege of Algiers in 1598 was a Koukou–Zwawa affair, whereas, as we have seen, it was a (brief) riposte by the Ath Abbas to Ottoman thrusts at Qal'a. The building of Ottoman forts at Borj Menaiel and Borj Hamza is likely to have alarmed the rulers of Koukou as evidence of Algiers's intentions towards them.

126 Boyer, *art. cit.*, 37.

127 *Ibid.*

and acquiring local supporters there. A later attempt of the same kind in 1607 was successful, however, but by 1608, to Spanish dismay, Ameur ou l-Qadi had switched sides and done a deal with the Regency. Boyer suggests that this deal was advantageous to Koukou, since he speaks of 'a reciprocal restitution of conquests',[128] but he does not specify what was 'restored' to Koukou in this way and adduces no evidence in support of this claim. What we do know, however, is that in 1607 an Ottoman force penetrated into Greater Kabylia as far as the important village of Jema'a n'Saharij,[129] the capital of the Ath Fraoucen, located in the foothills of the central massif overlooking the middle Sebaou valley and thus guarding the northern approaches to Koukou itself. It is likely that this striking event concentrated Ou l-Qadi's mind and brought home the need to seek terms with Algiers once more. This agreement proved insufficient to re-establish genuinely good relations, however. The following year Ameur ou l-Qadi renewed contact with the Spanish and this last round of exchanges continued into 1610, although without result, because of Spanish scepticism concerning the Ath l-Qadi's seriousness.[130] In the same year, Zwawa forces from Kabylia attacked the Mitija plain south of Algiers and the pasha, Mohammed Kouça, responded with an expedition which penetrated as far as Koukou itself, took the place by storm and forced the Ath l-Qadi to sue for terms again.[131]

The gist of previous accounts of the end of Koukou is that the Ath l-Qadi had exhausted their political capital by this stage and that the end was more or less inevitable, with the lords of Koukou succumbing to the simultaneous assaults of the Ottomans and local public opinion as articulated by leading *mrābtīn* of the region. This view of the matter rests on a very flimsy basis.

The first major intervention of *mrābtīn* in the Kabyle political sphere is recorded as having taken place in 1590, for it was in response to the urging of an unidentified *mrābit* in the Soummam valley that Kheder Pasha had agreed to a cease-fire and negotiated a settlement with the Ath Abbas.[132] The next intervention that certain traditions record was that of the *mrābtīn* of Greater Kabylia some 20–25 years later and it is widely suggested that this intervention was fatal to the Ath l-Qadi dynasty.[133] According to Boulifa, four saints – Sidi Abderrahmane, Sidi Ahmed Wedris, Sidi Ahmed ou Malek and Sidi Mansour – established themselves at some point in the early seventeenth century in a kind of hermitage at a deserted spot called Tizi Berth[134] on the main ridge of

---

128 *Ibid.*
129 Boyer, *art. cit.*, 38; Gaïd, 1974, *op. cit.*, 114.
130 Boyer, *art. cit.*, 39.
131 De Grammont, *op. cit.*, 137.
132 De Grammont, *op. cit.*, 130; Boulifa, *op. cit.*, 124–5.
133 Boulifa, *op. cit.*, 127–46; Genevois, 1974, *op. cit.*, 34–5
134 Boulifa, *op. cit.*, (198, fn 1) 135–6, fn 1. The largest scale maps of the region make no mention of this place.

the Jurjura near Tizi n'Ichelladen. From here they subsequently embarked on a campaign of propaganda – Sidi Abderrahmane and Sidi Ahmed Wedris among the Illoulen Oumalou, Sidi Ahmed ou Malek among the Ath Ijjeur, and Sidi Mansour among the Ath Jennad – which roused these populations against the increasingly intolerable exactions of the rulers of Koukou. It was in this context, when local opinion had turned against his dynasty that, in 1618, the third (or possibly fourth) ruler, Ameur ou l-Qadi, was assassinated and succeeded by his brother.

Although it has since been repeated as historical fact by numerous scholars, there are very strong reasons for rejecting Boulifa's account of the role of the *mrābtīn* in this affair. These include the fact that Sidi Ahmed Wedris had been dead for over 150 years by this time[135] and Sidi Abderrahmane was still a *tāleb* and an adolescent in 1618 and yet to acquire the status of a saint and the title 'Sidi', let alone found his *zāwiya*.[136] As for 'Sidi Ahmed ou Malek', Boulifa appears to have confused two quite different saints, Sidi Ahmed (or, in Thaqbaylith, 'Hend') ou Malek, a saint of the Azeffoun district in maritime Kabylia,[137] and Sidi M'Hand ou Malek, the founder of the *zāwiya* of Tifrit n'Ath ou Malek and the small *'arsh* of the same name belonging to the Ath Ijjeur confederation in the Akfadou district. The first lived some distance from and had little connection with the Ath Ijjeur and could not have mobilised them against the Ath l-Qadi and the second founded his *zāwiya* in the late fifteenth century CE[138] and so could not have mobilised the Ath Ijjeur against the Ath l-Qadi in the early seventeenth century.[139]

The only part of this legend that rings true concerns Sidi Mansour, who very probably did indeed mobilise and articulate the revolt of the Ath Jennad against the lord of Koukou.[140] It is also possible that the Ath Jennad's neighbours

---

135 Sidi Ahmed Wedris (or Oudris) lived in the fourteenth century and is mentioned by Ibn Khaldun in his *History of the Berbers*; see Hadibi, *op. cit.*, 95–110.

136 I discuss the role of Sidi Abderrahmane further in Chapter 7.

137 Mouloud Mammeri, *Les Isefra: poèmes de Si Mohand ou M'Hand* (Paris: François Maspero, 1969), 157.

138 According to the notice on this saint posted on the internet: http://fr.wikipedia.org/wiki/Sidi_M'hand_Oumalek.

139 Boulifa refers to Sidi M'Hand ou Malek in a later passage (*op. cit.*, 158), so his earlier reference to Sidi Ahmed ou Malek may have been simply a lapse on his part; but Sidi M'Hand's dates do not work for Boulifa's thesis in any case.

140 The *zāwiya* of Sidi Mansour at Timizar, in *'arsh* Ath Adas of the Ath Jennad confederation, has been one of the most important *zawāyā* in maritime Kabylia up until recently. Sidi Mansour's opposition to the lord of Koukou is documented by the notice on this *zāwiya*, which includes a brief life of the founder, written by Daoui Sid Ahmed Ben Mohammed, the then sheikh of the *zāwiya*, dated 22 April 1911 and included by Boulifa in the appendix of his book. The notice includes an account of Sidi Mansour's confrontation with Ameur ou l-Qadi, recording how he defied Ou l-Qadi and predicted his death, which this tradition claims occurred a few days later.

among the 'aarsh of maritime Kabylia supported this revolt, perhaps invoking the defunct Sidi Hend ou Malek or his successors. Given this saint's connection with Azeffoun, scene of the planned landing of the infidel Spanish forces in 1603, this makes good sense. But, once we discount Sidi Wedris, Sidi Abderrahmane and the *imrabdhen* of Tifrit n'Ath ou Malek, the evidence of a significant revolt against the Ath l-Qadi by the populations of the right bank of the Wad Boubehir evaporates completely.[141] In addition to the Ath Jennad and (possibly) their neighbours, there is evidence that public opinion among the Ath Yahia had turned sharply against Ameur ou l-Qadi and it is possible that local *imrabdhen* took a hand in articulating and even fomenting this. But the evidence that the *imrabdhen* led a region-wide popular revolt against the Ath l-Qadi disintegrates when we examine it.

Finally there is every reason to reject Boulifa's claim that, in supposedly acting to rid the region of the Ath l-Qadi's 'tyranny', the *mrābtīn* were establishing or re-establishing 'Kabyle independence'.[142] This is a *romance*. The political role of the *mrābtīn* of Kabylia from this point onwards was intimately connected to the Ottoman penetration of the region, as we shall see. The independence of Greater Kabylia was not (re-)established following the downfall of the Ath l-Qadi. And, if it may be said that the independence of the Igawawen was eventually re-established, a good deal later on, this, as we shall see, was achieved not under maraboutic leadership but at the expense of saintly hegemony, under the leadership of lay forces to which the *mrābtīn* were obliged to submit.

How, then, are we to understand the assassination of Sidi Ameur ou l-Qadi in 1618 and the fact that he was succeeded by his brother, Sidi Ahmed?[143] It is possible that Sidi Ahmed was acting to preserve the kingdom by co-opting popular resentment against his brother. The stories of the latter's exactions, at any rate among the Ath Yahia and the Ath Jennad, would explain such resentment. But it is at least as likely that the real matter at issue was the attitude of the Ath l-Qadi family to the Regency. It was Ameur ou l-Qadi who had intrigued for so long and to such little effect with the Spanish, thereby provoking the Ottomans' punitive expedition to Jema'a n'Saharij in 1607 and Koukou itself in 1610. That his policy was contested within his family is clear

---

141 As for the Ath Ghoubri, we can be sure they stayed loyal to the Ath l-Qadi. According to the notice on the *zāwiya* of Sidi Mansour included as Appendix II in Boulifa's book (*op. cit.*, 283–97), Sıdı Mansour first settled in the Ath Ghoubri village of Yakouren, but the villagers soon withdrew their welcome and he was obliged to move to the Ath Jennad, where he then founded his *zāwiya*. According to the notice, the people of Yakouren grew irritated by the numbers of people visiting the saint. But an alternative hypothesis that suggests itself is that they and the Ath Ghoubri in general remained loyal to the Ath l-Qadi and refused to harbour a saint preaching revolt against the dynasty.

142 See Boulifa, *op. cit.*, chapter VI: 'Les marabouts et l'indépendance kabyle'.

143 Tahar Oussedik, *Le Royaume de Koukou* (Algiers: Entreprise National du Livre, 1986), 43–6, 58, 65.

from the fact that the troops who, by defecting to the Ottomans, sabotaged the Spanish landing at Azeffoun in 1603 were commanded by one of his own nephews, Abdallah, and defected at the latter's instigation.[144] According to one source, it was the same Abdallah who personally assassinated Ameur ou l-Qadi.[145] There is every reason to think that Sidi Ahmed, who succeeded Ameur ou l-Qadi and was at least implicated in the assassination if not its principal instigator, was the father of this same nephew. If this reading is correct, it would follow that what lay behind the assassination of Ameur was a serious disagreement on strategy within the Ath l-Qadi family, and that the assassination was motivated by the concern to assure the Regency that the family regretted and would on no account resume its defiant flirtations with the Spanish and was seeking a fresh understanding with Algiers as a loyal client.

But, if this was the calculation, it did not buy the family much relief. In 1623–4, troops of the Ottoman Regency under Kosrou Pasha mounted another brief expedition to Koukou. This seems to have been simply a show of strength, presumably in order to reinforce the by now rather humiliating terms on which the Regency was prepared to recognise the lords of Koukou, for the expedition did not overthrow the Ath l-Qadi when it could have done. The fact of the matter is that neither the *imrabdhen* nor the Ottomans put an end to the kingdom of Koukou; the Ath l-Qadi, or rather a branch of the Ath l-Qadi, did this themselves.

When Ameur ou l-Qadi was assassinated, his widow, who was pregnant with their son, fled to Tunis, where her relations and the family's former patrons in Hafsid circles provided refuge. At some point in the 1630s – Robin says 1632–3 but it was probably as late as 1638[146] – the son, Sidi Ahmed 'El-Tounsi' ('the man from Tunis'), returned at the head of a small army and settled accounts with his father's murderers. But El-Tounsi did not stay at Koukou; he returned to the ancestral village of Aourir n'Ath Ghoubri instead before finally settling at Tifilkout in *'arsh* Illilten.[147] The era of Koukou as a political capital was over and it was an Ou l-Qadi who brought the curtain down.

Koukou defined

What, then, are we finally to make of the 'kingdom of Koukou' in the light of our exploration of the political history of Kabylia between 1509 and the 1630s?

---

144 Boyer (*art. cit.*, 37) mentions the nephew's role but not his name; Mercier, however, gives this (*op. cit.*, t. III, 174).

145 Boulifa, *op. cit.*, 145–6.

146 Robin, *op. cit.*, 142; Oussedik recounts (*op. cit.*, 60) that Sidi Ahmed El-Tounsi was 20 years old when he set out from Tunis to avenge his father; this would place these events in 1638–9.

147 Oussedik, *op. cit.*, 77.

Two issues have been the focus of earlier commentaries and call for clarification. The first concerns the relationship of the lords of Koukou to the Igawawen. The second is an instance of the much wider question of the relationship of politics and religion in the history of Kabylia, for it concerns the relationship of Koukou to the maraboutic movement.

In some of the Spanish documents which record Spain's dealing with the Ath l-Qadi, the latter are referred to not only as 'los reyes de Cuco' but also as the rulers of 'the kingdom ... of the Zwawa ('reino ... de Azuagos').[148] Masqueray dismissed this, arguing that the Ath l-Qadi dynasty ruled only over the valley of the Wad Sebaou and its uppermost reaches in the Wad Boubehir.

> Its influence no doubt extended much further but, in spite of its arquebusiers and cavalry, it was never master of the mountain of the Gaouaou.[149]

For this Masqueray has been taken to task by Genevois,[150] who appears to support Boyer's claim that the kingdom, while not including all the Kabyles, did comprise 'the tribes of maritime Kabylia and the confederation of the Zouaoua.'[151] But, since Boyer immediately added: 'Although the latter were allies rather than subjects,'[152] an admission which logically implies that the Igawawen were *not* under the rule of the Ath l-Qadi and their territory *not* part of the 'kingdom' of Koukou at all, Genevois's criticism of Masqueray's opinion appears to be an empty quibble. There are in any case other reasons for supposing that Masqueray was right.

First, although the Ath Yahia may be considered Igawawen in the extended sense of the term, they appear never to have been part of a *thaqbilth* grouping them with other *'aarsh*. It is inaccurate to speak of 'the confederation of the Zwawa'; the Igawawen never formed a confederation in the sense of a single *thaqbilth*. We know from Ibn Khaldoun that most of the Igawawen *'aarsh* were already grouped in a number of distinct *thiqbilin* – the Ath Irathen, the Ath Bethroun – in his time, long before the advent of the Ath l-Qadi, and these *thiqbilin* survived into the nineteenth century if not the twentieth. A dynasty based in the leading village of an important *'arsh* might well have been able to exercise a commanding authority over the entire *thaqbilth* to which the *'arsh* belonged and thereby acquire influence over the *thaqbilth*'s neighbours, but a dynasty based in a village of an *'arsh* that belonged to no *thaqbilth* at all was another matter.

---

148 Genevois, 1974, *op. cit.*, 4–5, citing the Spanish author Luis del Marmol Carvajal, *Descripcion General de Africa* (Granada, 1573), Libro II.

149 Masqueray, *op. cit.*, 142 (my translation). 'Gaouaou' is Masqueray's rendering of Igaouaouen (Igawawen).

150 Genevois, 1974, *op. cit.*, 6.

151 Boyer, *art. cit.*, 26 (my translation).

152 *Ibid.* (my translation).

Moreover, geographical as well as sociological factors militated against this. While the Ath Yahia might be considered to have been well placed to exercise a kind of leadership over the other Igawawen populations in their relations with Hafsid Bejaia (but less so with Ottoman Algiers), it is striking that the situation of Koukou made it about the worst placed Ath Yahia village from which to aspire to exercise a continuous *governing* authority over the populations to its west and south-west. Located on the far eastern edge of the series of high ridges, extending north from the central Jurjura, that constitutes the Igawawen district, Koukou is also one of the most easterly of the Ath Yahia villages, on the periphery of the *'arsh*, not at or near its centre.[153]

Second, there is no evidence whatever that the Ath l-Qadi levied taxes or in other ways exploited the economic activities of the *'aarsh* of the central Jurjura. All the oral traditions cited by Genevois regarding the Ath l-Qadi's economic exploitation and depredations concern the Ath Yahia and the populations of the middle and upper Sebaou. Indeed, it is very striking that Genevois is unable to cite any traditions concerning the Ath l-Qadi from sources in the central Jurjura other than the maraboutic hamlet of Bou Aggach, in the immediate vicinity of the Ath Yahia,[154] and the Illilten villages of Tifilkout and Tizit perched on ridges overlooking the head of the Boubehir valley.[155] Apart from Koukou itself, the other sources are from the Ath Ghoubri and the Ath Jennad.

Finally, it is striking that the Igawawen played no part in the overthrow of the Ath l-Qadi dynasty yet, had they been ruled by it, they should have been expected to do so. Traditions variously ascribe the assassination of Ameur ou l-Qadi in 1618 to his brother Ahmed or his nephew Abdallah, or to an Ath Yahia man acting with the encouragement of local opinion, exasperated by the Ath l-Qadi's exactions.[156] In any case, the rest of the Igawawen were not involved, nor were they involved in the Ottomans' expedition in 1623–4. All this indicates that the Igawawen were indifferent to the fate of the lords of Koukou, which in turn implies that, whatever their relations with them, they were never ruled by them. Thus the evidence supports Masqueray's opinion. It is clear that the Igawawen accepted the Ath l-Qadi's leadership early on in the jihad against

---

153 The social and political centre of the Ath Yahia is the large village of Taqa and its satellite hamlets.

154 Bou Aggach is a hamlet of the Ath Sidi Saïd, an important maraboutic family with settlements primarily in the Ath Menguellat near Aïn El-Hammam. Bou Aggach is situated on the south-western side of the valley separating the Ath Menguellat from the Ath Yahia; it is thus the Ath Sidi Saïd settlement closest to the Ath Yahia.

155 The Illilten occupy the south-easterly part of the Igawawen territory, the north-facing slopes of the high Jurjura between the Tirourda and Chellata passes. Their location at the head of the Boubehir valley is probably the premise of their connection to the Ath l-Qadi.

156 H. Genevois, *Légende des Rois de Koukou*, 19–21, 27, 31, 43.

the Spanish and subsequently in alternately serving and resisting the Turks. But they were not part of the 'kingdom' of Koukou in any other sense.

This brings us to the second point at issue, which can be broken down into two questions. How are we to characterise the Ath l-Qadi's 'kingdom' and what was its relationship to the maraboutic movement? Our answer to the first question will depend on our answer to the second. To arrive at this we need to finish clearing the decks as far as the family's maraboutic lineage is concerned, for a corollary of the thesis that the Ath l-Qadi's power was religious in origin is that the kingdom they ruled was a maraboutic state and thus a variant of the phenomenon already noted and documented in respect of Morocco in the cases of Boujad, Dila and Zawiya Ahansal.

I have already explained why the Ath l-Qadi's maraboutic lineage does not account for their rise to political prominence. To this we may add that the evidence concerning the behaviour of the dynasty is inconsistent with the thesis that it ruled a maraboutic state. The oral traditions are especially eloquent about the despotic, capricious and unpopular nature of their rule in the upper Sebaou, at any rate in its latter period.[157] And, above all, there is no trace of any religious activity properly so-called, apart from the initial mobilisation of the population for the jihad against the Spanish aggressions at Bejaia and Algiers and the Genovese at Jijel. There is no evidence of the foundation of a *zāwiya* by the Ath l-Qadi at Koukou or anywhere else. Finally, to conceive of the 'kingdom of Koukou' as a maraboutic state is to imply that it was part of the maraboutic movement which swept Kabylia from the turn of the fifteenth and sixteenth centuries onwards. That this is to misconceive its nature and to mistake the essentially political and military logic of its genesis I have already made clear. The fact that it fell foul of Sidi Mansour, a leading light of this movement in the early seventeenth century, can be seen as applying the *coup de grâce* to this misconception.

The balance of evidence therefore suggests that we should understand the kingdom of Koukou as the achievement of an adventurous fragment of the old Hafsid order that managed to carve out a position for itself by mobilising local popular support and anti-Spanish feeling and then to sustain this position for three or four generations primarily by honouring its understanding with the Regency for as long as this was possible, but which had been strategically weakened by the disappearance of its original patrons, the Hafsids in Tunis, in 1574 and, given the drawbacks of entering into a genuine alliance with the Spanish, got into severe difficulties soon after the Regency adopted a more aggressive policy towards Kabylia.

If we are to encapsulate the nature of the 'kingdom of Koukou' in a brief formula, it emerges that what we have been examining was not a maraboutic state

---

157　H. Genevois, *op. cit.*, 19–35.

but the realm of a dynasty of warlords – a *mujahid* command. The foundation of Ahmed ou l-Qadi's power in Kabylia was his status as the commander of a jihadi army. While he failed to achieve either of his principal ambitions, of making himself a force in a liberated Bejaia – although his descendants at least temporarily achieved this objective as vassals of the Ottomans – or of establishing his own enduring rule in Algiers, he created a sufficiently solid power base in Greater Kabylia for himself and his family as the leading pretenders to one or other of these positions that his descendants were able to sustain their hegemony in the region for over a century. That they did so cannot be credited simply to the solidity of their internal support in the region. On the contrary, the survival of Koukou after 1525–7 clearly owed a great deal to external recognition, endorsement and support, whether that of the Ottoman Regency in Algiers or that of its adversaries (Hafsid Tunis and, very accessorily, Spain). In the relative weight of internal and external support, moreover, it might be said that the realm of Koukou increasingly came to resemble the early Ottoman Regency itself.

CHAPTER 7

~

The Reconstitution of Greater Kabylia after 1640

Al-haqīqa lubb al-Sharī'a (Truth is the heart of the law).
Hussein Al-Warthilani[1]

On a huge hill,
Cragged and steep, Truth stands, and he that will
Reach her, about must and about must go.
John Donne[2]

The origins of an originality

At some point in 1765 CE the *'ulamā'* of Bejaia expressed an opinion about the state of affairs in Kabylia. It is not clear that this amounted to a *fatwā*. Houari Touati has inferred that they considered the region to be 'un pays de mission',[3] which might be understood to mean that they regarded Kabylia as no longer firmly part of *Dār al-Islām* but rather a land whose inhabitants needed to be re-converted to the true faith. This would not necessarily mean that they regarded the Kabyles as apostates, but that they considered them at least to have strayed and to need to be brought back to the right path through the good offices of the religious mission, *al-da'wa*. But the matter was not exactly of this kind.

The source of this report is the fancily titled *Nuzhat al-anzār fī fadhl 'ilm al-tārīkh wa 'l-akhbār* ('Promenade of the eyes with the benefit of the study of history and news'), commonly known as the *Rihla*, of Sheikh Hussein Al-Warthilani. A *rihla* is a journey that an *'ālim* or *tāleb* or sufi adept makes in search of knowledge and enlightenment, visiting renowned scholars and sufi masters to learn from them; by extension, it is also the written narrative of

---

1   Hussein Al-Warthilani, *Rihla*, edited by M. Ben Cheneb (Algiers: P. Fontana, 1908), 179.
2   John Donne, *Satire III*.
3   Houari Touati, *Entre Dieu et Les Hommes. Lettrés, saints et sorciers au Maghreb (17ᵉ siècle)* (Paris: Éditions de l'École des Hautes Études en Sciences Sociales, 1994), 91, n. 81.

that journey. Hussein Al-Warthilani was from a cultivated family of maraboutic lineage,[4] an *'alīm* who was also a sufi master, an adept of the Shadhiliyya order[5] and the sheikh of a *zāwiya* at Borj Zemoura, at the foot of the Atlas on the edge of the Mejana plain in Lesser Kabylia.[6] He was born in 1710 and died in 1779. His family, which claimed sharifian status, was originally from Mila in the Constantinois but subsequently settled at Zemoura. As his *nisba* indicates, Hussein himself developed a connection, as the sheikh of a second, smaller, *zāwiya*, with the Beni Warthīlān, known by the French as Beni Ourtilane and in *Thaqbaylith* as Ath Warthīrān, a respected but rather reclusive *'arsh* of Lesser Kabylia, discreetly tucked away in the folds of the Guergour mountains to the east of the Soummam valley, about 30 miles south of Bejaia. He set off on his journey – which took him on an extended tour of Kabylia before joining a caravan of pilgrims to Mecca – in the year 1179 of the Hegiran calendar, corresponding to 1765–6 CE, and completed his account of this in 1768. The reference to the *'ulamā'* of Bejaia appears early on in his narrative and he cites their opinion with approval.[7]

Before examining this incident in its context, let us seek our wider bearings by briefly glancing ahead. Some 170 years later, in the 1930s, concern about the standing of Islam in Kabylia would be expressed by the Islamic reformers inspired by the Salafiyya movement and organised from 1931 onwards in Sheikh Abdelhamid Ben Badis's Association of the Algerian Muslim *'ulamā'* (*Association des Oulémas musulmans algériens*, AOMA).[8] This fact may be misunderstood as lending support to the suggestion not only that the Islamic faith of the Kabyles was questionable but also that this was a constant, permanent, aspect of Kabyle society and culture. But this would be to overlook the difference between the judgment of the *'ulamā'* of eighteenth-century Bejaia and that of their twentieth-century counterparts.

In the view of Ben Badis and his associates, the waning or undermining of the Islamic faith of the Kabyles had causes that were quite recent, for they could be attributed to the activity of Christian missionaries in the region in some degree but above all to the influence of France's secular culture, transmitted

---

4   Adli, *op. cit.*, 217 n. 25.
5   Mahammad Hadj Sadok, 'A travers la Berbérie Orientale du XVIIIe Siecle avec le Voyageur Al-Warthîlanî', *Revue Africaine* 95 (1951, 3rd and 4th quarters), 315–99: 321, n. 13; for the Shadhiliyya, see P.J. André, *Confréries religieuses musulmanes* (Algiers: Éditions La Maison des Livres, 1956), 27.
6   Mahammad Hadj Sadok, 'Avec un cheikh de Zemmorah à travers le ouest constantinois du dix-huitième siècle', *Bulletin de la société historique et géographique de la région de Sétif* (1935), 45–59.
7   Al-Warthilani, *op. cit.*, 8.
8   Ali Merad, *Le Réformisme Musulman en Algérie de 1925 à 1940; Essai d'histoire religieuse et sociale*, 2nd edition (Algiers: Éditions El Hikma, 1999), 301–5.

to the population in part through French schoolteachers imbued with the secularist principles of French Republicanism but mainly as a side-effect of the reorientation of Kabyle labour migration to France from 1914 onwards (a factor the AOMA could do nothing about and did not emphasise).[9] The view of Ben Badis & Co. should therefore not be read as providing belated vindication of the views of the late nineteenth-century French adepts of the Kabyle myth such as Sabatier. But to say this is not to end the matter.

I have described the French belief, central to the Kabyle myth, that the Kabyles were not 'really' Muslims as a hallucination. But, while maintaining this judgment, I consider that a plea of mitigation could be entered here on the mythmongers' behalf. For, unlike the view of the twentieth-century *'ulamā'*, that of the eighteenth-century *'ulamā'* may appear, at any rate in Touati's account of it, to have provided an element of corroboration of this aspect of the Kabyle myth and to have done so, moreover, in advance. What the French adepts of the Kabyle myth believed to be true of the Kabyles in the matter of religious faith and observance, Algerian *'ulamā'* may appear to have already judged to be the case a century earlier. In other words, the septic question of the relationship of the Kabyles to Islam was not entirely an invention of French colonialism. This relationship seems to have exercised some at least of the *'ulamā'* of Ottoman Algeria long before it was problematised anew by the French.

It is clearly important for us to understand why. But before we address this question – and in order to address it fully – we need to consider a second question. To do this we must glance backwards from this event, to the Kabylia of some 100–130 years earlier – that is, of the period between *c.* 1630 and *c.* 1660 – and the situation, as this has been so far, rather vaguely, understood, in the aftermath of the end of Koukou. Boulifa presents this aftermath in positive, indeed lyrical, terms. Celebrating the maraboutic movement as the real artisan of the overthrow of the Ath l-Qadi's tyranny, he further presents the *imrabdhen* of Kabylia not only as preachers of the good word but as the architects of a new, just and harmonious order in the region and simultaneously as the guarantors of 'Kabyle independence' in relation to the Ottoman Regency.[10] The unreliable elements of this vision will be addressed presently. For the moment, let us face this question: if, as Boulifa claims and, I believe, is indeed the case, the *imrabdhen* were important social actors in Kabylia during the decline of Koukou and thereafter, why should the Islamic character of Kabylia have been in question 130 years later?

Let us in turn sharpen this question somewhat. To do so, we should bear in mind that at no point between 1514 and the 1630s that is, at no point during the protracted relationships between the Barbarossa brothers and their successors in the government of the Ottoman Regency on the one hand and

9   Merad, *op. cit.*, 301–3.
10 See note 142 in Chapter 6 of this volume.

the lords of Koukou and Qal'a on the other – were the Muslim credentials of the Kabyles at issue. Not even when Algiers and Koukou or Algiers and Qal'a were in armed conflict did the Regency seek to stigmatise or delegitimate as 'bad Muslims' either the Ath l-Qadi and Ath Abbas in particular or the Kabyles in general. Throughout the first century and more of Ottoman rule in Algeria, neither the religious faith nor, for that matter, the mother tongue of the Kabyles were at issue at all. In short, there was a Koukou question and a Qal'a question, but not a *Kabyle* question. Had some significant change taken place, then, in the character of Kabyle society by the mid-eighteenth century to warrant the raising of a Kabyle question, at any rate in the overlapping spheres of faith and law, by the *'ulamā'* of Bejaia and by Al-Warthilani himself?

Elements of two possible answers to this question can be found in Houari Touati's fascinating study of the religious life of Algeria in this period.[11] Touati presents evidence that, as early as the 1660s, the *'ulamā'* of Constantine were noting and denouncing the failure of the *mrābtīn* of the mountain districts to uphold Islamic law in their communities. The sources he draws on are two: the *Manshūr al-hidāya fī man idda'ā al-'ilm wa al-wilāya* ('Pamphlet providing guidance concerning those who pretend to knowledge and authority'), a tract written by a leading *'alīm* of Constantine, Abdelkrim Lefgoun (died 1073 AH/1663 CE), and the body of legal case histories known as the *Nawāzil* collected by his son, Mohammed Lefgoun (died 1114 AH/1702 CE), who inherited the title of *Shaikh al-Islām* as well as other titles to preeminent religious authority in the city, including the office of *imām* of the Great Mosque, on his father's death.

The principal concern expressed in the *Nawāzil* of Constantine was with the marriage customs of the Kabyles. The custom singled out for particular condemnation as contrary to Islamic law was the 'right of flight' accorded to a married woman oppressed or mistreated by her husband.

> One feature of their detestable conduct is the custom whereby the woman lives for a time with a man and that she subsequently leaves him by fleeing to the home of another man without divorcing …
>
> The runaway wife is debauched. The man who receives her is also debauched. And both of them are fornicators. There is no solution of tolerance for them, whether the wedding gifts are returned or not … It is consequently illicit for whoever justifies this irregularity, as is said to be the case of many tribal fakirs who meddle in this matter on the pretext of seeking piety and peace among the people.[12]

---

11 Touati, *op. cit.*
12 *Nawâzil, op. cit.*, 44–5, cited by Touati, *op. cit.*, 90–1 (my translation into English here and below).

That such concerns were expressed up to a century before the 'ulamā' of Bejaia delivered themselves of their opinion may suggest that the failure of the Kabyles to conform to orthodoxy in religion and law was chronic, a constant feature of their society. This is the interpretation to which Touati himself tends. In this light, the fact that Kabylia at this time was also producing a striking number of distinguished Islamic scholars and that scholars from elsewhere would come there to pursue their studies assumes, Touati suggests, the status of a paradox. As he puts it,

> this paradoxical Kabylia, at one and the same time land of Berber oral tradition and of scholarly Arab culture, of custom and of the study of Islamic law … In the entire Berber Maghreb at this time only the Moroccan Sous could rival Kabylia in its cultural originality.[13]

At the same time, however, Touati himself provides evidence that supports a different understanding of these matters.

First, it is not clear that the strictures of the 'ulamā' of Constantine applied to the society of Greater Kabylia. The corroboration of their concerns provided by Leo Africanus was limited to 'the mountains of the province of Constantine'.[14] This phrase would embrace the Edough, Collo and Ferjiwa in the north, the Mejerda mountains in the east, the massifs of the Aurès and Nememcha in the south, the Hodna in the south-west and the mountains of Lesser Kabylia in the west. But the Jurjura massif was not in the province of Constantine and it may be doubted that legal case histories collected in Constantine would include material relating to Greater Kabylia.

Second, even if these strictures were intended to apply to Greater Kabylia, we may well ask whether they were justified at the time and also, even if they were, whether they continued to be justified. The 'right of flight' of a desperately unhappy wife was indeed a recognised right in Greater Kabylia, as the qawānīn collected by Hanoteau and Letourneux documented.[15] But these same qawānīn imposed strict conditions on the exercise of this right: the unhappy wife might flee *only* to her parents' home. The woman who fled to an unrelated man with whom she then cohabited without securing a divorce from her husband was clearly condemned by the qawānīn, and the man who took her into his household was also condemned and severely penalised.[16] It is a misuse of language to describe as a 'custom' conduct that Kabyle law itself unequivocally condemned

---

13 Touati, *op. cit.*, 92.
14 As Touati himself observes, *op. cit.*, 89, n. 78.
15 Hanoteau and Letourneux, *op. cit.*, II, chapter XV: 'De la femme insurgée (*Thamenafekt*)', 182–4.
16 Hanoteau and Letourneux, *op. cit.*, II: qānūn of Ath Douala (183), qānūn of Agouni n'Taslent (184 and n. 1).

and punished. And if we assume – on the basis of no evidence and purely for the sake of argument – that the unconditional resort to this practice was indeed a 'custom' of the society of Greater Kabylia (with the occasional 'fornication' tacitly tolerated instead of penalised) in the seventeenth century, it had clearly ceased to be a custom by the nineteenth century, as the *qawānīn* in force by then make clear, in which case a significant change had evidently taken place in the mores of Kabyle society and moreover one which, if anything, enhanced rather than weakened the Islamic credentials of the society and its legal code.

Third, we may note that the preoccupations of the *'ulamā'* of Constantine as recorded in the *Nawāzil* and those of the *'ulamā'* of Bejaia and Al-Warthilani a century or so later were not identical. While the *Nawāzil* fulminate against the 'fakirs' for misguidedly tolerating the 'fornication' allegedly allowed by the 'right of flight', Al-Warthilani does not mention this nor was this what concerned the *'ulamā'* of Bejaia. The problem which exercised them was not that of the onset of unbelief either, but the fact that the Kabyles were constantly fighting one another, a problem Al-Warthilani and his companions undertook to address.

> So we departed with the intention of visiting and satisfying the needs of some Muslims in bringing accord between them, since fighting (*al-qītāl*) between Muslims in our country occurs often and conflict (*fitna*) is seldom lifted and disorder (*al-harj*) abounds – may Allah in His generosity and His grace lift that off them![17]

Al-Warthilani was quite clear where the root of the matter lay. It was not that the Kabyles lacked faith, but that

> the authority of the Sultan has no influence with them, as he fails to exercise it over them. Although the people in this region are close to Algiers, they have built themselves fortified places in the mountains. It is only the zeal of the righteous and of those people who do good that has had any effect with them. It is therefore the duty of those whose deeds are accepted by God the Almighty to go to those people and try to repair their situation and stop them from committing sins and disobedient acts; this is in accordance with the saying of the Prophet (peace be upon Him) that, when two Muslims fight, the slayer and the slain will be in Hell fire. And the *'ulamā'* of Bejaia have stated that it is the duty of the people of goodness and righteousness who are accepted to mediate and mend the rift between those Muslims, otherwise they would be considered as having disobeyed God, the Almighty.[18]

---

17 Al-Warthilani, *Rihla*, 8 (my translation).
18 *Ibid.*

This is the 'mission' to which Touati alludes.

So, insofar as Kabylia exhibited a scandalous aspect, this lay not in the fact that the Kabyles were not good Muslims, but, on the contrary, that, although Muslims, they were constantly fighting one another and defied the 'Sultan'. Al-Warthilani and the *'ulamā'* of Bejaia thus took it for granted that the Kabyles were Muslims; their faith (*al-īmān*) was not in question.

Other authors who have quoted this passage have accepted it as a reliable observation on the state of the region at the time.[19] But there is reason to doubt this, at least in respect of the Jurjura district. There is no significant evidence from another contemporary source to corrorborate this picture of Greater Kabylia as a scene of constant fighting and there is testimony from a slightly earlier source that it was not.

Thomas Shaw was the chaplain of the British factory[20] in Algiers between 1721 and 1733. He visited many parts of Algeria, including Greater and Lesser Kabylia, and noted an important difference between the latter. 'The Zwowah [*sic*; Zwawa]', he tells us, 'the richest and the most numerous Kabyles of this province, possess a large and impenetrable tract of mountains to the eastward of the Sebowe [Sebaou].' As for the 'Beni Abbess' (*sic*; Ath Abbas),

> These are almost as powerful Kabyles as the Zwowah, bringing into the field upwards of three thousand foot, and half the number of horsemen … However the Beni Abbess are not supposed to have the riches; It is certain, they enjoy not the quiet and tranquility of the Zwowah, who, from a more difficult situation, have not, for many years, been molested by the Algerines.[21]

Thus in the 1720s at least the Jurjura district was noted for its peacefulness. It is possible that the *'ulamā'* of Bejaia were projecting onto it the more anarchic conditions they were familiar with in Lesser Kabylia. But while Al-Warthilani, as a near neighbour of the Ath Abbas at Zemoura, might equally be inclined to this mistake, and cites several examples of lawlessness at Zemoura and in the Mejana nearby,[22] he also speaks explicitly of those Kabyles 'close to Algiers' – that is, of Greater Kabylia. This had indeed known a series of intense conflicts since Shaw wrote, especially in the decade from 1745 to 1755, as we shall see, and routine vendettas, short-lived clashes between *'aarsh* and villages, and occasional confrontations between certain *'aarsh* and the Ottoman authorities in the lowlands no doubt continued to occur. But there is no reason to suppose that Al-Warthilani's picture of an entire region in a state of constant warfare and

---

19 For example, Morizot, 1985, *op. cit.*, 91.
20 That is, the trade delegation.
21 Shaw, *op. cit.*, 101–2.
22 Al-Warthilani, *Rihla*, 36, 700.

chaos is a factually accurate one and good reason to discount it, especially in view of the ease with which he himself travelled across the region.

A little later Al-Warthilani emphasised a very different set of aspects of Kabylia:

> Our country is a good country that abounds with science, shows friendliness and generosity to strangers, and is full of olives, grapes, figs and the cultivation of land. Our country is greatly cherished and treasured by its people. The number of the population is great …[23]

But, he immediately reiterates,

> bereft of the Sultan and his authority; consequently, the country is lawless (*sā'ib*).[24] May God, the Almighty, cause it to thrive with the prescriptions of the *Sharī'a*, root out strife (*al-fitna*) and replace it with everlasting well-being (*al-ʿāfiya*).[25]

Thus the Kabyles were accused not so much of a few particularly 'detestable' customs contrary to Islamic law and morality but rather of general lawlessness, in the absence of the authority of the 'Sultan'. The condemnation of this state of affairs, Touati tells us, entailed – if it did not presuppose – a refusal to recognise the *qawānīn* as valid law. As Touati put it,

> the problem is not only that the region transgresses the rules of legal marriage,[26] but, more gravely, that its substitutes its own customary rulings, the famous kanouns [*sic*], for the *Sharī'a*, Islamic legality. Engaged in rebellion, *sība*, it recognizes neither 'the authority of the prince' nor 'legal qualifications'.[27]

At the same time, this disqualification of Kabyle law *en bloc* entailed a condemnation of the *thajma'th* in its role as promulgator of this flawed law.

> The champions of the *Sharī'a* cannot conceive of a worse transgression than that which makes law a product of a human institution and sets up the *tajma'at*, the Kabyle village assembly, as a legislator, as a source of juridical authority.[28]

---

23 Al-Warthilani, *Rihla*, 28.
24 This word, of the same root as the familiar *sība*, can mean 'loose', 'astray', 'lost' and even 'free'; Al-Warthilani presumably intends it in its stronger and negative meaning.
25 Al-Warthilani, *Rihla*, 28.
26 A charge which, as we have seen, is far from proved.
27 Touati, *op. cit.*, 90.
28 Touati, *op. cit.*, 92–3.

If there is a criticism to be made of Touati's otherwise admirable exposition, it is that by interweaving citations from the *Manshūr al-Hidāya* and the *Nawāzil* on the one hand and Al-Warthilani's *Rihla* on the other, he tends to elide the differences between them and thus obscures the element of change over time and other differences between the outlook of the *'ulamā'* of seventeenth-century Constantine and that of Al-Warthilani a century later.

Consider, for instance, the contemptuous reference that we find in the *Nawāzil* to some of the religious leaders of the society of the countryside (and especially of the mountains) as 'fakirs'.[29] The resort to this delegitimating term expressed the hegemonic ambitions of the urban *'ulamā'* and thus their claim to be the authoritative arbiters not only of Islamic orthodoxy but also of who was and who was not a true *'alīm*, combined with the standard urban prejudice against rural and provincial society. In Al-Warthilani's case, the matter was more complicated, for he was himself a 'provincial'; he was moreover of maraboutic lineage and enjoyed the company of those of his fellow *mrābtīn* he respected as true men of religion, *ahl 'ilm wa fadhl* ('people of knowledge and merit'),[30] making a point of visiting many such *mrābtīn* in the course of his journey through Kabylia, and was as inclined to criticise the urban *'ulamā'* (except those of Bejaia, with whom he had strong ties) as he was to denounce those *mrābtīn* who in his view failed in their proper, religious, mission or whose credentials were bogus. Clearly more discriminating in its choice of targets, Al-Warthilani's critique above all articulated an important shift in perspective, from a piecemeal condemnation of the mores and unorthodox customs of the mountain populations to a general criticism of the Kabyles for subsisting in a state of lawlessness. But the charge of 'lawlessness', we can now see, was essentially the logical corollary of the observable fact that the Sultan's writ did not run among them, and the exaggerated complaint that the Kabyles were forever 'fighting' was the corollary, owing as much to sophistry as to logic, of the charge of 'lawlessness'.

In short, by the 1760s the main issue was no longer the irregular marriage customs or the (allegedly) debauched sexual mores of the Kabyles, but rather the quite different question of legitimate authority in all matters of law. This issue was not, as has so often been mistakenly asserted, that of the opposition: *Sharī'a* vs *'urf*. As we have already noted in Chapter 3, it was entirely accepted that the custom of a country or region might be one of the sources of law. But Islamic legal theory, while recognising in principle the validity of law derived from custom, nonetheless sought to subject the process of derivation to certain

---

29 The Arabic word *faqîr* has the root meanings of 'poor' and 'pauper' and has the derived meanings of 'mendicant dervish' or 'Sufi mendicant'. It is thus a term of dismissal and contempt in the mouth of an urban *'alīm*.

30 Hadj Sadok, 1951, *art. cit.*, 331.

conditions. As Touati explains, the condition was that each derivation of law from local custom should be validated by a procedure known as *'amal*.[31] This procedure was the business of the qualified specialists, the *'ulamā'*. Thus at one level, the problem with the Kabyle *qawānīn* was that they had derived law out of custom without this necessary validating procedure. But underlying this problem was the more fundamental problem of legitimacy. The legitimate ruler had the right to promulgate a *qānūn* and in doing so would enlist the assistance of the *'ulamā'* to effect the required *'amal*; from the point of view of the central power and its doctors of law, a mere mountain village had neither the political authority to make *qānūn* law nor the properly qualified *'ulamā'* available to it to ensure the validating conditions.

This reasoning led logically to the condemnation of the Kabyle *thajma'th* and its law. But it should be noted that a premise built into this argument was that Kabylia was an integral part of the rightful jurisdiction of the Ottoman Regency of Algiers and its provincial and local representatives. In other words, the assemblies of Kabylia were, as legislatures, illegitimate whatever decisions they took and their laws invalid whatever their actual content, by virtue of the fact that, in seeking to preserve their system of sovereign self-government from interference by the Regency, the Kabyles were denying the latter's authority and *ipso facto* in a state of 'rebellion'. The political *parti pris* underlying Al-Warthilani's discourse should be clear. It was not that he was subjectively pro-Turk; indeed, the *Rihla* contains powerful criticisms of aspects of Turkish rule. But he was the sheikh of the *zāwiya* at Borj Zemoura, one of the most important outposts of Ottoman power on the southern marches of Lesser Kabylia, and, while critical of corruption and other bad practices, accepted the framework of the Regency as the object of political obligation. In line with classical Sunni teaching, he insisted on the religious duty of obedience to those who hold authority,[32] and in Algeria it was the Ottomans who did so. Thus in the conflict between Kabyle self-government and the claims of the Regency, he sided with the latter.

Paradoxes are tricks of the light, the light being manipulated by the author of the paradox. In reality, Achilles can easily outrun Zeno's tortoise. The fact that Kabylia in the pre-colonial period produced a striking number of distinguished religious scholars and that others came to the region to study there only appears paradoxical if the assumption is made that the Kabyles in general were bad Muslims in dire need of reconversion to the true faith. The basis of this assumption is the disdainful and partisan discourse of the *'ulamā'* of Constantine, the unreliability of which we have shown, and the critical discourse of Al-Warthilani. And a crucial premise of Al-Warthilani's critique turns out to be the determination of

---

31 Touati, *op. cit.*, 94–9.
32 Hadj Sadok, 1951, *art. cit.*, 338.

the Kabyles to make and preserve their own political order and to make their own law independently of the Regency, deriving part of this law from custom as they saw fit by means of careful deliberation in representative assemblies which carried an authority with the society that the Regency and its relays could not rival. Seen in this light, we might rather think that it is not at all surprising that a society that possessed the capacity to govern itself and to make its own law should also have produced doctors of law capable of distinguishing themselves elsewhere. It should also be clear that the origin of the 'cultural originality' of Kabylia of which Touati speaks was its *political* originality.

It remains for us to establish what prompted Al-Warthilani to develop his radical critique of Kabyle law. Had some development in the political life of the region occurred that acted as a catalyst to his thoughts and thereby radicalised the orthodox critique of Kabyle society? There is reason to believe the answer is yes and that the development in question was the decision of the Igawawen to break explicitly with the *Sharīʿa* in respect of the right of women to inherit. While Al-Warthilani does not refer to this development, we know he sided with those *mrābtīn* who, in the name of the *Sharīʿa*, opposed the exheredation of women,[33] and so he would certainly have been concerned by it. And it is reasonable to suppose that the matter would have been among those he discussed with the *mrābtīn* of Greater Kabylia whom he visited on his journey across the region.

For Al-Warthilani's promenade around Kabylia was not a conventional *rihla* in the sense of a quest for spiritual enlightenment, but a quest, as the title he gave his text makes plain, for *news (al-akhbār)* and expressed his interest in current affairs. It is striking that he wasted no time visiting the most eminent centres of spirituality and religious teaching, the *zawāyā* of Timizar n'Sidi Mansour, Tifrit n'Ath ou Malek, Sidi Wedris or Sidi Abderrahmane El-Illouli. Instead, in halting among the Ath Menguellat, the Ath Bethroun, the Ath Irathen, the Ath Fraoucen, the Ath Yahia and at Werja among the Ath Bou Youcef, in addition to the centres of Ottoman authority at Tizi Ouzou and Dellys,[34] he was visiting most of the principal collective actors in the story we are about to tell.

The Igawawen and the exheredation of the Kabyle woman

At an extraordinary deliberative assembly held in 1162 AH/1748–9 CE, the Ath Bethroun confederation – 'the heart of the Igawawen'[35] – together with four allied *ʿaarsh* proclaimed their decision to abolish the right of women to inherit. The

---

33   Hadj Saddok, 1951, *art. cit.*, 381.
34   Al-Warthilani, *Rihla*, 15–16; Hadj Saddok, *op. cit.*, 326–7 and map 1.
35   Devaux, *op. cit.*, 255.

question is: why? This decision placed Kabyle law in unprecedentedly explicit opposition to the *Sharīʿa*. To do this and to do it so openly was surely to invite trouble. What, then, motivated this decision?

Boulifa insisted that the decision was a response to the problem that arose when numerous Kabyles who had been held in captivity by the Spanish were finally released, for they found on their return to their villages that they had already been given up for dead, their 'widows' had remarried, in some cases outside the village or even the *ʿarsh*, and their property had been redistributed among their heirs, including their female heirs, and had in some cases passed into the hands of total strangers.[36] The gravity of the conflicts – within villages, between villages of the same *ʿarsh* and even between different *ʿaarsh* – that were precipitated on the return of the living dead accordingly prompted the decision to avoid a repetition of such problems by depriving all women of the right to inherit.

The first difficulty with this theory is that the release of the Kabyle captives occurred as a by-product of the treaty which the Regency concluded with Spain in 1767. Boulifa accordingly insisted that the conventional date of 1748 for the exheredation decision was wrong and that it must have been taken after 1767.[37] But this does not work. The text of the decision of the Ath Bethroun is both full of convincing detail and is dated 1162 AH – that is, in 1748–9 CE[38] – so it must have been prompted by something other than the locally inconvenient side-effects of the 1767 treaty. A second difficulty with Boulifa's theory is that only 1200 Algerian Muslim captives were released and many of these, perhaps more than half, will not have been Kabyles;[39] it may well be doubted that the return of a few hundred dispossessed men would have caused a problem big enough to prompt such a dramatic and controversial measure to remedy it.

---

36 Boulifa, *op. cit.*, 265, n. 2.

37 *Ibid.*

38 The French text of this decision is given by Hanoteau and Letourneux, *op. cit.*, vol. III, 451–4, and reproduced in Appendix I below. An abridged version is given in F. Patorni, 'Délibération de l'année 1749 dans la Grande Kabylie', *Revue Africaine* (1895), 315–20, and another slightly different abridged translation and abridged version of the Arabic original are given in Basagana and Sayad, *op. cit.*, 94–5. Hanoteau and Letourneux give the date of this event as 1748 CE (*op. cit.*, vol. II, 8, n. 1) and most subsequent authors have repeated this but, since the year 1162 AH began on 21 December 1748, the meeting in question was almost certainly held in the course of 1749, as the title of Patorni's article takes for granted.

39 De Grammont, *op. cit.*, 257, where he gives the date of the agreement with Spain as October 1768, speaks of the captives as 'Turks' and subsequently as 'Turks or Moors' and states that, reduced to penury, they took to crime, were driven from Algiers into the countryside 'then occupied by the Kabyles' and engaged in banditry until most of them were killed. This is a quite different picture from the one Boulifa paints of hundreds if not thousands of Kabyles returning to their own homes to find they had lost everything. But the key point is that, if the figure of 1200 is correct and many of these were not Kabyles, the problem that arose in Kabylia was not enough to cause the change in question.

An explanation that avoids Boulifa's problem with the chronology was advanced by another Kabyle writer, Oukhalfoun, who suggested that the issue arose simply as a consequence of a growing tendency of Kabyle women to marry into families from other villages or *'aarsh*.[40] This hypothesis resembles Boulifa's but does not need to posit the return of the living dead as catalyst and so can be squared with the conventional dates of the decision. The weakness of this explanation is that it fails to account for or even demonstrate the alleged new fashion of marrying into other villages and *'aarsh*. It is not as if young Kabyle women in those days were free to marry whomever they chose, irrespective of the wishes of their parents. I therefore regard Oukhalfoun's hypothesis as purely speculative and implausible. I also consider that Boulifa was displaying a sound instinct in looking for a specific event that might explain the Kabyles' resort to this drastic measure. If the later treaty with Spain will not do, can we find a convincing alternative?

Let us begin by considering what we know.

We know a great deal about the Ath Bethroun's deliberation, thanks to the survival of an extended record of the meeting. This knowledge includes the date and place of the meeting, the terms of the decisions taken, and the names of most of those who attended and of their villages of origin and thus, by derivation, the names of the *'aarsh* represented at the meeting.

We also know that there is a tradition among the Ath Irathen to the effect that they too held a similar meeting, which took an identical decision, at a place called Tizra Waguemoun.[41] The date of this meeting is not known, but it must have been no earlier than 1737, since there is evidence that the *qawānīn* of the Ath Irathen were in at least superficial conformity with the *Sharī'a* in respect of female inheritance at that time.[42] We should also note that it may have been held as late as 1748, close to the time of the Ath Bethroun meeting, except that there is reason to believe that the Ath Irathen held their assembly first, *before* the Ath Bethroun, a point to which I shall return.

Finally, we know that there used to exist an impressive monument to this affair in the shape of a large stone, known in French as *la pierre de l'héritage* ('the inheritance stone'), in the centre of the village of Jema'a n'Saharij,[43] the capital of the *'arsh* Ath Fraoucen, the immediate neighbours of the Ath Irathen

---

40 B. Oukhalfoun, in an article published in a local periodical in Kabylia in 1922, cited by J. Martin, *Djemaa-Saharidj au cours des siècles* (Fort National: Fichier de Documentation Berbère, 1971), 27–30.

41 Hanoteau and Letourneux, *op. cit.*, II, 8, n. 1.

42 *Ibid.*; that is, the *qawānīn* of the Ath Irathen at that time did not openly deny the right of women to inherit; they provided, however, for this aspect of the *Sharī'a* to be got round via the procedure of donation by the female heir of her share of the inheritance to her male relatives. This matter is discussed in detail below.

43 J. Martin, *op. cit.*, 19–33; this useful monograph contains a photograph of the stone in question.

to their east. This fact has fuelled various speculations. Some have suggested that the meeting claimed to have been held at Tizra Waguemoun among the Ath Irathen was really held at Jema'a n'Saharij. Others have apparently supposed that the decision recorded as having been taken by the Ath Bethroun in their own territory in the high Jurjura was really taken at Jema'a n'Saharij.[44] These speculations bear witness to a shared reluctance to accept that the people of Jema'a n'Saharij would have gone to the trouble of commemorating a decision taken elsewhere and by others.

I am inclined to agree with this. I see no reason to suppose that the 'inheritance stone' commemorates anything other than a decision taken at Jema'a n'Saharij itself. At the same time, I believe that this meeting should not be confused with either the meeting held by the Ath Irathen or the meeting held by the Ath Bethroun. In short, I submit that the evidence supports the view that three distinct assemblies occurred[45] and took, one after another, the same dramatic decision. I also believe, for reasons I shall explain presently, that the meeting at Jema'a n'Saharij was the last of the three and took place no earlier than 1752.

The next step we should take is to examine with care the precise decisions taken. The assembly of the Ath Bethroun and its allies actually resolved upon four distinct measures:

i.   to abolish the right of women to inherit;
ii. to abolish the right of everyone (i.e. men as well as women) to exercise *shefa'a*, the right of pre-emption, in respect of property made over to a *hubus*;
iii. to abolish the right of daughters, sisters and orphans to participate in the exercise of the right of pre-emption – *shefa'a* – of any property;
iv. to abolish the right of the wife who has been repudiated or widowed to have her dowry returned to her.

---

44 Ageron, *op. cit.*, t. 1, 288. Ageron's (unargued) opting for this view influenced others. Thus in his autobiography Augustin Ibazizen wrote that 'a congress of all the tribes decided [the exheredation of women] in 1748 at the historic assembly at Djemaa Sahridj' (*Le Pont de Bereq'mouch*, 242; my translation), despite the fact that the record of the Ath Bethroun's meeting makes clear that it was attended by representatives of Ibazizen's own 'arsh, the Ath Yenni.

45 There may have been more than three. Adli (*op. cit.*, 93) has come to Boulifa's rescue in some degree by suggesting that many of the Kabyle captives released in or after 1767 would have been from the maritime districts of Greater Kabylia and that their return home may have prompted the populations of these districts (Ath Jennad, Ath Waguenoun, Iflissen Lebahr, Izerkhfawen) belatedly to see virtue in the decisions taken by the Igawawen and to hold a meeting at this juncture to decide their own position on the matter. This is a plausible hypothesis, notwithstanding the lack of material evidence to support it; further research among the 'aarsh of maritime Kabylia might unearth such evidence.

In considering what prompted these decisions, we clearly should examine their likely effects. What did these measures actually achieve? Did they make any real difference to the material position of women in Kabyle society? Virtually all commentary has taken it for granted that they did. And virtually all discussion of this point has taken it for granted that, in disinheriting their women, the Kabyles were not only deviating from the *Sharīʿa* but also distinguishing themselves very radically from the other rural and mountain populations of the Maghrib.

Let us reconsider the latter point first. The central problem posed by the insistence of Islamic law on the right of women to inherit is that this threatened the integrity of the landholdings of the extended family. In order to preserve the family patrimony, especially its patrimony in land, it was necessary to deny to wives and daughters and sisters the right to any share of the inheritance. This problem did not confront the Kabyles alone; it also confronted the populations of the Oranie and Constantinois, to look no further. How, then, did these other populations deal with it?

In the Oranie, it appears that the standard ploy to get around this provision of the *Sharīʿa* was that the female heir would make a 'gift' of her share of the inherited property to her male kinsmen, in exchange for their commitment to provide for her for the rest of her life. This 'gift' was of course in many if not most cases an imposition on the woman concerned; under pressure from her family, she would have no choice but to make it. That this was how things worked emerges from the legal debate concerning this practice of 'donation' that took place in the district of Ghris, near Mascara in the central Oranie, in the second half of the seventeenth century and early eighteenth century. Touati remarks of the social context of this debate that 'we are in a country that disinherits its women'[46] and informs us that the debate turned on the following question:

> What is the point of view of the law with regard to the gift, *hiba*, that the daughters and sisters who live among their tribe make to their kinsfolk when the local custom, *'urf*, is to disinherit them?[47]

How that debate was concluded need not concern us here. The point is that it clearly emerges that the practice of denying women their right, under Islamic law, to inherit property was by no means confined to the Kabyles or even the Berbers in general; it was a characteristic feature of rural society in Algeria, if not the Maghrib, as a whole. The procedural device of female donation, *hiba*, appears

---

46 Touati, *op. cit.*, 62: 'nous sommes dans un pays qui exhérède ses femmes'; Touati is not speaking of Kabylia here; in its context this phrase can be read as referring to either the Mascara region or the Oranie or Algeria as a whole.

47 Touati, *ibid.*

to have been the standard one employed in western Algeria[48] but it was not the only expedient to which rural society might resort.

Mahé has suggested that, prior to the mid-eighteenth century assemblies that met to consider this question, the standard ploy in Kabylia was the resort to mortmain, *hubus*[49] – that is, the constitution of all or part of the family property as a bequest to a religious foundation such as a *zāwiya*.[50] The rule here was that the former owners would continue to enjoy use-rights to the property up until the extinction of the family, at which point (which of course might never be reached) the land in question would become the absolute property of the foundation to which it was bequeathed, unless kinsmen of the family that originally owned it exercised the right of *shefaʿa* in respect of it. Thus the device of *hubus* made it possible to arrange for women to be taken care of since they too might enjoy use-rights in the property, without this entailing the alienation of a part of the property to an unrelated family.[51]

Mahé accordingly asks the following pertinent question: given that the Kabyles could get round the *Sharīʿa* in the matter of female inheritance by the unobtrusive and licit means of the *hubus*, what could have motivated them to affront the *Sharīʿa* so openly by explicitly rejecting, in principle as well as in practice, women's right to inherit?[52] Mahé offers two hypotheses in answer to this question, both speculative and neither wholly persuasive.

The first is based on a document recording the decision taken in 1818 CE by the *thajmaʿth* of the largest of the Ath Yenni villages, Ath Lahcène, to go back on the decision to which it had been party in 1749 and to re-establish the right of women to inherit in the village's code of law. The document in question records that this decision was taken after a plague had broken out in the village. Mahé accordingly infers that this misfortune threatened to create a situation where a family might become extinct in the male line, leaving only women with no near relatives to take care of them, and he suggests that it was under the pressure of this threat that it was agreed to revert to the *Sharīʿa* on this point. As he himself remarks, however, 'this explanation seems insufficient' and how it might throw light on the earlier decision to disinherit women is unclear.[53]

---

48 Allan Christelow, *Muslim law courts and the French colonial state in Algeria* (Princeton: NJ: Princeton University Press, 1985), 75.
49 Usually written *habous* in Algeria; plural: *ahbās*; the equivalent of *waqf, awqāf* in the Mashriq.
50 Mahé, *op. cit.*, 68–73: 70.
51 Article 8 of the *qānūn* of the Maatqa explicitly enshrines this usage. Interestingly, article 13 affirms that the Maatqa have *always* ('de tout temps') refused the right of inheritance to their women. This version of their *qānūn* was drawn up after the French conquest; while the claim may well be true, it is doubtful that pre-1749 versions of the *qānūn* would have included such an explicit affirmation; see Louis Milliot, 'Le Qânoun des M'atqa', *Hespéris*, 2 (1922), 193–204.
52 Mahé, *op. cit.*, 70.
53 Mahé, *op. cit.*, 71.

Mahé's second suggestion is that the procedure of constituting landed property as *hubus* had inconvenient consequences which eventually became intolerable. Speculating that the resort to this expedient led to a proliferation of *ahbās*, he points out that this led at least by implication to a serious conflict of interests. As we have already explained in Chapter 2, all land held as *melk*, 'private property', ultimately belonged to the community. Thus when a family became extinct, its landholdings would revert to the village, which would then decide how to exploit or reallocate them. By making land over to a *zāwiya* or *ma'ammera* (Quranic school; in Thaqbaylith: *thim'ammerth*, plural: *thim'ammrin*) as mortmain, a family was implicitly arranging for this land to escape the ultimate ownership and control of the village community. Were this to happen on a large scale, the long-term consequences for the villages of Kabylia would be very serious, for it would entail the rise of the *zawāyā* as major landholders that were independent of and in at least latent rivalry with the *thudrin* of Kabylia.[54]

This is a far more interesting theory and persuasive in one respect, in the latent rivalry it tacitly posits between *thaddarth* and *zāwiya* in the society of the Jurjura. But it too fails to account for the decision taken to abolish the right of female inheritance. Even if we accept one of this theory's indispensable premises, that the *ahbās* had proliferated to an intolerable extent by *c.* 1748 (a premise for which there is no documentary support), it remains to explain why the Igawawen dealt with this problem as they did. It was, after all, open to them to place restrictions on the resort to *hubus* and encourage the practice of *hiba* as a preferable alternative. As we have seen, the Ath Bethroun did indeed place a restriction of a kind on the resort to *hubus* in the decisions they took in 1749. Why, then, did they also abolish the right of women to inherit, instead of simply relying on the customary practice of *hiba*?

There can be no doubt that the Igawawen were aware of this practice. Not only is this a reasonable inference from the fact that the Igawawen would by the mid-eighteenth century have acquired an extensive experience of western Algeria and its customary law as a by-product of their trading ventures there and also their military activities in the service of the Regency; it is also a fact documented by Hanoteau and Letourneux. For, in their discussion of the question of the exheredation of women in the case of the Ath Irathen, they record that, up until 1737 at least, the Ath Irathen relied on the procedure of female donation as their way of getting round the *Sharī'a* and preventing female inheritance.[55] It was because they were able to employ this expedient that their *qawānīn* did not openly conflict with the *Sharī'a* on this question. Why, then, did they not continue to do so? And why did the other Igawawen populations not resort to this procedure more extensively if they had reason to curb the recourse to *hubus*?

---

54 Mahé, *op. cit.*, 71.
55 Hanoteau and Letourneux, *op. cit.*, II, 8, n. 1.

Dissatisfied with his own hypotheses, Mahé goes on to suggest that we need to know more about the state of the religious field in Kabylia during this period in order to understand this event fully.

> Some supplementary elements of an explanation are certainly to be found in the religious situation of Kabylia at this time. The second half of the 18th century is precisely the beginning of a profound reconstitution of the religious leadership in Kabylia.[56]

But it is in the changes and developments of the first, not the second, half of the eighteenth century – and, for that matter, of the second half of the seventeenth century – that we must seek the supplementary elements, that is, the elements of the historical context, that we need in order to discern the chain of cause and effect and thereby make sense of these events. As we shall see, the changes and developments in question were predominantly political, not religious, in nature and Al-Warthilani was not alone in finding them disturbing.

The *imrabdhen* and the reordering of Kabylia

Between *c.* 1610 and *c.* 1760, a complex transformation occurred in the socio-political organisation of Greater Kabylia. This transformation established the premises both of Al-Warthilani's critique and of the 'Kabyle myth' of a century later. In doing so it also established several – but not all – of the premises of the Kabyle question, which emerged with the rise of popular nationalism from the 1920s onwards and remains unresolved.

The transformation was not the achievement of a single coherent force oriented by the purpose of reordering the region, let alone of a definite project made explicit in documents available for historians to contemplate. It was the product of the vigorous interaction of several distinct forces with competing interests – the *imrabdhen*, both as missionary movement and as locally notable lineages forming networks of complicity and influence; the Ottoman Regency, seeking to extend its control of the hinterland; the *jawād* families of the lowlands seeking to hold or gain power at the local level; and the egalitarian society of the highlands determined to preserve, in its system of representative and law-bound self-government, the political and juridical framework on which its complex economic activities depended. The respective purposes of these forces were rarely if ever made explicit and the processes of their interaction through which the new order in Kabylia was forged were correspondingly obscure and had a chaotic aspect.

---

56 Mahé, *op. cit.*, 72 (my translation).

These features of the story, together with the scarcity of written sources, has rendered the historian's task of doing justice to it an especially challenging one. In the absence of a reliable body of evidence, the tenuous historiography of the pre-colonial era has been enlisted by the opposed sides in the successive variants of the controversy over Kabylia that has been a constant of Algerian life for the last 250 years, and ahistorical and partisan theses have structured the debate at every stage.

These theses have proposed essentialist readings of Kabyle society and its religious and political organisation that are mutually exclusive because of the 'all or nothing' variety. To the French myth-monger Sabatier and his thesis – that 'the Kabyle is essentially anti-clerical' and his laws 'the most energetic negation of the fundamental principles of the Muslim code' – which reduced the Islamic dimension of Kabyle society and the Islamic factor in Kabyle history to virtually nothing, we find opposed Chachoua's comparable claim that the importance attached to the Kabyle *jema'a* by nineteenth-century French (and, by implication, all subsequent) observers was simply part of the same *bêtisier* ('collection of howlers') of which anti-clerical zealots such as Sabatier were guilty and that not only was Kabyle society profoundly Muslim but the *only* institutions it possessed in the pre-colonial period were the *zawāyā*.[57]

There can be no question of mediating such differences of opinion. The positions staked out by the protagonists of that debate are not to be reconciled. We must instead follow our own course while navigating between them, recognising that, while neither is true, both contain an element of truth which we can appreciate at its real value only within a soundly based historical vision of Kabylia which resolutely rejects essentialist theses. Such a vision will enable us to see that a tension between religious and lay leadership in Kabyle political life has been a feature of the society of Greater Kabylia throughout the period we are discussing. It will also allow us to notice that the balance between the two has varied from one period to another and also from one district to another and encourage us accordingly to ask the interesting question why that should be so and to attempt an answer to it. A provisional answer is that religious leadership has repeatedly come to the fore when lay political leadership has, for one reason or another, been weak or absent. This was actually the situation that prevailed in the immediate aftermath of the end of Koukou.

The re-emergence of the *imrabdhen* as major actors in Kabylia in the late sixteenth and early seventeenth century was not prompted by the need for an access of missionary zeal in the face of a region-wide loss of faith. Although a resumption of missionary activism was a feature of this period, faith as such was not the issue. Rather, the main cause of this development appears to have been the descent of the region into a condition resembling in some degree that of

---

57 Chachoua, *op. cit.*, 25–30: 29.

Morocco at the time of the 'maraboutic crisis' there, namely the opening up of a political vacuum in a context of growing social crisis.

Let us consider this social crisis first. While we must operate with little in the way of solid evidence and content ourselves with putting forward hypotheses rather than hard and fast assertions, we can be sure of the existence of this crisis in the first place and, in the second, reasonably confident that we understand its main elements.

One of these was the pressure on the socio-political order generated by the influx of immigrants into the region as a whole and into Greater Kabylia in particular. Bejaia after its fall to the Spanish was the first major source of these immigrants, in a process that involved simultaneously a degree of ruralisation of a previously urban population and a corresponding degree of 'urbanisation' of the society of the countryside and the society of the mountains above all.[58] In addition to the exodus from Bejaia from 1509, we may mention the return to the hill districts of many Kabyles drawn to Algiers in the heyday of good relations between Koukou or Qal'a on the one hand and the Regency on the other but who subsequently felt unwelcome and unsafe there when relations deteriorated from 1590 onwards, and the influx of the Moors of Andalusia after the last expulsion of the 'Hispano-Muslims' from Iberia in 1609–14,[59] some at least of whom arrived in Kabylia.[60] While we have no detailed accounts to rely on and no statistics at all, we can be confident that to a large extent the remarkable development of craft manufacturing in the Jurjura and also parts of Lesser Kabylia, notably among the Ath Abbas, owed much to this influx of refugees bearing elements of urban culture with them, as did, no doubt, the developments of certain centres of Islamic scholarship and teaching. As Morizot notes, there is evidence that in its heyday Qal'a n'Ath Abbas had both a Jewish quarter and an Andalusian quarter and the

---

58 Witness to this is overtly borne by the hamlet of Alma ou Hadri ('the meadow of the townsman') in the *tūfiq* of Iazzouguen, *'arsh* Ath Ghoubri, and by the large *tūfiq* of Ihadriin ('the descendants of the townsman') in the *'arsh* Ath Koufi of the Igouchdal confederation (Hanoteau and Letourneux, *op. cit.*, I, 333 and 341). These few examples greatly understate the population movement in question as most urban families that settled in the mountains will not have commemorated their origins in this way.

59 Hess, *op. cit.*, 120–1.

60 Most 'Andalusians' will have settled in the cities, Tlemcen especially but also Algiers and the other coastal towns. Some however settled in maritime Kabylia, as the hamlet of Ath Wandalous in the *tūfiq* of Ath Melloul in the *'arsh* Izerkhfawen (Hanoteau and Letourneux, *op. cit.*, I, 328) testifies, but also in the high Jurjura; the patron saint of the *zāwiya* at Zaknoun in *'arsh* Ath Bou Akkach is Sheikh Arezki n'Ath Wandelous and the people of Tifilkout in *'arsh* Illilten have a memory of a group of strangers called variously 'Ath Wandlous' or 'Ath Wandiouss' who tried to settle among them until the locals chased them away; see Madjid Tighilt, 'Les Aït Wandiouss ou les Maures d'Andalousie', Tifilkout.com, 15 September 2007 (www.tifilkout.com/ articles/327/1/Les-Ait-wandiouss-ou-les-maures-dandalousie/Page1. html) and 'Tifilkout: un village moderne, une cité ancestrale', *L'Authentique*, 25 August 2009.

sophisticated artisanate there included the manufacture of weapons[61] as well as the weaving of the fine burnouses for which the Ath Abbas became famous.[62] Finally, there is reason to believe that a significant element of the populations of the low-lying districts that saw most of the fighting of the Ottomans against Koukou and Qal'a and also between the latter in the various campaigns between 1518 and 1624 – the Sebaou, Wad Sahel and Soummam valleys, the Hamza and Mejana plains – fled to higher ground at various points and at least some of these will have settled in the mountain districts for good. Subsequent movements of population for similar reasons are likely to have occurred later also, during the conflict between rival factions of the Ath l-Qadi over the dynastic succession from the 1690s onwards and during the numerous conflicts arising out of the Ottoman penetration of the region from 1710 onwards, matters to which I shall return.

Thus the society of Greater Kabylia will have had to cope with a complex set of pressures arising from these population movements. Unlike the pressure of population movements in the Moroccan High and Middle Atlas, which were predominantly a series of migrations by one tribe after another from the south-east to the north-west, each successive migrant population pushing the one that went before it in a steady chain-reaction effect that occurred over four centuries,[63] the movements of population besetting Kabyle society were more abrupt and much more complex in their cultural and political impact and occurred in virtually all directions, with newcomers arriving from the east, the west and the south.[64] To these we should add the pressure of migration *within* the region. Some of this will have been caused by the need for individuals or

---

61 Also found among the Igawawen of the high Jurjura, as we have noted in Chapter 2.
62 Morizot 1985, *op. cit.*, 57–9, citing M. Eisenbeth, 'Les juifs en Algérie et en Tunisie au temps des Turcs', *Revue Africaine* (1952, 1st and 2nd quarters), 127 and 153.
63 David Hart, 'Four centuries of history on the hoof: the northwest passage of Berber sheep transhumants across the Moroccan Atlas, 1550–1912', *Morocco* (The Journal of the Society for Moroccan Studies), No. 3 (1993), 21–55.
64 Isherqien ('the easterners') is the name of villages of *'arsh* Ath Aïhmed of *thaqbilth* Iflissen Lebahr and of *'arsh* Maatqa; Igherbien ('the people from the west') is the name of a hamlet of *tūfīq* Ath Maamar, *'arsh* Ath Adas (*thaqbilth* Ath Jennad), of a *tūfīq* of *'arsh* Iltaien (*thaqbilth* Iflissen Oumellil) and of two hamlets (Igherbien Oufella and Igherbien Bouadda) in *tūfīq* Tasoukit of *'arsh* Ath Abdelmoumen (*thaqbilth* Ath Aïssi); the hamlet of Ibiskrien, *tūfīq* Ath El Adeur, *'arsh* Ath Kodhea (Ath Jennad) was founded by immigrants from Biskra on the edge of the Sahara (Hanoteau and Letourneux, *op. cit.*, I, 321, 327, 349, 362); the ancestors of the Ath Ali lineage at Ath Larba'a of *'arsh* Ath Yenni came from Bou Saada (Genevois, 1971, *op. cit.*, 5); those of the Ath Azzouz lineage which gave its name to the village of Taguemount Azouz came from Boghar in the southern Titteri region just north of the High Plateaux (Genevois, 1972, *op. cit.*, 36); Sidi Mansour, founder of the celebrated *zāwiya* at Timizar, came originally from Mniaâ, near El-Golea in the Algerian Sahara (Oussedik, 1986, *op. cit.*, 33); the ancestor of the Ouled Mahieddine of Taourga, the dynastic chiefs of the Iamraouien Bouadda, came from the *'arsh* Ouled Bellil of the southern side of the Jurjura (Feredj, *op. cit.*, 47).

entire families to escape vendettas, but much of it may have had economic motives, such as the migration of families into the fertile middle Sebaou valley from the mid-sixteenth century onwards as this began to be settled and farmed under the supervision of the Ath l-Qadi,[65] but also the migration of families from the more arid districts on the southern side of the Jurjura and in Lesser Kabylia to the verdant districts of Greater Kabylia north of the watershed. The names of several settlements bear witness to this, notably Ighil Oumecheddal,[66] 'the ridge of the man from the Imecheddalen'; Isikhen Oumeddour,[67] 'the escarpments of the man from the Ath Meddour'; Imelikchen,[68] 'the descendants of the man from the Ath Melikech'; Bou Aïdel,[69] 'the place of the man from the Ath Aïdel'; and Iwennoughen,[70] 'the descendants of the man from the Wennougha'.[71] The same is true of the names of quarters or neighbourhoods within villages: at Jema'a n'Saharij, part of the quarter of Hallawa is called l-Hara guizerkhfawen ('the neighbourhood of the Izerkhfawen'): its inhabitants are the descendants of families who migrated to the village from the 'arsh Izerkhfawen of the Azeffoun district in maritime Kabylia.[72] No doubt further research in the field would discover more such cases.

We evidently cannot know the particular motives in each case, but we can observe that movement occurred not only from lower to high ground but also from the high Jurjura to lower-lying areas and from one part of the Jurjura to another. The villages of Ourthi Bouakkach ('the orchard of the man from the Ath Bou Akkach') of 'arsh Ath Khelifa of the Maatqa confederation overlooking the Sebaou valley, Ath Ougawa ('the descendants of the Agawaw'[73]) of the *tūfīq* of Tahanouts, 'arsh Ath Aïssa ou Mimoun of the Ath Waguenoun confederation (also overlooking the Sebaou), Aafir Oukoufi ('the entrenchment of the man from

---

65 Feredj, *op. cit.*, 32; some of the settlers in the Sebaou valley were Arabic-speakers from outside Kabylia (*ibid.*).

66 Hanoteau and Letourneux, *op. cit.*, I, 303; a hamlet in *tūfīq* Tizi Rached, 'arsh Ath Akerma, *thaqbilth* Ath Irathen.

67 *Op. cit.*, I, 317: a village of the Iamrawien Oufella, south-east of Tizi Ouzou.

68 *Op. cit.*, I, 324 and 347: a hamlet of the *tūfīq* of Akaoudj, 'arsh Ath Aissa ou Mimoun (*thaqbilth* Ath Waguenoun) and a village of 'arsh Imkiren (Iflissen Oumellil).

69 *Op. cit.*, I, 310 and 358: a hamlet of *tūfīq* Taourirt n'Ath Ali ou Naceur of 'arsh Ath Itsouragh and a hamlet of the *tūfīq* Beni Athman of 'arsh Isser Droua.

70 *Op. cit.*, I, 360: a village of 'arsh Ath Mekla of the Iflissen Oumellil confederation. There is also a maraboutic lineage of this name at Taourirt Amrane in 'arsh Ath Bou Youcef (Salhi, *op. cit.*, 206).

71 The Ath Meddour, Imecheddalen and Ath Melikech are all 'aarsh of the southern slopes of the Jurjura; the Ath Aïdel are an 'arsh of the Guergour east of the Soummam valley; the Wennougha is a district to the south of the Jurjura and to the south-west of the Biban.

72 Interview at Jema'a n'Saharij in July 2012 with Mme Cherifa Zerraf, who confirmed Genevois (1958, *op. cit.*, 38–9).

73 Singular of Igawawen; pronounced 'Agawa' (the final 'w' is almost silent) and often written this way.

the Ath Koufi'), of *'arsh* Ath Slegguem in north-western Kabylia, Ath Illoul ('the descendants of the man from the Illoulen'), of the *tūfiq* of Ath Melloul of *'arsh* Izerkhfawen, and the village of Ibouyoucefen ('the descendants of the man from the Ath Bou Youcef') in *'arsh* Ath Hantala of the Ath Ijjeur confederation, all testify to the first tendency. In the Kouriet district of the central Jurjura, the *'arsh* Ath Ali ou Illoul ('the descendants of Ali the son of the man from the Illoulen') of the Ath Sedqa confederation bears witness to the second, which undoubtedly was far more frequent and important than may be suggested by the rare cases that explicitly commemorate it in this way.

Some of these movements of population will have taken place after the period we are presently considering, but many of them undoubtedly occurred between 1510 and 1630. We can also be confident that the most important direction of movement was into the highlands and that this movement, by greatly increasing the population density of the mountain districts, both created a problem of social order in these districts and furnished elements of a solution to this problem through the quantitative and qualitative development of craft manufacture and the development of commercial migration associated with this that would ultimately enable the economy of the mountains to support their greatly increased population. In the meantime, however, these population movements and the endless jostling and frictions that they will have occasioned undoubtedly posed problems of order and security. These problems can only have been aggravated by the side-effects of the end of Koukou.

The fact that the Ath l-Qadi did not govern the Igawawen did not mean that the society of the Jurjura was not adversely affected by the end of their kingdom. From 1529 to the 1630s the Ath l-Qadi were the Ottomans' principal interlocutors in Greater Kabylia. As such, they were the guarantors of the security of the Zwawa residents of Algiers and other towns under Ottoman control and of the security of Zwawa traders as they travelled outside the region. In acting as recruiting sergeants for the Ottomans' campaigns to establish their rule over the interior of the country, they were undoubtedly able to acquire and maintain considerable influence with the *'aarsh* of the Jurjura that furnished the main body of auxiliary troops. These circumstances will have enabled the lords of Koukou to maintain a degree of order in the Jurjura, as well as the other districts of Greater Kabylia, even while refraining from levying taxes on the Igawawen or interfering in their internal affairs. Not only did they mediate relations between the population of the region and the Ottoman authorities, but they also were available to mediate and had an interest in mediating relations between the *'aarsh* of which this population was composed. In addition, their control of the communication routes made them the principal guarantors of the safety of travellers throughout the region. The end of Koukou deprived the society of the Jurjura of these mediating functions and guarantees of security at precisely the time when the stresses to which this society was subject made them more than ever indispensable.

To these urgent problems the society of the Jurjura found an at least partial solution through an expansion of the presence and social role of the *imrabdhen*. This expansion comprised several elements, notably the founding of *zawāyā* in the full sense of the term, the founding of Quranic schools, *thim'ammrin*, and the establishment of maraboutic settlements – that is, hamlets or sometimes full villages composed exclusively of maraboutic families; these saintly settlements were and still are commonly called *zawāyā* also, whether or not they regularly receive visitors and offer instruction or other distinctive religious services.

An illustrious instance of the first is the celebrated *zāwiya* of Sidi Abderrahmane el-Illouli near the hamlet of Ihamziin of *tūfīq* Abourghas in *'arsh* Illoulen Oumalou. Sidi Abderrahmane was a native of this *'arsh*, born in 1601 in the hamlet of Ikherdouchen of the *tūfīq* of Ighil Gueltounen. He became a *tāleb* (student of Islamic theology and law) and studied first at the nearby *zāwiya* of Sidi Ahmed Wedris and then under Sidi Mohamed Saadi al-Bahlouli in the Mizrana district of maritime Kabylia. He subsequently returned to his *'arsh* of origin and founded his *zāwiya* in 1635 CE.[74] In doing this, he had of course been preceded by Sidi Mansour, who founded his *zāwiya* at Timizar in *'arsh* Ath Adas of the Ath Jennad confederation about 20 years earlier. Some 65 years later, in 1700 CE,[75] another *zāwiya* which was to prove extremely influential, that of Sidi Mohammed Ben Ali Cherif, was established near Tizi n'Ichelladen (the Chellata pass) amongst the Illoulen Ousammeur.[76]

Most of the *thim'ammrin* in the Igawawen region were established on its northern edges, at or near the point of contact with the plain; this was the case of the *thim'ammerth* of the Ath Ameur of Tamazirt and the *thim'ammerth* at Adeni, both of *'arsh* Irjen; that of Arous, *'arsh* Ath Oumalou, and those of Chorfa and El-Kouadhi at Jema'a n'Saharij, *'arsh* Ath Fraoucen.[77] The main exceptions were two *thim'ammrin* established among the Ath Itsouragh (at Tizi Guefres and Ath El-Mançour) and that of Sidi Ali ou Taleb of Koukou, *'arsh* Ath Yahia.[78] According to the testimony of Si Yidir Brahimi of Koukou (a descendant of

---

74 'El Achoura en Kabylie: Les Saints ont toujours la côte', *El Watan*, 11 February 2006; see also article by Mohamed Bokreta, citing Mohamed Maimoun, *Zawiya Sidi Abderrahmane al-Illouli and its educative, cultural and influential roles in the Kabylia area* (Masters thesis, 2001, which I have been unable to consult) (www.scribd.com/SidiAl-Illouli/d/3194907+Illoula+or +zawiya+%22Sidi+Abderrahmane+%22&cd=1&hl= en&ct=clnk&gl=eg).

75 Salhi, *op. cit.*, 149.

76 Literally, 'the Illoulen of the sunlight', that is of the south-east-facing slopes of the Jurjura, as opposed to the Illoulen Oumalou, 'the Illoulen of the shadow', settled on the north-west-facing slopes. The boundary between the two *'aarsh* is the main watershed ridge. This is the only case of *'aarsh* that appear to be related, since bearing the same distinctive name, located either side of the Jurjura. I know of no attempt to account for this intriguing state of affairs, a striking lacuna in the literature on Kabylia.

77 Hanoteau and Letourneux, *op. cit.*, II, 110–12.

78 *Ibid.*

Sidi Ali), Sidi Ali lived at the time of the decline of the Ath l-Qadi. When Sidi Ahmed El-Tounsi decided not to stay at Koukou after avenging his father's death there, he bequeathed the palace of justice and gardens he inherited there to Sidi Ali ou Taleb, who established his school on this property.[79] The story neatly illustrates and symbolises the transition from the old authority of the warlords to the new authority of the pious and pacific *imrabdhen*. It also places Sidi Ali ou Taleb in time, since the encounter with Sidi Ahmed El Tounsi will have taken place no later than 1638–9. The *thim'ammerth* of Sidi Ali ou Taleb is credited with missionary influence in this period, for one of its *tolba* went on to found an important maraboutic centre in the *'arsh* Ath Douala of the Ath Aïssi confederation. This was Sidi Abdallah ou Hassan, from Igouras, *tūfīq* of Ath Mellal in *'arsh* Ath Yahia, who around the middle of the seventeenth century settled among the Ath Douala at Akal Aberkane and established nearby the village of Ath Bou Yahia, which is the most influential maraboutic settlement among the Ath Aïssi to this day.

With the case of Ath Bou Yahia we have begun to address the third aspect of the maraboutic expansion, namely the proliferation of saintly settlements in the mountains of Greater Kabylia. This proliferation exhibited very striking features in the Jurjura especially. The first is that the resulting distribution of such settlements is extremely uneven: certain *'aarsh* of the Jurjura contain several while others contain not one. Thus the Ath Menguellat, Ath Yahia and Ath Itsouragh have numerous exclusively maraboutic hamlets, whereas the Aqbil, Ath Bou Akkach and Ath Yenni have only one apiece and the Illilten, Ath Attaf, Ath Boudrar and Ath Wasif none at all. Clearly the distribution of these settlements has not reflected a standard requirement of the internal political organisation of each *'arsh*. What then might account for it?

As already mentioned, the Igawawen district consists of the system of high parallel ridges that extend northwards from the central spine of the Jurjura massif. By far the most important of these ridges is the one that extends from just below the Tirourda pass in a broadly north-westerly direction all the way to the Sebaou valley. This central ridge is occupied successively by different *'aarsh*. The highest and most southerly part of the ridge is the territory of the Ath Bou Youcef, which boasts in its second largest village, Tiferdoud, situated at an altitude of 1175 metres, the highest village in the whole of Kabylia. A secondary ridge branching off to the north-east culminates in a large outcrop that forms the territory of the Ath Itsouragh. To the north of the Ath Bou Youcef, the main ridge as well as a couple of secondary ridges that branch off from it are occupied by the Ath Menguellat, while another, very substantial, secondary ridge branching off to the north-east forms (with a few side branches) the territory of the Ath Yahia. Then, as the main ridge curves to the north-west, it becomes the territory of the Ath Irathen confederation, occupied first by the Aouggacha, then

---

79 Genevois, 1974, *op. cit.*, 24–6.

the Ath Akerma and finally 'arsh Irjen, with ridges branching off to the left and right forming the territories of the Ath Ousammeur and Ath Oumalou.

The location of saintly settlements along this main ridge from the southernmost point of the Ath Bou Youcef territory to the northern limits of the Ath Menguellat and Ath Yahia territories has corresponded to two historic imperatives: the need to guarantee safe passage for travellers on the roads[80] (especially those communicating between the Sebaou valley and the Tirourda pass) and the need to minimise frictions along the boundaries between neighbouring 'aarsh.

One of the first settlements encountered when descending the main ridge from Tizi n'Tirourda is the hamlet of Werja (Ourja), one of the constituent hamlets of the *tūfiq* Ath Khelifa and situated no more than a few dozen metres from the road. At first sight a modest and easily overlooked settlement, Werja is in fact the historic cradle of the most important saintly lineage in the Jurjura, the Ath Sidi Ahmed, which has numerous ramifications across the central Jurjura district.[81] It was a young woman of this lineage, Lalla Fadhma n'Ath Sidi Ahmed ou Meziane, more generally known as Lalla Fadhma n'Soumeur (1830–63), still very much celebrated to this day as 'Kabylia's Jeanne d'Arc', who inspired the resistance to the French in the Jurjura from 1849 to 1857. Her capture in the Illilten village of Thakhelijth n'Ath Atsou, on 11 July 1857, marked the completion of Randon's campaign and the end of 'la Kabilie indépendante'.[82]

In addition to its original settlement among the Ath Bou Youcef, the Ath Sidi Ahmed boast a cluster of small settlements among the Ath Menguellat (see Map 7.1), and the two settlements of the Ath Ahmed in 'arsh Ath Yahia are a branch of this lineage.

The presence of saintly settlements along 'arsh boundaries is a striking feature of this district. In addition to the Ath Sidi Ahmed settlements, which act as a line of buffer communities between the Ath Menguellat and its northern neighour ('arsh Aouggacha of the Ath Irathen confederation), the string of settlements of the Ath Sidi Saïd, the patron saints of Aïn el-Hammam,[83] line the boundaries with the Ath Yahia to the north-east and the Ath Bou Youcef to the south-east. They also straddle two important junctions of the main ridge road with side roads leading north-east via the Ath Yahia and the Ath Fraoucen to reach the Sebaou valley near Jema'a n'Saharij and south-west to the market

---

80 A point that has been made in general terms regarding the social function of maraboutic families by Michael Gilsenan, *Recognizing Islam* (London and Canberra: Croom Helm, 1983), 146.

81 Salhi, 1979, *op. cit.*, 213.

82 A native of Werja, she moved with her brother Sidi Tahar to the nearby village of Soumeur in 'arsh Ath Itsouragh, hence her name. She died in captivity. See M. Benbrahim, 'Fadhma n'Soumeur' in Chaker (ed.), *op. cit.*, 136–8. 'Lalla' (or 'Lla') means 'Lady', the female counterpart of 'Sidi' and the standard title of women of maraboutic lineage.

83 The great nineteenth-century poet Si Mohand ou M'Hand refers to this town as 'El-Hammam Aït Sidi Saïd' (Asefru No. 157 in Mouloud Mammeri, *Les Isefra: poèmes de Si Mohand-ou-M'Hand* (Paris: Maspero, 1972), 425).

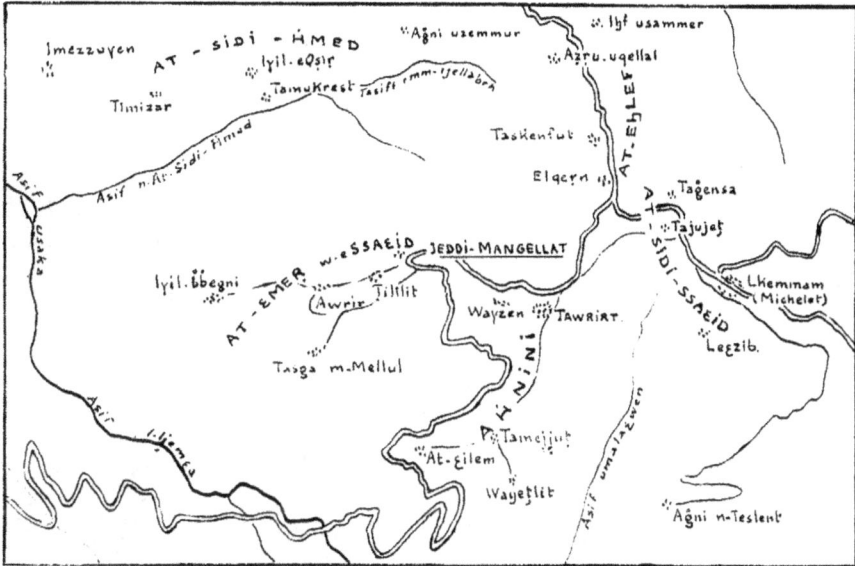

Map 7.1: The territory of *'arsh* Ath Menguellat, showing the settlements of the Ath Sidi Ahmed – Agouni Ouzemmour, Thamukrest, Ighil 'aqsir, Thimizar and Imezzoughen – and those of the Ath Sidi Saïd – El Qarn, Tagensa, Tajujet and La'azib (but omitting Bou Aggach, below Tagensa to its north). *Source*: Genevois, 1962, *op. cit.*

of Souq el-Jema'a and beyond that towards the Ath Wasif and Ath Yenni. The saintly settlements of Ath Ahmed, Ath Si Amara and Ath Bou Thetchour similarly guarantee *'arsh* boundaries by occupying the northernmost part of the Ath Yahia's territory (see Map 7.2) where this protrudes in a kind of salient separating the territories of the Ath Khelili to the north, the Ath Fraoucen to the west and the Ath Bou Chaïb to the east.

Many of the maraboutic villages and hamlets of the Ath Itsouragh perform the same function. The Ath Itsouragh inhabit an outcrop that is the culmination of a secondary ridge that extends from the main ridge just north of Werja (see Map 7.3). This outcrop resembles that on which the Ath Yenni are settled but, whereas the main Ath Yenni villages are perched on top of their mountain, the Ath Itsouragh villages are nearly all located on its slopes, like a series of pendants hanging from a girdle,[84] or at its foot, while the top of the mountain

---

84 The road that goes around the mountain is known locally as 'la ceinture des Ath Itsouragh'.

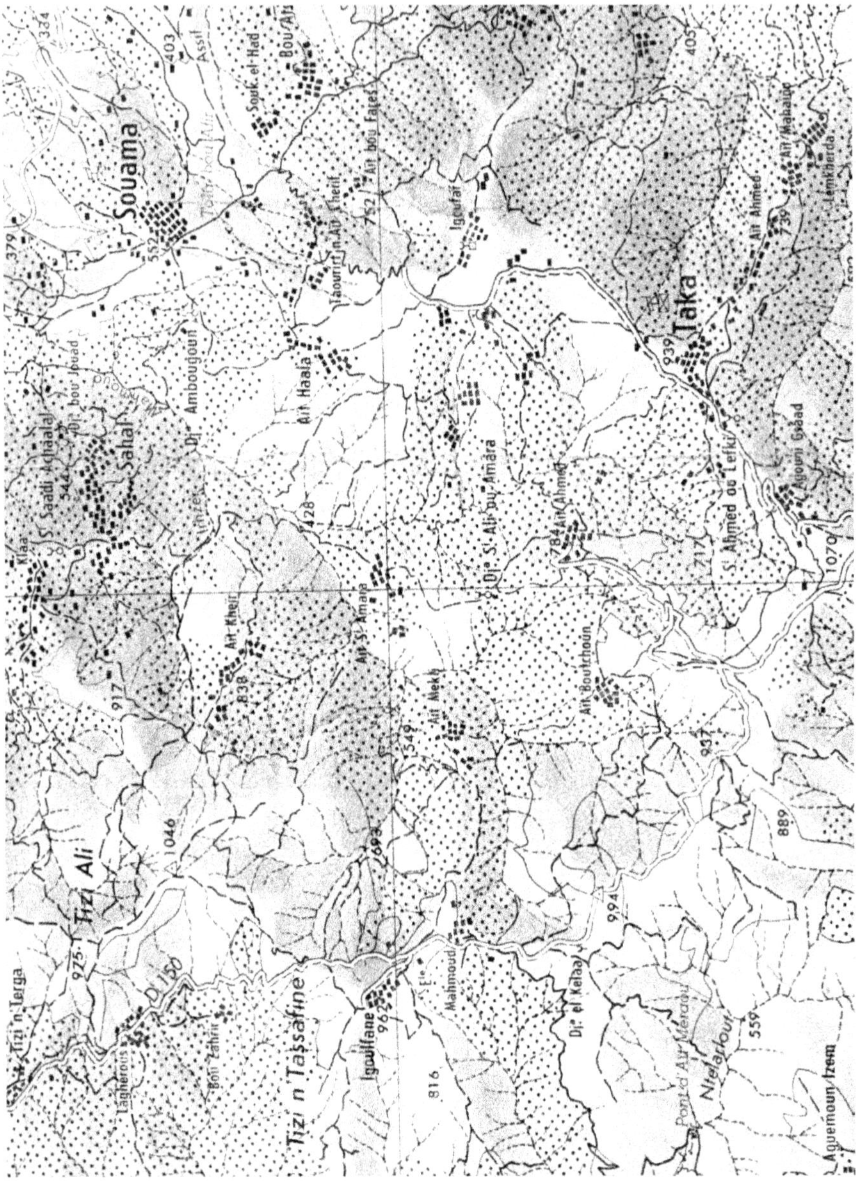

Map 7.2: Part of the territory of 'arsh Ath
Yahia, showing the saintly settlements –
Ath Si Amara, Ath Ahmed and Ath Bou
Thetchour (here misspelled as 'Boutchoun')
– on its northern frontier. The villages
to the east, north and west belong to the
'aarsh Ath Bou Chaïb, Ath Khelili and Ath
Fraoucen respectively.

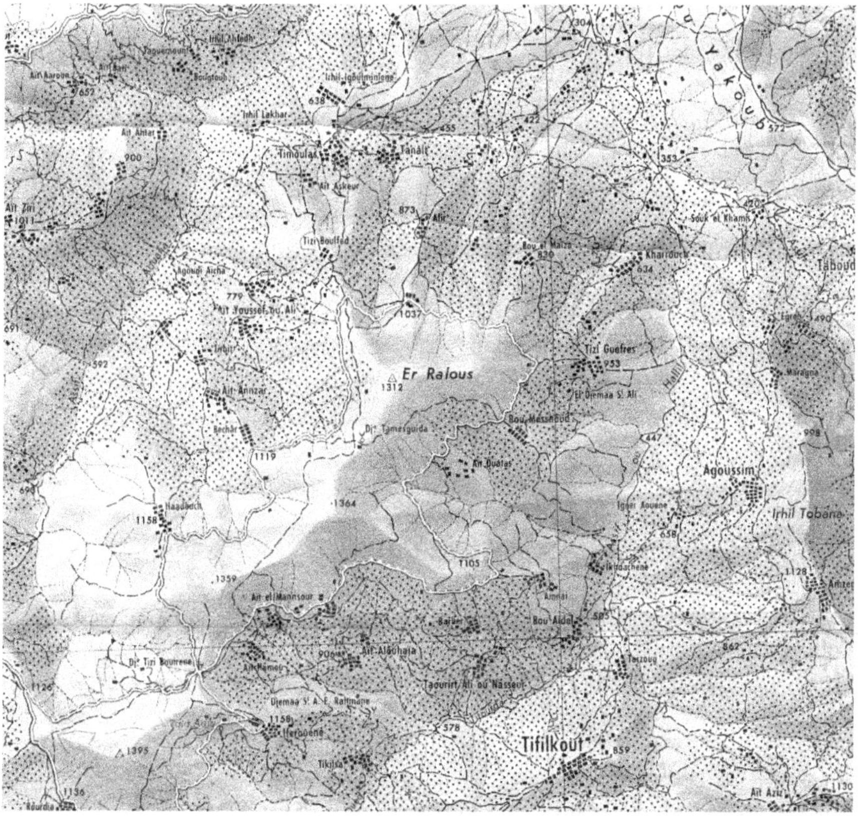

Map 7.3: The mountain outcrop that forms
the territory of the Ath Itsouragh, showing the
saintly settlements along the ῾arsh boundaries
with the Ath Yahia to the north-west (Tanalt,
Ath Asker, Ath Youcef ou Ali, etc.) and with
the Illoulen Oumalou to the east and Illilten to
the south-east (Ikhdachen, Bou Aïdel, Iberber).
The important maraboutic village of Werja can
just be seen (misspelled as 'Rourdja') next to the
road bottom left.

is bare of human settlement. It is probable that sheer altitude, around 1,300 metres, made the top of this mountain unsuitable for settlement; the highest Ath Yenni villages are at about 900 metres. Whatever the reason, the location of the Ath Itsouragh settlements on the slopes, with few higher villages to retreat to, made them vulnerable. The presence of the *imrabdhen* settlements along the boundaries with the neighbouring *'aarsh* compensated for this by guaranteeing these boundaries.

Thus, while *imrabdhen* elsewhere in the Jurjura have also performed this role of 'spiritual lords of the marches',[85] it was most highly developed and most visible among these three particular *'aarsh*, the Ath Menguellat, Ath Yahia and Ath Itsouragh, to a degree that distinguished them from the rest of the Igawawen.

Finally, a feature of this expanded presence of maraboutic lineages in the central Jurjura was the development of solidarities between maraboutic families that transcended *'arsh* divisions. The fact that branches of the Ath Sidi Ahmed were to be found in various different *'aarsh* (Ath Bou Youcef, Ath Itsouragh, Ath Yahia, Illilten, Aqbil and Ath Bou Akkach)[86] gave the lineage a capacity for political influence in the central Jurjura that was independent of *'arsh* interests. The same could be said of the Ath Sidi Saïd who, in addition to their settlements among the Ath Menguellat, also had (and still have) a settlement near the Aqbil village of Aourir Ouzemmour as well as branches of the family at Tiferdoud in *'arsh* Ath Bou Youcef and no doubt elsewhere.[87] In addition, intermarriage between the various maraboutic lineages soon created a very powerful network – or, rather, a series of overlapping or interconnecting networks – of maraboutic solidarity and influence. These alliances were especially important between the *imrabdhen* of the Ath Menguellat and those of the Ath Yahia on the one hand and those of the Ath Bou Youcef on the other.[88]

Putting definite dates to when this configuration and distribution of saintly settlements in the central Jurjura occurred is very difficult. Salhi, whose thesis is by far the most informative study available of the maraboutic lineages of Greater Kabylia, is unable to provide much information on this score. But there are grounds for believing the configuration was effected between *c.* 1600 CE and 1700 CE. We know that it was in this period that important maraboutic settlements were established elsewhere in Kabylia, notably the Ath Sidi Braham who, profiting perhaps from the loss of influence of the Ath Abbas, established themselves in the early seventeenth century near 'Les Portes de Fer', the crucial passage of the Algiers–Constantine road through the Biban mountains, a position that enabled them to levy toll payments in return for guarantees of safe passage.[89]

---

85 Gellner, 1969, *op. cit.*, 301.

86 Salhi, *op. cit.*, 213.

87 Salhi, *op. cit.*, 210.

88 For details, see Salhi, *op. cit.* 199 (Table VII), 201 (Table IX) and 206 (Table XV).

89 Yacine, *op. cit.*, 46 *et seq.*

In the Jurjura, the ancestor of the Ath Sidi Saïd is believed to have founded the first settlement of his lineage among the Ath Menguellat in the fifteenth century.[90] But the lineage will have taken time, two or more generations, to grow and expand on the ground and it is unlikely that the disposition of the Ath Sidi Saïd settlements as reported by Hanoteau and Letourneux in the 1860s (and as they have remained, largely unchanged, to the present) took shape before the large village of Taourirt, the capital of the *'arsh* Ath Menguellat, was established out of the regrouping and unification of previously scattered hamlets. This most probably occurred at some point in the early seventeenth century also, since local tradition firmly credits the founding of Taourirt as an integrated village to the action of a saint of a different lineage, Sidi L'Hadi Bou Derbal, who was born *c.* 1544 CE and is known to have died in 1637 CE.[91]

This bring us to the other main part which the *imrabdhen* played, or at least are said to have played, in the response of the society of the Jurjura to the pressures on the social order during this period, namely the reconfiguration of the settlement patterns of the lay population through the constitution of large, integrated villages (*thudrin*) out of previously dispersed hamlets (*ikhelijen*) linked if at all in the looser form of 'associations' (*tuwāfeq*).

We possess at present accounts of how this happened in only six cases, namely the local traditions collected by Genevois concerning the constitution of the present village of Taguemount Azouz of *'arsh* Ath Mahmoud; of Taourirt n'Ath Menguellat, as we have just noted, and of the three central villages of Ath Lahcène, Ath Larba'a and Taourirt Mimoun among the Ath Yenni, and a local tradition, which remains to be investigated and fully documented, that the village of Tifilkout in *'arsh* Illilten was reformed in the early seventeenth century as well as moved from an opposite slope to its present location.[92] All these traditions situate the events in question in the seventeenth century. The fact that these are the only such traditions we know of does not mean that other, similar, traditions do not exist elsewhere in the Jurjura or the broader Kabylia region.[93] The entire question is under-researched. But the coming into existence of what I have called the Igawawen *thaddarth* – that is, the large, highly integrated and nucleated village settlement that is not a kinship unit because composed of a plurality of *iderman* ('clans') that do not share a common ancestry – is not hypothetical but a palpable fact. Many of the villages

---

90 Salhi, *op. cit.*, 210.

91 The date of Sidi L'Hadi's death is given on the plaque erected in his honour at Taourirt some years ago; a photograph of this plaque can be seen on a website established by a descendant of the saint (http://sidilhadi.vip-blog.com).

92 Source: www.tifilkout.com/articles/327/1/Les-Ait-wandiouss-ou-les-maures-dandalousie/Page1.html.

93 Guenzet, the leading village of the Ath (or Ith) Yala in Lesser Kabylia, was also reconstituted out of scattered hamlets (Gaïd, 1990, *op. cit.*, 20).

Figure 7.1: Villages of the Illilten today:
Ath Adalla in the foreground and the very
important village of Tifilkout extending along
its ridge in the middle distance, with Agoussim
of 'arsh Illoulen Oumalou beyond.

of the Jurjura which are of this nature may have been formed later than the seventeenth century and, as I have suggested, constituted from the outset as nucleated settlements in imitation of an already established model. But the fact that all the traditions concerning the constitution of such villages out of previously dispersed and much smaller settlements locate these events in the seventeenth century supports the thesis that the initial development of the Igawawen *thaddarth* was a response to the crisis I have described arising out of the conjunction of the pressure of chaotic population movements and the aggravation of insecurity following the end of the 'kingdom' of Koukou. The fact that, in two of the cases cited, Ath Yenni and Taourirt n'Ath Menguellat, *imrabdhen* (Sidi Ali ou Yahia and Sidi L'Hadi Bou Derbal) are credited with instigating the change is, however, ironic. For the eventual effect of the change was not to reinforce the influence of the *imrabdhen* in general but to submerge them in the lay population and subordinate them to the interest of the village community and the authority of its *jema'a*.

Clearly this trend did not go far among the Ath Itsouragh, Ath Yahia and Ath Menguellat (where the case of Taourirt was exceptional). Something else happened instead. For these three *'aarsh* possess a level of internal organisation between that of the *'arsh* and that of the constituent settlements (whether *thudrin* or *tuwāfeq*) that no other *'aarsh* of the Jurjura have possessed. The Ath Itsouragh are composed of two 'fractions': the Imesdourar ('the highlanders') and Imessouhal ('the lowlanders'); the Ath Yahia of three: Imesdourar and Imessouhal again, and Taqa; the Ath Menguellat of four: Ahnini, Ath Ameur ou Saïd, Ath Ikhlef and the Ath Sidi Ahmed. One could reasonably say that they are 'segmented' into these fractions. The logic of this arrangement seems clear: consisting of unusually large numbers of small settlements, these *'aarsh* needed this extra level of internal organisation for the purpose of maintaining their internal equilibrium while the settlements in question needed, for their own security, to be grouped in this way to compensate for their small size. Thus these three cases resemble the 'segmentary' organisation Gellner describes in the case of the Central High Atlas of Morocco. The premises of their peculiarity in this respect are the near total absence of the 'Igawawen *thaddarth*' and the presence of numerous exclusively maraboutic settlements. The *imrabdhen* in these *'aarsh* clearly did not as a rule encourage the smaller settlements to combine to form larger ones, but seem to have exercised a conservative influence that impeded such a development.

It follows that what actually happened is that the society of the Jurjura responded in two quite different ways to the pressures it faced in the seventeenth century and produced in effect two different formulas for coping with these pressures. One formula was that of the *'aarsh* Ath Menguellat, Ath Yahia and Ath Itsouragh and involved the following features:

- a large presence of maraboutic lineages and a proliferation of exclusively saintly settlements located at points of high strategic or geo-political significance;
- a comparatively dispersed pattern of settlement on the ground, with the settlements being relatively small but numerous;
- the rarity or absence of the Igawawen *thaddarth*[94] and prevalence instead of the looser *tūfiq* as the political form linking settlements and the lineages inhabiting them;
- the consequent operation, at one level, of the 'segmentary' principle in the internal structure of the *'arsh*.

---

94 Taourirt n'Ath Menguellat and both Taqa and Ath Hichem among the Ath Yahia clearly qualified as instances of the 'Igawawen *thaddarth*' as I use this term by the time Hanoteau and Letourneux investigated the region, but as such they were untypical of their respective *'aarsh*, where far smaller settlements inhabited by kinship groups were the rule.

The second formula was the opposite of the first, viz.:

- the prevalence of the Igawawen *thaddarth*, ensuring that the population is concentrated in a small number of relatively large settlements;
- the corresponding rarity or absence altogether of the *tūfiq* form;
- the small proportion of the population belonging to maraboutic families;
- the rarity or total absence of exclusively maraboutic settlements; instead, maraboutic lineages are integrated into the Igawawen *thaddarth* as simply a street or quarter of this and more or less indistinguishable on the ground from the lay lineages.

The perfect illustration of the first formula is provided by the Ath Itsouragh. As Salhi notes, the maraboutic element of the population of this 'arsh has been very high indeed, no fewer than 2,489 persons representing perhaps as much as 40 per cent of the population of the 'arsh (and 31 per cent of the total maraboutic population of the Jurjura district), when this question was investigated in the late nineteenth century.[95] The dispersed settlement pattern is clearly shown in Map 7.3. Hanoteau and Letourneux identified no fewer than 34 settlements in this 'arsh; eight of these are listed as independent *thudrin*; the other 26 are grouped in 10 *tuwāfeq*. Seven of the eight *thudrin* are small; the largest, Ahfir, is credited with a population of 495; the average population of the *thudrin* is a mere 228, and all of them, except Ahfir, can be assumed to be kinship units. The average population of the 26 hamlets grouped in *tuwāfeq* is 115.[96]

The perfect illustration of the second formula is provided by the Ath Wasif. This 'arsh consists entirely of seven *thudrin*. When investigated by Hanoteau and Letourneux, the smallest *thaddarth* had 360 inhabitants, the largest 1,272; their average population was 790.[97] There were no exclusively maraboutic settlements. The *imrabdhen* represented about 3 per cent of the population in

---

95 Salhi, *op. cit.*, 189–91. This figure is derived from a study of the maraboutic families in the Commune Mixte du Jurjura carried out in 1895 by M. Pervieux de Laborde, who examined the 'aarsh Illilten, Ath Itsouragh, Ath Yahia, Ath Menguellat, Ath Bou Youcef, Aqbil, Ath Attaf, Ath Boudrar, Ath Yenni, Ath Bou Akkach, Ath Wasif and the 'Ath Sedka Ogdal' (*sic*) – that is, the three 'aarsh of the eastern Ath Sedqa: Aouqdal, Ath Ahmed and Ath Ali ou Illoul. The total maraboutic population of these 'aarsh was 7,896 persons; 2,489 were from the Ath Itsouragh; this would have represented 51 per cent per cent of the total population of the 'arsh, 4,697, *c.* 1868 (Hanoteau and Letourneux, *op. cit.*, I, 311); the 'arsh population can be assumed to have risen somewhat by 1895.

96 Hanoteau and Letourneux, *op. cit.*, I, 309–11.

97 Hanoteau and Letourneux, *op. cit.*, I, 306. Thus the smallest *thaddarth* of the Ath Wasif was one and a half times the size of the average *thaddarth* of the Ath Itsouragh, and the average *thaddarth* of the Ath Wasif was nearly three and a half times the size of the average *thaddarth* of the Ath Itsouragh.

the late nineteenth century[98] and they are all integrated into the various *thudrin* alongside the lay population.

Arguably these are both extreme cases. But the *'aarsh* of the Jurjura resemble the Ath Wasif far more than they resemble the Ath Itsouragh. This is true not only of the Ath Wasif's neighbours of the Ath Bethroun confederation (Ath Yenni, Ath Bou Akkach, Ath Boudrar) in the south-west of the Igawawen district, but also of the Ath Attaf and Aqbil of the Ath Menguellat confederation, the Illilten (southern neighbours of the Ath Itsouragh), the Ath Ousammeur and Irjen of the Ath Irathen confederation and the three *'aarsh* to the north of the Ath Yahia, namely the Ath Fraoucen, Ath Khelili and Ath Bou Chaïb. It is also true of the easternmost *'aarsh* of the Ath Aïssi confederation, namely the Ath Douala and the Ath Mahmoud, which, while not counted as Igawawen, are their close neighbours, facing the Ath Ousammeur and Ath Yenni across the Wad Aïssi valley. It is entirely possible that the regroupment of scattered hamlets into a large, tightly integrated village at Taguemount Azouz of the Ath Mahmoud was precisely a case of imitation of the model pioneered by the Igawawen and most probably by the *'aarsh* of the Ath Bethroun.

Thus, in the districts of Greater Kabylia identified with the Igawawen in the broader sense (the region that extends from the Sebaou valley to the main watershed ridge of the Jurjura), only a small minority of *'aarsh* conformed to the first formula. The socio-political and religious organisation of the Ath Itsouragh, Ath Menguellat and Ath Yahia was exceptional. Yet the location of these *'aarsh* – especially *'arsh* Ath Menguellat – in the vicinity of Michelet (now Aïn el-Hammam), the administrative centre of the high Jurjura, encouraged subsequent observers to overlook their peculiarities. Can it be that it is in large part their central position that accounts for the latter? To put it the other way round: may it be the case that it was above all in the *'aarsh* located on the edges of the central Jurjura region – the Irjen, Ath Ousammeur, Ath Yenni, Ath Wasif and Ath Bou Akkach on the western edge, the Ath Fraoucen, Ath Khelili and Ath Bou Chaïb on the northern and eastern edges, the Illilten, Aqbil, Ath Attaf and Ath Boudrar on the southern edge – that the need to regroup in a smaller number of larger villages was most pressing and accordingly acted upon? And is there any other evidence that supports the hypothesis of a significant dichotomy between the centre and the edges of the region in question at this period?

It is here that we should consider another ingredient of the crisis of the society of the Jurjura during the seventeenth and early eighteenth centuries. This was the conflict that broke out between the descendants of the lords of Koukou for control of what was left of the family's possessions and influence, for this

---

98 Salhi, *op. cit.*, 191; the 1895 study found a maraboutic population of 178 among the Ath Wasif, whose total population *c.* 1868 was 5,532 (Hanoteau and Letourneux, *op. cit.*, I, 306) and will have been higher than this by 1895.

conflict implicated most of the populations of the region as a whole, because it also involved the Ottoman Regency.

The Iboukhtouchen succession and the Ottoman penetration of Kabylia

The end of the kingdom of Koukou was not the end of the Ath l-Qadi. They were to remain a force in the political life of Greater Kabylia for a further 120 years, from the 1630s to the 1750s. And there is a case for saying that, over most of this period, they were the premier political force in the region.

This is not generally known. The truth of the matter has gone unrecognised, where it has not been denied, in the literature on pre-colonial Kabylia. It has been widely supposed that, after Koukou, the Ath l-Qadi disappeared into oblivion,[99] while the political life of the region was dominated by the *imrabdhen*, certain *jawād* families in the lowlands, and the Ottomans. Various authors have acknowledged the influence of a family known as the Ath Bou Khettouch or Iboukhtouchen, but the fact that these were the direct descendants and continuation of the Ath l-Qadi dynasty has not been generally understood and has been explicitly denied by some (notably Boulifa), while the extent and importance of their influence has not been fully appreciated. In addition, the conflict that erupted in Kabylia in the 1690s, and which began as a dispute within the Iboukhtouchen family itself before widening to implicate other forces, has been almost entirely neglected. In these ways, the political history of Kabylia has been relentlessly obscured.

As we have already seen, in 1632–3, or more probably a few years later than this,[100] the son of Ameur ou l-Qadi, known to history as Sidi Ahmed (or Hend[101]) El-Tounsi, returned to Kabylia with troops provided by his Tunisian connections, settled accounts with his father's murderers by killing them all, bequeathed his family's property at Koukou to Sidi Ali ou Taleb, and returned to the ancestral home at Aourir n'Ath Ghoubri before subsequently establishing himself at Tifilkout in *'arsh* Illilten.[102] At some point he acquired the sobriquet *Bou Khettouch* – 'the man with the lance' – and this eventually replaced Ath l-Qadi as the family name, at any rate of his direct descendants.

An alternative version promoted by Boulifa holds that *Bou Khettouch* was the sobriquet of one of Sidi Ahmed El-Tounsi's lieutenants who was not a

---

99   Mercier, *op. cit.*, 234.

100   1632–3, when Sidi Ahmed El Tounsi was 15 years old, is the date given by Robin (1873, *op. cit.*, 135 (1998, *op. cit.*, 42)). Tahar Oussedik claims (*op. cit.*, 60) that Sidi Ahmed was 20 years old when he set out from Tunis to avenge his father, which would place these events in 1638–9.

101   Hend or Hand is a standard Berber version of Ahmed, as Mohand is of Mohammed.

102   Oussedik, *op. cit.*, 77.

member of the Ath l-Qadi lineage, which soon died out and was supplanted by the descendants of Bou Khettouch, who somehow managed to appropriate the prestige and *baraka* and estates of the defunct Ath l-Qadi family. I do not believe this version at all, but rather that the Iboukhtouchen were and are (for they still exist) the lineal descendants of Sidi Ahmed El Tounsi ou l-Qadi.

The only evidence that can be cited for the existence of someone other than Sidi Ahmed called Bou Khettouch is the name itself and the fact that it became the name of the family which inherited the Ath l-Qadi's estates and influence. But 'Bou Khettouch' was originally a nickname. *Khettouch* is a typically Algerian and Kabyle deformation of the Arabic word *khattī*, meaning spear or lance, but the effect of the deformation (i.e. the suffix *-ouch*) is to make a diminutive.[103] Thus 'Bou Khettouch' really means 'the man with the *little* lance', which would have been a natural, ironic if also affectionate, nickname for a young princeling leading a small army and bent on revenge.

Second, it is established that both before and after settling accounts with his father's murderers Sidi Ahmed El Tounsi stayed at the Illilten village of Tifilkout, where a shrine to his memory exists to this day and is regularly visited by members of the Iboukhtouchen family of Jema'a n'Saharij.[104] This is evidence that he was indeed their ancestor, but it may be thought to be less than conclusive; a sceptic might suggest that the annual pilgrimage merely asserts rather than proves the Iboukhtouchen's claim and that this claim is false. But a problem with this (i.e. Boulifa's) thesis is that it is entirely unclear when the pretender Bou Khettouch is supposed to have supplanted the extinct Ath l-Qadi.

It is widely accepted that Sidi Ahmed El Tounsi lived to a ripe old age and died in 1696–7 and that he had two sons. The conflict referred to earlier assumed the form of a conflict between the latter in its early stages. But, if it was this fratricidal conflict which finally destroyed the Ath l-Qadi, it follows that Bou Khettouch took over the Ath l-Qadi inheritance only in the early 1700s. This timing is implausible, however, since a former lieutenant of El Tounsi would have been in his 80s by this point. The alternative is to suggest that Sidi Ahmed El Tounsi *was* Bou Khettouch *but not an Ou l-Qadi at all*. In that case, we are faced with several mysteries. If he was not an Ou l-Qadi, why should he have sought revenge on Ameur ou l-Qadi's assassins? Why should the Tunisian friends of the Ath l-Qadi have supported and equipped him? Why should he have returned to Aourir n'Ath Ghoubri? And if he had no title to the Ath l-Qadi's inheritance in the region, how did he manage to get hold of it all? I submit that Boulifa's thesis has no answer to these questions and holds no water. Reason and evidence support the straightforward view that *Bou Khettouch was simply a nickname of* Sidi Ahmed El Tounsi, that the latter was Ameur ou l-Qadi's son and heir and

---

103 This suffix is frequently found in given and family names (e.g. 'Amirouche', 'Didouche', 'Hamadouche' etc.).

104 Genevois, 1974, *op. cit.*, 62; Oussedik, *op. cit.*, 82.

as such had good title to what was left of the Ath l-Qadi inheritance, which was why he did in fact inherit it.

But an equally cogent objection to Boulifa's thesis is the fact that the crucial premise of his argument – that the Ath l-Qadi died out or at least disappeared – is simply untrue.

In the early part of his *Rihla*, devoted to his journey across Kabylia in 1765–6, Hussein Al-Warthilani speaks of visiting members of the Ath l-Qadi lineage in several localities and, in the first place, Jemaa n'Saharij, where he notes that he met 'the honourable and noble Sidi Mohammed Ibn el-Qadi Al-Sherif, Sultan of the Zwawa'.[105] The Ath l-Qadi lived at Jema'a n'Saharij and also among the Ath Bou Chaïb, which Al-Warthilani also visited (and where a lineage of the Iboukhtouchen exists to this day).[106] How is this to be understood? There is no suggestion that the lineage of the Ath l-Qadi that had been dispossessed by El-Tounsi in the 1630s had somehow regained primacy within the Ath l-Qadi as a whole. Clearly the Iboukhtouchen were themselves Ath l-Qadi and, moreover, recognised as the legitimate heirs to the main line of royal descent. So the two names – the broader one, Ou l-Qadi, and the more specific one, Ou Boukhtouch – could both be used by the decendants of Sidi Ahmed El-Tounsi, while descendants of the collateral branch(es) of the Ath l-Qadi had only the original lineage name available to them and kept it.

The inheritance El-Tounsi came into was considerable. It is generally acknowledged that the Iboukhtouchen continued to enjoy political pre-eminence in the middle and upper Sebaou for several generations, but no attempt has been made to assess this influence. Let us therefore do so now.

The family of Sidi Ahmed El-Tounsi and his heirs are associated with a large number of different places and credited with ownership of an impressive number of properties in Greater Kabylia. They possessed or acquired connections and in many cases properties or residences in the following places: Jema'a n'Saharij, the political capital of *'arsh* Ath Fraoucen;[107] Adeni, *tūfiq* of *'arsh* Irjen of the Ath Irathen confederation (in fact, the Irjen settlement closest to the Sebaou valley floor);[108] Souama, the principal village of *'arsh* Ath Bou Chaïb;[109] the village of Moknia in *'arsh* Ath Ghoubri (in addition to their pre-existing connections at Aourir, Achallam and Tabburt);[110] Tamda, village of the Iamrawien Oufella in

105 Al-Warthilani, *op. cit.*, 15–16. Sidi Mohammed's retention of the honorific title 'Sultan of the Zwawa' should not mislead us; his lineage had long ceased to possess a kingdom and its subsequent influence had waned by the 1760s.
106 Al-Warthilani, *op. cit.*, 16. See also notes 118 and 143 below.
107 Robin, *La Grande Kabylie sous le régime turc*, 42, n. 2; Boulifa, *op. cit.*, 174; Feredj, *op. cit.*, 34.
108 Robin, *op. cit.*, 62, 69; Feredj, *op. cit.* 39.
109 Robin, *ibid.*; Boulifa, *ibid.*
110 Boulifa, *op. cit.*, 156, speaks of a 'fortress' in this village; the Iannichen family of Moknia descends from members of Sidi Ahmed El Tounsi's army who stayed in Kabylia (Genevois, 1974, *op. cit.*, 33).

the middle Sebaou valley;[111] 'Borj Kara' in *'arsh* Ath Jennad[112] (most probably the village of Khahra, on the right bank of the Sebaou, due south of Timizar n'Sidi Mansour); a stronghold on Jebel Tamgout, the important mountain immediately to the east of the Ath Jennad;[113] a residence on Jebel Zeraïb, a mountain that forms the southern boundary of the *'arsh* Ath Fliq, north of Azazga;[114] Ath Aouana, a village of *'arsh* Asif el-Hammam, situated just east of the Ath Ghoubri village of Yakouren on the road that leads to Bejaia along the northern edge of the Ath Ghoubri territory;[115] Tifilkout, the principal village of *'arsh* Illilten;[116] Tizit, another important Illilten village, close to Tizi n'Ichelladen, and its satellite hamlet, Iqfilen.[117]

Several of these will probably have been in the possession of the Ath l-Qadi for some time before the 1630s, notably those in the vicinity of the Ath Ghoubri – at Ath Aouana, in the Jebel Tamgout and Jebel Zeraïb, and possibly also at Tamda in the Sebaou valley. It is also probable that a branch of the Ath l-Qadi was already settled at Jema'a n'Saharij before the 1630s. But there is no doubt that it was Sidi Ahmed El-Tounsi and the Iboukhtouchen who secured the bases at Iqfilen and Tifilkout in *'arsh* Illilten and at Adeni; there is no doubt that they also subsequently established themselves at Jema'a n'Saharij (whether or not other Ath l-Qadi already lived there) and at Souama;[118] and, if 'Borj Kara' is correctly identified with Khahra, the family's position there is likely to have been a late addition to its portfolio of bases and properties.

What, then, are we looking at? The answer is a redeployment of political assets and new political investments. Under Sidi Ahmed El-Tounsi, the Ath l-Qadi dynasty gave itself a new lease of life *qua* the Iboukhtouchen. The first step was the liquidation of an old and no longer profitable asset, the position at Koukou. As already noted, the choice of Koukou as the dynasty's political capital was predicated on the long-standing orientation of the society of Greater Kabylia to Bejaia and the Ath l-Qadi's ambition to recover and if possible

---

111 Robin, *ibid.*

112 Baron H. Aucapitaine, 1860, *art. cit.*, 454.

113 Robin, *ibid.*; Liorel, *op. cit.*, 135; Boulifa, *op. cit.*, 156.

114 Robin, *ibid.*

115 Robin, *ibid.*

116 Genevois, 1974, *op. cit.*, 30, 62; Oussedik, 1986, *op. cit.*, 68–77.

117 Genevois, 1974, *op. cit.*, 62; Oussedik, *ibid.*

118 The Iboukhtouchen have remained an important lineage at Jema'a n'Saharij to this day, occupying a large part of the quarter of the village called Madal (H. Genevois, *Djemaa-Saharidj* (Fort National: C.E.B., 1958), 8–10 and 27–9), as I was able to see for myself in a visit to the village in 2012. According to Salah Iboukhtouchen, whom I interviewed on 14 July 2012, the link with Tifilkout is maintained and other branches of the Iboukhtouchen family still live at Achallam (Ath Ghoubri) and Souama (Ath Bou Chaïb). In 2011, the President of the Popular Communal Assembly of Souama was a certain Mohand Boukhetouche (*L'Expression*, 9 March 2011).

improve upon their old position in the political dispensation centred on Bejaia. With the definitive defeat of the Hafsids, the decline of Bejaia and the rise of Algiers under the Ottomans, that strategic perspective had become obsolete and the mismanagement of matters by Ameur ou l-Qadi had alienated the Ath Yahia into the bargain. So the Koukou-Ath Yahia investment was finally written off[119] and new investments oriented by a new strategic perspective were made.

This new perspective evidently took as its premise the reorientation of the society of Greater Kabylia towards Algiers that had occurred since 1529. It probably also took as a further premise the vanity of intriguing with the Spanish and the danger in doing so, given the social influence of the maraboutic movement. The strategy accordingly appears to have been to negotiate a compromise with the Regency based on a balance of power in the region. Control of the Sebaou valley was the central issue around which this negotiation had to take place and the Iboukhtouchen made their investments accordingly.

Up to this point the Ottomans had established their presence on the marches of Greater Kabylia but had not tried to penetrate further into the region. The forts established at Borj Hamza (Bouïra) and at Sour el-Ghozlane to the south-west, like those further east on the southern edge of Lesser Kabylia at Borj Bou Arrerij and Borj Zemoura, had the purpose of protecting the routes from Algiers to Constantine. The fort at Borj Menaïel had established the Regency's authority over the westernmost marcher populations – the 'aarsh of the mainly Arabophone Isser confederation and of the western Iflissen Oumellil – and had the further function of giving warning of Kabyle incursions into the Mitija. East of Borj Menaïel they had mounted occasional punitive expeditions but had no permanent presence. This now began to change.

In 1640, the Regency established a military observation post at Tizi Ouzou.[120] In fact, there is no record of the existence of any settlement at Tizi Ouzou prior to the establishment of the Ottoman post there and it is possible that the village of Tizi Ouzou, subsequently incorporated into 'arsh Iamrawien Bouadda, grew up around the Ottoman military presence.[121] This move took the permanent Ottoman presence 20 miles further east from Borj Menaïel and into the middle Sebaou valley; it also brought representatives of Ottoman authority into regular contact with a new range of populations: the Iourgioun (Taourga) to the north-west, the Ath Waguenoun to the north, the eastern Iflissen Oumellil to the south-west, the Maatqa and Ath Aïssi confederations to the south, and the Ath Irathen to the south-east. This move thus had an audacious aspect and also a provocative or destabilising aspect. By moving into terrain previously controlled

---

119 But not for ever; at a much later date the Ath l-Qadi/Iboukhtouchen appear to have re-established themselves at Koukou in addition to the family's seats elsewhere. See below, p. 260 and note 143.
120 Feredj, *op. cit.*, 34.
121 *Ibid.*

by the Ath l-Qadi, the Ottomans were taking advantage of the vacuum that had opened up since the end of Koukou. The logic of this seems clear: if the pro-Ottoman lords of Koukou were no longer available to control the lowlands, the Ottomans would have to undertake this themselves. Their advance is likely to have been regarded by the Iboukhtouchen as a challenge they had to meet.

It was probably around this time that the family established itself at Jema'a n'Saharij and at Souama.[122] The first position gave them the perfect vantage point from which to reassert their influence in the middle Sebaou. With their establishment at Souama, the capital of the Ath Bou Chaïb, immediately to the north of the Ath Yahia and directly opposite the Ath Ghoubri, they could continue to control access to the Wad Boubehir, where they had in any case already reinforced their position through their new connections with the Illilten villages of Tifilkout, at the head of the valley, and Tizit, the village controlling the northern approach to Tizi n'Ichelladen, while their positions among the Ath Ghoubri, Ath Fliq and Asif el-Hammam will have enabled them to retain control over the main road to Bejaia.

The redeployment of the Iboukhtouchen in this way will have established a new balance of power in the Sebaou valley that at least contained the Regency's advance there, and this balance appears to have remained stable for the next four decades, until the 1690s. But this understanding did not extend to the south-western districts of Greater Kabylia. From their bases at Borj Hamza and Sour el-Ghozlane the Ottomans will already have gained some purchase over the populations of the southern side of the Jurjura. But this still left a vacuum. For neither the Ottomans' presence on the southern marches nor their understanding with the Iboukhtouchen addressed the issue of the political control of the other main low-lying district, the narrow but fertile plain that lies at the northern foot of the western Jurjura and extends from east of Draa el-Mizan through Boghni, Amechras and Tizi n'Tleta to just beyond Wadhia. At some point, most probably in the mid-1650s, the Regency took steps to deal with this.

An official decision dated 1659–60 CE is the earliest evidence we have of the assertion of Ottoman authority over this district by the creation, under the Regency's mandate, of the sheikhdom or chieftancy of *bled Guechtoula*, covering the *'aarsh* of the north face of the western Jurjura that formed a *thaqbilth* known in Thaqbaylith as the Igouchdal.[123] This was initially entrusted to a certain Sheikh Gacem Ben M'Hamed, who held this post for many years, at least until 1089

---

122 It may also have been at this time that the Iboukhtouchen established themselves at Adeni, in *'arsh* Irjen, so gaining the backing of the Ath Irathen confederation. But this is more likely to have occurred later (see below).

123 Robin, *op. cit.*, 43–4, citing documents dated 1070 AH/1659–60 CE and 1085 AH/1674–5 CE. These *'aarsh* were/are: Frikat, Ath Smaïl, Ath Bou Gherdane, Ath Mendas, Ath Koufi, Ath Bou Addou, Cheurfa Guighil Gueqqen, Amechras and Ighil Imoula. It is not certain that all nine *'aarsh* were included from the outset in the command established by the Ottomans.

AH/1678–9 CE,[124] if not till the month of *Sha'abān*, 1104 AH/1693 CE, when a certain Ferhat Ben Seghir Ben Ahmed was appointed Sheikh of the Guechtoula.[125] At some point, possibly from the outset, the Ottomans sought to levy taxes on the populations concerned.[126]

The timing of this development is interesting, for it was in 1659 CE that the form of government of the Regency underwent a major change, with the *agha* of the janissaries assuming supreme power in Algiers at the expense of the triennial pashas.[127] This new form of government proved short-lived: four *aghas* ruled, each of them briefly, before meeting violent ends in a bloody succession that lasted until 1671, when the *ra'īs al-tā'ifa* (admiral of the navy) finally intervened to introduce a new governing formula, the rule of the *deys*, elected by the armed forces as a whole.[128] It is possible then, that the creation of the command of *bled Guechtoula* expressed the more aggressive policy which the Ojaq had always favoured towards Kabylia and likely that this development was resented and discreetly resisted by the Iboukhtouchen.

It is also interesting to note that both of the sheikhs appointed to command *bled Guechtoula* were outsiders imposed on the Igouchdal by the Regency. According to Robin, Sheikh Gacem was from Meneja, which was near a place called Mehalet Ramdan; neither place can be found in the Igouchdal district. The first cannot be found at all on the maps of the region, and the nearest candidate for the second is Dechra Mehalla, on the south side of the Jurjura at its extreme westernmost point, adjacent to or possibly part of the *'arsh* Er-Rich to the north-west of Bouïra. As for Sheikh Gacem's replacement, Sheikh Ferhat, Robin describes him as from the Arib Ben El-Thaalibi tribe. The Arib were not Kabyles but an important Arabic-speaking population situated between Bir Ghbalou and Aïn Bessem, to the south-west of Bouira. That the Ottomans appointed such outsiders strongly suggests that they could not find suitable candidates for the post from the leaders of the Igouchdal *'aarsh* or anywhere else on the north side of the Jurjura for that matter. Could this be because the influence of the Iboukhtouchen was enough to ensure that no plausible local candidates put themselves forward? Moreover, in recruiting Sheikh Ferhat from the Arib, the Ottomans were having to seek much further afield than before. This suggests that it had become harder not easier to find appropriate candidates in Kabylia and that this was a side effect of a more general deterioration or crisis in relations between the Iboukhtouchen and the Regency. A reason for

---

124 Date of a third official document mentioning Sheikh Gacem as holder of this post, cited by
      Robin, 1998, *op. cit.*, 44.

125 *Ibid.*, citing a fourth official document bearing this date.

126 According to an official order (cited by Robin, *loc. cit.*) dated 1103 AH/1691–2 CE, requiring
      the Sheikh of the Guechtoula to make an annual payment to the Regency and certain other
      occasional payments.

127 Julien, 1970, *op. cit.*, 303.

128 *Ibid.*

entertaining this hypothesis is that the appointment of Sheikh Ferhat more or less coincided with the eruption of a major dispute within the Iboukhtouchen themselves, to which the Ottomans cannot have been indifferent.

The fact that a conflict among the Iboukhtouchen occurred in the 1690s and expanded for some time thereafter, drawing much of the population of Kabylia into a party division of a kind, is in itself well known. What is absent from the literature, however, is any understanding of the significance of this conflict. Instead, the practice has been to make a passing mention of the affair while admitting, usually quite frankly, that it is impossible to know what it was all about. I wish to show that it is, in fact, possible to work out what it was probably about and as a result to specify and evaluate its historical significance.

According to the tradition, one of Sidi Ahmed El Tounsi's sons, known to history as 'Ourkho', fell out with his father over a point of honour – the fact that his father had violated the *'anāya* (guarantee of protection) that 'Ourkho' had offered an unidentified third person – and left the region to establish his base in *'arsh* Ifenayen in the Soummam valley.[129] His conflict with his father continued after Sidi Ahmed's death as a conflict with his brother, Sidi Ahmed's other son, Si Ali, and the dispute divided the populations of Kabylia into two hostile camps, Ourkho's partisans being known as 'the upper party' – *saff oufella* – and Ali's supporters as 'the lower party' – *saff bouadda*.

It is not clear when exactly this conflict took place. It must have begun before 1696 CE, since Sidi Ahmed died in this year, and may well have begun in the early 1690s. According to the traditions collected by Hanoteau and Letourneux, it continued up to the end of the eighteenth century and so lasted for over a hundred years.[130] This claim is undocumented and hard to believe if all that was at issue was the wounded *amour-propre* of a son who had fallen out with his father and brother and I doubt that it is to be taken literally. In the oral culture of Kabylia, situations and events remembered would normally not go back beyond two or three generations. Thus informants questioned by French ethnographers in the 1860s would be unlikely to ascribe a memory to a time earlier than the late eighteenth century and would be inclined to bring a distant event remembered, however dimly, forward to a time when

---

129 'Ourkho' was certainly a nickname and I believe it to have been given the individual in question by his adversaries, who as the winners in the conflict will have determined the subsequent local tradition. In Thaqbaylith, *'our'* or *'ur'* is the negative particle; *'kho'* could well come from the Arabic for 'brother', making 'Ourkho' signify 'not a brother', i.e, stigmatising his behaviour as the opposite of fraternal. That he became an outcast from the family is clear from the fact that he had to go as far afield as the Soummam valley to find refuge and a base.

130 Hanoteau and Letourneux (*op. cit.*, vol. II, 17–20) mistakenly situated this conflict *before* the advent of Koukou and accordingly supposed that it had lasted «pendant plusieurs siècles»!

they or their parents or grandparents could have witnessed or heard tell of it and handed the tradition concerning it on to their own offspring. But the fact that there was a recollection of the *fitna* of the *sfūf* in the popular collective memory in the 1860s suggests that this event was important to the society, as does the fact that, according to Hanoteau and Letourneux, it was still possible at the time they undertook their research to specify the *saff* allegiances of all the main *'aarsh* of Greater Kabylia.

Like their mention of the four *saff* systems, the reference Hanoteau and Letourneux made to the division of the *'aarsh* of Kabylia into *saff oufella* and *saff bouadda* is brief and subsequent studies have taken scarcely any notice of it.[131] Our difficulty in interpreting this event is that we know very little about it beyond the fact that it occurred, the approximate timing of it and the support given by the populations of Kabylia to one side or the other as indicated by the enumeration of the *'arsh* allegiances that Hanoteau and Letourneux provided. These are shown in Table 7.1.

The information in Table 7.1 is intriguing. It does not suggest that the *saff* division was a kind of order-maintaining mechanism. Hanoteau and Letourneux explicitly dismiss Carette's earlier suggestion that the *saff* divisions in the Boghni district assumed a 'chess-board' pattern (an anticipation of Montagne's view of the *liff* alignments in south-western Morocco) and suggested that what we are looking at here were 'veritable leagues for attack and defence' – that is, the two sides of what may have amounted to a civil war. The data tabulated here supports their view.

For instance, we find that only one of the *'aarsh* of the Wad Boubehir district supported *saff oufella*, namely the Ath Yahia. All the other *'aarsh* of the Wad Boubehir lined up with *saff bouadda* – that is, stayed loyal to the main line of descent, now known as the Ath Bou Khettouch or Iboukhtouchen. Clearly there was no local 'chess-board' pattern in the district but near total unanimity.[132]

A second feature of the conflict is its sheer scale. Not only were the vast majority of *'aarsh* of Greater Kabylia implicated in the *saff* division, some of the populations of Lesser Kabylia were as well, including nearly all the *'aarsh* of the left bank of the Wad Sahel and the Wad Soummam and many of those of the right bank.

---

131 An exception is Alain Mahé, *op. cit.*, 59.
132 Boulifa's claim that the populations of the Wad Boubehir, led by their saints, had rebelled en masse against the Ath l-Qadi is emphatically contradicted by this evidence, which shows that, with the sole exception of the Ath Yahia, every *'arsh* of the district – Ath Ghoubri, Ath Bou Chaïb, the four *'aarsh* of the Ath Ijjeur confederation, Ath Ziki, Illoulen Oumalou, Illilten and Ath Itsouragh – remained loyal to the Ath l-Qadi/Ath Bou Khettouch.

Table 7.1: *Saff* allegiances of the *'aarsh* of Kabylia in the *fitna* of the Iboukhtouchen succession[133]

Saff Oufella (Ourkho)	Saff Bouadda (Ali)
1. 'aarsh and thiqbilin of Greater Kabylia	
Ath Yahia	Ath Irathen (*thaqbilth*: 5 *'aarsh*)
Ath Menguellat	Iamrawien
Ath Bou Youcef	Ath Waguenoun (*thaqbilth*: 7 *'aarsh*)
Ath Wasif	Ath Fraoucen
Ath Attaf	Ath Khelili
Ath Bou Akkach	Ath Bou Chaïb
Aouqdal	Ath Itsouragh
Ath Ahmed	Illilten
Ath Bou Addou	Illoulen Oumalou
Ath Mendas	Ath Ijjeur (*thaqbilth*: 4 *'aarsh*)
Ath Ismaïl	Ath Ziki
Iflissen Oumellil (*thaqbilth*: 14 *'aarsh*)	Ath Ghoubri
Ath Abdelmoumen	Iflissen el-Bahr (*thaqbilth*: 4 *'aarsh*)
Ath Jennad (*thaqbilth*: 3 *'aarsh*)	Ath Aïssi (*thaqbilth*: 3 *'aarsh*)[134]
Iazzouzen[135]	Maatqa
Ath Fliq	Ath Yenni
	Ath Boudrar
	Aqbil
	Iwadhien
	Ath Bou Gherdane
	Ath Koufi
	Ihassenawen
	Ath Zmenzer
	Amechras
	Ath Ameur ou Faïd

133 Hanoteau and Letourneux, vol. II, 19. The *'aarsh* not accounted for include Frikat and Cheurfa Guighil Gueqqen (both Igouchdal); Ath Bou Chennafa, Ath Chebla, Ath Ali ou Illoul and Ath Irguen (all Ath Sedqa); Ath ou Belkacem (Ath Bethroun) and Izerkhfawen.

134 The Ath Aïssi are listed as well as the Ihassenawen, Ath Ameur ou Faïd, Ath Zmenzer and Ath Abdelmoumen; these *'aarsh* belonged to *thaqbilth* Ath Aïssi by the 1860s. I assume the Ath Aïssi at this earlier stage consisted only of *'aarsh* Iferdiwen, Ath Douala and Ath Mahmoud, which are not listed separately, omissions not easily explained otherwise.

135 The text of Hanoteau and Letourneux says « Iazzouguen », the name of a village of *'arsh* Ath Ghoubri now known as Azazga; this must be a misprint for Iazzouzen, an *'arsh* of north-eastern Kabylia, eastern neighbour of the Ath Fliq.

Table 7.1 *continued*

2. *'aarsh* of Lesser Kabylia	
Illoulen Ousammeur	Asif el-Hammam
Ath Mellikech	Ath Tamzalt
Ifenayen	Ath Aïdel
Ath Ben Messaoud	Ourzellaguen
Imezzaïen	Iberbachen
Iznaguen	Ath Seliman
half of Ath Abbas	Ath Ameur
	Ath Waghlis

Examination of those *'aarsh* which did not take part provides clues to what may have been at issue in this conflict and why such a large proportion of the population of Kabylia was drawn into it. The *'aarsh* of those districts of Lesser Kabylia – the Biban, Guergour and Babor – where the lords of Koukou had never had any authority because pre-empted by the lords of Qal'a, did not take part in the conflict. Nor did the *'aarsh* of the north-western marches of Greater Kabylia north of Borj Menaïel[136] and the southern and south-western marches around Borj Hamza,[137] districts under Ottoman control since the 1590s if not earlier. The *'aarsh* of all the other districts did.

This suggests very strongly that it was the region-wide political influence of the Iboukhtouchen that was at stake and that the Ottomans had a very direct interest in the conflict and its outcome. The scale of the mobilisation on either side and the duration of the conflict – since it certainly lasted a considerable time (if well short of a century) – are impossible to explain if all that was at issue was the injured pride of a member of the Iboukhtouchen family. And if the political position of the family was at stake, we can be certain the Ottomans sought to influence the outcome and played a part in mobilising support for the *saff* which was challenging the family leadership, *saff oufella*. In short, there are grounds, for thinking that the dynastic conflict between the partisans of, successively, father and son and then opposed brothers masked a far broader and more significant conflict, between the pro-Ottoman and anti-Ottoman wings of Kabyle opinion.

That this was the truth of the matter is further suggested by another intriguing feature of the alignments tabulated above. This is the fact that all of the confederations on the northern and eastern edges of the Jurjura massif or outside it – the Ath Irathen, the Ath Ijjeur, Iflissen Oumellil, Iflissen Lebahr, Ath

---

136　That is, the Iourguioun (Taourga), Ath Slegguem and the *'aarsh* of the Isser confederation.
137　The Harchaoua, Ath Aïssa, Ath Meddour, Ahl l-Qsar, Imecheddalen, Ath Wakour and Ath Qani.

Waguenoun, Ath Jennad – acted in a united manner, rallying en bloc to one *saff* or the other, whereas those of the high Jurjura – Ath Menguellat, Ath Boudrar, Ath Sedqa and Igouchdal – displayed no such coherence and their constituent *'aarsh* were split between the two *sfûf*. A hypothesis that would explain this is that the *thiqbilin* that were either already in substantial contact with the Ottomans or occupied terrain of immediate strategic significance for the relationship between the Iboukhtouchen and the Ottoman Regency – those of western and maritime Kabylia and those immediately bordering the Sebaou and Boubehir valleys – were conscious of their collective interest in the *saff* conflict and chose their camp accordingly, whereas the *thiqbilin* of the high Jurjura, far removed from regular contact with the Ottomans and occupying terrain that was yet to assume geopolitical significance in relation to the Regency, felt no such compelling common interest and allowed other considerations to determine the allegiance of their constituent *'aarsh*.

This hypothesis would explain the split in the Ath Bethroun, with the Ath Yenni and Ath Boudrar taking their lead from the Ath Irathen to the north while the Ath Wasif and Ath Bou Akkach aligned themselves with their neighbours to the west (*'aarsh* Ath Ahmed and Aouqdal of the Ath Sedqa confederation). As for the split in the Igouchdal confederation, with the Ath Bou Addou, Ath Mendas and Ath Ismaïl (*sic*; i.e. Ath Smaïl) supporting *saff oufella* and the Ath Bou Gherdane, Ath Koufi and Amechras supporting *saff bouadda*, this is consistent with our surmise that the appointment by the Ottomans of outsiders to command '*bled* Guechtoula' signified that they were far from assured of its unanimous loyalty.

But the hypothesis that may explain the split in the Ath Bethroun does not fully account for the split amongst the *'aarsh* of the Ath Menguellat confederation, in which *'arsh* Aqbil supported *saff bouadda* while *'aarsh* Ath Attaf, Ath Bou Youcef and Ath Menguellat proper all supported *saff oufella*. For, whatever may have determined the Ath Attaf's alignment, the decision of the Ath Menguellat and the Ath Bou Youcef to choose *saff oufella* – that is, align themselves with the Ath Yahia – undoubtedly had something to do with the nexus of maraboutic connections which, as we have already demonstrated, was a major feature of these three *'aarsh* and a powerful link between them. There is evidence, moreover, that the Ath Menguellat and Ath Bou Youcef had displayed solidarity with the Ath Yahia on a previous occasion, namely the tradition, collected by Genevois,[138] that in order to settle accounts with his father's murderers, Sidi Ahmed El-Tounsi had first to fight not only the Ath Yahia, but also the Ath Bou Youcef and the Ath Menguellat. The source of this tradition was a certain Fodil Salem Ben Mouhoub from Bou Aggach, one of the exclusively maraboutic hamlets of the Ath Sidi Saïd of Taourirt n'Ath Menguellat. The implications are

---

138 Genevois, 1974, *op. cit.*, 27–9.

far-reaching. Far from the *imrabdhen* of the central Jurjura being hostile to and determined to overthrow the Ath l-Qadi of Koukou *en bloc* and for good and then assert Kabylia's independence against the Turks as Boulifa implied, they were, on the contrary, inclined to defend the family's position at Koukou *once the latter had got rid of Ameur ou l-Qadi*, and they were able to determine the policy of these three *'aarsh* in this matter. They accordingly opposed Sidi Ahmed El-Tounsi in the 1630s and again opposed him and his preferred son Si Ali in the 1690s and thereafter. Given that Ameur ou l-Qadi's murderers and usurpers were the pro-Ottoman wing of the family, it made perfect sense for the *'aarsh* influenced by these *imrabdhen* to support the pro-Ottoman *saff* in the 1690s, which is what they did, the outlook and implicit loyalties of the *imrabdhen* being the factors guaranteeing continuity in this respect.

The final feature of the data in Table 7.1 which calls for comment is the order in which the two *saff* alignments have been drawn up. The table scrupulously follows the order in which Hanoteau and Letourneux listed the component *'aarsh* and *thiqbilin* in each *saff*.[139] They themselves made no comment on this order; indeed, they made no attempt to make sense of the information they reproduced about this entire affair, which they clearly saw as irrelevant to the Kabylia of the 1860s and which they included in their discussion of the Kabyle *sfûf* mainly for the sake of completeness. And they made a point of remarking that they saw no rhyme or reason in the fact that the two *sfûf* in this case were traditionally known as the Upper *Saff* and the Lower *Saff*, anticipating by 90 years Pierre Bourdieu's attitude to the question of *saff* names. But the order is extremely interesting, for it contains a hidden logic which they clearly did not notice, and this logic enables us to understand the *saff* names among other things. Since it is reasonable to assume that Hanoteau and Letourneux reproduced the order given them by their informants,[140] we may imagine that the latter understood this logic even if they refrained from explaining it to the French ethnographers.

---

139 The only modifications I have made concern some spellings of names and the separation I have introduced between the populations of Greater Kabylia and those of Lesser Kabylia.

140 In the preface to the first edition of their book, Hanoteau and Letourneux acknowledged the especial help of Si Moula Naït Ameur, the secretary of the Bureau Arabe at Fort Napoléon, of the important maraboutic Aït Ameur family of Tamazirt, the leading Irjen village, who had rallied to the French after the conquest in 1857. Since Hanoteau and Letourneux display far more knowledge of the *imrabdhen* of the Ath Irathen than of those of the high Jurjura, it would seem that they came to depend heavily on the local maraboutic networks, largely limited to the Ath Irathen, to which Si Moula belonged, although they also employed as an interpreter a certain Si Saïd ou Ali, of a maraboutic family of Ighil Bouammas (Ath Boudrar). See Augustin Bernard and Louis Milliot, 'Les qânoûns Kabyles dans l'ouvrage de Hanoteau et Letourneux', *Revue des Études Islamiques*, 2 (1933), 1–44, and Général Maurice Hanoteau, 'Quelques souvenirs sur les collaborateurs de « La Kabylie et les coutumes Kabyles »', *Revue Africaine*, LXIV (1923), 134–49.

Given the traditions that Sidi Ahmed El Tounsi Bou Khettouch resided at Aourir n'Ath Ghoubri (and later Tifilkout) and that Ourkho found refuge among the Ifenayen, we might have expected the Ath Ghoubri (or the Illilten) to head one *saff* and the Ifenayen the other. This is not at all the case. As the table shows, Hanoteau and Letourneux place the Ath Yahia at the head of *saff oufella*, immediately followed by its close allies, the Ath Menguellat and Ath Bou Youcef, and the Ath Irathen confederation at the head of *saff bouadda*, immediately followed by the Iamrawien of the Sebaou valley and then the Ath Waguenoun confederation, whose southernmost villages (those of *'arsh* Ath Aïssa ou Mimoun) overlook the middle valley on its north side. These are followed by the Ath Irathen's immediate neighbour to the east, the Ath Fraoucen, and then by the *'aarsh* and confederations of the Wad Boubehir to the south-east.

The AthYahia's alignment with and leading role in *saff oufella* make good sense given that *saff bouadda* was identified first with Sidi Ahmed El-Tounsi Bou Khettouch and subsequently with the son who stayed loyal to his father and thus with the main line of descent from the assassinated Ameur ou l-Qadi.[141] It was natural that, with bad memories of Ameur ou l-Qadi – whether it was his 'tyranny' or his intrigues with the Spanish that were most held against him – the Ath Yahia should line up with the rebellious Ourkho rather than his father or brother.

The alignment and leading roles of the Ath Irathen, Iamrawien, Ath Waguenoun and Ath Fraoucen similarly make perfect sense. It was in the leading Ath Fraoucen village of Jema'a n'Saharij that the Iboukhtouchen had established the forward base from which to conduct their new strategy;[142] the Iamrawien had been settled in the valley by the Ath l-Qadi and were still loyal to the latter's principal descendants; and the Ath Waguenoun resented (as they subsequently made clear) the threat of Ottoman encroachment on their territory since the establishment of the post at Tizi Ouzou and naturally made common cause with the Iboukhtouchen as an important ally of the latter. As for the Ath Irathen, neighbours and long-standing allies of the Ath Fraoucen, it was natural that they should be in the pro-Iboukhtouchen and implicitly anti-Ottoman party. In addition, given their size and weight, as a powerful *thaqbilth* composed of five *'aarsh*, and their position, controlling the eastern side of the Wad Aïssi as well as the northernmost third of the central ridge that extends from the Jurjura to the Sebaou and thus both the low road and the high road into the central Jurjura districts, as well as a section of the southern side of the Sebaou valley, it was equally natural that they should have assumed the leadership of their *saff*. Finally,

---

141 We can be confident that the same consideration explained the alignment of the Ath Abbas with *saff oufella*.

142 According to Feredj (*op. cit.*, 34), the Iboukhtouchen were by the end of the seventeenth century *the* leading family of Jema'a n'Saharij. He also notes that another family in this village, called El-Qoadhi or Kouadi, was descended from the Ath l-Qadi as well.

it is very likely that it was at this time that a section of the Iboukhtouchen family established itself at Adeni, *tūfiq* of *'arsh* Irjen of the Ath Irathen confederation, the Irjen settlement closest to the Sebaou valley floor.

The headquarters of the anti-Iboukhtouchen *saff* in three *'aarsh* of the high Jurjura made it natural for it to be called *saff oufella*. And the headquarters of the pro-Iboukhtouchen *saff* in villages on both the edges and the floor of the Sebaou valley made it natural for it to be called *saff bouadda*. The *saff* names were not meaningless or arbitrary. The irony in them lies in the fact that it should have been certain *'aarsh* of the high Jurjura which, guided by their *imrabdhen*, organised support for the Ottoman interest in this affair. But that is what happened.

A remarkable by-product of the victory of *saff bouadda* is that it appears to have enabled the Ath l-Qadi/Iboukhtouchen family to return to Koukou. In his observations on Kabylia, Thomas Shaw notes the importance of 'The Jimmah at Saritch' (*sic*; Jema'a n'Saharij) but then adds that 'Kou-kou' (*sic*) 'where their Sheikh or Sultan as they call him, resides, is their principal village.'[143] Unless Shaw misunderstood his sources – were they speaking of the present or the past? – the implication is that the people of Koukou changed their attitude towards the Iboukhtouchen following the defeat of *saff oufella*, the party their *'arsh* (Ath Yahia) had favoured, and made the family welcome there anew, although to describe Koukou as the region's principal village was undoubtedly an anachronism by this time and perhaps simply a courtesy.

The *saff* conflict we have been examining can therefore be seen to have had three levels. In the first instance, it was a conflict *within* the Iboukhtouchen family which was almost certainly decided relatively quickly in favour of Sidi Ahmed and his son Si Ali and at the expense of Ourkho, who then disappeared from history. The second level pitted pro- and anti-Iboukhtouchen forces (whether or not the latter were bound to Ourkho: for example, the Ath Abbas of the Soummam valley) against each other in Kabylia. It is likely that it continued for a period of years, but that this aspect of the conflict was decided by the early eighteenth century CE, *c.* 1710 or 1715 at the latest, since this is when the Regency began an entirely new phase of its penetration of Kabylia. It is reasonable to suppose that Algiers waited to see whether the anti-Iboukhtouchen party, which it favoured, might prevail without (possibly embarrassing) Ottoman support, and that it resumed its forward policy on its own account only after and in reaction to the resolution of the conflict to the Iboukhtouchen's advantage.

This left the underlying third level of the dispute, between those forces allied to or implicated in the expansion of the Regency's presence and authority in the region and those forces resisting this (whether or not the latter were partisans of the Iboukhtouchen). This fundamental level of the conflict was, of course, not

---

143 Thomas Shaw, *op. cit.*, 101. This testimony also supports the thesis that the Iboukhtouchen were genuine Ath l-Qadi, since the people of Koukou would have been unlikely to accept them once more otherwise.

decided promptly at all. Indeed, it is in this respect that the tradition recorded by Hanoteau and Letourneux might best be understood, in that the conflict between pro- and anti-Ottoman interests and forces in Kabylia undoubtedly continued until the end of the eighteenth century, indeed beyond that date. While we know very little about the incidents that composed the first two aspects and phases of the conflict, we know substantially more about the last phase, since it embraced the rest of the history of Kabylia in the pre-colonial era.

The Ottoman dispensation and the supersession of the Iboukhtouchen

In 1127 AH/1715–16 CE, the village of Tikobaïn on the north-eastern edge of the Jebel Aïssa Mimoun was destroyed by order of the *qā'id* of Tazarart. This was undoubtedly a punitive measure, to teach a lesson; the people of Tikobaïn were able to rebuild their village subsequently. Despite its proximity to the settlements of *'arsh* Ath Aïssa ou Mimoun of the Ath Waguenoun confederation, Tikobaïn seems always to have belonged to the Iamrawien. By the time Hanoteau and Letourneux investigated these matters, it was much the largest settlement of the Iamrawien Oufella and it may well have been the leading village of the latter for long periods. The great eighteenth-century poet Youcef ou Kaci (b. *c.* 1680 CE)[144] sang the praises of the village, extolling the courage and honour of its inhabitants, especially the noble Azouaou family.[145] That the Ottoman-appointed *qā'id* decided that it needed to be destroyed suggests that Tikobaïn was at that time a centre of the resistance to the Regency's encroachment on the middle Sebaou.

The destruction of Tikobaïn in 1715–16 is the first we hear of the existence of the fort of Tazarart and its *qā'id* – that is, of the new forward position east of Tizi Ouzou which the Ottomans had established in Kabylia. The literature is unclear as to where exactly this position was, perhaps because of a mistaken transliteration of the place name. The spelling is that given by Robin, who reported that the fort was the first place occupied by the Ottomans on the right bank of the Wad Sebaou, opposite the confluence with the Wad Aïssi. The place which best corresponds to Robin's description is occupied by a small agglomeration called Tazmalt,[146] midway between Timizar Laghbar and Tala Atmane, on the right bank of the Sebaou, almost opposite the mouth of the Wad Aïssi and at the foot of the Jebel Aïssa Mimoun, where it could not have

---

144 According to Mammeri's calculations; see Mouloud Mammeri, *Poèmes kabyles anciens* (Paris: Maspero, 1980; 2nd edition, Paris: La Découverte & Syros, 2001), 66.

145 Mammeri, 2001 (1980), *op. cit.*, 75, 89, 90–3.

146 Not to be confused with the now sizeable town of this name in the Wad Sahel at the southern foot of the Jurjura.

failed to irk the Ath Waguenoun as well as the Iamrawien Oufella; its name – 'the little *zmāla*' – also corresponds to the function presumably performed by Robin's 'Tazarart', a *zmāla* (plural: *zmoul*) being a military encampment or base.[147]

Around this time a forceful personality emerges as the organiser of the Regency's drive to expand its authority in Greater Kabylia. His name was Ali Khodja – 'Ali the scribe' – but what his official status may have been is unclear. Robin notes that he described himself in his correspondence as 'emir el-outon' (*sic*) – that is, 'commander of the country' – but what exactly 'the country' ('el-outon', i.e. *el-watan*) referred to, we do not know. Robin also quotes Peysonnel as referring to Ali Khodja as having been appointed '*qā'id*' in Kabylia, an equally vague indication of his jurisdiction and responsibilities. Perhaps this vagueness was in the nature of the situation, in that the territory over which Ali Khodja had 'command' could only be defined after the event, the event being the transformation which it was his mission to bring about in the political character and geographical extent of the zone under Ottoman control. For there was nothing vague about the radical changes he proceeded to introduce.

In 1132 AH/1720–1 CE, Ali Khodja established the new fort of Borj Sebaou, midway between Borj Menaïel and Tizi Ouzou, on the right bank of the Sebaou near the point where it turns north and enters the final stretch of its course to reach the Mediterranean just west of Dellys. This was to become the headquarters of a new administrative jurisdiction, the qā'idate[148] of the Sebaou. In 1724 or 1725, a second fort, Borj Boghni, was established midway between Draa el-Mizan and Wadhia to be the headquarters of the qā'idate of Boghni and thus the centre of Ottoman authority in the southern plain.

With these two major initiatives, a new dispensation began to take shape in the lowlands. Between 1720 and 1730, Ali Khodja sought to assert Ottoman authority over the Iamrawien of the Sebaou valley and convert them into a *makhzen* tribe loyal to the Regency. In doing so, he inevitably clashed with the Iboukhtouchen and their allies and is recorded as having defeated them in two pitched battles, at Draa Ben Khedda near Borj Sebaou, and then at Bou Ilzazen near Jema'a n'Saharij.[149]

The co-optation of the Iamrawien involved two main elements. First, the land they farmed – 20,000 hectares in all – became *beylik* or state property;[150] thus

---

147 This is the Algerian usage of the term, which in classical Arabic means 'comradeship', 'fellowship', 'company'. In poor handwriting, 'Tazmalt' might be misread as 'Tazarart'. But the problem of identification may have arisen out of a simple change of name. 'Tazarart' is almost certainly a deformation of the Berber word *Tazaghart*, meaning 'the little plain'. Once the fort was built, it may have seemed natural to rename the place *Tazmalt*: 'the little fortified camp'.

148 My translation (by analogy with 'governorate') of the French term *caïdat*; the Arabic word is *qiyāda*.

149 Robin, *op. cit.*, 46.

150 Robin, *op. cit.*, 49.

the Regency was claiming and appropriating the Sebaou valley floor and part of its sides. Second, the Iamrawien villages were reconstituted as *zmoul*, military settlements; their inhabitants could keep their plots of land but had to undertake military service for the Regency, for which they were supplied with horses. According to Robin, 16 villages were reorganised in this way.[151] The remaining seven or eight villages, all from the Iamrawien Bouadda,[152] were not reconstituted as *zmoul* and had no horses.

In addition to suborning the Iamrawien, Ali Khodja imported a population of black slave descent and established it in the new settlement of Abid Chamlal to form a kind of advance observation post a few kilometres to the east of Tizi Ouzou on the left bank of the Sebaou close to the mouth of the Wad Aïssi, and thus on the northern edge of the territory of the Ath Aïssi confederation and just opposite the Irjen (Ath Irathen) villages on the Wad Aïssi's right bank. He also began to assert Ottoman control over the commercial life of the region by establishing new markets at Baghlia in the lower Sebaou valley and at Wad Defali (also known as Wad Sebt) between Draa Ben Khedda and Tizi Ouzou. Shortly afterwards, a second colony of blacks was established at Aïn Zawiya, south-west of Borj Boghni. We know from documents that a *qā'id* of the Sebaou was in post by 1136 AH/1723–4 CE at the latest[153] and a *qā'id* of Boghni was in post by the following year.[154]

The new qā'idate of the Sebaou covered the town of Dellys, the confederations of the Iflissen Oumellil, Ath Waguenoun, Iflissen Lebahr and Ath Jennad, and the following *'aarsh*: Ath Khalfoun; Beni Thour; Ibethrounen; Ath Khelifa; the northern part of *'arsh* Maatqa; Ath Aïssi; Ath Douala; Ath Zmenzer; Ath Ghoubri and 'the tribes of the Upper Sebaou and Asif el-Hammam'.[155] The qā'idate of Boghni covered, at least in principle, the Igouchdal confederation, the *'aarsh* Iwadhien, Ath Bou Chennacha, Ath Chebla, Ath Ali ou Illoul and Ath Irguen of the Ath Sedqa confederation,[156] the southern part of the *'arsh* Maatqa and *'arsh* Ath Abdelmoumen of the Ath Aïssi confederation. The qā'idate of Boghni was subordinate and answerable to that of Borj Sebaou, which in turn came under the authority of the bey of the Titteri.

---

151 Among the Amrawa Tahta (Iamrawien Bouadda): Borj Sebaou, Taourga, Kef el-Aogab, Draa Ben Khedda, Sidi Namane and Litama; among the Amrawa Fouaga (Iamrawien Oufella): Oulad Bou Khalfa, Tizi Ouzou, Abid Chamlal, Timizar Laghbar, Sikh ou Meddour, Ighil ou Radjah, Tala Athmane, Tikobaïn, Tamda and Mekla (Robin, *op. cit.*, 49).

152 Namely Kettous, Oulad Ouaret (Ath Wareth), Zimoula, Tala Mokkor (Tala Moqran), Bordim (Bou Redim), Irjaounen n'Techt, Irjaounen El-Bour (*ibid.*) This list omits the maraboutic village of Agouni Bou Mehala.

153 Robin, *op. cit.*, 46.

154 *Ibid.*

155 Robin, op. cit., 48–9.

156 But not, apparently, *'aarsh* Aouqdal and Ath Ahmed of this confederation.

Map 7.4: Western Kabylia: section of a French
map showing – from left to right – Borj Menaïel,
Naciria (Haussonvillers), Borj Sebaou, Draa Ben
Khedda (Mirabeau), Tizi Ouzou and Abid Chamal,
with Baghlia (as Rebeval) and Taourga (Horace
Vernet) to the north-west and north-east of Borj
Sebaou and Boghni as the principal settlement
in the southern plain. The settlements from Borj
Menaïel south-east to the forest of Bou Mahni are
those of the Iflissen Oumellil confederation. The
settlements from Tizi Ouzou south-west to Bou
Mahni are those of the Maatqa confederation,
including the important *zāwiya* of Sidi Ali ou
Moussa in the hills NNE of Boghni.

In both cases, the *qā'id* would appoint sheikhs responsible for particular *'aarsh* or confederations, charged with maintaining order and also with collecting taxes annually and any other moneys due on occasion, although it was some time before the actual collection of taxes became possible. In this way, the new administrative structures generated as their political corollary the constitution of sheikhdoms which, since they tended to remain in the same family from one generation to another, favoured the development of aristocratic dynasties in the society of the lowlands.

There was, of course, a 'divide-and-rule' aspect to this, particularly in the middle and upper Sebaou, so long the *chasse gardée* of the Ath l-Qadi and their successors, the Iboukhtouchen. In order to suborn the Iamrawien Oufella effectively, it was necessary to enable new political loyalties to supersede the old, and these new loyalties had to be local ones; reliable loyalty to the frequently rotating Ottoman personnel was not to be expected and the Regency itself was scarcely a regime to evoke enthusiasm. And so, among the populations of the Sebaou valley, the piedmont and the lesser ranges of the mountains in the northern and western districts, this period witnessed the emergence of new local power-holders drawn from or acquiring the status of the *ajwād*, the warrior nobility,[157] and suddenly the political life of these populations acquired colour and its own dramatic interest in tandem with the *dramatis personae* who appeared, in such marked contrast to the anonymity that had obscured its actors in all previous epochs.

From around 1730 onwards, the political history of the lowlands is the story of the relations of the Ottomans with the Mahieddine family of Taourga (the chiefs of the Iamrawien Bouadda); the Ath Kaci or Oukaci family of Tamda and Mekla; the Azouaou family of Tikobaïn, rivals of the Ath Kaci for the leadership of the Iamrawien Oufella; and, dominating the western approaches to Kabylia from Borj Menaiel to Draa Ben Khedda, the Ben Zamoum family of Tighilt Iternach, Tigounatine and Naciria, the chiefs of *'arsh* Ath Amrane of *thaqbilth* Iflissen Oumellil and rapidly established as the dynastic chiefs of the entire confederation, a position they would maintain to the very end of the Ottoman period, as their role in mustering and co-ordinating Kabyle military support for the Regency against the French in 1830 would testify.[158]

While the emergence of these *ajwād* families owed a great deal to the developing fluids of Ottoman favour, this by no means ensured their loyalty. The chiefs of the Isser confederation and the Iamrawien Bouadda, already in the zone of Ottoman authority for some time, were reliably docile, but those of the Iflissen

---

157 As distinct from the *shurāfa'*, the *noblesse de robe*.

158 Joseph Nil Robin, *Notes historiques sur la Grande Kabylie de 1830 à 1838* (republication in one volume with an introduction by Alain Mahé of articles originally published in *Revue Africaine*, 20 (1876), 42–56, 81–96 and 193–219) (Éditions Bouchène, 1999), 29 and 31; see also Robin, *La Grande Kabylie sous le régime turc*, 135–54: 'Les Oulad ben Zamoum'.

Oumellil and the Iamrawien Oufella were another matter, about as troublesome vassals as might be. But it would be a mistake to interpret the rebellions which punctuated the history of their relations with the Regency for the next century as expressions of a will to genuine independence; they were more in the nature of political *strikes*, the manifestations of a temporary withdrawal of loyalty pending a renegotiation of the terms of allegiance.

It is likely that a key variable here was the burden of taxation. The system introduced by the Ottomans was a system of tax-farming, with the *qā'id* obliged by the dey in Algiers or the bey of the Titteri in Medea to raise a certain amount each year and he in turn requiring the sheikhs under his command each to furnish their parts of this, while keeping a smaller part, usually 10 per cent, for themselves. In years of good harvests, the burden may have been borne with equanimity, but in bad years some sheikhs will have found it hard to collect the expected amount. The refusal of the *'aarsh* in their charge to deliver would put their own authority in question, inclining some of them at least to place themselves at the head of the revolt against the *qā'id* rather than meekly admit their inability to satisfy their Ottoman patrons, for by leading the rebellion they could hope to make themselves indispensable to the process of bringing it to an end. Such rebellions were thus manœuvres, in which the vigorous demonstration of nuisance value would normally be followed by renewed acceptance of co-optation on more acceptable terms or even the same terms as before if nothing better was to be had.

In all these respects, the society of the lowlands and the lesser ranges of north-western Kabylia, once incorporated into the Ottoman system in this way via the institution of initially appointed but subsequently hereditary chieftaincies, came to resemble much of the rest of Ottoman Algeria. There was, however, an important difference between the Iflissen Oumellil and the Iamrawien Oufella which was simultaneously a difference in their relations with neighbouring *'aarsh* and a difference in their relations with the Ottomans.

In the 1860s, the Iflissen Oumellil confederation counted no fewer than 14 *'aarsh*, much the largest *thaqbilth* in Greater Kabylia, with a total population of over 24,000. It is likely to have had comparable dimensions a century earlier. Its settlements are spread over both the north-west and south-east slopes of a long mountain ridge known as Sidi Ali Bou Nab and to the south-east extend beyond the Wad Bougdoura-Asif Tleta-Wad Ksari[159] river to the Bou Mahni forest. These circumstances gave its chiefs, the Ben Zamoum, a degree of strategic depth and tactical flexibility in their relations with the Regency that the Iamrawien Oufella, confined to the middle Sebaou valley with few if any settlements occupying high ground, never possessed. To compensate for this lack, the Iamrawien Oufella had

---

159 These are names of one and the same river. It is common to find a river given different names by the distinct communities settled along successive sections of its course.

to rely on their alliances with the confederations controlling the high ground in their vicinity, the Ath Waguenoun and the Ath Jennad to the north and the Ath Irathen to the south, a state of affairs that qualified their status as a *makhzen* tribe and complicated their relations with the Ottomans. These alliances also eventually implicated them, as we have seen, in the *saff* systems of both the Ath Irathen and maritime Kabylia. In contrast, the Iflissen Oumellil were big enough to act independently; they did not often need allies and there were no *saff* systems among any of the populations to the west of the Maatqa.

Thus for the Regency its dealings with the Iflissen Oumellil were a comparatively straightforward affair. The confederation had taken the anti-Iboukhtouchen and pro-Ottoman side in the conflict between the *sfūf* in the 1690–1710 period but, thereafter, whether inclined to be amenable or refractory, its behaviour was its own affair rather than a function of complex alliances. With the Iamrawien Oufella, matters were uncertain from the Ottomans' point of view. The '*arsh*'s dependence on its relations with its southern and northern neighbours involved it in their strategies and calculations and so made its behaviour unpredictable. Dispossessing the Iboukhtouchen and promoting new *jawād* chieftaincies had not resolved the Regency's problem in the middle Sebaou at all; arguably it had simply fragmented it and made it more complicated. It had not even dealt with the Iboukhtouchen fully, since they remained a leading family among the Ath Fraoucen, Ath Irathen, Ath Ghoubri and Ath Bou Chaïb and still had cards to play, and may well have used this influence from time to time to remind the Ottomans of the fact by making a nuisance of themselves with the Iamrawien Oufella. The Ottomans accordingly resolved, eventually, to do what they had so far mainly fought shy of doing, namely take on the '*aarsh* and *thiqbilin* of the mountains.

The man who incarnated this resolution was Mohammed Ben Ali, who was appointed *qā'id* of the Sebaou in 1150 AH/1737–8 CE. He held this position for eight years and was then promoted to the position of Bey of the Titteri, but continued to direct Ottoman policy in Greater Kabylia, since the new *qā'id* of the Sebaou, El-Hadj Mohammed Ben Hassan, was under his authority.

Born at Blida *c.* 1700, Mohammed Ben Ali had studied at the *zāwiya* of the Ath Amar – a maraboutic lineage whose ancestor was a Turk – at Adeni in '*arsh* Irjen, and in the course of this he had got to know the Iboukhtouchen family.[160] After his appointment as *qā'id*, he first concentrated on strengthening the Ottoman order in the lowlands, distinguishing himself by the severity of the summary justice he meted out and so earning the sinister nickname *Ed-Debbah*, 'the throat-cutter'.[161] He then turned his attention to the populations of

---

160 Robin, 'Le bey Mohammed ben Ali Ed-Debbah', in Robin, *La Grande Kabylie sous le régime Turc*, 61–71.

161 According to a notice on Mohammed Ben Ali written by a marabout of the Ath Sidi Ali ou Moussa who was his contemporary, cited by Robin (1998, *op. cit.*, 47), Ed-Debbah was credited with personally executing more than 1200 people by cutting their throats.

the mountains. Before doing so, however, he had asked for and obtained the hand of the daughter of Si Amar ou Boukhettouch, who directed the Iboukhtouchen family fortunes from his seats at Aourir and Jema'a n'Saharij and an additional residence at Adeni. Ben Ali thus sought the neutrality if not the support of the Iboukhtouchen and those 'aarsh and *thiqbilin* under their influence, notably the Ath Irathen and Ath Fraoucen. This seems to have been forthcoming at first, undoubtedly because Ben Ali's initial campaigns targeted the populations to the west of the Wad Aïssi – the Ath Aïssi and Maatqa confederations of the central massif and the Igouchdal and Ath Sedqa confederations of the western Jurjura – and left the Igawawen alone.

According to Robin, Ben Ali began with the Ath Aïssi and did so with vigour, mobilising two columns of troops, one commanded by Ahmed Agha and the other by Ali, the Bey of the Titteri. The campaign met with initial success, obtaining the submission of the 'aarsh Ath Zmenzer, Ath Douala and Iferdiwen in a single day.[162] But it encountered fierce resistance from the villages of Taguemount Azouz and Ath Khalfoun of 'arsh Ath Mahmoud and was unable to overcome this. At this point, the *qā'id* Mohammed Ben Ali was promoted Bey of the Titteri at Ali Bey's expense. He soon resumed his campaign, now targeting the Igouchdal and the Ath Sedqa of the south-west with a view to consolidating Ottoman authority in the qā'idate of Boghni. In this he was successful, obtaining the submission of the Igouchdal and certain 'aarsh of the Ath Sedqa (Ath Bou Chennacha and Ath Ali ou Illoul), although apparently leaving the Iwadhien alone, and imposing a fairly light obligation to pay taxes to the Regency.

A significant feature of Ben Ali's strategy in this campaign was his harnessing of the influence of the major maraboutic lineage of the western half of the central massif, the Ath Sidi Ali ou Moussa of the southern Maatqa.

We have already seen, in the cases of the *imrabdhen* of the 'aarsh Ath Menguellat and Ath Bou Youcef of the high Jurjura, that important maraboutic lineages were disposed to align themselves with the pro-Ottoman point of view at critical junctures, such as the *fitna* of the *sfūf* disputing the Iboukhtouchen succession. There can be no doubt that the Ottomans were alive to the potential of this and were interested in enlisting the good offices of *imrabdhen* from an early stage, perhaps seeing them as cards to be played against the Ath l-Qadi at some point. The mosques of least two of the Ath Yenni villages, Taourirt Mimoun and Ath Larba'a, were built on the initiative of the Ottoman authorities, most probably in the mid-seventeenth century.[163] Well before this, in 1582, the

---

162 Robin, 1998, *op. cit.*, 63.

163 According to the local tradition collected by H. Genevois (1971, *op. cit.*, 35–40), Taourirt's mosque was built during the time of Sidi l-Mouhoub, the son of Sidi Ali ou Yahia. Since Sidi Ali's arrival at Taourirt is located 'shortly before 1616' (*op. cit.*, 20), this could place the building of the mosque in the 1630s or 1640s, around the time of the Iboukhtouchen succession. Mouloud Mammeri, who was himself from Taourirt Mimoun, placed it 'vers [around] 1630' (Mammeri, 2001, *op. cit.*, 66).

Regency's preliminary dealings with the populations of north-western Kabylia had included an apparent attempt to acquire the goodwill and services of one of the latter's *imrabdhen* when Jaffar Pasha authorised the sale of land at Sebaou El-Kedim (see Map 7.4) on the west bank of the lower Sebaou to a certain Si Ali Ben Haroun of the Iflissen Oumellil.[164]

We know of no subsequent dealings with the *imrabdhen* of this confederation, however. It would appear that the recourse to *jawād* families and the recourse to maraboutic lineages were alternative ploys, each appropriate in particular cases but not to be combined in a single case. In the lowlands and piedmont districts from the 1720 onwards if not earlier, the Ottomans consistently gave priority to the *ajwād* as their preferred interlocutors. This practice was not without producing, sooner or later, certain ironies. According to an official document dated the month of Ramadan 1136 AH/1724 CE, the *qā'id* of the Sebaou, a certain Mahmoud, charged the *qā'id* (or sheikh?) of the Guechtoula, Gacem Ben Aïssa, to arbitrate and settle a dispute over inheritance among none other than the Ath Sidi Ali ou Moussa; thus were the mediators mediated.

But this and other evidence shows that the Ottomans had been developing their relations with the Ath Sidi Ali ou Moussa for at least two decades by the time Mohammed Ben Ali launched his campaign against the Ath Aïssi in 1745. According to Robin, the assistance of these *imrabdhen* secured for the Ottomans the levée of native troops from the Maatqa, who proceeded to play a large part in the crushing of the Igouchdal and Ath Sedqa, and it was as a reward for these services that the Bey Mohammed had the *zāwiya* of Sidi Ali ou Moussa rebuilt and its cupola restored, all at his own expense. Adli suggests this was done before the campaigns in which Maatqa fighters participated; Robin that it was immediately afterwards. Either way, there was a clear *quid pro quo*. And we can in any case be confident that the Bey Mohammed had assured himself, through the Ath Sidi Ali ou Moussa, of the benevolent neutrality of the Maatqa early on, around the time that he secured that of the Iboukhtouchen, so that he might take the Ath Aïssi in a pincer movement, having deprived them of possible allies on both their eastern and western flanks from the outset. The Ottomans' failure to reduce the Ath Mahmoud at the first attempt, while standing out from their general success, only delayed matters. Before long, Ben Ali returned to this unfinished business, again deploying two columns, captured Taguemount Azouz and Tizi Hibel, and the Ath Mahmoud submitted.

It was at this point, which we can date approximately as late 1746 or 1747 CE, that the Bey finally decided to take on the Igawawen, which he did, not by attacking the Ath Irathen from the Sebaou valley floor, as Randon would do 110 years later, but by first mounting an expedition against the Ath Wasif, which ended in a deadly fiasco for the Ottomans, who were obliged to withdraw.[165]

---

164 Robin, 1998, *op. cit.*, 40.
165 Robin, 1998, *op. cit.*, 65–6.

I believe that it was in the wake of this event that the first of the assemblies held by the 'aarsh of the Igawawen to decide on the exheredation of their women took place, and that this was the assembly of the Ath Irathen at Tizra Waguemoun.

The assemblies of the Igawawen and their purposes

It is an interesting fact that Robin, whose account of Ottoman policy in Kabylia at this time is indispensable and much the best that exists, should say nothing about the meetings that proclaimed the exheredation of women. The most natural explanation for this striking omission is, I believe, the true one: he did not know about them. He certainly can have had no motive for suppressing this information. We can infer that he simply did not possess it. But it is odd that he should not have possessed it. Is it possible that his informants possessed it and withheld it?

Robin's principal source for his account of the Bey Mohammed Ben Ali was, as he acknowledges, a certain Mohammed Ben Mohammed Ben Belkacem El-Zouggari, a *mrābit* of the Ath Sidi Ali ou Moussa lineage who was the Bey Mohammed's contemporary and wrote a set of notes about him which were preserved and made available to Robin a century or so later.[166] Had these notes made any mention of the exheredation of women and the Igawawen assemblies that resolved on this, we can be sure that Robin would have included this in his account. The omission of this important topic could have been due to ignorance in the case of the *mrābit* as well. We do not know when he died, and he may have died around the time the Bey died (1754 CE), before hearing of the assemblies and their decisions. But it seems far more likely that he would have known about these assemblies and either omitted any discussion of them from his notes or that this part of his notes was withheld from Robin. For the Ath Sidi Ali ou Moussa would have had a motive for suppressing this information as we shall see.

We know for a fact, supported by documentary evidence, that such an assembly was held by the Ath Bethroun confederation together with allied 'aarsh of the eastern Ath Sedqa, almost certainly in 1749. We know, in addition, of the oral traditions among the Ath Irathen and the Ath Fraoucen that they too held assemblies to take the same decision, the former at Tizra Waguemoun and the latter at Jema'a n'Saharij, although no documents have come to light and neither of these traditions specifies the year the assembly took place. We also know that the exheredation of women was a common practice in other parts of the Algerian countryside and was already established practice in Kabylia and that

---

166 Robin, 1998, *op. cit.*, 61.

the Kabyles, like their counterparts in other regions, had the procedures known as *hiba* and *hubus* at their disposal to enable them to get around the stipulations of the *Sharīʿa* without flagrantly breaching them. So we still have not elucidated the reason for these assemblies and their decisions.

Let us therefore now reason about all this from what we have established concerning the historical context of these events. Two questions need to be answered. What was the object of these exercises? And in what order did these assemblies take place?

I shall argue that they took place in the following order: first, the assembly of the Ath Irathen, in 1747 or 1748; second, the assembly of the Ath Bethroun and their allies, in 1749; and, third, the assembly of the Ath Fraoucen and their eastern and southern neighbours some time later, most probably in 1752–3. My hypothesis concerning the order and timing of these assemblies is connected to what I think the object of these exercises was.

We know that the object of the exercise was not to exheredate Kabyle women, since they had long been denied the right to inherit. Thus Hanoteau and Letourneux were mistaken in supposing that these assemblies were restoring an ancient customary law. What possible benefit, therefore, could these confederations and *ʿaarsh* have been seeking in taking and proclaiming a decision that was, in content, largely if not entirely superfluous and, in form, a public scandal? If we give further consideration to the record of the Ath Bethroun's deliberations, we shall find elements of an answer.

The text of the French translation of this record as given by Hanoteau and Letourneux is reproduced in Appendix 1. It will be seen that it contains not the slightest attempt to explain or justify the four measures upon which the Ath Bethroun had resolved, beyond the most perfunctory and cryptic reference to 'that which is a permanent cause of brawls, troubles and discords in the villages', a phrase which seems to allude, or so the reader may infer, to the right to inherit which women had enjoyed up until then. But we know that they did not, in actual fact, enjoy this right for practical purposes, so even this reference to the problem to be dealt with explains nothing. The record then specifies the four decisions taken and does so very briskly, in a mere five lines. These are followed by a remarkable passage.

These dispositions being accepted by a common accord, only an iniquitous man could wish to revive those which they have abolished. Now, iniquity is a thing that is condemned. The authority of usage and custom is inviolable and immutable like the authority of a king. Whoever will wish to infringe and violate the aforementioned rules will become for his fellow men a cause of misfortunes and discords. Now, 'discord is a fire', according to the words of the Prophet (blessings and peace be upon Him). 'Discord is a fire; may God's curse be upon him who lights it, and his mercy upon the man who restores peace.' Whoever will wish to violate these laws, God will crush him under the weight of abjectness, of poverty, of hunger and of misfortune in this world and the next, whether the culprit is one of us, or one of our children, or one of our children's children, for as long as one generation replaces its predecessor. If any one of the marabouts or the notables of the villages does not conform to the above-mentioned dispositions, God will hold him accountable.[167]

The length and tone of this passage suggests that, although the decisions were formally unanimous, these measures were in fact controversial, and a disposition to defy them in some quarters was anticipated. The gist of the passage is clear: whoever defies these new rules is a trouble-maker and God is not on his side. Thus the validity of the new rules from the point of view of religion is clearly in question and this passage is a warning to those disposed to dispute the decisions in the name of the *Sharī'a* that if they do so they will be precipitating *fitna* (discord, division of the community of believers) and so putting themselves in the wrong in God's eyes. In effect, the doctrinal debate concerned the relative importance of the letter of the *Sharī'a* and the preservation of the community, with the decision taken giving emphatic priority to the second.

The concern to represent the decisions as valid in relation to religious orthodoxy is evident throughout the document. The meeting which took the decision is described as 'an assembly of the marabouts of the Beni Bethroun, assisted by the sages of their villages and the imam of the mosque'. In the detailed enumeration, village by village, of those who were present at the meeting, the *imrabdhen* are always mentioned first, followed by the *'udūl*,[168] if any, and then the lay *'uqqāl* (sages, elders). The sherifian status (descent from the Prophet) of the *imrabdhen* is stressed wherever this obtained, as well as their invariable honourableness. The author of the record of the meeting, Sidi Ameur ben Sidi Ahmed ben Yahia of Tiqichourt, makes a point of referring to himself as 'the honourable, the rightly guided, the erudite, *the orthodox*' (my emphasis), terms also applied to another *amrabedh* cited as present when the original document was copied in 1225 AH/1810 CE. And, in case the warning in the earlier paragraph is not clear enough, it is repeated in pithy terms at the end:

It is by the order of the above-named marabouts and sages that the aforementioned customs have been abolished; whoever, among the descendants, would violate the new dispositions, God will hold him to account. Goodbye!

---

167 My translation.

168 *'ādil*, plural: *'udūl*, meaning good, upright, just, a person of good reputation etc., has the additional specific meaning in the Maghrib of an assistant to a *qādi*; it thus implies the possession of qualifications in matters of Islamic law.

The fact that this assembly was a public meeting of *imrabdhen* has gone entirely unremarked in the literature on the history of Kabylia. But it is a fact of the first importance. The assembly of a village consists of the officers of the *thajma'th* (the *amīn*, *wakīl* and *aberrah*), the *temman* of the various lineages and perhaps a number of other *'uqqāl*; in plenary session (*aberrah*), it consists of all adult males of the village. The assembly of the *'arsh*, an infrequent event, would consist of the *umanā'* – the presidents of the *thijemmu'a* – of the constituent villages, the meeting electing an *amīn el-umanā'* – 'the president of the presidents' – to take the chair and possibly hold office for the duration of whatever emergency (such as a war with a neighbouring *'arsh*) provoked the assembly in the first place. In both cases, the actors in these instances would be lay Kabyles, not the *imrabdhen*, whose role, if they attended, would be confined to the ritual recital of the *Fātiha* at the beginning of the meeting. For the *imrabdhen* to be the principal actors and participants in an assembly held as a public event to debate and resolve questions of policy and law and placed on record in writing was entirely unprecedented. If the meeting of the Ath Bethroun was, as I believe, the second in the series, after that of the Ath Irathen, the latter was a precedent for the former, but the point of course is that these meetings, taken, as they should be, as a unified series, were events without precedent and, we might add, without sequel. What, then, can have induced or prompted the *imrabdhen* of the Ath Bethroun to assemble, deliberate, resolve and, crucially, bear witness, through the written record, to their resolutions as they did?

In abolishing the right of women to inherit, the assembly of 1749 made no practical difference to the material condition of the women of the Ath Bethroun and their allies. But the explicit abolition of this right in Kabyle law obviated all future recourse to the expedients previously employed to get round the *Sharī'a*. In particular, it obviated recourse to the expedient of *hubus*. There was no longer any need for a family to bequeath its property to a religious foundation in order to avoid the division of the patrimony and the alienation of part of it through marriages of daughters into other families. The beneficiaries of the practice of *hubus* were the religious foundations to which such properties were bequeathed, the *thim'ammrin* and *zawāyā* of the *imrabdhen*. There could be no question of abolishing the practice of *hubus* in itself; but abolishing one of the main reasons – the right of women to inherit – for lay families to resort to it was another matter.

Moreover, as we have seen, the assembly of 1749 did not only abolish this reason; it also abolished the right of *shefa'a* by anyone, man or woman, in respect of property already made over to a religious foundation as *hubus*. Previously, should a family that had bequeathed a property as *hubus* and thereafter enjoyed use-rights in this property become extinct, its nearest relatives in the male line of descent would have the right to buy this property and so pre-empt the definitive acquisition of the property in question by the foundation concerned. The right of pre-emption in this specific case was now abolished. At first sight, this measure might appear to be to the advantage of the religious foundations, which could henceforth expect to secure absolute ownership of *hubus* properties without the interference of pre-empting relatives. But the matter is at least ambiguous, for the fact that a family or quite possibly several families no longer had the right to buy a cousin's property once this was bequeathed to a *zāwiya* as *hubus* would give them a strong incentive to dissuade their cousin from making this bequest in the first place. In short, while the first measure removed a major motive for making bequests to religious foundations, the second measure created a socially potent disincentive to do so.

These measures can hardly have been welcome to the *imrabdhen* families connected to those *zawāyā* and *thim'ammrin* that benefitted or stood to benefit from the practice of *hubus*. How, then, can we explain the pre-eminent role of the *imrabdhen* of the Ath Bethroun and their allies in the taking of these decisions?

Given the controversial character of the decisions taken, it is entirely unrealistic to suppose that they were not discussed and largely resolved upon well in advance of the assembly held at Souq el-Sebt n'Ath Wasif. We can be confident that this assembly was preceded by numerous other meetings, very probably in the *thajma'th* of every village of every *'arsh* of the Ath Bethroun and their Ath Sedqa allies. We can also realistically suppose that there are likely to have been reservations about and opposition to the proposals, at least at first, and that much of this came precisely from the *imrabdhen*, concerned as they would naturally be both about possible loss of material benefits connected to the *ahbās* and also about their credentials as the local representatives of Islamic doctrine. We can therefore most realistically understand the assembly that was finally held as having the function of *consecrating* the decision taken – that is, the measures favoured by the majority opinion among the *'aarsh* concerned, by formally establishing these measures as being unanimously agreed and by inducing the *imrabdhen* to do the honours in taking responsibility for promulgating the new laws and so both validating them from the point of view of religion and publicly implicating themselves in the agreed change.

It was, I believe, the last point that was crucial. By consecrating the decisions, affirming their validity in respect of Islam and bearing witness to their own role, the *imrabdhen* of the Ath Bethroun and their allies were making themselves immediately and massively vulnerable to critical attack by the urban guardians of orthodoxy, the *'ulamā'* of Algiers and Bejaia. In inducing their *imrabdhen* to do this, then, the Ath Bethroun and their allies were inducing them to break with and openly defy the Regency and its religious scholars and to take sides in the developing conflict between the coalition of forces supporting the Ottoman penetration of Kabylia and the emerging resistance to this.

Thus the Ath Bethroun and their allies found a way of putting their *imrabdhen* on the spot and obliging them to declare their political allegiance. But why did they think they needed to do this?

It is possible that it was the Bey Mohammed's attack on the Ath Wasif that concentrated minds and triggered the Ath Bethroun's response. But the timing does not work very well, since the Bey's attack will have taken place no later than 1747, and the meeting at Souq el-Sebt was most probably held in 1749. And it is not evident that the attack on the Ath Wasif, which was repulsed effectively, would have been enough on its own to galvanise the entire *thaqbilth* of the Ath Bethroun, not to mention its Ath Sedqa neighbours, into taking such a far-reaching and audacious decision. I therefore believe that something else happened in the interim and that this was the meeting of the Ath Irathen, which then served as an example for the Ath Bethroun to follow. For the expedition against the Ath Wasif will have given food for thought to the Ath Irathen as well.

Let us consider how the Bey's behaviour will have appeared to the Ath Irathen. He first married the daughter of Si Amar Ou Boukhettouch and, through this family connection and the Iboukhtouchen's connection at Adeni, obtained the Ath Irathen's neutrality in respect of the campaigns he then undertook. At the same time, he enlisted the assistance of the Ath Sidi Ali ou Moussa and, through them, the southern Maatqa. By doing this, he isolated and encircled the Ath Aïssi and proceeded to crush them and then crushed the Igouchdal and part of the western Ath Sedqa with the help of Maatqa auxiliary forces. By this stage, the Bey's strategy will have become clear to all observers and it is unrealistic to suppose that the Ath Irathen will have looked on complacently as if none of this concerned them in the slightest. By neutralising the Ath Irathen and crushing the Ath Aïssi, the Bey had made himself master of the Wad Aïssi valley leading into the heart of the high Jurjura. By crushing the Igouchdal and western Ath Sedqa, he had further gained control of the southern plain, the other line of access to the central high Jurjura. These two routes, from the north and the west, converge at Takhoukht, in the valley below the Ath Yenni and the 'arsh Ath Ousammeur of the Ath Irathen, which is where the expeditionary force sent against the Ath Wasif will have been mustered prior to launching its attack. By this stage, however, it must have dawned on the Ath Irathen that the Bey was systematically depriving them of potential allies to their west, south-west and south and simply leaving them till last while steadily encircling them. Although they may have been comparatively indifferent to the fate of the distant Igouchdal, the fate of the Ath Bethroun was another matter, for they constituted the Ath Irathen's own strategic hinterland. This is something that may have alarmed some 'aarsh of the Ath Irathen more immediately than others. It would be natural for the Ath Ousammeur, the 'arsh directly neighbouring the Ath Bethroun, to be more sensitive to what was happening than the Irjen, where the Iboukhtouchen had their seat at Adeni, on the edge of the Sebaou valley. The Bey's expeditionary troops will have marched south up the Wad Aïssi valley directly under the Ath Ousammeur villages of Ath Ferah, Ath Atelli and Taourirt Amoqran and the Ottoman troops' engagements with the Ath Wasif will have been hot news in the *thijemmu'a* of these villages and the subject of intense debate. This debate will undoubtedly have spread eventually to the other 'aarsh of the confederation before culminating in the historic assembly at Tizra Waguemoun, 'the rocks of Aguemoun'.

The village of Aguemoun is neither in 'arsh Irjen nor in 'arsh Ath Ousammeur, but in 'arsh Ath Akerma, whose settlements extend all the way from the very edge of the Sebaou valley floor (the hamlets of *tūfiq* Tizi Rached) to the high central ridge where the French built their town of Fort Napoléon after the conquest in 1857. Aguemoun is the highest of all the Ath Akerma villages (905 metres) and one of the most southerly, near the point of contact with both 'arsh Ath Oumalou to the east and 'arsh Ath Ousammeur to the south-west, while belonging neither to the Ath Ousammeur nor the Irjen and so in that respect neutral ground. It was therefore a very apt place at which to hold a general assembly to decide the strategy of the *thaqbilth* as a whole.

My hypothesis, then, is that a reaction set in among the Ath Irathen against the policy favoured by the Iboukhtouchen. The latter were comparative newcomers to the Ath Irathen and their deal with the Bey, which amounted to a policy of appeasement, would no longer have been seen as working in the general interest of the Ath Irathen as a whole. I further believe that it would most likely have been the southernmost 'aarsh of the confederation, the Ath Ousammeur and the Aouggacha, immediate neighbours of the Ath Yenni, which pressed most energetically for a change of policy. The long experience that the Ath Irathen possessed of dealing with the central power – formerly the Hafsids at Bejaia and now the Ottomans in Algiers – would have equipped them with the political sophistication to work out what their alternative strategy should be. Since the Bey was working his connections with influential maraboutic lineages, the Iboukhtouchen and the Ath Sidi Ali ou Moussa, it was imperative to put a stop to that and pre-empt any fresh attempt by him to suborn the *imrabdhen* of the Ath Irathen or those of their neighbours among the southern Igawawen.

This, I submit, was the true rationale and function of the meeting at Tizra Waguemoun, to force the *imrabdhen* to clarify and then affirm their loyalties. Were they the Ottomans' fifth column, aligned with the Regency and its *'ulamā'*, in the name of the *Sharī'a* and scriptural orthodoxy? Or were they aligned with the Ath Irathen, whose patron saints they claimed to be, in the name of the general interest of the community in which they lived? In going along with the proclamation of the exheredation of women, the *imrabdhen* of the Ath Irathen repudiated the Iboukhtouchen's policy, burned their bridges with the Regency and committed themselves to the anti-Ottoman resistance.

In view of the Ath Irathen's leading role in *saff bouadda* in the 1690–1710 period, it may not have been very difficult for the Ath Irathen and their *imrabdhen* to agree on this position, which amounted to reverting to their previous independent and anti-Ottoman policy while disconnecting this from support for the Iboukhtouchen family interest, since the latter no longer coincided with the former. Matters stood very differently in this respect with the Ath Bethroun.

In the *fitna* of the *sfūf*, the Ath Bethroun had been divided, as we have noted. Their northernmost 'arsh, Ath Yenni, had aligned itself with the Ath Irathen in *saff bouadda* and the Ath Boudrar had followed the Ath Yenni's example, as had most probably the Ath ou Belkacem.[169] But its two westernmost 'aarsh, the Ath Wasif and Ath Bou Akkach, together with their nearest neighbours of the eastern Ath Sedqa, 'aarsh Ath Ahmed and Aouqdal, had gone the other way, rallying to *saff oufella*, the implicitly pro-Ottoman *saff* headed by the Ath Yahia, Ath Menguellat and Ath Bou Youcef, the three 'aarsh whose position in this matter had been determined by the influential nexus of maraboutic families in the central Jurjura. Thus for the Ath Bethroun and its allies to take a unified position against the Ottoman Regency in 1749 was not at all easy; it required an about-turn in the position of the Ath Wasif, Ath Bou Akkach and their Ath Sedqa neighbours. This is why it is doubtful that this would have occurred had the Ath Irathen not already set an example with their own assembly and thereby exerted a powerful influence. And these considerations explain the very striking fact that, in the record of the assembly of the Ath Bethroun in 1749, the list of participants begins with the Ath Bou Akkach and Ath Wasif and mentions them in considerable detail and then continues immediately with the 'aarsh of the eastern Ath Sedqa, for it is the representatives of these 'aarsh that were required to bear public witness to their commitment to the new position. This was probably easier for the eastern Ath Sedqa, since the Bey Mohammed's crushing of the western Ath Sedqa will have concentrated their minds, so it was above all the position of the Ath Wasif and the Ath Bou Akkach that had to be reversed, which is undoubtedly why the Ath Bethroun chose to hold its meeting on the Ath Wasif's territory, thereby implicating the latter to the utmost degree. The mention made of the representatives from the other Ath Bethroun 'aarsh – Ath Yenni, Ath ou Belkacem and Ath Boudrar – was perfunctory because their position had not changed and was not the problem; their commitment was already established and could be taken for granted.

The third assembly, at Jema'a n'Saharij, took place not long afterwards. The local tradition credits the Iboukhtouchen family with the initiative of holding this assembly.[170] If this is reliable, the assembly may have been held shortly

---

169 The Ath ou Belkacem do not figure among the 'aarsh in Saff Bouadda in Table 5.1 since they are not mentioned by Hanoteau and Letourneux in this context; this can be explained by the fact that this 'arsh no longer existed when they were investigating the region and their informants from the Ath Irathen had probably forgotten about it. But since its villages – Ath Ali ou Harzoun, Tassaft Waguemoun, Ath Eurbah and Takhabit – were situated between the Ath Boudrar and the Ath Yenni, they almost certainly took the same side as their immediate neighbours.

170 Genevois, 1958, *op. cit.*, 9; B. Oukhalfoun, *art. cit.*, cited in J. Martin, *Djemaa-Saharidj au cours des siècles*, Fort National, Fichier de Documentation Berbère, No. 110 (1971), 28–9; O. Naït-Djoudi, 'At-Lqadi: Les « rois » de Koukou', in Chaker 2001 (ed.), *op. cit.*, 78.

before Si Amar ou Boukhettouch finally took a stand against his son-in-law the Bey, which happened in 1753, when the Bey sent forces to crush rebellions by the Ath Jennad and Iflissen Lebahr and Si Amar sided with and actively aided the rebels.[171] Given the Iboukhtouchen's role in calling this assembly and the tradition that it was a gathering of many 'aarsh, it is likely that the participants included those 'aarsh to the east and south-east of the Ath Fraoucen with which the Iboukhtouchen were connected, notably the Ath Bou Chaïb and the Ath Ghoubri.[172] It is likely that Ou Boukhettouch finally decided to lead the Ath Fraoucen and their allies into emulating the Ath Irathen and Ath Bethroun as a way of mobilising the largest possible alliance to support his siding with the anti-Ottoman rebellion in maritime Kabylia. The following year, 1754, the Bey Mohammed finally attacked the Ath Irathen, beginning – rather pointedly, one might think – with the village of Adeni. His troops had taken a number of villages when the Bey himself suddenly fell dead, shot, apparently by one of his own soldiers;[173] his troops, demoralised, abandoned the attack and withdrew.

The success of the Igawawen in weathering the Ottoman assault and the news of the Bey's death triggered a general rising across the region, in which even the Iflissen Oumellil joined, while the 'aarsh of the qā'idate of Boghni attacked and destroyed the Borj there and killed the Turkish qā'id. When the rebels turned south and tried to repeat this success at Borj Hamza, it took three columns of Ottoman troops to stop them and quell the revolt.

The Ottoman authorities were to make no further attempt to subdue the Igawawen and incorporate them into their system of rule on the same basis as the lowland populations. They contented themselves with developing a *modus vivendi* with them, respecting their sovereignty over their own territory while negotiating certain matters, such as the passage of Ottoman troops between Tizi Ouzou and Bejaia along the periphery of the Igawawen district, negotiations in which certain *imrabdhen* provided their good offices.[174] The independence of the Igawawen, asserted with such success in this way in 1747–54 CE, was to last another century, together with the political arrangements which had been forged in the fire of these events.

If the Iboukhtouchen did indeed promote the assembly at Jema'a n'Saharij, they were, as Algerians today would put it, jumping on a moving train. A

---

171 Robin, 1998, *op. cit.*, 66.

172 It would probably have also included the Ath Khelili, situated between the Ath Fraoucen and the Ath Bou Chaïb.

173 Robin, 1998, *op. cit.*, 69–70; Feredj, *op. cit.*, 40.

174 Robin (1998, *op. cit.*, 57) mentions in this regard the *imrabdhen* of the village of Ath Zellal of 'arsh Ath Bou Chaïb and those of the Ath Ijjeur, presumably the saints of Tifrit n'Ath ou Malek. Since the role of interlocutors with the Regency authorities of these *imrabdhen* of the Wad Boubehir district would have presupposed the eclipse of the Iboukhtouchen, we can date the development of these relations to the second half of the eighteenth century or later.

political process had been set in motion by the Ath Irathen and given further momentum by the Ath Bethroun and their allies and it is likely that the other 'aarsh of the Igawawen region would have followed suit sooner or later in any event. It was politically astute of Si Amar ou Boukhettouch to act as he did but, while it put his family on the winning side, it made little difference to its own political prospects in the longer term. For the change which had begun to take place spelled the end of the Ibouktouchen as a major force in Kabyle political life.

This is because the assemblies of the Igawawen established the foundations of two of the four *saff* systems described in Chapter 4 and triggered the formation of the other two, and these systems consolidated the democratic character of the form of government of Igawawen society by ensuring that in future the relations this society entertained with the Ottoman Regency would be determined by assemblies representing public opinion instead of being decided by a dynasty acting in its own interest. The rise of the *saff* systems signified the eclipse of the dynastic principle in the highlands. While the political life of the lowlands becomes personalised at this time, a colourful drama dominated by the Ben Zamoums and Mahieddines and Oukacis, that of the Jurjura becomes depersonalised or, one might well say, institutionalised, an affair of 'aarsh and *thiqbilin* and *sfūf*.

None of the 'aarsh which assembled at Jema'a n'Saharij were united in *thiqbilin*. In consequence, the endorsement by this assembly of the position already proclaimed at Tizra Waguemoun signified in effect the acceptance by the Ath Fraoucen and their eastern and south-eastern neighbours of the leadership of the Ath Irathen as the *thaqbilth* dominating the southern side of the middle Sebaou valley and the northern approaches to the Jurjura district. At the same time, the Ath Irathen had themselves been acting to restore their relations with the Ath Aïssi to their west and did so with success. In this way, the Ath Irathen *saff* system, which embraced all these populations, was brought into being. So powerful was the gravitational pull of the Ath Irathen as a consequence of these events that even the Maatqa were drawn into their *saff* system.[175]

In the high Jurjura, matters were, once again, more complicated. It is a striking fact that there is no oral tradition whatever – let alone a written record – of any assembly to resolve upon the exheredation of women among the 'aarsh to the east of the Ath Bethroun, those of the Ath Menguellat confederation and the 'eastern Igawawen' – that is, the Ath Yahia, the Ath Itsouragh and the

---

175 This state of affairs would explain the lacuna we have noted in Robin's account, the absence of any reference to the assemblies that resolved on the exheredation of women. If, as seems likely, this was due to the matter being suppressed by his informant from the Ath Sidi Ali ou Moussa, this omission makes sense given the Maatqa's rallying to the anti-Ottoman line taken by the Ath Irathen, on the principle that, where a change of heart has occurred, as one of Jane Austen's characters observes, 'a good memory is unpardonable'.

Illilten. Given the unusual degree of political influence of the *imrabdhen* among several of these *'aarsh* (Ath Menguellat, Ath Bou Youcef, Ath Itsouragh), this is very understandable. In effect, the confederation of the Ath Menguellat proved quite unable to emulate the Ath Bethroun in this respect. As a result, the Ath Bethroun were able, like the Ath Irathen to their north, to exert a considerable gravitational pull on the *'aarsh* to their east. It was the Ath Bethroun who had given a lead in the high Jurjura in defining the attitude to be taken towards the Ottoman Regency's ambition to subdue the region and this lead remained uncontested locally. At the same time, the dissociation of this anti-Ottoman position from its former connection to the Iboukhtouchen interest made it possible for *'aarsh* which had taken the anti-Iboukhtouchen side in the *fitna* of the *sfūf* to abandon their old attitude and gravitate towards the Ath Bethroun. As a result, the Igawawen *saff* system that came into being was in reality an extension of the *saff* system of the Ath Bethroun confederation, enlarged to include its eastern neighbours. At the same time, however, the Ath Wasif, the *'arsh* which had hosted the assembly of 1749 and taken the lead in sealing the Ath Bethroun's alliance with the eastern Ath Sedqa, was itself undergoing a dramatic internal change arising out of its own enlargement to absorb the villages of Tassaft Waguemoun and Ath Eurbah, formerly of the *'arsh* Ath ou Belkacem, which had disintegrated and disappeared. This change set up a new basis, in the *Igherbien* vs *Isherqien* rivalry, for the *saff* division within the Ath Wasif as we have seen and this then became the division structuring the Igawawen *saff* system as a whole.

As for the *saff* system of the eastern Jurjura and Akfadou district, this appears, given the scarcity of information available, to have been constituted almost by default. One factor was the decline of Iboukhtouchen influence in the Wad Boubehir district: while this was still strong enough among the Ath Ghoubri to draw them into the Ath Irathen system, it clearly no longer had any purchase on the Ath Ijjeur. The ability of the Ottomans to negotiate their relations with the Ath Ijjeur directly, through the latter's own *imrabdhen*, was an index of this change. Above all, the Ath Ijjeur were a confederation in their own right, comprising four *'aarsh*; their collective self-respect may have ruled out their implication in the Ath Irathen system but in any case they occupied a quite distinct piece of terrain, the western side of the Akfadou district, and their geo-political situation naturally inclined them to give precedence to their relations with their southern neighbours, the Ath Ziki and the Illoulen Oumalou. As for the Illilten, who might otherwise equally have entered the Igawawen system, it would appear that it was their close relations with the Illoulen Oumalou which decided their choice of *saff* system.[176]

---

176 A factor in this may have been the connections between *imrabdhen* families; of the 26 marriage alliances of the *imrabdhen* of Illilten with maraboutic families of other *'aarsh* examined in 1895, only seven were with families from the Igawawen *'aarsh* to their west and

Finally, it was natural enough that the *thiqbilin* and *'aarsh* of maritime Kabylia should constitute a *saff* system of their own. They may have done this merely in imitation of the populations to the south. If Adli's hypothesis that the return of Kabyles from Spanish captivity in the late 1760s prompted the *thiqbilin* and *'aarsh* of this district to hold their own assembly to resolve upon the exheredation of their women, this may well have precipitated the formation of their *saff* system. But two of the *thiqbilin* in the district, the Iflissen Lebahr and Ath Jennad, had already engaged in united action in the rebellion against the Bey Mohammed in 1753, so the nucleus of a unified *saff* system already existed in some degree.

Thus the political process initiated at Tizra Waguemoun and then generalised to other districts of Greater Kabylia had a number of crucial effects that one might call revolutionary. It completed and consolidated the system of political organisation and government founded on representative assemblies at village, *'arsh* and *thaqbilth* level by adding a fourth, higher, level, that of the *saff* systems. In doing this, it substituted the democratic principle of represention of public opinion for the aristocratic and dynastic principle – incarnated in the Ath l-Qadi and subsequently the Ibouktouchen – that had predominated at this level up until this moment. In the process, the systems of representative government that had developed in the highlands of Greater Kabylia domesticated the *imrabdhen* by subordinating them to the general interest of the community as determined by its *thijemmu'a*. They thus asserted the primacy of the political field over the religious field. In so doing, the Kabyle polity was in a sense mirroring the Regency itself, for there can be no doubt that, for the rulers of the Regency, religion was subordinate to and an instrument of *raison d'état*, as official Islam has been in all Muslim states in the post-colonial era.

The decision of the Igawawen in their historic assemblies to subordinate the letter of the *Sharī'a* to the preservation of the community and the defence of the general interest did not mean that the Kabyles were not good Muslims. It meant merely that they could henceforth be attacked by the urban *'ulamā'* as bad Muslims or misconceived a century later by French administrators as trans-Mediterranean Auvergnats who were not really Muslims at all. But the Kabyles who acted in this way were undoubtedly as pious and as devout as any of the other populations of the countryside and mountains of Algeria and their polity was a Muslim polity. They had acted to preserve the political and juridical framework which was necessary to the orderly reproduction of the very particular society that had developed in the mountains and, in respect of the right of women to inherit, they had differed from the other rural populations of Algeria only in frankly proclaiming their decision not to uphold that right.

---

north-west, while 19 were with families from their neighbours to the east and south-east: Illoulen Oumalou: seven, Illoulen Ousammeur: four, Ath Qani: four, Ath Melikech: two, Cheurfa: two (Salhi, *op. cit.*, 202). But these relations may have been as much an effect as a cause of their choice of *saff* system.

In declaring that 'the authority of usage and custom is inviolable and immutable like the authority of a king', the Igawawen were in effect claiming for their assemblies, as the creations of custom and the institutional agents of the transmutation of custom into law, precisely 'the authority of the prince' that the urban *'ulamā'* and Al-Warthilani reproached them for defying. They were, of course, simply defying the pretension to authority of the Regency in the name of the substantial authority their representative assemblies possessed. And the fact that the audacious and controversial decisions taken at Tizra Waguemoun and at Souq el-Sebt n'Ath Wasif were then accepted and adopted by all the other populations of Greater Kabylia is a very clear index of the hegemony of the Igawawen over the society of the region as a whole.

~

CHAPTER 8

Transcending Kabylia

The Constitutional Tradition
and the Exceptional Tradition

The polity – the particular form of political community, specified and sustained by the particular form of government – which I have described in Chapters 2 to 4 of this book was not the epiphenomenal corollary of some sociological law, let alone the emanation or expression of some racial genius, but the product of the complex history which I have outlined in Chapters 5 to 7. This polity attained its final form in the second half of the eighteenth century CE, with the crystallisation of the four *saff* systems in the wake of the extraordinary assemblies of 1748–53. As far as I can see, no qualitative change to this polity occurred prior to the French conquest of the Jurjura in 1857.

The Kabyle polity that I have described was a very remarkable one. Its form of government combined a stable distribution of authority founded on consent, a mode of legitimation predicated on a principle of political representation, a procedure of public deliberation and decision-making that was respectful of public opinion, a corpus of man-made law that carried authority, and rudimentary political parties – the *sfūf* – that structured public opinion, concentrated debate and transcended kin-based fault lines in the community and thereby facilitated its government.

The remarkable qualities of the political organisation of the Kabyles and of the Igawawen above all were recognised by some of the French ethnographers and administrators of the early colonial period. I do not consider that their admiring references to the Kabyle 'republics' were misconceived. Among the Igawawen certainly, and in varying degrees among the populations of most other districts of Kabylia, government was indeed *res publica*, the business of the people, because it was conducted by assemblies in which the people were regularly and effectively represented as of right.

The society of the Kabyle highlands and of the Jurjura especially had lived and evolved within the framework of this polity for about a century by the time Randon's campaign ended Kabylia's independence in 1857. And it had already lived and evolved within earlier and less complete versions of this political organisation for several centuries beforehand. The perfecting of this political organisation by the Igawawen in the mid-eighteenth century and the resort to open defiance of the Regency and explicit rejection of an aspect of the *Sharīʿa* had the effect of raising the Kabyles' own awareness of both the necessity and the specificity of their political arrangements at the same time that they constituted these into a scandal in the eyes of Al-Warthilani and the urban *ʿulamāʾ*. They thereby established the Kabyles' attachment to these arrangements as a fact in the social consciousness – that is, as a political tradition. This tradition has survived to the present day.

That these democratic republics had an archaic aspect, which, as Masqueray suggested, recalled the city-states of classical antiquity, may be conceded. But the two mistakes that this recognition tended to encourage must be corrected.

The archaic aspect of the Kabyle republics induced observers to assume that they had been in existence for very many centuries, if not indeed since before the arrival of the Arabs and Islam in North Africa in the seventh century CE. They accordingly led the same observers to infer that the political organisation of the Kabyles was the product of the 'genius' of the Berber race, a notion that wilfully ignored, among other things, the fact that, in itself, self-government by the *jemaʿa* was a feature of many Arabic-speaking populations in the Maghrib and by no means an exclusively 'Berber' practice. But a corollary of this mistaken notion has been the failure to recognise that the 'democratic' or 'republican' tradition of the Kabyles has not been the only political tradition that has existed in Kabylia and has had purchase on their reflexes.

The 'democratic' tradition in Kabylia is a tradition of law-bound or constitutional government. The fact that the constitution has been an unwritten one is neither here nor there. The constitution of the political community has existed, as Masqueray appreciated, 'in the heart of all the free men who compose it'. But something else has also existed in the hearts of all these free men, the fact that they have also been members of a much wider community, the community of believers, the Islamic *umma*.

The Kabyle polity was a Muslim polity. Only Muslims could belong to it. That the urban *ʿulamāʾ* could fault the political arrangements and the corpus of law of these 'republics' did not alter the fact that the Kabyles considered themselves to be, indeed took it for granted that they were, perfectly good Muslims. Their legal codes embodied the notions of good and evil and right and wrong given them by their Islamic faith, and membership of the wider community defined by this faith was a condition of membership of each and every *ʿarsh* in the Jurjura and throughout the region. Accordingly, the Kabyles could on occasion be mobilised in the name of this faith to fight for something other than the defence of their own laws and sovereign territories. And what this meant is that, in addition to the constitutional tradition, there has long existed an exceptional tradition, the tradition of mobilisation to honour the political obligation to the wider community, the *umma*, a mobilisation expressed most explicitly in the jihad.

The 'kingdom' of Koukou had its origins in this exceptional tradition. For as long as a connection could continue to be perceived between the power of the Ath l-Qadi and their original role and authority as leaders of a jihad, their political pre-eminence was accepted despite its dynastic and undemocratic character. The failure of previous observers to understand fully the origin, nature and logics of the 'kingdom' of Koukou had as one of its consequences a failure to appreciate the latent vitality and force of this exceptional tradition. In the case of the French after 1857, it made the subsequent rebellions of the Kabyles against French rule, in 1871 and 1954, difficult to conceive until they happened.

This exceptional tradition had its natural origin and anchorage in the religious sphere. Their membership of the wider community of Muslims was a premise of the Kabyles' ability to move around Algeria, the wider Maghrib and indeed North Africa as a whole with confidence. And it made it natural for Kabyles to affiliate to religious orders, *turuq*, that transcended Kabylia and linked Kabyles to their fellow Muslims elsewhere in wider communions.

A couple of years before Sheikh Hussein Al-Warthilani penned his critique of Kabyle law and morality, a member of a maraboutic lineage from the '*arsh* Ath Smaïl of the Igouchdal confederation of the western Jurjura returned to his native hearth to found a new *zāwiya* and a new religious order there, after a sojourn of 30 years in the Middle East. Sidi M'Hammed Ben Abderrahmane el-Guechtouli el-Jurjuri el-Azhari Bou Qobrin, as he is known to history, was born in 1715 or 1720 and died in 1793. After studying at the *zāwiya* of Sheikh Arab in '*arsh* Ath Oumalou (Ath Irathen), he continued his studies at Al-Azhar in Cairo, and became an adept of the Khalwatia *tarīqa*, on behalf of which he performed many missions, in the Hijaz, the Sudan and Turkey, before finally returning to Kabylia *c.* 1765, a few months at most before Al-Warthilani set out on his *rihla*. The order he founded, known after his death as the Rahmaniyya, was initially limited mainly to western Kabylia and the adepts of the second *zāwiya* Sidi M'Hammed had founded at Hamma near Algiers, but it expanded very rapidly after the French capture of Algiers in 1830 to become the largest *tarīqa* in the whole of Algeria, massively dominant in Kabylia but also in the Constantinois as well.

The history of the Rahmaniyya belongs primarily to the colonial period and accessorily to the post-colonial period as well, since the order still exists, so this is not the place to attempt to do justice to it.[1] Its relevance to the argument of this book lies in the fact that the story of the Rahmaniyya after 1830 illustrated the exceptional tradition in action.

The massive expansion of the order between 1830 and 1871 was very largely

---

1 Very substantial justice has already been done to it by Mohamed Brahim Salhi in his remarkable doctoral thesis (Salhi, 1979, *op. cit*). It is earnestly to be hoped that this fine study will soon at last be published.

due to the role it played in the resistance to the colonial conquest. By the 1850s if not sooner, virtually all the leading maraboutic families and *zawāyā* of Kabylia had affiliated to it. These included the especially influential network of maraboutic lineages of the *'aarsh* Ath Bou Youcef, Ath Yahia and Ath Menguellat of the high Jurjura and in particular the Ath Sidi Ahmed of Werja, who produced, in Sidi Tahar and his sister, Lalla Fadhma n'Soumeur, two of the most prominent leaders and inspirers of the Kabyle resistance to the French from 1849 to 1857. The same Kabyle 'republics' that had, in the assemblies of 1748–53, acted to assure themselves of the political loyalty of their *imrabdhen* against the Ottomans, unhesitatingly mobilised their fighting men against the French under the banner of Islam and the leadership of their *imrabdhen* in 1857 and were willing to do so again in 1871, when an important current of maraboutic opinion in the Jurjura was against the rebellion and ignored the Rahmaniyya's call to jihad.[2]

Moreover, the fact that it is a question of a long-standing tradition, rather than a series of peculiar episodes, is demonstrated by the rapidity and completeness of the mobilisation of the Igawawen to come to the defence of the Regency in Algiers, alongside the contingents furnished by the *'aarsh* and confederations of the low-lying districts, in July 1830.

As the story of the Ath l-Qadi and Koukou illustrated, the exceptional tradition is not a tradition that gives rise to democratic or even constitutional government. Since 1962, Kabylia has, once again, been subject to rule by a regime that is a product of this exceptional tradition. The fact that the Kabyles played an immense role in the national revolution and in both the rank and file and the leadership of the wartime FLN and ALN, a fact known to all and widely acknowledged, did not make it any easier for them to accept for long the form of government of the state that was constituted by the FLN-ALN at Independence. Since then, Kabyle resistance and opposition to this state have ultimately been based upon the constitutional tradition that has its origins in the remarkable polity that has been the subject of this book. But the premise of much of the contemporary preoccupation of the Kabyle intelligentsia with *l'amazighité*, the Berber identity, has been the belief that, as one Kabyle political activist put it, 'the identity claim constitutes the foundation of the democratic claim'.[3] It will be seen that this idea has recycled, whether consciously or unconsciously, the old French notion that the Kabyles were democratic because they were Berbers.

---

2 With the death of Lalla Fadhma in 1863, the leadership of the Ath Sidi Ahmed was in effect assumed by the most prominent saint of another branch of the lineage, Sheikh Mohand ou el-Hocine of Taqa, *'arsh* Ath Yahia, who, though affiliated to the Rahmaniyya, advised against the 1871 revolt and was widely credited with sagacity after its failure. Sheikh Mohand's nephew was subsequently appointed *qā'id* by the French; the latter's son, Hocine Aït Ahmed, became a leader of the nationalist movement in Kabylia after 1945 and of the FLN in 1954.

3 Cited in International Crisis Group, *Algeria: Unrest and Impasse in Kabylia*, Middle East/ North Africa Report No. 15 (Cairo/Brussels: 10 June 2003), 11.

The fact that the Algerian state has proved able to accommodate 'the identity claim' by recognising *l'amazighité* as one of the three constitutive elements of the Algerian national identity (along with the Arab and Islamic elements)[4] and has even recognised *Thamazighth*, the Berber language, as a national language,[5] without becoming substantially less undemocratic or less arbitrary in its form of government, is evidence that this belief and the strategy predicated upon it have been mistaken. I have accordingly long been convinced that it is necessary to distinguish between the question of identity and the question of democracy and law-bound government and consider and debate them separately, each on its own merits.

I have sought in this book to do justice to the remarkable political organisation of the Kabyle highlands in the pre-colonial period and provide an historical explanation of its genesis and development, in order that others may conceive this polity more realistically, in its own, historical, terms and thereby better understand and appreciate the constitutional tradition that has originated in it.

---

4   In the constitutional revision of November 1996.
5   In the constitutional revision of April 2002.

Appendix

Déclaration abolissant le droit d'héritage des femmes[1]

Louange à Dieu. Que Dieu répande ses bénédictions sur Mohammed, l'élu ! C'est votre secours que nous implorons, ô Dieu de bonté.

Ceci est la copie[2] d'un acte transcrit par nécessité, de peur que le texte de la minute ne s'altère et ne s'efface, et par crainte des vicissitudes des temps.

Louange au Dieu unique. Toute puissance lui appartient. Que Dieu répande ses bénédictions sur celui après lequel il n'y a plus de prophète !

Salut sur quiconque lira notre écrit. Le Dieu très haut, dans les décrets de sa toute-puissance, ayant voulu rendre prospère le marché du samedi des Beni Ouasif, il s'y tint une assemblée des marabouts des Beni Bethroun, assistés des âk'al de leurs villages et de l'imam de la mosquée de Tahammamt.[3]

Chacun exposa ce dont il avait à souffrir, se plaignant de ce qui était une cause permanente de rixes, de troubles et de discordes dans les villages, les tribus et la confédération des Beni Bethroun. Chaque village était représenté à l'assemblée. Celle-ci, à l'unanimité des voix, abolit, chez les Beni Bethroun et leurs voisins et alliés, le droit d'héritage (pour les femmes), le droit de chefâa sur les bien h'abous (pour tout le monde), et tout droit de chefâa pour les filles, les sœurs et les orphelins; enfin la dot de la femme répudiée ou veuve fut déclarée perdue pour elle. Ces dispositions étant acceptées d'un commun accord, il n'y a qu'un homme inique qui puisse vouloir faire revivre celles qu'elles ont abolies. Or l'iniquité est une chose réprouvée. L'autorité de l'usage et de la coutume est inviolable et immuable comme l'autorité d'un roi. Quiconque voudra enfreindre et violer les règlements précités deviendra pour les hommes une cause de malheur et de discordes. Or, « la discorde est un feu, » selon la parole du Prophète (sur lui

---

1 Source: Hanoteau and Letourneux, *op. cit.*, III, 451–4; for « âk'al » in the text, read *'uqqâl* ('sages').

2 [Note by H&L] L'acte original est entre nos mains ; il est un peu détérioré par le temps et plusieurs mots manquent. On peut cependant le lire facilement, et nous avons pu constater que la copie est bien exacte.

3 [Note by H&L] Cette mosquée est située chez les Aït Ouasif, près de la rivière.

soient les bénédictions et le salut). « La discorde est un feu; que la malédiction de Dieu soit sur celui qui l'allume, et sa miséricorde sur celui qui l'apaise ! » Quiconque voudra violer ces lois, Dieu l'écrasera sous le poids de l'abjection, de la misère, de la faim et du malheur dans ce monde et dans l'autre, que le coupable soit un d'entre nous, ou un de nos enfants, ou un des enfants de nos enfants, tant que les descendants remplaceront les ascendants. Si quelqu'un des marabouts ou des grands des villages ne se conforme pas aux dispositions susdites, Dieu lui en demandera compte.

Chacun des assistants dit alors trois fois: amen ! amen ! puis on enregistra le nom des marabouts et des grands du village présents au conseil.

Sont venus du village de Tiguemmounin (les petits mamelons): le chérif, l'honorable Sidi Lounis; les âk'al : Kassi ben Ali, Ahmed Amzian, Bel Kaçem ben Lalam,[4] Mohammed ben Bel Abbas, Mohammed ben Mesbah,[5] le chérif, l'honorable Sidi El-Haoussin ben Bel Kaçem, Sidi Ali ben Abbas;

Du village de Tirouel: le chérif, l'honorable Sidi Ahmed Zerrouk, Sidi Çadok; l'âdel favorisé de la grâce divine, El-Haoussin ben Salem, Messaoud Naït Hamdan, Chalal ben Yakoub;

Du village de Zaknoun: le chérif, l'honorable Sidi Mohammed ben Touâti, Sid Ahmed ben Andalous; l'âdel favorisé de la grâce divine, Mohammed ben Saadi ou Ali,[6] Mohammed ben Allal, El-Haoussin ben Rahmoun, Ibrahim ben Aïssa, Ameur ben Medjebeur, El-Mouhoub ben Châban;

Du village de Tikichourt: Sâïd ben K'adhi, Mohammed ben Mohammed Sâïd, Châban ben Youcef, Ahmed ben Hamadouch et l'écrivain du présent;

Du village de Tiqidount: le chérif, l'honorable Sidi Abd el-Kader ben Ali, et les âk'al, savoir : Ahmed ben Chalal, Mohammed Naït Ahmed, Slimane Naït Hamadouch ou Mâamar, Mohammed Sâïd ben Bekkouch, Mohammed ou Hammour;

Du village de Bou Abd er-Rahman: le chérif, l'honorable Sidi Mohammed Iriz, et les âk'al, savoir: Mohamed ou Sâïd, Mohammed Sâïd ben Amara, Amara Naït Bel Kaçem, Ahmed ou Mohammed, Ameur ou Goujil;

Du village de Zoubga: Sidi El-Arbi ben Mansour, Ali ou Sliman;

Du village des Beni Abbas: le chérif, l'honorable Sidi Aïssa, et les âk'al, savoir: El-Mouffok ben Yahia, Mohammed ben Si Ahmed, Mohammed ben Sidhoum.

Telles sont les personnes venues des tribus des Beni bou Akkach et des Beni Ouasif.

Du chez les Beni Sedka, adhérents et alliés des Beni Bethroun, sont venus:

Du village de Timer'eras: le chérif, l'honorable Sidi El-Haoussin ben el-K'adhi et Sidi Mohammed el-Haoussin ben Kar;

---

4   I have inserted this comma in the text which appears to run two names together here.
5   The text says 'ben Mesbas' but this is a typographical error.
6   I have inserted this comma in the text which appears to run two names together here.

Du village de Bou Mahdi: Sidi El-Mokhtar ben Sidi Ali; les deux âk'al, Ameur ou El-Haoussin et Mohammed Sâïd ben Mohammed et le chérif, l'honorable Sidi Mohammed ben Bel Kaçem;

Du village des Beni Chebla : l'astre, objet de la miséricorde divine, la brillante étoile polaire, Sidi Ameur ben Bel Kaçem, Mohammed ben el-Tir, Ameur Amokran ;

De la tribu des Aoukdal, du village des Aït Amran, sont venus : le chérif, l'honorable Sidi Taïeb, Sidi Mohammed ben Allouan et les âk'al, savoir : Bou Sâad Ikellalen, Ibrahim ben Chemmoun, Mohammed ben Sliman ou Tâleb, Ahmed ben Ibrahim ;

De la tribu des Beni Irguen : le chérif, l'honorable Sidi Ameur ben Ahmed ben Youçef, l'âdel favorisé de la grâce divine, Mohammed ou Ameur ben Hammou, Ameur Ihaddaden ;

Du village de Iguer Adloun : l'âdel favorisé de la grâce divine, Ahmed ou Sâïd ben Abed, Addouch ben Ouarich ;

Du village de Bou Adnan : Bel Kaçem ben Mohammed ou Sâïd, Ali ben Abd el-Selam, Sâïd ben Sâada ou Ismaïl ;

Du village des Beni Ali ou Harzoun : le chérif, l'honorable Sidi Abd er-Rahman ben Sidi Mâamar, Sidi Mohammed ben Bou Abd Allah, et les âk'al, savoir : Sliman ben Kaçi, Ali ben Sliman, Mohammed ben el-Amara, Madhi ben Hammou, Bou Bekeur Naït Ahmed ou Ameur, Ameur Naït Tarhift, El-Haoussin Naït Hammou, Bel Kaçem ben Kaçi, ainsi que d'autres personnes.

Le manque d'espace ne nous permettant pas d'énumérer tous ceux qui sont venus des tribus des Beni Bel Kaçem et des Beni Yenni jusqu'au village des Beni el-Hassen, nous n'en mentionnerons que quelques-uns, savoir : Abd er-Rahman ben Arab, Yahia Naït Ahmed, El-Haoussin ben Youçef et Ibrahim ben Amara, des Beni Bel Kaçem. Parmi les gens des Beni Yenni, on remarquait : le chérif, l'honorable Sidi Mohammed Amzian, et les âk'al de son village, savoir : Mohammed ben Jaber, El-Haoussin ben Mâamar, Mohammed ben Messaoud. Il y avait encore d'autres personnes, sur la mention desquelles nous ne nous étendrons pas.

C'est par l'ordre de tous les marabouts et âk'al susnommés qu'ont été abolies les coutumes précitées ; quiconque, parmi les descendants, voudrait violer les dispositions nouvelles, Dieu lui en demandera compte. Salut !

Voila ce que nous avons trouvé dans la minute.

L'acte copié a été écrit par le sieur, le bien dirigé, le savant, l'orthodoxe Sidi Ameur ben Sidi Ahmed ben Yahia, en l'an 1162.[7] Il a été transcrit, pour éviter les inconvénients signalés plus haut, par l'excellent Ebn Ahmed ben Abd el-Kader ben Ali, de la tribu des Beni Ouasif, que Dieu lui pardonne et améliore sa parole

---

7 [H&L] Le premier jour de l'année 1162 de l'hégire correspond au 21 décembre 1748 de J.-C.

et ses actes, amen ! à la date de l'année 1225,[8] que Dieu nous accorde le bien et nous préserve du mal qu'elle apporte, amen !

Ont assisté comme témoins à la transcription dudit acte : le sieur, le bien dirigé, le savant, l'orthodoxe Sidi El-Mokhtar ben Abd el-Malek, du village de Bou Abd er-Raman ; Sidi Bel Kaçem ben Ameur et Sidi Bouzid, tous deux de la famille de Sidi Ali ben Yahia ; Ali Naït Ali ou El-Mouffok et Ibrahim ben el-Hadj, du village de Taourirt Mimoun ; Sliman Naït Kaçi ou Ali, du village des Beni Lahssen.

Salut de la part de celui qui s'est nommé dans la minute.

---

8   [H&L] Le premier jour de l'année de l'hégire 1225 correspond au 5 février 1810.

Glossary

Arabic words

'abd, pl. *'abīd*   servant, slave

'āda, pl. *'ādāt*   custom

'ādil, pl. *'udūl*   good, upright, just; (in the Maghrib) an assistant to a *qāḍi*

aghā, pl. *aghawāt*   lord; commander (military rank) in Ottoman Algeria

'alim, pl. *'ulamā'*   knowing, learned; (as substantive) religious scholar, doctor of Islamic law

'amal   action; labour, work;

amīn, pl. *umanā'*   trustee; a person entrusted with responsibility; the man who presides the *jema'a* in Kabylia

amir   commander; prince

'anāya   care, concern, consideration, regard; (derived meaning) protection

'aqil, pl. *'uqqāl*   wise, possessing judgment; sage, elder

'arsh, pl. *'arūsh*   throne; in Algeria: a political community; in Kabylia this consists of a number of villages sharing a common territory

'āshūrā'   10 Muharram in the Islamic calendar, a day of fasting; the anniversary of the martyrdom of Hussein and so a day of mourning sacred to the Shi'ites

baldi   (Algerian colloquial, from classical Arabic *baladī*): townsman

baraka   blessing, divine grace, charisma; the miraculous power associated with possession of this

ben, pl. *beni*   son

beylik   the jurisdiction of a bey, governorate; (loosely) the government, state; in Ottoman Algeria: one of the three provinces of the Regency

bilād (colloquial: *bled*) land, country

bled el-makhzen   'the land of government', the area controlled by the central power and paying taxes to it

bled es-sība   (Morocco) 'the land of dissidence' (or disorder or « the free-flowing of things »): the area of the country resisting the central power and refusing to pay taxes

bled el-baroud	(Algeria) 'the land of gunpowder': the Algerian equivalent of *bled-es-sība*
dār	house
Dār el-Islam	The Abode of Islam; the Islamic world, those countries and population under Islamic government
dhāmin	responsible, answerable for; guarantor, surety
dīwān	council
Fātiha	The first sura (verse) of the Qur'ān
gharb	the west
haqq	truth; rightness, right, rightful possession, one's due
hiba	gift, donation
hubus, pl. *ahbās*	religious endownment, estate in mortmain entailed so that its proceeds accrue to the members of the donor's family
horma	sanctity, inviolability, that which is sacrosanct, honour
'īd, pl. *a'yād*	feast, festival, feast day, holiday
'īd el-adhā	the feast of the sacrifice, commemorating Abraham's sacrifice of the ram
'īd el-fitr	the feast of the breaking of the fast at the end of Ramadan
imām	imam, prayer leader, religious leader
jawād, pl. *ajwād*	good; noble, of the (military) aristocracy
jebel, pl. *jibāl*	mountain
jema'a, pl. *jemāya'*	assembly, council (e.g. of a village or an *'arsh*)
jihad	struggle, battle; holy war on behalf of the *umma* (q.v.)
kamel	perfect, finished, accomplished
kanun	hearth, fireplace
khalīfa	lieutenant
khammes	agricultural worker receiving one-fifth of the crop as wages
khammesat	share-cropping arrangement where the worker receives a fifth
khams khmas	five fifths; a feature of the organisation of certain Berber tribes in Morocco.
khattī	spear, lance
liff, pl. *ilfūf*	(from *laff*: circumvention, subterfuge) in Morocco: political alliance, faction or pact
ma'ammera	Quranic school
mahkama, pl. *mahākim*	law court
makhzen	store, storehouse, treasury; (derived meaning) the state apparatus of the central power
melk	land held in private possession
mrābit, pl. *mrābtīn*	holy man, saint
nisba	attribution; sobriquet denoting origin
qabīla, pl. *qbā'il*	tribe

qādi, pl. *qudāh*	judge
qā'id	commander
qā'ida	foundation; precepts, manners, mode, customs
qal'a	fortified place, stronghold, citadel
qānūn, pl. *qawānīn*	code of (man-made) law, regulations, by-laws
ra'īs	head, chief, leader; president
ra'īs al-tā'ifa	commander of the navy, admiral
ra'īya	flock, herd; subjects
Rebbi	My Lord
reqba	revenge
saff, pl. *sfūf*	row, alignment; party
sālih	good, right, virtuous, pious, saintly, venerable
shahāda, pl. *shahādāt*	bearing witness; the first duty of a Muslim: bearing witness to the oneness of God
Sharī'a	the Sharia, the revealed law of Islam
sharif, pl. *shurafā'*	noble; one able to claim descent from the Prophet; used in the Maghrib to indicate the religious aristocracy
sharq	east
shefa'a	the right of pre-emption of real estate enjoyed by agnates of the vendor
sīdī	'My lord', term of respect used especially when addressing saints or holy men (*mrābtīn*)
sultān	ruler, sultan
tāleb, pl. *tolba*	student
tarīqa, pl. *turuq*	path, way; a religious (Sufi) order
tawfīq	adjustment, settlement, peacemaking, reconciliation
twīza (Alg. colloquial)	mutual aid, reciprocal assistance
umma	the community of believers, the Islamic community
'umrān	inhabitedness; culture, civilisation
'umrān badawī	rural life, the civilisation of the Bedouin or country-dwellers
'umrān hadarī	urban life; the society or civilisation of the towns
'urf	usage, custom; local customary law
'urfi	pertaining to secular legal practice, customary
wakīl	agent, deputy, administrator; head clerk, secretary
walī	near, close; a man close to God, saint; patron, protector, governor
watan	country, nation
wilāya, pl. *wilayāt*	rule, government; the charge or jurisdiction of a *wali* (q.v.), guardianship, supervisory authority; governorate, administrative region
wujāq (Turkish: *ojaq*)	stove, kitchen, galley; the corps of the Janissaries

zāwiya, pl. *zawāyā*	nook, corner; small mosque; religious lodge established near shrine of a saint; a settlement composed wholly or overwhelmingly of saintly families
Zwawi, pl. *Zwawa*	someone from Greater Kabylia; someone from the central Jurjura
zmāla, pl. *zmoul*	fellowship, comradeship, company; in Algeria: a military camp or base

Berber words

(including Berberised borrowings from Arabic)

aberrah	public crier; meeting of the village assembly by convocation
adrum, pl. *iderman*	usually translated as 'clan': kinship unit grouping several lineages
adrar, pl. *idurar*	mountain
afrag, pl. *ifraguen* or *ifergan*	lineage; kinship unit grouping several households
agouni, pl. *ignān*	elevated but level ground, plateau
aguemoun	hillock
agurram, pl. *igurramen*	(Morocco): saint, holy man
aït	see *ath*
akharrub, pl. *ikharban*	lineage; kinship unit grouping several households
akhkham, pl. *ikhkhamen*	house, household, family
akli, pl. *aklan*	slave; black; butcher
alemmas, pl. *ilemmasen*	middle, centre
amazigh, pl. *imazighen*	literally 'free'; used to mean 'Berber'
amrabedh, pl. *imrabdhen*	saint, holy man, marabout; applied to members of a saintly lineage
aqbayli, pl. *leqbayel*	Kabyle, a Kabyle man
argaz, pl. *irgazen*	man, husband; as a term of respect: 'man of honour'
'arsh, pl. *'aarsh*	stable political unit grouping several villages sharing a common territory
ath (singular: *ou* or *u*)	the Berber equivalent of *banu* or *beni*, used in names of families, settlements and larger units (*'arsh*, *thaqbilth*, q.v.): the sons/children of, the people of
'attar, pl. *i'attaren*	pedlar
awrir	high ground, hill, spur of a mountain
azaghar	plain
azniq	street
igherm (Mor.)	large house of notable family; fortifed village; citadel
ighil	literally: arm, forearm; used to mean a spur of a mountain, rise, hill, ridge
imoula	forest

lemluk	cultivable land in private possession
meshmel	the common lands of a community
ou, pl. *ath*	son
oufella	above, on high, higher, upper
oumalou	side of a mountain that receives less sun, in the shadow, north side
seksu	couscous
tafsut	spring (the season);
tafsut Imazighen	'the Springtime of the Berbers', i.e. the wave of protests in Kabylia in March–April 1980.
tamen, pl. *temman*	the man who answers for a lineage in the village *thajma'th*
tamgout	the summit or peak of a mountain
taoussa	gift (of food but sometimes money) presented as participation in a feast or celebration
tazaghart	little plain
thaddarth, pl. *thudrin* or *thuddar*	
	village in the sense of nucleated settlement or agglomeration
thaguemounth, pl. *thiguemounin*	
	diminutive of *aguemoun*: a little hill, hillock
thajma'th, pl. *thijemmu'a*	the governing assembly or council of a village
thajma'th l-'uqqāl	literally: 'the assembly of the sages'
thakharrubth, pl. *thikharrubin*	
	diminutive of *akharrub*: lineage
thakhelijth, pl. *ikhelijen*	hamlet; small settlement, usually a dependent satellite of a *thaddarth*
thala	fountain
thamurth	land, country
Thaqbaylith	the Kabyle dialect; the quality of being Kabyle, 'Kabyleness' – the ensemble of Kabyle culture and values
thaqbilth, pl. *thiqbilin*	confederation grouping several *'aarsh* in a stable alliance for attack and defence
thaqel'ath (Chaouia)	a Chaouia village; its collective storehouse
thashmelith	collective work on a communal project
thawrirth (often written *taourirt*)	
	a small hill
thighilt	diminutive of *ighil* (q.v.)
thim'ammerth	Quranic school
thiwizi	mutual aid; gift of labour which will later be reciprocated
tighermt	see *igherm*
tizi	mountain pass
tsaar	vengeance, vendetta

tūfīq, tuwāfeq group of hamlets occupying a common territory and forming a political unit

wadda (ou adda) low, below, lower down

bouadda lower, occupying the lower ground

Bibliography

Primary sources

Dossiers du Sénatus-Consulte des Tribus d'Algérie
(French National Archives, Annexe d'Aix-en-Provence):

Series M 36	*Letter from jema'a of Aït Ouabane to the Governor-General of Algeria*, Michelet, 25 May 1895.
	Letter from the President and members of the jema'a of the tribe of the Beni Bou Drar to the Governor-General of Algeria, Michelet, 2 July 1895.
	Letter from jema'a of Aït Ouabane to the Governor-General of Algeria, Michelet, 11 April 1896.
	Letter from the Administrator of the Commune-Mixte du Djurdjura to the Governor-General of Algeria, Michelet, 15 April 1896.
	Letters from jema'a of Aït Ouabane to the Governor-General of Algeria, Michelet, 30 December 1896.
	État de noms d'indigènes de la tribu des Beni Bou Drar, Algiers, 23 February 1897.
	Letter from jema'a of Aït Ouabane to the Official Inspector, Aït Ouabane, 22 July 1897.
	Rapport sur l'application du Sénatus-Consulte dans la tribu des Beni Bou Drar, Algiers, 14 August 1897.
Series M 96/242	*Minute de rapport sur la délimitation et la répartition du territoire de la tribu des Beni Bou Drar*, Algiers, 19 February 1900.
Series M 96/244	*Minute de rapport sur la délimitation et la répartition du territoire de la tribu des Beni Bou Attaf*, 19 March 1900.
Series M 98/264	*Letter from jema'a of Aït Mislaïen to the Governor-General of Algeria*, Khenchela, 9 September 1909.
Series M 190/3	*Decree of 25 May 1889 constituting the jema'a of the douar Beni Idjeur Sahel.*
Series M 231/125	*Decree of 28 June 1890 constituting the jema'a of the douar Beni Bou Drar.*

                                    État statistique concernant la tribu des Beni Bou Drar, Michelet,
                                    4 May 1896.

Series 6Mi/64/L125   *Note from Victor Cuvellier concerning the douar Beni Bou Drar*,
                                    Algiers, 1 January 1898.

            Fichier du Personnel Administratif du Département d'Alger:

Series C: *Communes Mixtes et Communes de Plein Exercice:* C 566 and C
                                    666.

Unpublished theses and dissertations

Amrane Ben Younès   *Émigration et Société: un village de Kabylie,* Mémoire pour
                                    le Diplôme d'Études Supérieures en Sciences Politiques,
                                    Université d'Alger, Institut des Sciences Juridiques, Politiques
                                    et Administratives, June 1977.

Khelifa Bouzebra   *Impact socio-économique des Coopératives Agricoles de
                                    Production de la Révolution Agraire dans les campagnes: le
                                    cas de la commune de Berrouaghia,* University of Algiers,
                                    Mémoire de Diplôme d'Études Approfondies, October 1975.

Khelifa Bouzebra   *Culture and political mobilisation in Algeria,* University of East
                                    Anglia, PhD, 1982.

Hugh Roberts   *Political Development in Algeria: the region of Greater Kabylia,*
                                    Oxford University, D.Phil., 1980.

Mohamed Brahim Salhi   *Étude d'une confrérie religieuse algérienne: la Rahmania à la
                                    fin du XIXe siècle et pendant la première moitié du XXe siècle*
                                    (thesis for doctorat de 3ᵉ cycle), Paris, École des Hautes Études
                                    en Sciences Sociales, 1979.

Reports

International Crisis Group   *Algeria: Unrest and Impasse in Kabylia,* Middle East/North
                                    Africa Report No. 15, Cairo/Brussels, 10 June 2003, 41pp.

Other primary sources and manuscripts

Hussein Al-Warthilani   *Rihla,* edited by M. Ben Cheneb, Algiers, P. Fontana, 1908.

Fadhma Aïth Mansour   *My Life Story,* English translation by Dorothy Blair, London,
Amrouche   The Women's Press, 1988.

Baron Henri Aucapitaine	'Kanoun du village de Thaourirt Amokran chez les Aïth Irathen (Kabilie)', *Revue Africaine*, 7, 1863, 279–85.
Si Amar ou Saïd Boulifa	*Recueil de Poésies kabyles*, with introduction by Tassadit Yacine, Paris, Awal, 1990.
Diego de Haedo	*Topographie et histoire générale d'Alger*, translated into French from the Spanish text (Vallodolid, 1612) by Dr. Monnereau and A. Berbrugger, *Revue Africaine*, 1870–1; republished with introduction by Jocelyne Dakhlia, Saint-Denis, Éditions Bouchène, 1998.
Diego de Haedo	*Histoire des Rois d'Alger*, translated from the Spanish by Henri de Grammont (Algiers, Jourdan 1881), republished with an introduction by Jocelyne Dakhlia, Saint-Denis, Éditions Bouchène, 1998.
Abou Ali Ibrahim El-Merini	*Unwān el-Akhbār fimā marra ala Bijāya*, translated by Laurent-Charles Féraud and published in two parts as 'Exposé des évènements qui se sont passes à Bougie', *Revue Africaine*, 1868, 242–56 and 337–48.
H. Genevois	*Djemaa-Saharidj*, Fort National, C.E.B., 1958.
H. Genevois	*Tawrirt n'At Mangellat: notes d'histoire et de folklore*, Fort National, Fichier de Documentation Berbère, 1962.
H. Genevois	*At-Yänni – Les Beni Yenni: Eléments historiques et folkloriques*, Fort National, Fichier de Documentation Berbère, 1971.
H. Genevois	*Taguemount Azouz des Beni Mahmoud: notes d'histoire et de folklore*, Fort National, Fichier de Documentation Berbère, 1972.
H. Genevois	*Légende des Rois de Koukou: Si Amar ou el Qadi, Si Ahmed El Tounsi*, Fort National, Le Fichier Périodique, 1974.
A. Hanoteau	*Poésies Populaires de la Kabylie du Djurdjura*, Paris, Imprimérie Impériale eds, 1867.
Mouloud Mammeri	*Les Isefra: poèmes de Si Mohand ou M'Hand*, Paris, François Maspero, 1969.
Mouloud Mammeri	*Poèmes kabyles anciens*, Paris, Maspero, 1980; 2nd edition, Paris, La Découverte & Syros, 2001.
Luis del Marmol Carvajal	*Descripcion General de Africa*, Granada, 1573.
J. Martin	*Djemaa-Saharidj au cours des siècles*, Fort National, Fichier de Documentation Berbère, 1971.
Louis Milliot	'Les Qânoun des M'âtqa', *Hespéris*, 2, 1922, 193–204.
Youssef Nacib	*Chants Religieux du Djurdjura*, Paris, Sindbad, 1988.
Louis Piesse	*Itinéraire historique et descriptive de l'Algérie, comprenant le Tell et le Sahara*, Paris, Hachette, 1862, 2nd edition 1881.
Thomas Shaw	*Travels and Observations Relating to Several Parts of Barbary and the Levant*, Oxford, Theatre Editions, 1738.
Sinān-Chaouch	*Fondation de la Régence d'Alger, Histoire des Frères Barberousse* (French translation from Arabic of *Kitab Ghazawāt Aruj wa Khayr al-Dīn*), translated by Jean-Michel Venture de Paradis,

edited by Sander Rang and Ferdinand Denis, Paris, J. Angé, 1837; republished with a preface and additional notes by Abderrahmane Rebahi, Algiers, Éditions Grand-Alger Livres, 2006.

Books

Jamil M. Abun-Nasr	*A History of the Maghrib*, Cambridge, Cambridge University Press, 1971, 2nd edition, 1975.
Jamil M. Abun-Nasr	*A History of the Maghrib in the Islamic Period*, Cambridge, Cambridge University Press, 1987.
Stephen Adler	*International Migration and Dependence*, London, Saxon House, 1977.
Younes Adli	*La Kabylie à l'épreuve des invasions: des Phéniciens à 1900*, Algiers, Zyriab Éditions, 2004.
Charles-Robert Ageron	*Les Algériens musulmans et la France*, 2 vols, Paris, Presses Universitaires de France, 1968.
Hocine Aït Ahmed	*Memoirs d'Un Combattant*, Paris, Sylvie Messinger, 1983.
Madawi Al Rasheed	*Politics in an Arabian Oasis: The Rashidis of Saudi Arabia*, London, I.B.Tauris, 1991.
General P.J. André	*Confréries religieuses musulmanes*, Algiers, Éditions La Maison des Livres, 1956.
Walter Bagehot	*The English Constitution*, with an introduction by R.H.S. Crossman, Glasgow, Fontana, 1963.
Ramon Basagana and Ali Sayad	*Habitat traditionnel et structures familiales en Kabylie*, with a preface by Mouloud Mammeri. Algiers, Mémoires du Centre de Recherche Anthropologiques, Préhistoriques et Ethnographiques, XXIII, 1974.
Moulay Belhamissi	*Histoire de la marine algérienne (1516–1830)*, Algiers, ENAL, 1983.
Youssef Benoudjit	*La Kalaa des Beni Abbès au XVIe Siècle*, Algiers, Éditions Dahlab, 1997.
Louis-Adrien Berbrugger	*Les époques militaires de la Grande Kabylie*, Algiers, Bastide, 1857.
Jacques Berque	*Structures Sociales du Haut-Atlas*, Paris, Presses Universitaires de France, 1955, 2nd edition 1978.
Jacques Berque	*French North Africa: the Maghrib between two world wars*, translated by Jean Stewart, London, Faber and Faber, 1967
Jacques Berque	*Maghreb, histoire et sociétés*, Belgium, J. Duculot and Algiers, SNED, 1974.
L. Bouffard	*Atlas de l'Algérie*, Paris and Algiers, Librairie de la Hachette, 1847.

Si Amar Boulifa — *Le Djurdjura à travers l'histoire (depuis l'Antiquité jusqu'à 1830): organisation et indépendance des Zouaoua*, Algiers, J. Bringau, 1925; reprinted Algiers, Berti Editions, *c.* 2000.

Pierre Bourdieu — *Sociologie de l'Algérie*, Paris, PUF, 1958.

Pierre Bourdieu — *The Algerians*, Boston, MA, The Beacon Press, 1962.

Pierre Bourdieu — *Esquisse d'une théorie de la pratique*, Paris and Geneva, Librairie Droz, 1972.

Pierre Bourdieu — *Algeria 1960*, Cambridge, Cambridge University Press, 1979.

Ferdinand Braudel — *The Mediterranean and the Mediterranean World in the Age of Philip II*, translated from the French by Siân Reynolds, 2 vols, London, Collins, 1972.

Michael Brett and Elizabeth Fentress — *The Berbers*, Oxford, Blackwell, 1996, p/b 1997.

L. Carl Brown — *The Tunisia of Ahmed Bey, 1837–55*, Princeton, NJ, Princeton University Press, 1974.

Robert Brunschvig — *La Berbérie orientale sous les Hafsides, des origines à la fin du XVe siècle*, tome 1, Paris, Adrien Maisonneuve, 1940.

Gabriel Camps — *Berbères: Aux marges de l'Histoire*, Paris, Éditions des Hespérides, 1980.

Ernest Carette — *Études sur la Kabilie proprement dite*, Paris, Imprimerie Nationale, 2 vols., 1848.

Émile Carrey — *Récit de Kabylie (Campagne de 1857)*, Paris, Michel Lévy Frères, 1857; new edition 1876; republished Algiers, Epigraphe, 1994.

A. Cauneille — *Les Chaanba, leur nomadisme*, Paris, Éditions du C.N.R.S., 1968.

Kamel Chachoua — *L'Islam Kabyle. Religion, Etat et société en Algérie. Suivi de l'Epître (Rissala) d'Ibnou Zakri (Alger 1903), Muphti de la Grande Mosquée d'Alger*, Paris, Maisonneuve & Larose, 2001.

Salem Chaker (ed.) — *Hommes et Femmes de la Kabylie*, tome 1, Paris, INALCO and Aix-en-Provence, Édisud, 2001.

Corinne Chevallier — *Les Trente Premières Années de l'État d'Alger*, Algiers, Office des Publications Universitaires, 1988.

Allan Christelow — *Muslim law courts and the French colonial state in Algeria*, Princeton, NJ, Princeton University Press, 1985.

Brendan Clifford — *James Connolly: The Polish Aspect*, Belfast, Athol Books, 1985.

Fanny Colonna — *Instituteurs Algériens, 1883–1939*, Paris, Presses de la Fondation des Sciences Politiques, 1975.

Fanny Colonna — *Les Versets de l'Invincibilité: permanence et changement religieux dans l'Algérie contemporaine*, Paris, Presses de la Fondation des Sciences Politiques, 1995.

J.M. Dallet — *Dictionnaire Kabyle-Français: Parler des At Mangellat*, Paris, SELAF, 1982.

Eugène Daumas and M. Fabar	*La Grande Kabylie: Études historiques*, Paris, Hachette, 1847.
John Davis	*Libyan Politics*, London, I.B.Tauris, 1989.
Henri-Delmas de Grammont	*Histoire d'Alger sous la Domination Turque 1515–1830* (1887), reissued with an introduction by Lemnouar Merouche, Algiers, Éditions Bouchène, 2002.
Charles Devaux	*Les Kebaïles du Djerdjera*. Marseilles, Camoin, and Paris, Challamel, 1859.
Ross E. Dunn	*Resistance in the desert: Moroccan responses to French imperialism, 1881–1912*, Madison, University of Wisconsin Press, 1977.
Émile Durkheim	*De la division du travail social*. Paris, 1893; English translation: *The division of labour in society*, New York, The Free Press, 1964.
Dale F. Eickelman	*Moroccan Islam: tradition and society in a pilgrimage center*, Austin, University of Texas Press, 1976.
Dale F. Eickelman	*The Middle East and Central Asia: an anthropological approach*, 3rd edition, New Jersey, Prentice-Hall, 1998.
Bruno Etienne	*L'Algérie, cultures et revolution*, Paris, Éditions du Seuil, 1977.
E.E. Evans-Pritchard	*The Nuer*, London, Oxford University Press, 1940.
E.E. Evans-Pritchard	*The Sanusi of Cyrenaïca*, Oxford, Clarendon Press, 1949.
Mouloud Feraoun	*La Terre et le Sang*, Paris, Éditions du Seuil, 1953.
Mouloud Feraoun	*Le Fils du Pauvre*, Paris, Éditions du Seuil, 1954.
Mouloud Feraoun	*Jours de Kabylie*, Paris, Éditions du Seuil, 1954.
Laurent-Charles Féraud	*Histoire de Bougie* (republication of *Histoire des Villes de la Province de Constantine: Bougie*, Constantine, Imprimerie L. Arnolet, 1869), with an introduction by Nedjma Abdelfettah Lalmi, Algiers, Éditions Bouchène, 2001.
Mohamed Seghir Feredj	*Histoire de Tizi Ouzou des origines à 1954*, Algiers, ENAP, 1990.
Kamel Filali	*L'Algerie mystique: des marabouts fondateurs aux khwan insurgés XVe-XIXe*. Paris, Publisud, 2002.
Mouloud Gaïd	*L'Algérie sous les Turcs*, Tunis, Maison Tunisienne de l'Édition, and Algiers, SNED,1974.
Mouloud Gaïd	*Les Berbers dans l'Histoire*, tome III: *Lutte contre le colonialisme*, Algiers, Éditions Mimouni, n.d. but *c*. 1990.
Mouloud Gaïd	*Les Beni Yala*, Algiers, Office des Publications Universitaires, 1990.
René Gallissot and Gilbert Badia (eds)	*Marxisme et Algérie*, Paris, Union Générale d'Éditions, 1976.
Ernest Gellner	*Saints of the Atlas*, London, Weidenfeld & Nicolson, 1969.
Ernest Gellner	*Muslim Society*, Cambridge, Cambridge University Press, 1981.

Ernest Gellner	*Culture, Identity and Politics*, Cambridge, Cambridge University Press, 1987.
Ernest Gellner and Charles Micaud (eds)	*Arabs and Berbers from tribe to nation in North Africa*, London, Duckworth, 1972.
Ernest Gellner, Jean-Claude Vatin *et al.*	*Islam et Politique au Maghreb*, Paris and Aix-en-Provence, Éditions du CNRS, 1981.
Michael Gilsenan	*Recognizing Islam*, London and Canberra, Croom Helm, 1983.
Mohamed Akli Hadibi	*Wedris, une totale plénitude*, Algiers, Éditions Zyriab, 2005.
J.A Hall and J.A. Jarvie (eds)	*The social philosophy of Ernest Gellner*, Poznan Studies in the Philosophy of the Sciences and Humanities, 48, Amsterdam, Rodopi, 1996.
Adolphe Hanoteau and Arisitide Letourneux	*La Kabylie et les coutumes kabyles*, Paris: Challamel, 3 vols, 1872–3, 2nd edition, 1893.
Mohammed Harbi	*Le FLN: mirage et réalité*, Paris, Éditions J.A., 1980.
David Hart	*The Aith Waryaghar of the Moroccan Rif: an ethnography and history*. Tucson, University of Arizona Press, 1976.
David Hart	*Dadda 'Atta and his Forty Grandsons: the socio-political organisation of the Aït 'Atta of southern Morocco*, Wisbech, MENAS Press, 1981.
David M. Hart	*Qabila: tribal profiles and tribe-state relations in Morocco and on the Afghanistan-Pakistan frontier*, Amsterdam, Het Spinhuis, 2001.
Andrew C. Hess	*The Forgotten Frontier: A history of the sixteenth-century Ibero-African frontier*, Chicago and London, University of Chicago Press, 1978, p/b 2010.
Thomas Hobbes	*Leviathan*, edited with an introduction by C.B. Macpherson, London, Penguin, 1968.
Augustin Ibazizen	*Le Pont de Bereq'mouch ou le bond de mille ans*, Paris, Éditions de la Table Ronde, 1979.
Ibn Khaldun	*The Muqaddimah: An Introduction to History* (translated from the Arabic by Franz Rosenthal, edited and abridged by N.J. Dawood), London, Routledge & Kegan Paul, 1967.
Ibn Khaldun	*Histoire des Berbères, et des dynasties musulmanes de l'Afrique septentrionale*, translated by Le Baron de Slane, 4 vols, Paris, Paul Geuthner, 1968.
Halil İnalcık	*The Ottoman Empire: The classical period, 1300–1600*, translated by Norman Itzkowitz and Colin Imber, New York, Washington, Praeger Publishers, 1973; 2nd edition, New Rochelle and New York, Orpheus Publishing Co., 1989.
Raymond Jamous	*Honneur et baraka: les structures sociales traditionnelles dans le Rif*, Paris, Éditions de la Maison des Sciences de l'Homme, Cambridge, Cambridge University Press, 1981.
Charles-André Julien	*Histoire de l'Algérie Contemporaine: La conquête et les débuts de la colonisation, 1827–1871*, Paris, Presses Universitaires de France, 1964.

Charles-André Julien   *History of North Africa: From the Arab Conquest to 1830*, edited and revised by R. Le Tourneau (translated by John Petrie, edited by C.C. Stewart), London, Routledge & Kegan Paul, 1970.

Mahfoud Kaddache   *L'Algérie Durant la Période Ottomane*, Algiers, Office des Publications Universitaires, 1998.

Immanuel Kant   *Idea For A Universal History From A Cosmopolitan Point Of View*, 1784, in *Kant On History*, USA, Liberal Arts Library, 1963.

Mohand Khellil   *L'Exil kabyle*, Paris, L'Harmattan, 1979.

Mohand Khellil   *La Kabylie, ou l'ancêtre sacrifié*, Paris, L'Harmattan, 1984.

Camille Lacoste-Dujardin   *Le Conte kabyle*, Paris, Maspero, 1970, 2nd edition 1982.

Camille Lacoste-Dujardin   *Un village algérien*, Algiers, SNED, 1976.

Camille Lacoste-Dujardin   *Opération oiseau bleu: des kabyles, des ethnologues et la guerre d'Algérie*, Paris, La Découverte, 1997.

Jules Liorel   *Kabylie du Djurdjura*. Paris, Ernest Leroux, 1893.

Patricia Lorcin   *Imperial Identities: Stereotyping, prejudice and race in colonial Algeria*, London and New York, I.B.Tauris, 1995.

Alasdair MacIntyre   *After Virtue*, London, Duckworth, 1981, 2nd edition 1985.

Alain Mahé   *Histoire de la Grande Kabylie, XIXe-XXe siècles: anthropologie historique du lien social dans les communautés villageoises*, Paris, Éditions Bouchène, 2001.

Karl Marx   *Pre-capitalist economic formations*, edited by E.J. Hobsbawm, London, Lawrence and Wishart, 1964.

Émile Masqueray   *Formation des Cités chez les populations sédentaires de l'Algérie*, Paris, Ernest Leroux, 1886 ; republished with an introduction by Fanny Colonna by the Centre de Recherches et d'Études sur les Sociétés Méditerranéenes, series 'Archives Maghrébines', Aix-en-Provence, Edisud, 1983.

René Maunier   *La construction collective de la maison en Grande Kabylie*, Paris, Institut d'Ethnologie, 1926.

James McDougall   *History and the Culture of Nationalism in Algeria*, Cambridge, Cambridge University Press, 2006.

Ali Merad   *Le Réformisme Musulman en Algérie de 1925 à 1940; Essai d'histoire religieuse et sociale*, Paris-Mouton-La Haye, 1967; 2nd edition, Algiers, Éditions El Hikma, 1999.

Ernest Mercier   *Histoire de l'Afrique septentrionale depuis les temps les plus reculés jusqu'à la conquête française*, Paris, E. Leroux, 3 tomes, 1881–91.

Robert Montagne   *Les Berbères et le makhzen dans le sud du Maroc: Essai sur la transformation politique du groupe Chleuh*, Paris, Félix Alcan, 1930.

Robert Montagne   *The Berbers: their social and political organization*, translated and with an introduction by David Seddon, London, Frank Cass, 1973.

Jean Morizot	*L'Algérie kabylisée*, Paris, J. Peyronnet, 1962.
Jean Morizot	*Les Kabyles: propos d'un témoin*, Paris, Centre des Hautes Études sur l'Afrique et l'Asie Modernes (CHEAM), 1985.
Jean Morizot	*L'Aurès, ou le mythe de la montagne rebelle*, Paris, L'Harmattan, 1991.
Sir Oswald Mosley	*My Life*, London, Nelson, 1968.
Friedrich Nietzsche	*Beyond Good and Evil*, London, Penguin, 1973.
Daniel Nordman	*Tempête sur Alger: L'expédition de Charles Quint sur Alger*, Éditions Bouchène, 2011.
Aïssa Ouitis	*Les Contradictions Sociales et Leur Expression Symbolique dans le Sétifois*, Algiers, Documents du C.R.A.P.E., III, SNED, 1977.
Tahar Oussedik	*Le Royaume de Koukou*, Algiers, Entreprise National du Livre (ENAL), 1986.
Karl Popper	*The open society and its enemies: vol. I: Plato*, London, Routledge & Kegan Paul, 1945; 5th edition (revised), 1966.
William Quandt	*Revolution and Political Leadership: Algeria 1954-1968*, Cambridge, MA and London, England, MIT Press, 1969.
Yahia Rahal	*Histoires du Pouvoir: Un géneral témoigne*, Algiers, Casbah Éditions, 1997.
Karim Rahem	*Le Sillage de la Tribu: imaginaires politiques et histoire en Algérie (1843-1993)*, Paris, Riveneuve Éditions, 2008.
Ramdane Redjala	*L'Opposition en Algérie depuis 1962, t. 1: Le PRS-CNDR et le FFS*, Paris, L'Harmattan, 1988.
Hugh Roberts	*The Battlefield: Algeria 1988-2002. Studies in a broken polity*, London and New York, Verso, 2003.
Joseph Nil Robin	*La Grande Kabylie sous le régime turc* (republication in one volume with an introduction by Alain Mahé of articles originally published under the title 'Note sur l'organisation militaire et administrative des Turcs dans la Grande Kabylie' in *Revue Africaine*, 1873, 132–40 and 196–207), Éditions Bouchène, 1998.
Joseph Nil Robin	*Notes historiques sur la Grande Kabylie de 1830 à 1838* (republication in one volume with an introduction by Alain Mahé of articles originally published in *Revue Africaine*, 1876, 42–56, 81–96 and 193–219), Éditions Bouchène, 1999.
John Ruedy	*Modern Algeria: the origins and development of a nation*, Bloomington, Indiana University Press, 1992, 2nd edition 2005.
Marshall D. Sahlins	*Tribesmen*, Englewood Cliffs, NJ: Prentice-Hall 1968.
Judith Scheele	*Village Matters: knowledge, politics and community in Kabylia, Algeria*, Woodbridge, Suffolk and Rochester, New York, James Currey, 2009.
J.D. Seddon	*Moroccan peasants: a century of change in the eastern Rif, 1870–1970*, Folkestone, Kent, Dawson, 1981.

Benjamin Stora	*Dictionnaire Biographique de Militants Nationalistes Algériens, 1926–1954*, Paris, L'Harmattan, 1985.
Houari Touati	*Entre Dieu et Les Hommes. Lettrés, saints et sorciers au Maghreb (17ᵉ siècle)*, Paris, Éditions de l'École des Hautes Études en Sciences Sociales, 1994.
Jean-Claude Vatin *et al.*	*Connaissance du Maghreb: sciences sociales et colonisation*, Centre de Recherches et d'Études sur les Sociétés Méditerranéenes; Paris, Éditions du CNRS, 1984.
Eugène Vaysettes	*Histoire de Constantine sous la domination turque de 1517 à 1837*, Paris, Challamel, 1869, republished with an introduction by Ouarda Siari-Tengour, Éditions Bouchène, 2002.
Amal Rassam Vinogradov	*The Aït Ndhir of Morocco*, Ann Arbor, Michigan, 1974.
Hans Wehr	*A Dictionary of Modern Written Arabic*, edited by J. Milton Cowan, Wiesbaden, Otto Harrassowitz; London, George Allen and Unwin, 1971 (3rd impression).
Shelagh Weir	*A Tribal Order: Politics and Law in the Mountains of Yemen*, London, The British Museum Press, and Austin, The University of Texas Press, 2007.
Tassadit Yacine	*Poésie berbère et identité: Qasi Udifella, Héraut des At Sidi Braham*, Paris, Éditions de la Maison des Sciences de l'Homme, 1987.
Ali Zamoum	*Tamurt Imazighen: mémoires d'un survivant 1940–1962*, Algiers, Rahma, 1993.
Ahsène Zehraoui	*Les travailleurs algériens en France: étude sociologique de quelques aspects de la vie familiale*, Préface de Maxime Rodinson, Paris, Francois Maspero, 1971.
Sami Zubaida	*Law and Power in the Islamic World*, London, I.B.Tauris, 2003.

Articles

Dj. Aïssani	'El-Ghobrini' in Salem Chaker (ed.), *Hommes et Femmes de la Kabylie*, tome 1, Paris, INALCO and Aix-en-Provence, Édisud, 2001, 132–5.
Baron Henri Aucapitaine	'Notice sur la tribu des Aït Fraoucen', *Revue Africaine*, 1860, 446–58.
M. Benbrahim	'Fadhma n'Soumeur' in Chaker (ed.) 2001, *op. cit.*, 136–8.
Augustin Bernard and Louis Milliot	'Les qânoûns kabyles dans l'ouvrage de Hanoteau et Letourneux', *Revue des Études Islamiques*, 1933, 2, 1–44.
Jacques Berque	'Qu'est-ce qu'une « tribu » nord-africaine?' in *Maghreb, histoire et sociétés*, Belgium, J. Duculot and Algiers, SNED, 1974, 22–34.
Pierre Bourdieu	'Le sens de l'honneur' in Bourdieu, P., *Esquisse d'une théorie de la pratique*, Paris and Geneva, Librairie Droz, 1972; republished in English translation as 'The sense of honour' in Bourdieu P.,

	Algeria 1960, Cambridge, Cambridge University Press, 1979, 95–132.
Pierre Bourdieu	'The Kabyle house or the world reversed', in Pierre Bourdieu, *Algeria 1960*, Cambridge, Cambridge University Press, 1979, 133–53.
Pierre Boyer	'Espagne et Kouko. Les Négociations de 1598 et 1610', *Revue de l'Occident Musulman et de la Méditerranée*, No. 8, 2nd quarter, 1970, 25–40.
Edmund Burke III	'The image of the Moroccan state in French ethnological literature; a new look at the origin of Lyautey's Berber policy', in Gellner and Micaud (eds), *op. cit.*, 175–99.
Fanny Colonna	'Rituels et Histoire: à propos d'un ancien pélérinage aurasien', in Ernest Gellner, Jean-Claude Vatin *et al.*, *Islam et Politique au Maghreb*, Paris and Aix-en-Provence, Éditions du CNRS, 1981, 91–9.
Robert Descloitres and Laïd Debzi	'Système de parenté et structures familiales en Algérie', *Annuaire de l'Afrique du Nord*, Paris, CNRS, 1963.
Ross E. Dunn	'Berber imperialism: the Aït Atta expansion in southeast Morocco' in Gellner and Micaud (eds), 1972, *op. cit.*, 85–107.
M. Eisenbeth	'Les juifs en Algérie et en Tunisie au temps des Turcs', *Revue Africaine*, 1952, 1st and 2nd quarters.
Friedrich Engels	'The Moorish War', *New York Daily Tribune*, 17 March 1860, reprinted in Shlomo Avineri (ed.), *Karl Marx on Colonialism and Modernization*, New York, Anchor Books, Doubleday & Company, 1969, 416–21.
Jeanne Favret	'La segmentarité au Maghreb', *L'Homme*, 6, 2, 1966, 105–11.
Jeanne Favret	'Relations de dépendance et manipulation de la violence en Kabylie', *L'Homme*, 8, 4, 1968, 18–43.
Laurent-Charles Féraud	'Conquête de Bougie par les Espagnols d'après un manuscript arabe', *Revue Africaine*, 1868, 245–56 and 337–49.
Laurent-Charles Féraud	'Histoire des Villes de la Province de Constantine: Gigell', *Recueil des Notices et Mémoires de la Société Archéologique de la Province de Constantine*, vol. XIV, 1870.
René Gallissot	'L'Algérie pré-coloniale' in Centre d'Études et de Recherches Marxistes, *Sur le féodalisme*, Paris, Éditions Sociales, 1971, 147–79; published in English translation as 'Precolonial Algeria', *Economy and Society*, vol. 4, no. 4, November 1975, 418–45.
Ernest Gellner	'The sociology of Robert Montagne' in Ernest Gellner, *Muslim Society*, Cambridge, Cambridge University Press, 1981, 179–93.
Ernest Gellner	'The roots of cohesion', *Man*, 20, 1985, 1, 142–55, reprinted in Ernest Gellner, *Culture, Identity and Politics*, Cambridge, Cambridge University Press, 1987, 29–46.
Ernest Gellner	'The Maghreb as mirror for man', *Morocco*, 1, 1991, 1–6.
Ernest Gellner	'Reply to critics', in J.A Hall and J.A. Jarvie (eds), *The social philosophy of Ernest Gellner*, Poznan Studies in the Philosophy

of the Sciences and Humanities, 48, Amsterdam, Rodopi, 1996, 649–51.

Mahammad Hadj Saddok — 'Avec un cheikh de Zemmorah à travers le ouest constantinois du dix-huitième siècle', *Bulletin de la société historique et géographique de la région de Sétif*, 1935, 45–59.

Mahammed Hadj Saddok — 'A travers la Berbérie orientale du XVIIIe siècle avec le voyageur Al-Warthilani', *Revue Africaine*, 95, 1951, 3rd and 4th quarters, 315–99.

Abdallah Hammoudi — 'Segmentarité, stratification sociale, pouvoir politique et sainteté', *Hespéris-Tamuda*, Rabat, vol. XV, 1974, 147–79.

Général Maurice Hanoteau — 'Quelques souvenirs sur les collaborateurs de *La Kabylie et les coutumes kabyles*', *Revue Africaine*, 1923, 134–49

David Hart — 'Segmentary systems and the role of 'five fifths' in tribal Morocco.' *Revue de l'Occident Musulman et de la Méditerranée*, 3, 1, 1967, 65–95.

David Hart — 'Clan, lineage, local community and the feud in a Rifian tribe (Aith Waryaghar, Morocco)', in Louise Sweet (ed.), *Peoples and Cultures of the Middle East*, Garden City New York, The Natural History Press, 1970, vol. II, 3–75.

David Hart — 'The tribe in modern Morocco: two case studies' in Gellner and Micaud (eds), *op. cit.*, 25–58.

David Hart — 'Four centuries of history on the hoof: the northwest passage of Berber sheep transhumants across the Moroccan Atlas, 1550–1912', *Morocco*, The Journal of the Society for Moroccan Studies, No. 3, 1993, 21–55.

Wolfgang Kraus — 'Contestable identities: tribal structures in the Moroccan High Atlas', *Journal of the Royal Anthropological Institute* (N.S.), 1998, 4, 1–22.

Yves Lacoste — 'Rapports plaine-montagne en Grande Kabylie', in Lacoste, Y., *Unité et diversité du Tiers Monde*, Paris, La Découverte, 1984, 470–539.

Camille Lacoste-Dujardin — 'Géographie culturelle et géopolitique en Kabylie', *Hérodote*, 103, 2001.

Camille Lacoste-Dujardin — 'Grande Kabylie: du danger des traditions montagnardes', *Hérodote*, 107, 2002.

Karl Marx — 'Notes sur l'ouvrage de Kowalewski' in Gallissot and Badia (eds), 1976, *op. cit.*, 193–228.

Henry Munson — 'On the irrelevance of the segmentary lineage model in the Moroccan Rif', *American Anthropologist*, 91, 1989, 386–400.

Henry Munson — 'Rethinking Gellner's segmentary analysis of Morocco's Aït 'Atta', *Man* (N.S) 28, 1993, 267–80.

O. Naït-Djoudi — 'At-Lqadi: Les « rois » de Koukou', in Chaker (ed.) 2001, *op. cit.*, 78.

F. Patorni — 'Délibération de l'année 1749 dans la Grande Kabylie', *Revue Africaine*, 1895, 315–20.

| William Quandt | 'The Berbers in the Algerian political elite' in Gellner and Micaud (eds), *op.cit.*, 285–303. |

Hugh Roberts — *Notes on relations of production, forms of property and political structures in a dissident region of Algeria: pre-colonial Kabylia*, University of East Anglia, Development Studies Discussion Paper No. 38, 1978, 33pp.

Hugh Roberts — 'Towards an understanding of the Kabyle question in contemporary Algeria', *The Maghreb Review*, V, 5/6, September–December 1980, 115–24.

Hugh Roberts — 'The unforeseen development of the Kabyle question in contemporary Algeria', *Government and Opposition*, XVII, 3, Summer 1982, 312–34.

Hugh Roberts — 'The economics of Berberism: the material basis of the Kabyle question in contemporary Algeria', *Government and Opposition*, XVIII, 2, Spring 1983, 218–35.

Hugh Roberts — 'The FLN: French conceptions, Algerian realities' in George Joffé (ed.), *North Africa: nation, state and region*, London, Routledge, 1993, 111–41; republished in corrected version in H. Roberts, *The Battlefield: Algeria 1988–2002. Studies in a broken polity*, London and New York, Verso, 2003, ch. 2.

Hugh Roberts — 'A propos de la jema'a et de la Kabylie', 23 May 2001, Algeria-Watch (www.algeria-watch.org/farticle/kabylie/roberts_jemaa.htm).

Hugh Roberts — *Co-opting identity: the manipulation of Berberism, the frustration of democratisation and the generation of violence in Algeria*, London School of Economics and Political Science, Development Research Centre, 'Crisis States Programme' Working Paper No. 8, 46pp., December 2001.

Hugh Roberts — 'La Kabylie à la lumière tremblotante du savoir maraboutique', *Insaniyat: Revue algérienne d'anthropologie et de sciences sociales*, 16, January–April 2002, 99–115.

Hugh Roberts — 'Perspectives on Berber politics: on Gellner and Masqueray, or Durkheim's mistake', *J. of the Royal Anthropological Institute* (N.S.) 8, 2002, 107–26.

Hugh Roberts — 'De la segmentarité à l'opacité: à propos de Gellner et Bourdieu et les approches théoriques à l'analyse du champ politique algerien', *Insaniyat, Revue algérienne d'anthropologie et de sciences sociales*, 19–20, January–June 2003, 65–95.

Mohamed Brahim Salhi — 'Modernisation et retraditionalisation à travers les champs associatif et politique: le cas de la Kabylie', *Insaniyat, Revue algérienne d'anthropologie et de sciences sociales*, 8, May–August 1999, 21–42.

Benjamin Stora — 'Contribution de l'immigration en France à la construction du nationalisme algérien: étude sur les différentes générations de dirigeants nationalistes algériens dans l'immigration

(1926–1954)'. Paper presented to the Colloque International sur la Révolution Algérienne, Algiers, 24–28 November 1984.

Lucette Valensi — 'Le Maghreb vu du centre: sa place dans l'école sociologique française' in Jean-Claude Vatin *et al.*, *Connaissance du Maghreb: sciences sociales et colonisation*, Centre de Recherches et d'Études sur les Sociétés Méditerranéenes, Paris, Éditions du CNRS, 1984.

Amal Rassam Vinogradov — 'The socio-political organisation of a Berber 'Taraf' tribe: pre-Protectorate Morocco' in Gellner and Micaud (eds) 1972, *op. cit.*, 67–83.

E. Watbled and Dr Monnereau — 'Négociations entre Charles-Quint et Kheir-Ed-Din (1538–1540)', *Revue Africaine*, 1869, 139–48.

Newspaper and on-line articles

- 'El Achoura en Kabylie: Les Saints ont toujours la côte', *El Watan*, 11 February 2006

- 'Tifilkout: un village moderne, une cité ancestrale', *L'Authentique*, 25 August 2009.

Madjid Tighilt — 'Les Aït Wandiouss ou les Maures d'Andalousie', *Tifilkout.com*, 15 September 2007 (www.tifilkout.com/ articles/327/1/Les-Ait-wandiouss-ou-les-maures-dandalousie/Page1.html)

Index

www.ingramcontent.com/pod-product-compliance
Lightning Source LLC
Chambersburg PA
CBHW070901080426
R18103400001B/R181034PG41932CBX00006B/11